The Diary of

HENRY CRABB ROBINSON

AN ABRIDGEMENT

Henry Crabb Robinson at the age of 54

From the crayon drawing made at Goethe's request in 1829 by Johann Joseph Schmeller (1796–1841)

The Diary of
HENRY CRABB ROBINSON

AN ABRIDGEMENT

Edited
with an Introduction by
Derek Hudson

LONDON
Oxford University Press
NEW YORK TORONTO
1967

Oxford University Press, Ely House, London W.1
GLASGOW NEW YORK TORONTO MELBOURNE WELLINGTON
CAPE TOWN SALISBURY IBADAN NAIROBI LUSAKA ADDIS ABABA
BOMBAY CALCUTTA MADRAS KARACHI LAHORE DACCA
KUALA LUMPUR HONG KONG TOKYO

This selection
© *Oxford University Press* 1967

The text of the Diary has been abridged from *Henry Crabb Robinson on Books and their Writers*, edited by Edith J. Morley (1938), by kind permission of Messrs. J. M. Dent and Sons Limited.

942·073 ROB
CLASS NO. ~~B/ROB~~

ACC. NO. 26527

KING ALFRED'S COLLEGE
WINCHESTER.

PRINTED IN GREAT BRITAIN
BY EBENEZER BAYLIS AND SON, LTD.
THE TRINITY PRESS, WORCESTER, AND LONDON

CONTENTS

Illustrations

INTRODUCTION

1. Henry Crabb Robinson

An intensely sociable person; a determined inquirer in most fields of human activity (especially the literary); a vigorous bachelor, healthy, high spirited; a journalist, a barrister, a Nonconformist, an educationist; an inexhaustible talker, diarist, correspondent, and traveller; a great lover of liberty; above all, to many a firm and reliable friend, assiduous in the 'little, nameless, unremembered acts'—Crabb Robinson was all these.

He was the companion whose 'buoyant Spirit' cheered Wordsworth, whose 'kindnesses that never ceased to flow' and whose 'prompt self-sacrifice' Wordsworth gratefully acknowledged; the friend who, visiting Mary Lamb in her affliction after her brother's death, was warmly greeted with 'Oh, here's Crabby'.

Carlyle once said that 'he could talk by the gallon in a minute'. Of an evening at Lamb's, P. G. Patmore scathingly remarked that, when H.C.R. arrived, 'there was an end of general conversation, he took it all to himself!' Noting such 'uncivil' criticism, Crabb Robinson remained unmoved. He felt that he must be accepted as he was, with all his faults; and, a century after his death, we find ourselves essentially in agreement. The largeness of the man overrides incidentals. It is impossible not to have affection for him.

He lived to be 91. The span of his life from 1775 to 1867 covered a period of radical change and development, all faithfully reflected in his thought and writings. As a young man he came under the spell of William Godwin's *Political Justice*, which made him feel 'more generously'. His own subsequent acquaintance with Godwin proved a sad disillusionment; on Godwin's death he wrote, 'I had lost all my personal respect for him'. It is intriguing to follow the ups-and-downs of Crabb Robinson's friendships in his unstudied diary. Although Dr. Arnold of Rugby is at first 'not very much to my taste', his untimely death is reported as 'a really afflicting event'. The shape of his relationships was hammered out in day-to-day contacts. For some, like Wordsworth and Lamb, he always shows an unswerving affection. With Hazlitt, 'a man for whom I once had kindness', he is latterly not on speaking terms.

Crabb Robinson set down his personal progress with complete frankness. The Gothic revival duly influenced his youthful taste; the French

Revolution made a temporary Republican of him, as with greater men; at the end of his life he was happily reading Trollope. Where a genius might have lacked detachment, it is the 'ordinariness' of this level-headed, intelligent, middle-class Whig that accounts in part for the value of his record; yet only in part, for there was something extraordinary about his curiosity and persistence. He himself continually underrated his own powers, and was painfully aware of his limitations. While Carlyle and Macaulay grew in fame, he lamented in his reminiscences: 'I who was thought fit to be the companion of these men have only remained stationary. . . .'

True, we read him now less for himself than for what he had to say of others. But in one respect at least, Crabb Robinson's literary achievement is secure. As a young man he spent five years (1800–1805) in Germany, where he met many of the leading writers of the time and closely studied German life and literature. For the rest of his days he considered it his mission to act as an intellectual mediator between England and Germany. 'To him, more than to anyone else,' wrote Professor Edith Morley, 'is due the influence of German thought and German literature in England in the first quarter of the nineteenth century'. It is a claim which the late Dr. Hertha Marquardt's monumental work *Henry Crabb Robinson und seine deutschen Freunde* is now bringing home to German readers. As the advocate of Goethe and Kant, and the purveyor of German transcendentalism, Crabb Robinson has his place in European literary history.

Other enduring achievements arose from Crabb Robinson's steady campaign to relieve the disabilities of Nonconformists, culminating in the passing of the Dissenters' Chapels Act of 1844; and from his years of endeavour on behalf of University College, London, of which he served as vice-president of the senate from 1847 to 1866. University College, especially its Flaxman Gallery, and University Hall (now Dr. Williams's Library)—opened in 1849 as a hall of residence for students of University College without sectarian restrictions, with Arthur Hugh Clough as its first principal—are still memorials to his enthusiasm. His sympathy for the undergraduates was warmly practical; he entertained them socially, and he helped some of them financially.

It was part of Crabb Robinson's modesty to consider himself an ugly man. In fact, though not strikingly handsome, he had an agreeable, interesting face, with features that eventually became distinguished. A number of drawings of him have been published; two by Masquerier are personable enough; a watercolour in John Walter's collection shows a strong dependable profile; only a sketch by Scharf presents a knobbly, gnome-like ancient, and this has the elements of caricature. But I prefer to these a drawing I have chosen as a frontispiece, which, to the best of my knowledge, has not been reproduced before—that made by Johann Joseph Schmeller at Goethe's request on Crabb Robinson's German visit of 1829. The drawing conveys something of his stamina, his humour, and his gravity; typically, H.C.R. called it 'frightfully ugly and very like'. I have added one of the several photographs of his old age. This, again, I have not seen published, though it was used by Edward Armitage as the basis of the fresco of Crabb Robinson, surrounded by thirty-four of his distinguished friends, which, until it decayed, adorned Dr. Williams's Library.

Henry Crabb Robinson was born at Bury St. Edmunds, 13 May 1775, into a comfortable middle-class family of Dissenters. He was the youngest son of Henry Robinson, a tanner; and his mother, whose good influence on him he remembered to the end of his life, had the excellent name Jemima. Another important boyhood influence came from a girl several years older than himself, Catherine Buck; she lent him books, and later, after her marriage to Thomas Clarkson, the founder of the society for the abolition of the slave trade, she did him the inestimable service of introducing him to Coleridge and to Charles Lamb (who in turn introduced him to Wordsworth). This friendship with Mrs. Clarkson, and with her husband, forwarded Crabb Robinson's lifelong ardour for abolition, and inspired him eventually to take up the cudgels on Clarkson's behalf when he was involved in controversy.

Crabb Robinson's schooling was slight. He spent three years at an 'academy' kept by an uncle at Devizes, before being articled in 1790 to a Colchester attorney. At Colchester in that year he heard John Wesley preach: 'His feeble voice was barely audible. But his reverend countenance, especially his long, white locks, formed a picture never to be forgotten'. During the 1790s Robinson, like so many young people, was a convinced revolutionary. Though he adopted Godwin's idea of justice, he never became an atheist. At this time he met William Taylor, the German scholar, and Amelia Alderson, the blue-stocking friend of Catherine Buck, who later married the painter John Opie.

In the spring of 1796 he came to London, hoping to find a job in a lawyer's office. Failing in this attempt, he eventually obtained work as a 'writing-clerk', which supported him in London until the end of 1797. He went often to the theatre, forming a passionate admiration for Mrs. Siddons; and he joined debating societies, where he discovered a gift for public speaking. An important acquaintance made during this stay in London was J. D. Collier of *The Times*; and thus he came to know his son John Payne Collier, who eventually attained notoriety for his Shakespeare forgeries but in whose integrity Crabb Robinson, in his old age, preserved an obstinate faith.

Early in 1798, H.C.R. received a legacy of about £100 a year from an uncle. This greatly affected the course of his life. With strict economy, he was able to live on his modest income, and, finding no particular liking for the law but considerable facility and pleasure in writing, he embarked on a desultory career in literature and journalism.

In April 1800, he went on a visit to Germany, which was prolonged for five years, and whence he sent home contributions to J. D. Collier's *Monthly Magazine*. He stayed in Hamburg, Frankfurt, Grimma, Weimar, Marburg, and elsewhere; and finally in Jena, where he seriously studied Latin and Greek, the new transcendental philosophy, and German literature. Though he did not attempt to earn a doctorate, he mastered the language and made himself a cultured, well-read man. There is a hint, but no more, of a possible love-affair. He undertook long tours and walking trips through the country, sometimes in company with Christian Brentano—the brother of the poet Clemens Brentano and of Goethe's friend Bettina von Arnim. H.C.R.'s letters to his brother Thomas give a remarkable picture of contemporary German social and literary life. In the course of these years he met Goethe, Schiller, Herder, Wieland, Voss, Knebel, and Madame de Staël, to mention only a few celebrities. His description of his first visit to Goethe at Weimar—'the Athens of Germany', as he called it—in 1801 deserves to be quoted (I have lengthened the abbreviations and added some punctuation):

> . . . I sat a quarter of an hour with him & did not open my Lips. I was so awed & oppressed by the 'manly grace' of his figure, which according to Milton's testimony is so superior to female beauty, that I believe I should have forgotten my German had I attempted to speak. Goethe is about 50 & he begins to be corpulent. His features are regularly handsome, majestic & commanding. After a courteous bow to each of us he sat—would you believe it?—precisely in the posture in which Kemble seats himself in *Measure for Measure* when he judges the Judge—i.e. with his bent fist on his Knees & with his burning Eyes fixed on the person he was speaking to. I can't more strongly express my feelings than by saying that I felt in beholding Goethe during a most insignificant conversation precisely what I have felt in seeing Mrs. Siddons with all the pomp & corroborative aid of Scenery & decorations. And not contemplating him as we do the Actor at a distance, as an object we pay for seeing, being in his presence & subject to be observed by him, I was painfully oppressed by my admiration of him—And was really glad when I was away. . . .

But their acquaintance advanced, despite this oppressive start. Two years later, he again met Goethe, at the theatre in Weimar, when Goethe graciously remarked to him: 'Mr. Robinson, you have been as I hear a long time in our Neighbourhood & have never once paid me a visit.' An invitation to dinner followed: 'Goethe said nothing which *un de nous autres* could not have said too. And yet everything was of infinite importance, *for Goethe said it*. . . .' Frankly disapproving of the great man's morals, and of what he considered his excessive admiration of Byron, Crabb Robinson never faltered in devotion to Goethe's genius.

Back in London, he continued his busy, garrulous life. He met Mrs. Barbauld; and he accompanied the Lambs to the first performance of Lamb's disastrous comedy *Mr. H——*. At the beginning of 1807, Crabb Robinson was invited by John Walter, the proprietor of *The Times* (to whom he had been introduced by J. D. Collier), to go out to Altona as the correspondent of the paper, a mission lasting six months which he accomplished with credit. A *rencontre* at Bury that autumn with the sportsman Sir Charles Bunbury must be mentioned, if only to justify the inclusion of a delightful story about Lamb. 'I met him in London a few months afterwards, when I was walking with Charles Lamb. . . .' wrote Robinson in his reminiscences. 'Lamb was all astonishment. "I had no idea that you knew Sheridan." "No more I do. That's Sir Charles Bunbury." "That's impossible. I have known him to be Sheridan all my life. That shall be Sheridan. You thief! You have stolen my Sheridan." He seemed quite vexed. . . .'

Robinson's connexion with *The Times* continued. At the end of 1807 he was made 'a sort of foreign editor'; indeed this is the highest place at Printing House Square accorded him by such reference books as the Dictionary of National Biography. But we now know that on 25 January 1808, he was able to tell his brother Thomas that John Walter had 'intimated a wish that I would take a more responsible part in the conduct of the paper. . . . He then asked me whether I should have any objection to answering letters, occasionally make calls upon persons of respectability, etc., etc. I observed that in case I did anything of that kind I must appear in a certain character—He answered very quickly "Certainly you can't appear otherwise than as a principal, you might be known expressly as the Editor." Then, I replied, I saw no objection to it. . . .'

It was an offhand method of appointment; but it seems that this dialogue means that we must insert Crabb Robinson's name on the honourable roll of Editors of *The Times*. Yet the editorship in 1808 was not the responsible post that it later became. Its character was experimental and tentative. Robinson might be known as the 'ostensible editor', but John Walter remained in control, and he did not give Robinson the task of writing the more important leading articles.

H.C.R. paid a flying visit to Corunna as a special correspondent. In the office he wrote odds-and-ends; he read and corrected proofs; he opened letters to the Editor and made 'charming bonfires of them'. He got on very well with Walter and his colleagues. His evening office hours were variable, but not exacting, and 'I enjoy it much'.

The honeymoon period on *The Times* nevertheless proved short. Crabb Robinson soon showed, like other literary types in journalism, that he could not cope with the political side of the editorial job, for which he lacked enthusiasm, and which may occasionally have disturbed his conscience. In 1809 John Walter told him that he was 'no longer in want of that constant attendance for which I have been so much obliged to you'; and Robinson replied that he would 'close my attendance with the current quarter'. He made it clear, however, that he had done his best: 'I most heartily wish that whoever occupies my seat in future may discharge his obligations with the same scrupulous attention and much greater ability.' The proprietor resumed the editorial function, 'ostensible' or otherwise. He and Robinson remained friends.

Meanwhile, something much more important to Crabb Robinson personally had happened. He had met Wordsworth. His letter to his brother of March 1808, recording that first meeting, should be quoted (and again I have regularized abbreviations and punctuation):

> . . . I breakfasted with Wordsworth at Charles Lamb's on Tuesday And walked with him to Mrs. Clarkson afterwards who was at Hatcham house. Wordsworth begged me to come for him yesterday. I accordingly dined at Mr. Hardcastles & Wordsworth & I returned together. We had therefore two long têtes à têtes. I feel obliged to Mrs. Clarkson for she must have spoken of me very kindly. Wordsworth gave me his hand with cordiality on meeting, he was confidential with me, has promised to call on me & made advances which were, from my high opinion of him, certainly very flattering. My Esteem for Wordsworth's *mind*, his philosophic & poetic view of things, is confirmed & strengthened by these interviews. And I rejoice that you are so far initiated into a sense of his poetry that you can sympathise with my pleasure—Wordsworth is most opposite to Southey in his appearance. He is sloven & his manners are not prepossing [*sic*], his features are large & course [*sic*]; his voice is not attractive, his manners tho' not arrogant yet indicate a sense of his own worth, he is not attentive to others and speaks with decision his own opinion. He does not spare those he opposes, he has no respect for great names, And avows his contempt for popular persons as well as favorite books which must often give offence. Yet with all this, I should have a bad opinion of that person's discernment who should be long in his company without contracting an high respect, if not a love for him. Moral purity & dignity & elevation of Sentiment are the characteristics of his mind & muse. . . .

This critical note on Wordsworth, made after such short acquaintance, has lasted well, as is often the case with Robinson's off-the-cuff pronouncements. The friendship thus begun—soon to be extended to the ladies of Wordsworth's household—was to continue for more than thirty years with increasing intimacy. It would have been surprising if Wordsworth's reactionary gloom had had no effect on H.C.R.'s liberalism, but it does not seem to have had much.

Having learned from his experience on *The Times* that an active journalist's life was not for him, Crabb Robinson, in November 1809, decided to make one more attempt on the law; he began to eat his dinners at the Middle Temple. He continued to contribute to magazines, and translated a fairy tale from the German (*Amatonda*); but the financial failure of the translation further discouraged him in his literary ambitions; he became a pupil in a barrister's chambers, and in 1813 was called to the Bar.

As a barrister he had only one object—to build up a small fortune as quickly as possible, so that he could pursue his favourite life of 'busy idleness'. He achieved exactly this. His legal knowledge may not have been deep, but he 'knew the practice'; and he had the probity, eloquence, and native shrewdness to attract clients. By 1825 he was earning £700 a year and was a leader on the Norfolk Circuit. In 1828 he retired with a capital of about £8,000. No more need be said of his career at the Bar, except to add that his legal experience was henceforth always at the disposal of his friends.

Crabb Robinson's return to the law more or less coincided with his decision to commence his diary at the beginning of 1811. 'This year I began to keep a Diary,' he wrote. 'This relieves me from one difficulty, but raises another. Hitherto I have had some trouble in bringing back to my memory the most material incidents in the proper order. It was a labour of *col*lection. Now I have to *se*lect. When looking at a diary, there seems to be too little distinction between the insignificant and the important, and one is reminded of the proverb "The wood cannot be seen for the trees".' It is an interesting comment for the maker of this abridgement; but in general Crabb Robinson seems to have followed the rule, 'If in doubt, put it down'; which from an historical point of view is probably the soundest policy.

The opening of the diary shows him already firmly established as the friend of Lamb, Wordsworth, and Coleridge. We soon see his gifts of mediation demonstrated by the understanding way in which he sought to compose the differences between Wordsworth and Coleridge. He is also still on good terms with Godwin and Hazlitt. He had known Hazlitt personally longer than he had known Godwin; he had admired and encouraged the youthful Hazlitt, while Hazlitt had influenced his literary taste; but his relationships with both men deteriorated henceforth.

The existence of the diary makes it unnecessary to sketch Crabb Robinson's biography in further detail, though it must be remembered that the mainly literary excerpts in this volume only hint at the spread of his daily activity—his membership of the Athenaeum Club (1824), for example, was a landmark in his social life. Nor do they show H.C.R adequately in relation to contemporary changes in transport, communication, and scientific invention, on which his papers are a mine of historical evidence. In due course omnibus rides took the place of long walks to his friends in the suburbs. His account of his first railway journey, from Liverpool to Manchester in 1833, is worth quoting:

> . . . We travelled in the second class of carriages.—There were 5 trams linked together on each of which were placed open seats for the traveller 4 and 4 facing each other and of these *24* in each tram but not all were full—and besides there was a close carriage and one other machine for luggage. The company not genteel.—The fare 4/- for the 31 Miles.
>
> Everything went on so rapidly that I had scarcely the power of observation. The road begins at an excavation thro rock and is generally to a certain extent insulated from the adjacent country.—It is occasionally placed on bridges—and is frequently intersected by ordinary roads.—Not quite a perfect level is preserved.—On setting off there is a slight jolt arising from the chain catching each tram but once in motion we proceeded as smoothly as possible. For a minute or two the pace is gentle, and is constantly varying.—The machine produces little smoak or steam.—First in order is the tall chimney.—Then the boiler—a barrel like vessel. Then an oblong reservoir of water—Then a vehicle for coals and then come of a length infinitely extendible the trams on which are the carriages. Our train would have carried if all the seats had been filled about 150 passengers. . . . But, after all, the expense is so great, that it is considered uncertain whether the establishment will ultimately remunerate the proprietors. . . . Of the rapidity with which the journey will be made I had better experience on my return; but I may say now that it is certain that stoppages included the journey may be made 20 miles an hour!!! . . .
>
> I should have remarked before that the most remarkable moments of the journey are those when trains met. The rapidity is such, that there is no recognising the features of a traveller.—The noise on several occasions of the passing engine was like the whizzing of a rocket.

Crabb Robinson's efforts for the Nonconformist cause, for the abolition of slavery, and for University College, London, are touched on only in passing in this book. But the lecture-attending, theatregoing, book-reading Robinson, but busy conversationist and tireless friend, should be sufficiently revealed.

Two friends of his later years have left recollections[1] of him—Augustus De Morgan and Walter Bagehot. The former stresses his genial good-

[1] They are included in *The Life and Times of Henry Crabb Robinson*, by Edith J. Morley (1935).

humour and charm as a host, the companionship of his conversation, his hidden charities, his sturdy independence. He was eighty before De Morgan ventured to help him on with his overcoat. Crabb Robinson waved him off, saying: 'I look upon every man who offers to help me with my coat as my deadly enemy.'

Walter Bagehot, a little more exacting, saw him as a 'character', 'old Crabb', affectionately studying his gestures and eccentricities. He recorded the simplicity of his tastes, his love of young people. He remembered his recurrent anecdotes; his use of the chin at a conversational crisis, how at the point of a story he 'pushed it out, and then very slowly drew it in again, so that you always knew when to laugh, and the oddity of the gesture helped you in laughing'. He remembered the 'wonderful and dreary faces which Clough used to make' when H.C.R. insisted on reading Wordsworth in the middle of a meal. Of Robinson's expositions of German philosophy, Bagehot thought little; on the other hand, he felt that he much underrated his own legal knowledge and ability. The essential modesty of his old friend had made him nervous about the publication of his memoirs; but Bagehot, when he discovered Crabb Robinson's 'excellent power of narrative-writing', was surprised and pleased. Twice Bagehot nearly quarrelled with him; once when Bagehot wrote in favour of Louis Napoleon; once when he maintained that Hazlitt was a much greater writer than Charles Lamb. 'You, sir,' cried Robinson, 'you prefer the works of that scoundrel, that odious, that malignant writer, to the exquisite essays of that angelic creature!' But Bagehot, in conclusion, saw through the old-age infirmities of the man to 'the image of his buoyant sagacity, and his wise and careless kindness'.

Crabb Robinson died at 30 Russell Square on 5 February 1867, and was buried in Highgate Cemetery. 'He honoured and loved the great and noble in their thoughts and characters', states a tombstone inscription, more accurate than many. 'His warmth of heart and genial sympathy embraced all whom he could serve, all in whom he found response to his own healthy tastes and generous sentiments. His religion corresponded to his life; seated in the heart, it found expression in the truest Christian benevolence'. If there was a nimiety, a certain too-muchness, about Crabb Robinson (which could help to explain his Germanism), his goodness remains unassailable.

2. Text of the Diary

The papers left behind by Crabb Robinson are now preserved at Dr. Williams's Library, 14 Gordon Square, London, W.C.1. They include thirty-five volumes of his diary begun in 1811; thirty volumes of travel journals; thirty-two volumes of letters; four volumes of reminiscences; and a volume of anecdotes. Soon after Crabb Robinson's death in 1867, Dr. Thomas Sadler (1822–1891), a distinguished Unitarian minister, the author of various devotional works, prepared a comprehensive selection from the papers which appeared as the *Diary, Reminiscences, and Correspondence of Henry Crabb Robinson* (Macmillan, 3 vols., 1869). A third edition in two volumes was published by the same firm in 1872. Dr. Sadler's work was praiseworthy for its time; he contributed an excellent preface, and he succeeded in his main aim of establishing Crabb Robinson as a man to be reckoned with; but he was hardly a systematic editor, and, a century later, readers may well find his *omnium gatherum* somewhat old-fashioned and unattractive. Nor can his text be entirely relied on. Fifty years were to elapse, however, before Crabb Robinson's editorial saviour, Professor Edith Morley, appeared.

She proved to be as devoted a sponsor and admirer as H.C.R. could ever have dreamed of. Crabb Robinson's name is now inseparably linked with hers. In 1922 Professor Morley published a preliminary selection from his papers, especially those concerned with Blake, Coleridge, Wordsworth, Lamb, etc. (Manchester University Press). She followed this with his *Correspondence with the Wordsworth Circle* (Oxford University Press, 2 vols., 1927); his correspondence from Germany with his brother Thomas in 1800–1805, *Crabb Robinson in Germany* (Oxford University Press, 1929); a biography called *The Life and Times of Henry Crabb Robinson* (Dent, 1935); and the substantial selection from the diaries and reminiscences entitled *Henry Crabb Robinson on Books and their Writers* (Dent, 3 vols., 1938), on which the present abridgement is based. The diary extracts are confined to the first two volumes; the third volume consists of a number of appendices and a general index to the whole publication. The appendices include an index to mentions of writers and books in the volumes of Crabb Robinson's correspondence at Dr. Williams's Library, which has since been usefully supplemented by an index compiled by Inez Elliott of many other correspondents of Robinson's whose letters are preserved in the library (Dr. Williams's Trust, 1960).

Professor Edith Morley (1875–1964) came from a Jewish household, of families long settled in England. She held the professorship of English Language at the University of Reading from 1908 until 1940. Extremely generous and conscientious in all that concerned her teaching, she still found time to play a part in the Women's Movement, as a member of the Fabian Society, and as a founder-member of the British Federation of University Women. She became a magistrate, and she devoted herself for many years to the care of refugees from Nazi Germany. In her youth Professor Morley had spent three years in Hanover; throughout her life, Germany remained a major interest. Her knowledge of that country, and of education in England, was of particular value in her refugee work; while her German interest was again relevant in her prolonged study of Henry Crabb Robinson, where it was combined with her other major concern, English literature of the Romantic period.

I should like to pay the highest tribute here to Professor Morley's work for Crabb Robinson. The bibliography which I have added at the end of the book shows how much an inquirer must depend on the fruits of Professor Morley's labours. Her editorial resource and integrity inspire every confidence.

Nevertheless, H.C.R.'s testimony is less familiar to the general reading public than it might be; and this one-volume abridgement of *Henry Crabb Robinson on Books and their Writers* has been undertaken with the object, which I hope would have had Professor Morley's approval, of making his diary more widely known in the centenary year of his death. An abridgement that has reduced Professor Morley's eight hundred pages to the dimensions of the present book has had to be severe; interesting material has inevitably had to be excluded; and Professor Morley's volumes have been in no sense superseded. She set herself the task, which she successfully completed, of 'a comprehensive publication of everything that Crabb Robinson had to say about the books he read and the writers he met'. But Crabb Robinson wrote thousands of words about everything under the sun, and I seriously considered whether I should make my selection from his *Nachlass* as a whole. I soon decided, however, after dipping into the ocean of words at Dr. Williams's Library, that this would be a pointless exercise. On writers and their works Crabb Robinson is an irreplaceable commentator and witness—on other subjects he is interesting but dispensable. Besides, the theme of books and writers makes a wide field of reference, and the extracts in this book, which include several accounts of continental travel, do add up to a sort of social commentary on the years 1811 to 1867.

Professor Morley interspersed her excerpts from the diary and travel journals with passages from the reminiscences which Crabb Robinson compiled with their aid between 1845 and 1853. These I have ignored, apart from quoting them in this Introduction and in one or two footnotes. The diary has the great advantage of immediacy; of conveying first impressions, which must, to my mind, take precedence over afterthoughts. The reminiscences often add supplementary detail and a balanced summary; but on the whole they are of secondary value.

I have followed Professor Morley's text faithfully, inserting a few further names of people, places, etc., between square brackets, to assist readers of the abridgement. I have deleted the angle brackets used by Professor Morley to indicate a relatively small number of passages written either entirely in shorthand or in a mixture of shorthand and longhand in the manuscript. For the footnotes I must assume responsibility. Some of Professor Morley's footnotes have been displaced by the abridgement, but I have gratefully taken over many others, often in full, sometimes adapted or condensed. I have added many new footnotes of my own, either to explain or amplify points of detail, or to identify people in the diary. These footnotes tend to concern the lesser personalities; like Professor Morley, I have not thought it necessary to explain such outstanding figures as Wordsworth, Coleridge, Lamb, or Blake. If there is a certain inconsistency in this footnoting, owing to the quantity of names mentioned (often only surnames), I would add that the full names can usually be obtained from the index.

In making the abridgement, I have endeavoured to consider the diary as a whole, and especially to bear in mind that Crabb Robinson's close friendship with Wordsworth is its crowning glory. Although some cuts have been necessary, I have retained the greater part of the record of Wordsworth's activities and conversation. Similarly, I have kept virtually everything about Blake and Goethe, on both of whom H.C.R. is absorbingly interesting. References to Charles and Mary Lamb are extremely frequent, and often trivial—some of these have had to go; the same applies to a certain extent to Coleridge and Southey. Of H.C.R.'s accounts of the books he had been reading, I have been able to present only a small selection. I have given preference to his direct descriptions of men and events. It has been natural, perhaps, to concentrate on what he says about the major figures, but I have borne in mind that one of the charms of the diary lies in its references to minor characters.

In its early years the diary provides a fascinating account of the Regency and Georgian writers; and as gradually the great men disappear from the scene—Wordsworth one of the last—the interest is well sustained by the appearance of Carlyle, Landor, Dr. Arnold, Lady Blessington, Dickens, Emerson, Clough, the Brownings, George Eliot, Lady Byron, George MacDonald, Bagehot, and many more. In his old age H.C.R. could not get about as much as he used to, though he still 'cabbed it' to the Athenaeum; yet his candid comments on the latest contemporary offerings by the Victorian writers have a lasting value. I hope I have been able to convey, on a small scale, the importance and the unique quality of this record by a detached and discerning witness.

I am grateful to the Rev. Roger Thomas, the librarian, and to Miss Inez Elliott of the staff of Dr. Williams's Library, for much kind advice and assistance, and especially for drawing my attention to the two illustrations included in this volume. Schmeller's drawing of Crabb Robinson is reproduced by permission of the Goethe Collection, Weimar, and the photograph of him in his later years by courtesy of Dr. Williams's Library.

DEREK HUDSON

The Diary

1811

JAN. 8th . . . Spent part of the evening with Charles Lamb (unwell) and his sister. . . .

We spoke of Wordsworth and Coleridge. Lamb, to my surprise, asserted Coleridge to be the greater man. He preferred the *Mariner* to anything Wordsworth had written. Wordsworth, he thought, is narrow and confined in his views compared with [Coleridge]. He does not, like Shakespeare, become everything he pleases, but forces the reader to submit to his individual feelings. This, I observed, lies very much in the lyrical character, and Lamb concluded by expressing high admiration of Wordsworth. He had read many of his things with great pleasure indeed, especially the sonnets, which I had before spoken of as my favourites. Lamb also spoke in high praise of *Hart-leap Well* as one of Wordsworth's most exquisite pieces, but did not think highly of the *Leech-gatherer*. . . .

The other day Lamb related to me a droll anecdote of Smith, whom we met at Godwin's on Sunday, the 31st ult. He had been showing Smith an engraving of a female figure which he deems handsome, and on leaving it exclaimed: 'Well, what do you think of *my beauty*?' Smith became quite grave and embarrassed and said: 'Why, sir, from all I have heard of you, as well as from what I have myself seen, I certainly entertain a very high opinion of your abilities, but I confess that I have not yet thought or formed any opinion concerning your *personal pretensions*.' . . .

JAN. 29th Dined at Rickman's. Messrs. Proby, Hill, Wild, and Coleridge, who alone contributed with my host to my gratification.

Coleridge, as we walked, talked on Shakespeare, particularly his fools. These he considered as supplying the place of the ancient chorus. The ancient drama, he observed, is distinguished from the Shakespearian in this, that it exhibits a sort of abstraction, not of character, but of idea. A certain sentiment or passion was exhibited in all its purity, unmixed with anything that could interfere with its effect. Shakespeare imitates life, mingled, as we find it, with joy and sorrow. We meet with characters who are, as it were, unfeeling spectators of the most passionate situations, constantly in life. The fool serves to supply the place of some such uninterested person, where all the characters besides have interest. The most genuine and real of Shakespeare's fools is in *Lear*. In *Hamlet* the fool is, as it were, divided into several parts, dispersed through the piece. . . .

FEB. 2nd . . . Finished *Kehama.*[1] . . . My opinion of this poem has not changed on the second perusal. The faults are inherent in the subject. . . .

FEB. 27th . . . *Kehama*, I find, has a chance of becoming a fashionable poem. . . .

MARCH 4th . . . After dinner (the Gilberts here) I took tea with W. Hazlitt and had two hours' pleasant chat with him. Hazlitt spoke of Coleridge with the feelings of an injured man. Hazlitt had once hopes of being patronized by Sir George Beaumont. Coleridge and he were dining with him when Coleridge began a furious attack on Junius. Hazlitt grew impatient at Coleridge's cant and could not refrain from contradicting him. A warm and angry dispute arose. The next day Coleridge called on Hazlitt and said: 'I am come to show you how foolish it is for persons who respect each other to dispute warmly, for after all they will probably think the same.' Coleridge produced an interlined copy of *Junius* full of expressions of admiration, from which it appeared that Coleridge himself really agreed with Hazlitt. 'But,' added Hazlitt to me, 'Sir George Beaumont is a High Tory and was so offended with me, both for presuming to contradict and interrupt Coleridge and for being so great an admirer of Junius, that in disgust he never saw me afterwards. And I lost the expectation of gaining a patron.'

MARCH 8th . . . Called on W. Hazlitt. Learnt that Miss Lamb had had a renewal of her attack. . . .

Hazlitt thinks that poor Miss Lamb, as well as her brother, is injured by Coleridge's presence in town and their frequent visits and constant company at home, which keep their minds in a perpetual fever.

MARCH 10th . . . I showed Hazlitt Blake's *Young*. He saw no merit in them as designs. I read him some of the poems. He was much struck with them and expressed himself with his usual strength and singularity. 'They are beautiful,' he said, 'and only too deep for the vulgar. He has no sense of the ludicrous, and, as to a God, a worm crawling in a privy is as worthy an object as any other, all being to him indifferent. So to Blake the Chimney Sweeper, etc. He is ruined by vain struggles to get rid of what presses on his brain—he attempts impossibles.' I added: 'He is like a man who lifts a burden too heavy for him; he bears it an instant, it then falls on and crushes him.' W. Hazlitt preferred the *Chimney Sweeper*. . . .

At night wrote a letter to Southey thanking him for and praising his *Curse of Kehama*.

MARCH 13th . . . A call on Coleridge and a long chat on German poetry

[1] Robert Southey's chief epic poem.

and literature. He praised my translation of *Amatonda*,[1] and said there were only three or four faults in it. . . .

March 16th Charles Lamb . . . accompanied me and Mrs. Collier to Covent Garden. *Cato* was acted; a duller play than I was aware of. Kemble[2] gave me no pleasure, because the character could give me none; for *a priori* one might have thought that Kemble would have been a good Cato. He looked well. . . . Perhaps his performance throughout was faultless, but it was for me in general without beauties.

Bluebeard followed, to the delight of a crowded audience. Lamb was seemingly very merry. His sister's illness, I dare say, leaves him in no other state than outward affliction, or violent and false spirits which he works himself into, to subdue his real feelings.

March 29th . . . Spent evening with W. Hazlitt. Smith, his wife and son, Hume, Coleridge, and afterwards Lamb were there.

Coleridge philosophized as usual. He said that all systems of philosophy might be reduced to two, the dynamical and the mechanical, the one converting all quantity into quality, the other *vice versa*. He and Hazlitt joined in an obscure statement concerning abstract ideas. Hazlitt said that he had learnt from painting that it was difficult to form an idea of an individual object, that we had first only a *general idea*, that is, vague broken and imperfect recollection of the individual object. This, I had observed, was what the mob generally meant by a general idea, and Hazlitt said he had no other. Coleridge spoke of the impossibility of referring the individual to the class without having a previous notion of the class. But I doubt the concurrence of this explanation of a general idea with the Kantian theory. . . .

Before Lamb came, Coleridge had spoken with warmth of his excellent and serious conversation. Hazlitt imputed his puns to humility.

Coleridge declaimed about Rogers, whom he represented as most feelingly alive to criticism and public opinion. At first, he warmly eulogized Bloomfield, whom he neglected the moment he saw the world neglect him. . . .

March 30th . . . Accompanied Lamb to the Lyceum. *The Siege of Belgrade* afforded me considerable amusement. . . .

When Dignum and Mrs. Bland came on the stage together Lamb exclaimed:

> 'And lo! two puddings smoked upon the board.'

On returning to Lamb's, found Coleridge and W. Hazlitt there. A half-hour's chat. . . .

[1] A fairy tale by Anton Wall, published by Longmans.

[2] John Philip Kemble.

Coleridge spoke with severity of those who were once the extravagant admirers of Godwin,[1] and afterwards, when his fame declined, became his most angry opponents. . . . I noticed the infinite superiority of Godwin over the French writers in moral tendency and feeling. I had learned to hate Helvétius and Mirabeau and retained my love for Godwin. This was agreed to as a just sentiment by Coleridge, etc. Coleridge said there was more in Godwin after all than he was once willing to admit, though not so much as his enthusiasts fancied. He had declaimed against Godwin openly, but visited him notwithstanding he could not approve even of Wordsworth's feelings and language respecting Godwin. Southey's severity he ascribed to the habit of reviewing. Southey had said of Coleridge's poetry that he was a Dutch imitator of the Germans. Coleridge quoted this, not to express any displeasure, but to show in what way Southey could speak even of him.

We spoke of national characters, national dislikes, etc. Coleridge playfully said: 'I always say "a *Scotch* rascal," as if the infamy lay in the being *Scotch*.' Coleridge's antipathy to the Irish I cannot share in. But then, he has no aversion to Turks or Jews, so I am the best Christian after all.

APRIL 15th . . . Godwin related me an anecdote concerning Hazlitt. The painting he had made of . . . a handsome young man had been sent home with an abusive letter by the mother. Poor Hazlitt left town in great agony. He has not sent my brother's picture,[2] and I fear does not mean to let it go out of his hands; perhaps he has already destroyed it. And I fear he had not the money to refund. I saw also today Mr. Howel's portrait. It is a good caricature likeness, but a coarse painting. I fear poor Hazlitt will never succeed. With very great talents and with uncommon powers of mind I fear he is doomed to pass a life of poverty and unavailing repinings against society and his evil destiny. . . .

APRIL 16th . . . A pleasant gossip with Lamb, who talked seriously on his own affairs, etc. I am pleased to find that he is not imprudent in conduct. . . .

MAY 6th . . . Evening Charles Lamb called. I sat and chatted some time and at ten I called on Godwin, from whom I borrowed catalogues which I lounged over till late.

Coleridge, I learn, had from today undertaken to write occasionally in the *Courier*. He will at least have a motive to exertion which, while it lasts, must benefit his health and his pocket, though with such powers of mind, it cannot but be lamented that they should be so wasted.

[1] William Godwin (1756–1836), the philosopher and novelist.

[2] Crabb Robinson's brother Thomas had recently sat to Hazlitt.

MAY 11th . . . Called on Charles Lamb, gratified by finding Miss Lamb returned. . . .

MAY 15th . . . A very pleasant call on Charles and Mary Lamb. Read his version of the story of Prince Dorus—the long-nosed king. Gossiped about writing. Urged him to try his hand at a metrical *Umarbeitung* of *Reynard the Fox*. He believed, he said, in the excellence, but he was sure it would not succeed now. The sense for humour, he maintained, is utterly extinct. No satire that is not personal can possibly succeed. I spoke of *Rameau's Nephew*. He spoke highly of it without knowing it was translated by me; having no idea where he had seen it. He urged me to show him whatever I had written about the German authors and literature. This advice comes rather untimely; nor ought I to yield to it to any great degree to the derogation of my law reading, to which I am sufficiently disinclined. . . .

MAY 28th . . . A call on Coleridge. . . . He expressed liberal opinions on politics, and I doubt not the *Courier* would assume a different air if he were allowed to give it his complexion; but a prudent and shrewd man (Street) is always at his elbow, and knows sometimes how to make use of his talent, but more frequently rejects it as not suiting his purpose. . . .

JUNE 6th . . . At the exhibition, where I found but little to gratify me. Coleridge there: he pointed out to me the 'vigorous impotence' of Fuseli, whose 'Macbeth' is, indeed, a very disgusting production. The armed head is not amiss, but Macbeth is not human, and the more prominent witch has a vulgar sneer on her lip. Coleridge said: 'She is smelling a stink.' A ridiculous Achilles in the trenches looked like a soldier undergoing military discipline. 'The art of painting,' said Coleridge, 'it seems, is still to be recreated.' A fine picture of two boys by Lawrence delighted me, and there were also some excellent portraits. . . .

JUNE 11th . . . Coleridge read me a very beautiful essay on the reappointment of the Duke of York, which, however, had not been inserted in the *Courier*, though promised long since. He seemed dissatisfied with his situation. . . .

JUNE 13th . . . A call on Charles Lamb, his brother with him. A chat on puns. . . . The large room in the accountant's office in the East India House is divided into boxes or divisions in each of which sit six clerks (Charles Lamb himself is one). They are called *compounds*. The meaning of the word was asked one day there. Lamb said it was evident—'A *collection of simples*'. . . .

JUNE 20th . . . Finished Miss Edgeworth's *Leonora*. It is one of her least agreeable [narratives]. There is a great coarseness in the contrast between the good wife and the seductive mistress. . . . It wants the comic talent Miss Edgeworth so frequently displays, and as a novel is dull and tiresome. . . .

JUNE 21st . . . Charles and Mary Lamb, Dr. and Mrs. Adams, Barron Field, Wright, and M. Andrews spent the evening. At whist, which I enjoyed.

We sat up late. Lamb was very merry; his puns were more numerous than select; he made one good pun. Field had said: 'Whoever puns will steal. I always button my pockets when in company with a punster.' Someone said: 'Punsters have no pocket.' 'No,' said Lamb, 'they have no pocket; they carry only a ridicule.' . . .

JULY 12th Forenoon at law till twelve. A call on Coleridge; he conversed with me confidentially. The article about the Duke of York published in the *Courier* on Friday appeared only in about 2,000 copies of the paper. The day before it was to appear Mr. Arbuthnot from the Treasury, having obtained notice of the article, called on Stuart and insisted that it should not be published. Stuart resisted a long time, but at last yielded, and the greater number of the copies were cancelled. This compliance of Stuart with the will of the ministry Coleridge thinks is owing to Stuart's laziness, and not choosing to quarrel with Street,[1] . . . whom Coleridge considers as altogether a corrupt man. This affair makes Coleridge feel uncomfortable. He would gladly exchange his situation for that of *The Times*, but I informed him that Walter will not want him while Fraser remains with him. This conversation with Coleridge increased a great deal my good opinion of him. . . .

JULY 18th . . . I dined with Southey at Mr. Thelwall's; I enjoyed the day tolerably though the society was not the best for possessing the poet's company. Bakewell was there and not more pleasant than usual: he was not loud or frequent in the expression of his political feelings, but he sufficiently betrayed them to be, I believe, as little acceptable, though not so offensive personally, to Southey as myself. Southey's hopes of the Spaniards' final success are unchanged. But he is moderate and reasonable in his expectations. His opinions on the Bullion question are decided, and his reprobation of Lord King's conduct was marked and severe; he approves of the writings of Blanco White, and on the whole, I believe, I concur with him on the great questions of foreign and domestic policy. He spoke respectfully of Walter Scott (who wrote the *Quarterly* review of *Kehama*), considered him as having strength of delineation and the same kind of merit in his poems which Lewis has in his dramatic writings—rather an insidious [*sic*] comparison, I think. The *Vision of Don Roderick*

[1] Daniel Stuart, the original proprietor of the *Courier*, was a supporter of Coleridge, but Peter Street had recently acquired part-ownership.

he represents as an unsubstantial and insignificant performance. It will not maintain the poet's reputation. He spoke with great respect of William Taylor. Had not seen *Who is the father of Jesus Christ?* The *Edinburgh* reviewers, or rather Jeffrey, he says, having pledged himself to adopt a certain course in reviewing his poems, is obliged to persist in that course, though he would be glad to alter his tone if it were in his power. Southey's next poem will have a Quaker for the hero. I intimated the disadvantage he sustains from doing no homage to public opinion. He said: 'I think nothing about it.' He spoke highly of W. S. Landor, the author of *Gebir*, whom he is going to visit. Landor wrote lately a tragedy which Longman and Rees refused to publish. In consequence, Landor threw another tragedy into the fire which he had just composed. Southey would hardly allow him to be among the decided lunatics; though he admitted the first impression from his poem was to that effect. . . . Perhaps I took, however, too much of Southey's conversation to myself, for Bakewell, in a very gross way, reproached me with it afterwards. . . .

JULY 24th . . . Returned late to Charles Lamb's. Found a very large party there. Southey had been with Blake, and admired both his designs and his poetic talents, at the same time that he held him for a decided madman. Blake, he says, spoke of his visions with the diffidence that is usual with such people, and did not seem to expect that he should be believed. He showed Southey a perfectly mad poem called *Jerusalem*—Oxford Street is in Jerusalem.

Landor, Southey says, is by no means a madman in common life, but is quite discreet and judicious. . . .

Southey spoke of Wordsworth in a way that convinced me there is no great attachment between them. Wordsworth, he says, has the fault of overrating his works. He has by him poems that would be universally admired, but he has a miserly feeling concerning them, as if by being published they would cease to be his own.

He thinks the very worst of his works good enough to be published. Southey would not write a review of his pamphlet, because he knew Wordsworth would not be satisfied with the praise he should give it. I should add that Southey spoke enthusiastically of the pamphlet and of Wordsworth's genius, and said the fault of attaching too great importance to his own writings is his only one. . . .

Of Coleridge, Southey spoke as I expected he would. 'With a strong sense of duty,' said he, 'he has neglected it in every relation of life': he wishes him to finish his Greek Grammar, which he says would be most excellent, and would introduce a new mode of teaching the language.

JULY 31st . . . A call on Godwin. He looks ill, and I fear he is so broken in constitution that further intellectual exertion is not to be expected from him; perhaps not even the ordinary functions of an ordinary mind! Poor man! His latter days, if they be long, will be gloomy. He is not supported by enthusiasm, or the cheering hopes of a mild and sober faith. Nor will he be comforted by the kindness and respect of numerous friends. Though radically a man of integrity and principle, and endued with strong powers of mind, which he has *sometimes* employed for the benefit of society, yet in his decline the priest and the Pharisee will not merely turn *aside*, but will boast and make a merit of so doing. The selfish will be glad of an excuse for deserting an acquaintance who may be burthensome to them. And he is poor and has a numerous family, and his means of providing for them are very precarious.

AUG. 3rd . . . Chatted till eleven with Charles Lamb. He was serious and therefore very interesting. He corrected me not angrily, but as if really pained by the expression 'poor Coleridge,' I accidentally made use of. 'He is a fine fellow, in spite of all his faults and weaknesses. Call him Coleridge —I hate "*poor* Coleridge." I can't bear to hear pity applied to such a one.' . . .

AUG. 8th . . . Afterwards stepped to Charles Lamb's; Coleridge there. A short but interesting conversation on German metaphysics. He related some curious anecdotes of his son Hartley, whom he represented as a most remarkable child—a deep thinker in his infancy; one who tormented himself in his attempts to solve the problems that would equally torment the full-grown man, if the world and its cares and pleasures did not distract his attention. Hartley, when about five, was asked a question by someone concerning himself calling him 'Hartley.' 'Which Hartley?' asked the boy. 'Why, is there more than one Hartley?' 'Yes,' he replied, 'there is a deal of Hartleys.' 'How so?' 'There's Picture Hartley' (Hazlitt had painted a portrait of him) 'and Shadow Hartley, and there's Echo Hartley, and there's Catch-me-fast Hartley,' at the same time seizing his own arm with the other hand very eagerly, an action which shows that his mind must have been drawn to reflect on what Kant calls the great and inexplicable mystery, viz. that man should be both his own subject and object, and that these should yet be one. At the same early age, says Coleridge, he used to be in an agony of thought, puzzling himself about the reality of existence, as when someone said to him: 'It is not now, but it is to be.' 'But,' said he, 'if it *is* to be, it *is*.' Perhaps this confusion of thought lay not merely in the imperfection of language. Hartley when a boy had no pleasure in *things*; they made no impression on him, till they had undergone a sort of process in his mind and were become thoughts or feelings.

With a few abatements for the fatherly feeling (which I was glad to see in Coleridge), I have no doubt Hartley is a remarkable child. But of his subsequent progress Coleridge said but little.

SEPT. 22nd . . . Read also first volume Moore's *Epistles*, *Odes*, etc. This 'elegant voluptuary,' as my sister called him, must be allowed to possess great beauty of style and much grace of manner, and with a portion of talent that we regret to find without the higher qualities of the soul. His *Epistle*, sixth against America, is unlike his other works.[1] It is reasoning and serious and partakes of the gravity of a thinking man and the sternness of a moralist. He illustrates from the present character of the United States the vanity of relying on the perfectibility of man. . . .

SEPT. 26th . . . Pleasant evening. I read a number of Moore's poems, which I found very excellent, and though on the verge of indecorum, they were enjoyed by the ladies.

OCT. 20th . . . A party at dinner. . . . Coleridge, as usual, absorbed the conversation, but he was less interesting as he spoke on subjects of a technical kind; with Dr. Adams on medicine, etc. Manning called in after dinner and stayed the evening. Coleridge spoke of poetry, and gave an opinion of Southey, seemingly with reluctance, and not before he was urged to it, even more unfavourable than I expected. He had before denied all merit to Scott, saying that to judge of his beauties you must strike out all the names of places, of ancient armour—all the interesting *names* in fact, and seek for his images and sentiments. You would then perceive how little or nothing is in him—he nevertheless did not seem inclined to place Southey above Scott. He considered neither of them as poets. Coleridge spoke of his own poems with seeming disesteem. He published his first volume from poverty merely; he wanted £20. Yet the *Edinburgh* reviewers had considered him as the head of a class. By the bye, there was some self-complacency in this complaint. He mentioned that when his poems were first published he was accused of being inflated and bombastical in his style; but now he is ranked with those who delight in false simplicity.

Coleridge *wurde eingeladen etwas aus Christabel herzusagen aber er konnte die Worte nicht erinnern. Zum ersten Mahl sah ich ihn offenbar v. Getränk affizirt. Doch sagte er nichts Unschickliches.* The company remained till twelve.

OCT. 30th . . . Coleridge showed me an annunciation of lectures on poetry, etc., to be delivered this winter, fifteen of them; subscription, a lady two guineas; gentleman, three guineas, with power to bring a lady, four guineas. I *must* subscribe, though I ought not.

[1] *To the Lord Viscount Forbes from the City of Washington.*

Nov. 13th . . . Fraser desired me to take a ticket for him for Coleridge's lectures. This was handsome in him, the more so as he is very far indeed from being a friend to Coleridge. . . .

Nov. 14th . . . Walked into the city to distribute Coleridge's bills, some of which I left at C. Aikin's and Hamond's and with Evans. . . . Chatted a little with Charles Lamb, who expressed himself morally concerning both Hazlitt and Coleridge and their habits. I had afterwards occasion to write to Coleridge, and I was made low-spirited by the reflections which attending to the concerns of such a man naturally awoke. That a man of pre-eminent talents should be reduced to the necessary of soliciting for guineas and even for dollars is a most painful thing to see. The truth has been taught a thousand times in books, but I never felt before how inadequate the highest powers of the mind are to produce felicity without the concurrence of prudence. *Nullum numen abest si sit Prudentia!*

After dinner, at Flaxman's. I read to Flaxman Charles Lamb's very fine essay on Hogarth (*Reflector*, 3), which I had read before with great delight. Flaxman acknowledged the literary merit of the piece, but he by no means concurred in the opinion Charles Lamb maintains, that Hogarth is a moral painter. On the contrary Flaxman asserted that he was a very wicked though most witty artist. At first I was disposed to consider his remarks as founded on enthusiastic feeling and narrow conceptions concerning religion, but I found after a time that his censure of Hogarth rested on principles like those on which I had been accustomed to arraign Voltaire, especially in his *Candide*, viz. that Voltaire teaches that the most degrading vices and most horrid crimes that man can commit are objects of fun and ridicule. . . .

Nov. 18th . . . With Walter[1] to request he would put in a paragraph for Coleridge this evening. He hesitated and I was hurt. He consented, not with a good grace; and after the lecture I sent an article. . . . In the meanwhile Walter had become more civil, and left a note saying any article I might send should appear. Wrote my article at M. Andrews's.

Of Coleridge's lecture itself I fear the general opinion is not very favourable. It wanted popularity. And the moral remarks he made were not shown to have an immediate bearing upon the subject. I cannot myself well judge of the effect such remarks might have on strangers, for to me almost every individual observation was familiar. I had heard the same things from Coleridge in private conversation, and frequently in a better style than in the lecture itself. There was throughout too much

[1] John Walter II (1776–1847), son of the founder, and at this time the editor, of *The Times*. With Thomas Barnes, editor from 1817, he established the independent traditions of the paper.

apology, too much reference to what he had before written, too much promise of what was to come. This is his great fault. In the *Friend* he was guilty of it; he will commit it in his lectures. The observations he made were, in the main, just and often striking. But the lecture hardly equalled his conversation. . . .

NOV. 21st . . . Evening at Coleridge's second lecture, which was a vast improvement on the first. It was delivered with ease, was popular and contained interesting matter on that which the auditors wished to hear about. . . .

DEC. 5th . . . Accompanied Mrs. Rutt to Coleridge's lecture. In this he surpassed himself in the art of talking very amusingly without speaking at all on the subject to which the audience were especially invited. According to advertisement, Coleridge was to lecture on *Romeo and Juliet* and Shakespeare's female characters. Instead, he began with a defence of school flogging, at least in preference to Lancaster's mode of punishing, without pretending to find the least connection between that topic and poetry. Afterwards he remarked on the character of the age of Elizabeth and James I at the commencement in which intellect predominated, over that of Charles I, in which moral feeling prevailed. He distinguished between wit and fancy, not very clearly; he discoursed on the character of the different languages of Europe, attacked the fashionable notion concerning poetic diction, and abused Johnson's lines, '[Let] Observation with extensive view,' etc., ridiculing the tautology. And he commented on the alleged impurity of Shakespeare, and vindicated him against the charge with warmth!

The man is absolutely incorrigible. But his *vitia* are, indeed, *splendida.* I would have reported for the *Morning Chronicle* but it was too late. While Coleridge was so irrelevantly commenting on Lancaster's mode of punishing boys, Charles Lamb whispered: 'It is a pity he did not leave this till he got to *Henry VI* and then he might say he could not help taking part against the Lancastrians.' And afterwards, when Coleridge was so extravagantly running from topic to topic without any guide whatever, Charles Lamb said: 'This is not so much amiss. Coleridge said in his advertisement he would speak about the nurse in *Romeo and Juliet*, and so he is delivering the lecture in the character of the nurse.' . . .

DEC. 9th . . . Tea with Rough. Accompanied Mrs. Rough to Coleridge's seventh and incomparably best lecture. Coleridge declaimed with great eloquence on love, without wandering from his subject, *Romeo and Juliet.* He was spirited for the greater part, intelligible though profound, and he was methodical. . . . Drew up a hasty report of the lecture for the *Morning Chronicle*, which was inserted.

Dec. 30th . . . Allowed to make my retreat to Coleridge's lectures, went with Miss Benger, who called for me. I had drunk too much to be quite clear-headed. However, I was pleased to find Coleridge very methodical. He kept to his subject, and, in conformity with an opinion I gave him, intimated his intention to deliver two lectures on Milton. He had written to me stating his dilemma—having so much to do in so little time—and I wrote to him in answer in which I gently hinted at his digressions, those *splendida peccata*, which his friends best apologised for by laying the emphasis on the adjective.

1812

Jan. 14th . . . Tea with Charles Lamb. . . . Went to Hazlitt's first lecture on the History of English Philosophy. He read ill a very sensible book; and, as he seems to have no conception of the difference between a lecture and a book, his lectures cannot possibly be popular, hardly tolerable. He read a sensible and excellent introduction on philosophy and on Hobbes; but he delivered himself in a low, monotonous voice, with his eyes fixed intently on his book, not once daring to look on his audience. He read, too, so rapidly that no one could possibly follow him; at the same time, the matter he read was of a kind to require reflection. No subject is in itself less adapted to a lecture than metaphysical philosophy; no manner less adapted to recommend abstruse matter than Hazlitt's. So that it is impossible Hazlitt's lectures should not altogether fail of their subject, unless he should alter his style and delivery, which I fear is hardly in his power. With all these exceptions to his lectures, as such, the matter was in general, as far as I could force my attention to comprehend it, very excellent. . . .

Jan. 15th . . . Tea with the Lambs. An evening at cards. . . . Hazlitt there, much depressed. Dr. Stoddart had left a letter of advice to him on his lecture, which hurt him apparently, and the conversation that afterwards took place irritated him greatly. He seemed disposed to give up the lectures altogether, at least in the Russell Institution. He blamed himself for yielding to Dr. Stoddart in delivering them there, and considered the size of the room, the nature of the audience, etc., as the occasions of his not succeeding. He was told by Flack, the secretary, as he began to lecture, that he must limit himself to an hour. This made him read so rapidly. His lecture, read slowly, would (without any curtailments) have lasted three hours. I observed on the difference between a book and a lecture, and, perhaps more than I intended, betrayed my opinion. I spoke of the compassion I felt beholding Hazlitt so oppressed in delivering the lecture, and this he misunderstood. For Miss Lamb told me the following day that he had been hurt by this, and, in consequence, I wrote a letter to him explaining what I had said. . . .

JAN. 17th . . . Dinner at J. Buck's. Mr. and Miss Buck, Coleridge, the Gores, Jameson, and Aders. Coleridge was less profound than usual, but exceedingly agreeable. He recollected in whose company he was, and made himself pleasant by avoiding offensive topics. He related anecdotes of himself. He was arrested as a spy at Fort St. George. The governor immediately as he saw him, said: 'An ill-looking fellow.' Everything that Coleridge could say for himself was ingeniously perverted and applied against himself, till a card he accidentally had by him from a person of quality convinced the governor he was a gentleman, and procured him an invitation to breakfast the next morning. Coleridge then asked the governor what it was in his appearance that induced him to say 'an ill-looking fellow.' 'My dear sir,' said he, squeezing him by the hand, 'I lost my eyesight nearly, in the West Indies, and cannot see a yard before me.' Coleridge, when at Bristol, delivered lectures in conjunction with Southey. A fellow came and hissed him, and an altercation ensued. The man sneered at Coleridge for professing public principle, and said: 'Why, if you are so public-spirited, do you take money at the door?' 'For a reason,' said Coleridge, 'which I am sorry in the present instance has not been quite successful—to keep out blackguards.'

. . . At ten went to Barron Field's (No. 4 Hare Court, Temple). Charles Lamb and Leigh Hunt[1] and Mr. Hills there. Lamb and Hunt I found had had a contest about Coleridge. Hunt had spoken of him as a bad writer, Lamb as of the first man he ever knew. The dispute was revived by me, but nothing remarkable was said. Charles Lamb, who soon became tipsy, in his droll and extravagant way abused every one who denied transcendency, while Hunt dryly denied the excellency of his writings, and expressed his regret that he did not know him personally. Hunt took Lamb's speeches in good part, evidently by his manner showed his respect for his talents; while Lamb, to make his freedoms endurable, praised Hunt's remarks on Fuseli (a praise Hunt seeemed to relish).

JAN. 20th . . . Evening Coleridge's lecture, conclusion of Milton. Not one of his happiest lectures. Among the audience Lord Byron and Rogers the banker. . . .

JAN. 21st . . . Hazlitt's second lecture which I heard. He delivered him-

[1] James Henry Leigh Hunt (1784–1859), the essayist, critic, and poet, best considered in Edmund Blunden's biography (1930).

self well, that is, loud, and with a tone of confidence which, being forced, had sometimes the air of arrogance. This, however, did not offend (except perhaps a few), and he was interrupted by applauses several times. His lecture was on Locke. . . .

On the whole Hazlitt improved vastly in his present lecture, and I hope he will now get on.

JAN. 27th . . . Coleridge's concluding lecture. . . . The lecture was exceedingly well attended: and Coleridge was very animated in parts; his development of the character of Satan, his apology for Milton's mode of treating the character of the Supreme Being, etc., were excellent. There were some excrescences in the lecture, and he offended me by an unhandsome and unmanly attack upon Mrs. Barbauld. He ridiculed some expressions in her *Ode to Content*, 'The hamlets brown, primrose and violet,' etc.—'criticisms,' he added, 'which Wordsworth made to me at Charles Lamb's two years ago.' That he should select among the living authors, a woman, and that woman a lady who has been among his admirers formerly, and I believe always showed him civilities, is ungenerous and unworthy of his better feelings. He analysed a passage in Pope's *Homer* (a description of moonlight) and showed its want of propriety and taste with great spirit. At the same time he introduced this censure with a very insincere eulogium. . . .

MARCH 16th . . . Returned to Charles Lamb, with whom were Barron Field, Leigh Hunt, and Barnes.[1] Barnes, with a somewhat *feist* appearance, has a good countenance, and is a man who I dare say [will] make his way in the world. He has talents and activity and inducement to activity.

He has obtained high honours at Cambridge and is now candidate for a fellowship. He reports for Walter. These are all promising *indicia*. Neither he, however, nor the others said anything remarkable. Charles Lamb was in his best humour; very good-humoured, but at the same time solid. I never heard him to greater advantage. He wrote last week in the *Examiner* some capital lines, *The Triumph of the Whale*, and they occasioned the conversation to take more of a political turn than is usual with Lamb. Leigh Hunt is an enthusiast. He is very well-intentioned, and I believe prepared for the worst. He said pleasantly enough: 'No one can accuse me of *not* writing a libel. Everything is a libel, as the law is now declared; and our security lies only in their shame.' Lamb talked on the theatre, and showed his great superiority on these points over the others.

MARCH 30th . . . Stepped late to Barron Field's chambers. Barnes, Lamb, and J. Collier. We talked about Hunt, whose indiscreet articles

[1] Thomas Barnes, editor of *The Times*, 1817–1841.

against the Prince even his friends censure. Lamb and Barnes disputed about Wordsworth. Barnes's notions and feelings are quite commonplace, but he has a great deal of knowledge and converses well.

May 3rd . . . Coleridge spoke to me for the first time about Wordsworth's quarrel with him, and with permission for me to repeat to Wordsworth all he said. Coleridge has no objection whatever to see Wordsworth, either alone or in the presence of friends, but he will not consent to the proposal made that he should meet Wordsworth with Montagu[1] in order that he and Montagu should be confronted. . . .

. . . Coleridge also said: 'One of these three things must be true—a fourth is not possible. Either Wordsworth has treated me most unkindly and in a manner which no friend ought to have done, or I am a most ungrateful and vile wretch' (the words were more emphatic than these), 'or Montagu is a liar.' The result of all was a reiteration of his willingness to see Wordsworth; his determination not to see Montagu. I should add that throughout he spoke with strong feeling of reverence for Wordsworth. 'I complain of Wordsworth's conduct towards me. I have nothing to say against him. I should not have been almost killed by this affair if it had not been that I had loved Wordsworth as a great and good man. I would have sacrificed even my external reputation for him. And I should not have felt as I have done if I had not felt that I must love Wordsworth less than before.' Coleridge then burst into strong exclamations: 'What friend have I ever lost! Who that ever did love me has ever ceased to love me!' . . .

May 8th Intended to devote this day to business, when I was interrupted by a visit from Wordsworth, who stayed with me in chambers from between twelve and one till past three, and I then walked with him to Newman Street. His conversation with me was long and interesting. He spoke of his own poems with the just feelings of confidence that a sense of his own excellence gives him. He is now convinced that he never can derive emolument from them; but being independent now, he willingly gives up all idea of deriving profit from them. He is convinced that if men are to become better and wiser, the poems will sooner or later find their admirers; but if we are to perish and society is not to advance in civilization it would be wretched selfishness, said he, 'to deplore the want of any personal reputation.' The approbation he has met with from *some* superior persons compensates for the loss of popularity, though no man has completely understood him—Coleridge not excepted, who is not happy enough to enter into his feelings. 'I am myself,' said he, 'one of the happiest of men, and no man who does not partake of that happiness, who

[1] Basil Montagu. See *infra*, p. 53 note.

lives a life of constant bustle, and whose felicity depends on the opinions of others, can possibly comprehend the best of my poems.'

I urged an excuse for those who can really enjoy Wordsworth's better pieces, and who yet are offended by a language they have, by early instruction, been taught to consider as *unpoetical*. And Wordsworth seemed to tolerate this class, and to allow that his admirers should be taught and undergo a sort of education to his works. We spoke of a few living people. Wordsworth is not reconciled to Mrs. Barbauld; his chief reproach against her now is her having published pretty editions of Akenside, Collins, etc., with critical prefaces which have the effect of utterly forestalling the natural feeling and judgment of young and ingenuous readers. This practice he considers as absolutely shocking. The practice may be bad, but it seems to me still absurd to make it a charge against an individual. This is carrying intolerance further than I ever knew it carried. No allowance is made for the infinite bearings and relations and points of view in which anything may be contemplated, according to every one of which an act may be irreproachable morally, though according to some there may be inconveniences and even ultimately bad effects. Wordsworth expressed a wish to see Mrs. C. Aikin, though he laughed at the 'caste of writers': he would have no objection to meet Mrs. Barbauld, but he does not choose to seek her. . . .

I delivered Coleridge's message to Wordsworth, and this led to a long conversation, and to a commission which Wordsworth gave me, viz. in answer to Coleridge's message to say to him the following:

1. That he, Wordsworth, denied most positively having ever given to Montagu any commission whatever to say anything as from him, Wordsworth, to Coleridge; that he said nothing to Montagu with any other than a friendly purpose towards both Coleridge and Montagu, that he was anxious to prevent Coleridge's going into Montagu's family, because he knew that such an intimacy would be broken as soon as it was formed, and lead to very painful consequences. Under this impression only, he spoke with Montagu. But he takes blame to himself for being so intent upon attaining this object as to forget that Montagu was not a man whose discretion could be safely trusted with even so much as he did say to him.

2. He denies having ever used such a phrase as *rotten drunkard*; such an expression he could not, as a man of taste, merely, have made use of.

3. Neither did he ever say that Coleridge *had been a nuisance in his family*. He might, in the course of conversation, and in reference to certain particular habits, have used the word 'nuisance,' which is a word he frequently makes use of, but he never employed it as the result or summary of his feelings towards Coleridge. He never said *he* was a nuisance

4. Further, he wished me to inform Coleridge that he no longer wished to confront him and Montagu. He was content to leave undetermined who had erred, but he expected from Coleridge that when he, Wordsworth, had made this declaration, he, Coleridge, would give him credit for the truth of it, and not continue to use that language about him which he had done.

These points I distinguish from the rest of Wordsworth's statement, because they are those I did afterwards repeat to Coleridge. Except perhaps the conclusion of the last, which I might not distinctly state to Coleridge.

Wordsworth added other remarks, which I was careful not to repeat, as they could not tend to the reconciliation so desirable, and perhaps so important to the future happiness of Coleridge. Wordsworth did not deny having said he had no hopes of Coleridge. And with respect to the phrase 'rotting out his entrails by intemperance,' he does not think he used such an expression, but the idea might be conveyed in what he said, and Montagu might give that as the conclusion from all he said. . . . Coleridge's habits had, in fact, been of a kind which he, Wordsworth, could not have endured but for the high estimation he had formed of Coleridge. Wordsworth, with no faint praise, then spoke of Coleridge's mind, the powers of which he declared to be greater than those of any man he ever knew. From such a man, under favourable influences, everything might be looked for. His genius, he thought to be great, but his talents still greater, and it is in the union of so much genius with so much talent that Coleridge surpasses all the men Wordsworth ever knew. In a digression to which this remark led, Wordsworth observed of himself that he, on the contrary, has comparatively but little talent; genius is his characteristic quality. If genius (in this relation) be creation and original production from the stores of individual mind, and talent show itself in the power of appropriating and assimilating to itself the product of foreign minds, and by so imbibing and adding to its own possessions the attainments of other minds—then I have always given to Wordsworth and Coleridge the respective superiority in genius and talents. . . .

. . . I walked with him to Newman Street, and proceeded immediately to Coleridge. What I said to him is already stated in the preceding account of my conversation with Wordsworth. Coleridge manifested certainly much more feeling than Wordsworth. He was greatly agitated and affected, even to tears. He promised to draw up the brief statement Wordsworth requested, and I am to have this on Sunday morning. But Coleridge received Wordsworth's declarations with less satisfaction than I could have wished. He said: 'Had Wordsworth *at first* denied using the language employed by Montagu, had he stated, "I said what I did say purely out of friendship, and I regret having said so much to a man like Montagu,' the only [whole?] affair would have been as a cobweb between Wordsworth and my love of him.'

Coleridge then burst into strong expressions of his love for Wordsworth. . . .

MAY 9th . . . A call on Charles Lamb. Found Miss Lamb with him, to my great satisfaction. I chatted a short time. He is of opinion that any attempt to bring Wordsworth and Coleridge together must prove ineffectual. Perhaps he thinks it mischievous. He thinks Wordsworth cold. It may be so; healthful coolness is preferable to the heat of disease. . . .

MAY 10th Called by appointment on Coleridge. I found him writing the promised statement, which he read to me, but was too much affected to be able to proceed. The statement contained the most indubitable internal evidence of truth. The facts are nearly those anticipated in Wordsworth's denial on Friday. And the paper, though not elaborately drawn up, or artfully written, produced the due effect on Wordsworth's mind, to whom I carried it immediately, and with whom I spent the remainder of the morning. Wordsworth's conversation was very interesting; much was confidential. . . .

MAY 11th At half-past ten with Wordsworth by appointment, and left him in Oxford Road past two. The morning was spent in answering Coleridge's statement, which Wordsworth had great difficulty to do because he had to reconcile things very difficult to unite—the most exact truth and sincerity with the giving his friend the least possible pain. The objections, therefore, that were made to particular expressions that might be liable to one of two [*sic*] obvious objections were innumerable. The purport of the letter was a denial most direct and comprehensive, that he had given to Montagu any commission whatever to say to Coleridge anything whatever, and a denial, as to the particular words alleged, that any of them were used in the spirit imputed to them. . . .

I should add that the great part of the letter was written by me. Wordsworth being by no means tenacious of what he had written [erasure] willing to say anything he could truly, to give Coleridge satisfaction.

Dr. Wordsworth joined us and we walked into Oxford Street together. Coleridge was not at home. After an early dinner, and a short call at chambers and tea, I went again to Coleridge, where I found the Lambs. I had just heard of what had taken place about an hour and half before, the assassination of Mr. Perceval. This news shocked Coleridge exceedingly. He spoke with great warmth of esteem for Perceval, much more indeed than I think in any way merited by Perceval. Coleridge was at once ready to connect this murder with political fanaticism, Burdett's speeches, etc. Charles Lamb was apparently affected, but could not help mingling with humour his real concern at the event, for he talked of loving his Regent.

Coleridge said to me in a half whisper that Wordsworth's letter had been perfectly satisfactory to him, and that he had answered it immediately. I flatter myself, therefore, that my pains will not have been lost, and that through the interchange of statements, which but for me would probably never have been made, a reconciliation will have taken place most desirable and salutary.

MAY 13th . . . Lounged with Rough at his chambers. At four the Wordsworths came to the serjeant's to dinner. . . . Our afternoon was very pleasant. Wordsworth talked at his ease, having confidence in his audience. He spoke with respect of Landor's power. The tragedy which he is now publishing has very fine touches, he says. He spoke of Kirke White. Both he and Rough agreed in considering him as a man of more talents than genius, and that the great correctness of his early writings was a symptom unpromising as to his future works. He would probably have been rather a man of great learning than a great poet. He would not have been more than a Southey, said Rough. 'And that would have been nothing after all,' said Wordsworth,—'when speaking of the highest excellence,' he added. He however spoke afterwards of the 'genius' of Southey. In walking afterwards, Wordsworth spoke with great contempt of Scott, and illustrated his remarks on a phrase, 'kindling a spark'—it is with a spark we kindle a fire, etc. He assented to the observation 'that the secret of Scott's popularity is the vulgarity of his conceptions, which the million can at once comprehend.' . . .

Wordsworth accompanied me to Charles Aikin's. We found there Mrs., Miss, and Arthur Aikin, Misses Jane Porter, Benger, Clarke, Smirke, Messrs. Cullen, Roscoe (son of the Liverpool Roscoe), and Yates from Liverpool, and Montgomery[1] the poet and Mrs. Barbauld. The conversation was not very interesting. I did not hear Miss Porter speak, nor scarcely Montgomery. He looks like a methodist parson, and has what Wordsworth expressed the appearance of a feeble and amiable man. Wordsworth gave him his hand at once with cordiality, and Montgomery showed marks of great pleasure when Wordsworth entered. Indeed, the attention showed Wordsworth and the homage involuntarily paid him were the most agreeable circumstances during the evening. Everybody was anxious to get near him. . . .

MAY 19th . . . Wordsworth has seen Coleridge several times, and been much in his company, but they have not yet touched upon the subject of

[1] James Montgomery (1771–1854).

their correspondence. Thus, as I hoped, the wound is healed; but, as I observed to Mrs. Clarkson, probably the scar remains in Coleridge's bosom. . . .

MAY 24th A very interesting day. Rose late; at half-past ten joined Wordsworth in Oxford Road, and we then got into the fields and walked to Hampstead. We talked of Lord Byron. Wordsworth allowed him power, but denied his style to be English. Of his moral qualities we think the same. He adds that there is insanity in Lord Byron's family, and that he believes Lord Byron to be somewhat cracked. I read Wordsworth some of Blake's poems; he was pleased with some of them, and considered Blake as having the elements of poetry a thousand times more than either Byron or Scott; but Scott he thinks superior to Campbell. I was for carrying down the descent to Rogers, but Wordsworth would not allow it. Rogers has an effeminate mind, but he has not the bad, obscure writing of Campbell. Wordsworth says a very large proportion of our noble families are affected by hereditary insanity, as well as the royal families of Europe.

We met Miss Joanna Baillie and accompanied her home. She is a little woman with a mean, shuffling walk, and no exterior sign of literary talent; but on the other hand her manners are those of a well-bred gentlewoman, and she has none of the unpleasant airs too common to literary women. Her conversation is sensible; she possesses apparently considerable information, promptitude without forwardness, and a fixed judgment of her own, without any disposition to force it on others.

. . . Wordsworth, when alone, speaking of S.,[1] said he is one of the cleverest men that is now living. At the same time he justly denied him ideality in his works. He never inquires, says Wordsworth, on what idea his poem is to be wrought, what feeling or passion is to be excited; but he determines on a subject, and then reads a great deal and combines and connects industriously, but he does not give anything which impresses the mind strongly and is recollected in solitude. This was always my opinion of S.[1]

We talked of Unitarians, etc. Wordsworth said he could not feel with the Unitarians in any way. Their religion allows no room for imagination, and satisfies none of the cravings of the soul. 'I can feel more sympathy with the orthodox believer who needs a Redeemer and who, sensible of his own demerits, flies for refuge to Him (though perhaps I do not want one for myself) than with the cold and rational notions of the Unitarian.' Parken the other day speaking of Wordsworth, spoke of his pride. How would he triumph at such a confirmation of his charge.

MAY 29th . . . After a mere look at the office, at Morgan's, where I

[1] Presumably Southey.

spent the evening, and made a call for half an hour on Mr. [Parken?]. He had heard Coleridge's lecture in the morning, but thought him infinitely inferior to Campbell, who it appears is exceedingly admired. P[arken?] thinks Coleridge makes a sad confusion of mythology, metaphysics, etc. This, I have no doubt, is the general opinion, nor is it unfounded. With such powers of original thought and real genius both philosophical and poetical, such as few men in any age have possessed, Coleridge wants certain low and minor qualities which render his great powers almost inefficient and useless, while most subordinate persons obtain all the fame he merits. Returned to Morgan's. A pleasant chat with Coleridge apart, and afterwards with Wordsworth more generally. Coleridge very metaphysical; he adheres to Kant notwithstanding all Schelling has written, and maintains that from Schelling he has gained no new ideas, all Schelling has said he having either thought before or found in Jacob Boehmen.

Wordsworth talked very freely on poetry. He praised Burns for his introduction to *Tam o' Shanter*. He had given a poetical apology for drunkenness by bringing together all the circumstances which can serve to render excusable what is in itself disgusting, thus interesting our feelings and making us tolerant of what would otherwise be not endurable:

> The night drave on wi' sangs an clatter,
> And aye the ale was growing better:
> The landlady and Tam grew gracious,
> Wi' favours secret, sweet, and precious;
> The souter tauld his queerest stories;
> The landlord's laugh was ready chorus:
> The storm without might rair and rustle,
> Tam did na mind the storm a whistle.
> Care, mad to see a man sae happy,
> E'en drown'd himself amang the nappy;
> As bees flee hame wi' lades o' treasure,
> The minutes wing'd their way wi' pleasure;
> Kings may be blest, but Tam was glorious,
> O'er a' the ills o' life victorious!

Wordsworth also praised the conclusion of *Death and Dr. Hornbook*. Wordsworth compared this with the abrupt prevention of the expected battle between Satan and the Archangel in Milton; but this remark did not bring its own evidence with it. I took occasion to apply the praise given to Burns for the passage quoted to Goethe, and this led to my warm praise of him. Coleridge denied merit to *Torquato Tasso*, and Wordsworth seemed disposed to think low of him. Coleridge talked of the impossibility of being a good poet without being a good man, and urged the immorality of Goethe's works as a proof he is not a good poet. This I demurred to.

MAY 31st A day of great enjoyment. . . . At Hamond's found Wordsworth demonstrating to Hamond some of the points of his philosophical theory. Speaking of his own poems, Wordsworth said he principally valued them as being *a new power* in the literary world. Hamond's friend, Miller, esteemed Wordsworth for the pure morality of his works. Wordsworth said he himself looked to the powers of the mind his poems call forth, and the energies they presuppose and excite, as the standard by which they are to be estimated. Wordsworth purposes as soon as the two last volumes are out of print to reprint the four volumes, arranging the poems with some reference either to the fancy, imagination, reflection, or mere feeling contained in them. *The Kitten and the Falling Leaves* he spoke of [as] merely fanciful, *The Highland Girl* as of the highest kind being imaginative, *The Happy Warrior* as appertaining to reflection. In illustration of his principle of imaginative power he quoted his *Cuckoo*, and in particular the 'wandering voice,' as giving local habitation to an abstraction. I stated as a compression of Wordsworth's rather obscure account of poetic abstraction the following as the operation. The poet first conceives the essential nature of his object and strips it of all its casualties and accidental individual dress, and in this he is a philosopher; but to exhibit his abstraction nakedly would be the work of a mere philosopher; therefore he reclothes his *idea* in an individual dress which expresses the essential quality, and has also the spirit and life of a sensual object, and this transmutes the philosophic into a poetic exhibition. Wordsworth quoted the picture of the Old Man in his Leech Gatherer and the simile of the stone on the eminence as an instance of an imaginative creation.

Wordsworth spoke with great contempt of Campbell as a poet, and illustrated his want of truth and poetic sense in his imagery by a close analysis of a celebrated passage in *The Pleasures of Hope*, 'Where Andes, giant of the Western star,' etc.,[1] showing the whole to be a mere jumble of discordant images, meaning, in fact, nothing, nor conveying very distinct impression, it being first uncertain who or what is the giant, and who or what is the star. Then the giant is made to hold a meteor-standard and to sit on a throne of clouds and look (it is not apparent for what) on half the world. Gray's line, speaking of the bard's beard, which 'streamed like a

[1] Now on Atlantic waves he rides afar,
Where Andes, giant of the western star,
With meteor-standard to the winds unfurl'd,
Look from his throne of clouds o'er half the world.
The Pleasures of Hope. Part I, ll. 56-59.

meteor to the troubled air,' Wordsworth also considered as ridiculous, and both passages he represented to be unmeaningly stolen from a fine line by Milton, in which a spear is for its brightness only compared to a meteor. Wordsworth spoke with great feeling of the present state of the country. He considers the combinations among journeymen, and even the Benefit Societies and all associations of men, apparently for the best purposes, as very alarming: he contemplates a renovation of all the horrors of a war between the poor and the rich, a conflict of property with no property. Hamond believes that if masters have so great influence over their servants [and] if they do not forfeit it by gross misconduct, that the lower classes might be easily kept in order. I objected the vast extent of business carried on by manufacturers for foreign consumption. The ancient relations between master and servant are utterly lost among this class. And Wordsworth contemplated the manufacturing system as a most menacing evil. Wordsworth spoke in defence of Church establishment, and on the usual grounds said he would shed his blood for it. He declared himself not virtuous enough for a clergyman. Confessed he knew not when he had been in a church at home—'All our ministers are such vile creatures'—and he allowed us to laugh at this droll concession from a staunch advocate for the establishment.

The mischief of making the clergy depend on the caprice or fashion of the mob he considered as more than counterbalancing all other evils. And I agree with him. . . .

Dined at Mr. Carr's, and a very interesting afternoon—more from the persons than from their conversation. Sir Humphry and Lady Davy. Sir Humphry has a fine expressive eye, and his manners are not unpleasing, though there is a tendency to the coxcomb in them. Lady Davy I found more agreeable than when I first saw her; she and Sir Humphry seem to have hardly survived the honeymoon: their reciprocal endearments the other day induced Miss Joanna Baillie to say to Wordsworth: 'They had witnessed a picturesque happiness.' Lady Davy was my companion at table. I did not, I believe, *this* time offend by keeping her too frequently silent. Miss Baillie and Miss Joanna Baillie. The poetess looked amiably, but I hardly heard a word from her. She was engaged with Wordsworth. Miss Baillie is also a gentlewoman, rather more Scottish in her dialect and precise in her manners, but with a friendly countenance, though far from handsome. Mr. Duppa, who actually honoured me with his hand; meeting me at a dinner party, he may, perhaps, think me a person to be acknowledged. He calls Wordsworth his *friend* in his life of Michael Angelo. No one today would have thought they had been acquaintances. Mr. Stable, a young man of genteel appearance, but silent. His sister, a large, no longer young, nor perhaps a handsome, but a most elegant figure and fine, interesting face: her looks delighted me more than the words of the rest of the party. Mr. Burrell, whom I was much pleased with. Our host and hostess, who behaved with politeness, formed the party. We had little or no conversation. Davy and Wordsworth spoke in very depreciating terms of Mrs. Walter Scott, whom Joanna Baillie and Lady Davy, on the contrary, defended. Miss Baillie said: 'When I visited Mrs. Walter Scott, I thought I saw a great deal to like. She seemed to look up to and admire her husband. She was very kind to her guests, her children were well bred, and the house was in excellent order. And she had some smart roses in her cap, and I did not like her the worse for that.' After dinner the company was increased. Mr. Hoare the banker came: he said he knew that the Prince had been too much occupied by the installation of the Knights of the Bath to be able to form a ministry. . . .

June 3rd . . . At four went to Rough's. The poet and Dean Wordsworth and Cargill[1] dined with us. A very pleasant and interesting afternoon. Wordsworth talked much about poetry. He was made to explain *fancy* as opposed to *imagination*, from which it results that fancy forms casual and fleeting combinations in which objects are united, *not* on a permanent relation which subsists and has its principle in the capacity of the *sensible* produced to represent and stand in the place of the abstract intellectual conception, but in a voluntary power of combination which only expresses the fact of the combination with little or no import beyond itself. This is the best explanation I can give. Wordsworth quoted as instances a fine description of cold from Cotton's *Winter* (his own *Kitten and the Falling Leaves* I have mentioned before). After tea he read us *Benjamin the Waggoner*, a tale of more naiveté than Wordsworth often displays, and with a fine description of a sailor travelling with his ship in model: but I shall refer to it again. Walked with the Doctor to Lambeth Palace and then with Wordsworth to the end of Oxford Road. He talked much of poetry and with great and, to me, laudable freedom of his own poems. He said that perhaps there is as *intense* poetical feeling in *his* as Shakespeare's works, but in Shakespeare the poetical elements are mixed up with other things and wrought into greater works. In him the poetry is *reiner* [more pure]. He contrasted some fine lines from his verses on the Wye, with a popular passage from Lord Byron on solitude. Lord Byron's is a coarse but palpable assertion of the nature of solitude, with an epigrammatic conclusion. In Wordsworth the feeling is involved and the thought clothed in poetic shapes. It is, therefore, no wonder that

[1] Richard Cargill, a native of Jamaica, who became a barrister and afterwards took Holy Orders.

Wordsworth's description should be forgotten, and Lord Byron's in general circulation.

Wordsworth asserted that Southey was no judge of *his* poems, writing too many of his own to enter into his mind. And on my saying that Southey had praised his unpublished poems as superior to those published, Wordsworth seemed to resent this rather as a depreciation of the latter than a praise of the former. He could not surpass what he had already written. They are the utmost energies of his mind. Before his ballads were published Tobin implored Wordsworth to leave out *We are Seven* as a piece that would damn the book. It became one of the most popular. He related this in answer to a remark that by only leaving out certain poems at the suggestion of someone who knows the public taste he might avoid giving offence. Rogers has said the same, but Wordsworth gives no credit to the assertion. His sonnet in which the wild rose is compared to a village girl[1] he says is almost the only one of pure fancy. I also mentioned the one on the ship.[2] He said it expressed the delight he had felt on thinking of the first feelings of men before navigation had so completely made the world known, and while a ship exploring unknown regions was an object of high interest and sympathy.

JUNE 5th A short time in chambers only. At Coleridge's *last* lecture of his first course: he promised to speak of *Othello*, but wasted his time on *The Winter's Tale*. He digressed excessively, so that he hardly allowed himself time to point out the contrast between the jealousy of the husband of that play and that of *Othello*. In the future lectures money is to be taken at the door. I doubt much whether the experiment will succeed. He announced his lectures ill, as if he felt degraded by allusion to money matters; I felt degraded at hearing a great man refer to such a subject.... Went to Flaxman's. Read there *Peter Bell*—interrupted by Rogers the poet.[3] The conversation chiefly about Hayley the poet. Oh, these catalogued poets! It is quite profanation to use the word with a mind full of such men as Wordsworth and Coleridge! Rogers's manners have something of the coldness of riches and rank: he speaks like a sensible man, but certainly his exterior presents none of the indications either of poetry or genius....

JUNE 6th . . . Return to chambers after dinner for a short time. With Charles Lamb. Lent him *Peter Bell*. To my surprise he finds nothing in it good. He complains of the slowness of the narrative, as if that were not the

[1] *How sweet it is, when mother Fancy rocks.*

[2] *Where lies the Land to which yon Ship must go?*

[3] Crabb Robinson's first meeting with Samuel Rogers (1763–1855), whose hospitality he was often to enjoy in later years.

art of the poet. Wordsworth says he, has great thoughts, but *here* are none of them. He has no interest in the ass. These are to me inconceivable judgments from Charles Lamb, whose taste in general I acquiesce in, and who is certainly an enthusiast for Wordsworth. But I know no resource against the perplexity arising from the diversities of opinion in those I look up to, but in determination to disregard all opinions and trust to my own unstudied suggestions and natural feelings. The Colliers, Wordsworth, and the Lambs joined to tea and supper at Anthony Robinson's, and the evening passed off pleasantly enough. Wordsworth spoke freely on the character of Fox, to whom he denied the higher qualities of the mind, philosophy, and religion, and with reason denied his assertion of human rights in matters of religion to be a proof of religion. On politics of the time of the French Revolution he also spoke and attempted, but unsuccessfully, against Anthony Robinson's attacks, to defend Coleridge's consistency. He spoke of Johnson's style, etc., and denied him style as well as poetry; allowed his excellence in conversation and considered his false notions concerning the dignity of writing as the cause of his bad writing. There was, however, no offensive opposition of opinion during the evening. Charles Lamb was very pleasant and comfortable, and we broke off at the right time for him. . . .

June 11th At chambers I was unexpectedly visited by Wordsworth. He was come up from Bocking suddenly in consequence of tidings of the sudden death of his daughter Catherine, a girl of four years of age, and he was going to Wales to Mrs. Wordsworth. His spirits were properly affected, and his language that which became a man both of feeling and strength of mind. I walked with him to Coleridge. And he called on a Mr. De Quincey,[1] friend who had lately visited the Lakes, and was greatly attached to the little child. Mr. De Quincey burst into tears on seeing Wordsworth and seemed to be more affected than the father. He had received a letter from Miss Wordsworth. . . .

June 17th . . . At four o'clock dined in the hall with De Quincey, who was very civil to me, and invited me cordially to visit his cottage in Cumberland. De Quincey is, like myself, an enthusiast for Wordsworth; his person is small, his complexion fair, and his air and manner those of a sickly, enfeebled man. From which circumstances his sensibility, which I have no doubt is genuine, is in danger of being mistaken for a puling and womanly weakness. At least, coarser and more robustly healthful persons will think so. His conversation is sensible, and I *suppose* him to be a man of information on general subjects. His views in studying the law will never, I think, be realized. He has a small independent fortune, and the

[1] Thomas De Quincey (1785–1859), author of *Confessions of an Opium Eater.*

only thing he wants is a magnificent library; this he is willing to purchase by giving for it a few years close attention to the law. But he is resolved on no account to put himself under a special pleader, nor will he live more than six months during the year in London. I represented to him that I feared *nothing* could be expected from the law *so* studied. A man must be altogether or not at all a lawyer. . . .

JUNE 19th . . . Before the debate, an hour's lounge with Stephen[1] in Lincoln's Inn garden. He is an amiable, respectable, promising man. And I have no doubt will rise in his profession. . . . Stephen is not yet awakened as to poetry. He does admire Campbell and does not know anything of Wordsworth. . . .

AUG. 13th . . . I went by appointment to Coleridge, with whom I spent several hours most agreeably alone. I read to him a number of scenes out of the new *Faust*. He had read before the earlier edition, and he now acknowledged the genius of Goethe in a manner he never did before. At the same time, the want of religion and enthusiasm in Goethe is in Coleridge's mind an irreparable defect. The beginning of *Faust* does not please Coleridge, nor does he think Mephistopheles a character. I urged that Mephistopheles ought to be a mere abstraction, and no character, and Coleridge had nothing satisfactory to oppose to this remark. I read to Coleridge the *Zueignung*, and he seemed to admire it greatly. He had been reading Stolberg lately, of whom he seems to have a sufficiently high opinion. He considers Goethe's *Mahomets Gesang* as but an imitation of Stolberg's *Felsenstrom*, [not] considering that the *Felsenstrom* is but a piece of animated description, without any higher import, while Goethe's poem is a profound and significant allegory, exhibiting the nature of religious enthusiasm. The Prologue in Heaven to *Faust* did not offend Coleridge as I thought it would, notwithstanding it is a parody on Job. Coleridge said of Job: 'This incomparable poem has been most absurdly interpreted. Job, far from being the most patient of men, was the most impatient of men, and he was rewarded for his impatience: his integrity and sincerity had their recompense, because he was superior to the hypocrisy of his friends.'

Coleridge praised *Wallenstein* but censured Schiller for a sort of ventriloquism in poetry,—by the bye, a happy term to express that common fault of throwing the feelings of the writer into the body, as it were, of other personages, the characters of the poem. In *Ruth*, as it stands at present, there is the same fault; Wordsworth had not originally put into the mouth of the lover many of the sentiments he now entertains, and which would better have become the poet himself. . . .

[1] Afterwards Sir James Stephen.

OCT. 13th Rode on the outside of the Bury coach to Bocking. Read great part of the first volume of *Evelina*. Not at all pleased with it. No discrimination of character like that which renders *Cecilia* so excellent. . . .

On the coach, Fitzgerald, the loyal poet.[1] He did not trouble us with many recitations of his own poems, but appeared to be a vain, good-natured man. He related that Pye the poet laureate has a singular diseased affection: the sight of any extended plain, either the sea, or a heath, throws him into a nervous disorder amounting to convulsion. Fitzgerald was himself once with him when they were crossing Blackfriars Bridge by moonlight. Pye caught a glimpse of the water with the reflection of the moon upon it, and sank down into the carriage pretending to look for his glove in order to conceal the trouble the sight gave him. . . .

NOV. 3rd . . . At Coleridge's first lecture on Belles Lettres at the Surry Institution. It was a repetition of former lectures, and dull. He enlarged on the vagueness of terms and their abuse, and in defining taste gave the Kantian theory as to the nature of judgments of taste. He introduced, I had almost said cantingly, some pious parenthesis about religion *à la* Wood, and did not, on the whole, gratify me exceedingly. He walked with me to Anthony Robinson's for *Spinoza*, which I lent him. In the course of a few minutes, while standing in the room, Coleridge kissed Spinoza's face at the title-page, said his book was his gospel, and in less than a minute added that his philosophy was, after all, false. . . .

Coleridge informs me his tragedy[2] is accepted at Drury Lane. Whitbread admires it exceedingly, and Arnold, the manager, is confident of its success. Coleridge now says he has five or six pieces ready for representation! At the same time he is about to compose lectures, which are to be the product of all his talent and power, on education; and each lecture is to be delivered as it may be afterwards sent to the Press. For this purpose he wants *Spinoza*.

Afterwards sat an hour with Godwin . . . Godwin had been to see Betty on his return to the theatre as a man after he had been so famous as a boy. Godwin was pleased with him, though he does not think he will be a Garrick. . . .

NOV. 17th . . . Took tea with Rough, for I was stupid with the little wine I had taken after dinner; and then at Coleridge's lecture, where I slept. . . .

DEC. 24th . . . Called late on Charles Lamb. The party there. Hazlitt, I was gratified by finding in high spirits; he finds his engagement with Perry as Parliamentary reporter very easy, and the four guineas per week keep his head above water. He seems quite happy. I therefore ventured to

[1] William Thomas Fitzgerald. [2] *Remorse.*

ask about my brother's picture which he promises me; and I believe I shall get it.

DEC. 28th . . . Looked over an old copy of Coleridge's tragedy. The passages very beautiful, and on a reference to the incidents, I even hope it may succeed at Drury Lane this winter.

DEC. 31st . . . Late, called on Charles Lamb. He and his sister were very friendly and communicative. *Sie sprach von sich selbst und ihren Umständen.* Charles received from the India House rather more than £300 a year. He has spent this last year only £40 above his regular income.

1813

JAN. 23rd . . . Evening at Drury Lane, the first performance of Coleridge's tragedy, *Remorse.* Sat with Amyot, the Hamonds, Godwins, etc. My interest for the play was greater than in the play, and my anxiety for its success took from me the feeling as a mere spectator I should have had. I have no hesitation, however, in saying that its poetical is far greater than its dramatic merit; that it owes its success rather to its faults than its beauties, and that it will have for its less meritorious qualities applause which is really due for its excellencies. (*Mem.* It was subsequently acted [twenty] nights during the season.) Coleridge's great fault is that he indulges before the public in those metaphysical and philosophical speculations which are becoming only in solitude and with select minds. His two great characters are philosophers of Coleridge's own school, the one a sentimental moralist, the other a sophisticated villain; both are dreamers. Two experiments made by Alvar on his return, the one on his mistress by relating a dream, and the other when he tries to kindle remorse in the breast of Ordonio, are too subtle and fine-spun to be intelligible. So when Ordonio enigmatically reproaches Isidore with his guilt he tries the cunning of the audience to find out his drift. However, in spite of these faults, of the improbability of the action, of the clumsy contrivance with the picture, and the too ornate and poetic diction throughout, the tragedy was received with great and almost unmixed applause, and was announced for repetition without any opposition. . . .

JAN. 26th . . . In the evening heard Coleridge's concluding lecture at the Surry Institution. He was received with three rounds of applause on entering the lecture room, and very loudly applauded at the close. During the evening he gained great applause by some eloquent *moral* reflections, and he, this evening as well as on the three or four preceding nights, redeemed the reputation he lost at the commencement of the course. That Coleridge should ever become a popular man would once have been thought a very idle speculation. It depends on himself, and if he would make a sacrifice of some peculiarities of taste (his enemies assert he has made many on essential points of religion and politics) he has talents enough to command success; but he must also add the power of repressing the avowal of his own favourite peculiarities in opinion and feeling, which I doubt he will never be able to obtain. His general notions on party topics will suit a large proportion of the public, and though he is not yet a favourite, there is a general opinion in favour of his genius. . . .

FEB. 7th . . . A call on Godwin. From him I learnt that Coleridge was to receive for his tragedy £100 for the third, sixth, ninth, and twentieth nights of performance. There is every reason now to suppose the play will reach its twentieth night, and thus he will have £400. . . .

FEB. 23rd . . . A Mr. Talfourd called with a letter from Mr. Rutt. He is going to study the law, and wants information from me concerning economical arrangements. He has been some time Dr. Valpy's head boy,[1] and wishes for a few years to occupy himself by giving instruction or otherwise, so as to be no encumbrance to his father, who has a large family, and at the same time be pursuing the study of the law. He is a very promising young man, indeed, has great powers of conversation and public speaking; not without the faults of his age, but with so much apparent vigour of mind that I am greatly mistaken if he do not become a distinguished person. . . .

MARCH 2nd . . . In the evening accompanied Aders to see Coleridge. Coleridge was very eloquent, and on music, of which he seemed to speak with more feeling than knowledge. Purcell was his hero. He spoke with more than usual candour of Goethe, and said if he spoke in seeming depreciation of him, it was only because he compared him with the very greatest poets. He said that Goethe appeared to him from a sort of caprice to have underrated the kind of talent he had in his youth so eminently displayed, viz. the power of exhibiting man in a state of exalted sensibility as in *Werther*. Afterwards he delighted to exhibit objects in which a pure sense of the beautiful was chiefly called into exercise. These purely *beautiful* objects—not objects of desire or passion—he coldly delighted to exhibit as a statue does his succession of marble figures, and therefore he called Goethe picturesque. He spoke of Lessing's *Laocoön* as very unequal and in its parts contradictory; his examples destroying his theory. He spoke of *Reinecke Fuchs*, and said the moral of the piece is that if there

[1] Thomas Noon Talfourd was at Reading School.

be a conflict between dull blundering knaves, such as Isegrim the Wolf and Bruin the Bear, and such complete clever scoundrel[s] as Reynard, Reynard ought to be victorious. It is the prize due to his talents, and though poor and defenceless creatures like the hare, the hens, etc., must perish, for such is the constitution of nature, such creatures do not excite our sympathy. I never before heard him argue in favour of Buonaparte. He accused Schlegel of *Einseitigkeit* [narrowness] in his exclusive admiration of Shakespeare, and in his former work about the Greek poetry.

MARCH 11th . . . Mrs. Clarkson called on me. I accompanied her to Coleridge. She had received very distressing letters from the Lakes, and her object was to induce Coleridge to go and comfort Wordsworth, who was deeply afflicted by the loss of a second child.[1] And she afterwards informed me she succeeded in her undertaking. Wordsworth had expressed the strongest desire to see Coleridge, and the ladies thought it would be the greatest possible relief to him.[2] . . .

MARCH 24th . . . Called on Miss Lamb. I had received a letter from Mrs. Clarkson informing me that Lord Lonsdale had given Wordsworth the place of distributor of the stamps for Cumberland, worth £400 per annum. This news rejoiced me exceedingly, and I communicated it with joy to the Lambs. Wordsworth will now be independent of the world, and may devote himself to poetry without any of the cares and anxieties of penury, and I have no doubt his moral feelings will be improved by the improvement of his condition. He will mix more with the world and lose those peculiarities of feeling which solitude and discontent engender; while all that is beautifully individual and original in the frame of his mind and character will display itself with ease and grace. The Lambs think that this event will render Coleridge's going down less important. . . .

APRIL 29th . . . Spent the evening, which I have not done for a long time before, at Charles Lamb's—at whist as usual. Chat with Hazlitt, who finds himself made comfortable by a situation which, furnishing him with the necessaries of life, keeps his best faculties not employed, but awake; and I do not think it is much to be feared that his faculties will, therefore, decline. He has a most powerful intellect, and needs only encouragement to manifest this to the world by a work which could not be overlooked.

Read lately Charles Lamb's *Confessions of a Drunkard*, a very striking composition, and calculated to do good generally, though it will hardly be thought so near a correct representation of a fact as it really is.

It is sometimes painfully eloquent.

MAY 2nd . . . A call on Morgan. Coleridge, I see, will not go to the

[1] Thomas.

[2] But see *infra*, May 2nd, 1813.

Lakes. Of course, I did not press the subject any further. He will certainly have his £400, and the managers were almost offended when a doubt was implied whether the tragedy would be acted the twentieth night. . . .

JUNE 5th . . . She [Mrs. Gregory] said archly, speaking of the celebrity Miss Edgeworth[1] has now in London, being sought after at all the fashionable parties: 'She has quite supplanted the Cossack.' . . .

By the bye, Edgeworth, the father, has by no means gained the general favour which his daughter possesses. He is said to be exceedingly ill-bred. He must, too, be remarkably ostentatious. Hamond says he said in his presence: 'I have been forced this morning to be broiling in the sun along a dead wall because two dukes think proper to live at different ends of [P]ark Lane.'

JUNE 11th . . . When I came home Charles Lamb was here. His sister had been taken ill and he had brought her from Windsor. . . .

JUNE 26th . . . Mrs. Porden lent me this evening Lord Byron's *Giaour*, a Turkish tale (a fragment only). With a few energetic lines expressing a diseased state of feeling, the thing is as worthless and unmeaning as I should have expected, even from Lord Byron. A man must have a very mistaken notion of the importance of his writings who supposes that a few broken parts of a tale, wanting on that account the gross material interest of a story, and not having the recommendation of teaching any moral truth, or of exhibiting any picture delightful to the imagination or exciting the sympathy, can be in any way worth the attention of cultivated minds. For of the higher objects and views of poetry Lord Byron pretends not to entertain a notion.

OCT. 16th . . . Called on Godwin. He had seen Madame de Staël. He considers her as a woman of talents, but very coarse. . . .

NOV. 5th . . . Dined at Amyot's with a large party. *Inter alia* the poet laureate elect, Southey. He was seemingly jaded by having been too much in society lately, and did not exert himself much in conversation. He had a dispute with Mr. Byng (son of Lord Torrington) on the English soldiery, whom he accused of having been guilty of great excesses in Spain, and whom Byng defended. Byng was offended by Southey's manner, which I did not perceive to be unbecoming. We all concurred in expressions of joy at the late events;[2] and Southey, Amyot and others emulated each other in maledictions on Napoleon. . . .

[1] Maria Edgeworth (1767–1849), the novelist.

[2] The battle of Leipzig, where Napoleon was defeated on 19th October.

1814

JAN. 22nd . . . I repeated to Madame de Staël Wordsworth's sonnet on the King, and spoke warmly in his praise. She says Sir James Mackintosh also speaks of him as a man of great talents. But she asked if Wordsworth's style were good, without which, she said, no writer can have immortality. She spoke with satisfaction of W. Taylor's review of her book on Germany. . . .

FEB. 7th . . . Dined at the Hall, after which De Quincey, Cargill [and others] . . . came home with me. We drank tea together, and stayed till late, our conversation chiefly on Lord Byron, to whom we were not favourable, and on Wordsworth, whose admirers were more zealous than his adversaries. De Quincey has a fine and very superior mind. He talks about Wordsworth with the zeal and intelligence of a well-instructed pupil, and his style, with a mixture of pedantry and high-flown sentimentality, evinces a man who thinks while he talks and who has a discriminating judgment and delicate taste. . . .

FEB. 12th . . . De Quincey came by appointment, and we went together to Lamb, with whom we drank tea and stayed till nine. I returned to Lamb and stayed till eleven. This was contrary to my intention, and the evening was rather dull. De Quincey is a dry, solemn man, whose conversation does not flow readily, though he speaks well enough and like a sensible man. He is too much a disciple and admirer to have anything of his own. But he is still an amiable man, and, though it is an effort to keep up a conversation with him on general subjects, he is an interesting companion. After De Quincey was gone, knowing Lamb's feeling on such a subject, I felt it my duty to stay with him. . . .

MAY 15th . . . Concluded the evening by calling on the Colliers, with whom I found the Lambs. . . .

Lamb and his sister this evening expressed great kindness towards me, and it gave me great pleasure. They indeed belong to the very best of persons. Their moral qualities are as distinguished as their intellectual.

MAY 23rd . . . As I was about to leave chambers De Quincey called on me and stayed several hours. . . . De Quincey is a tedious proser though a sensible man. He wearies by the uniformity of his homilies, and he has no measure in his talk. His admiration of Wordsworth is not the only interesting trait in his character, I believe, had I knowledge enough of him to take an interest in his character. . . .

MAY 28th . . . I was today greatly pleased with Gainsborough's 'Quin,' but Lamb thinks Hogarth's 'Captain Coram' superior. . . .

Accompanied Charles and Miss Lamb to Dr. Aikin's. The visit was highly agreeable to all parties. Lamb was quite on his good behaviour. He kept within bounds and yet was very pleasant. He related a droll history of a clerk in the India House suspected of living on human flesh, and he introduced the whimsical conceit that among cannibals a man who would not join in the common diet would be called a misanthropist. Lamb abused Gray's poetry, but the Aikins did not take up the assertion, and the doctor's favourite opinion of the unimprovability of mankind met with no opposition from the Lambs. Miss Aikin admired both the wit and the fine face of Lamb, and he was pleased with the family, particularly the old lady. I believe they will renew their visits. . . .

JUNE 29th . . . A . . . call on . . . Lamb till late; found Lamb as delighted as a child with a garret he had appropriated and adorned with all the copperplate engravings he could collect, having rifled every book he possessed for the purpose.

It was quite delightful to observe his innocent delight. Schiller says all great men have a childlikeness in their nature.

JULY 3rd A day of great pleasure. Charles Lamb and I walked to Enfield by Southgate, after an early breakfast in his chambers. We were most hospitably received by Anthony Robinson and wife, and after tea, at which we were joined by the Freemans, Lamb and I returned. The whole day most delightfully fine, and the scenery very agreeable. Lamb enjoyed the walk more than the scenery, for the enjoyment of which he seems to have no great susceptibility. His great delight, even in preference to a country walk, is a stroll in London. The shops and the busy streets, such as Thames Street, Bank Side, etc., are his great favourites. He for the same reason has no relish for landscape painting. But his relish for historic painting is exquisite. Lamb's peculiarities are very interesting. We had not much conversation. He hummed tunes, I repeated Wordsworth's *Daffodils*, of which I am become very fond. Lamb can relish the thieves in the last stage of avarice,[1] . . . which is beyond me. At the same time he censures Wordsworth's narrative. Lamb praised T. Warton's sonnet in Dugdale[2] as of first-rate excellence. It is a good thought, but I find nothing exquisite in it. He praised Prior's courtly poems: his *Down Hall*, his fine application of the name of Marlborough as not so ill-sounding as to be offensive to the ears of Boileau[3]; his dedication to Lord Halifax, etc.

[1] *The Two Thieves, or The Last Stage of Avarice.*

[2] T. Warton the Younger. *Written in a Blank Leaf of Dugdale's Monasticon.*

[3] And is there not a Sound in Marlbro's Name,
Which thou and all thy Brethren ought to claim,
Sacred to Verse, and sure of endless Fame?

Letter to Monsieur Boileau.

Lamb and Anthony Robinson agreed together and seemed to enjoy the afternoon. Lamb expressed himself strongly against the keeping a mistress as more degrading and immoral than the most promiscuous intercourse, in which Anthony Robinson agreed. The holding a woman at once so near and yet at so great a distance is the most scandalous injustice and greatest wickedness. . . .

AUG. 13th . . . I stole out of the theatre to call on Madge, at whose apartments I found the new great poem of Wordsworth, *The Excursion*. I could only look into the preface, and read a few extracts with Madge. It is a poem of formidable size, and I fear too mystical to be popular. But it will, however, put an end to the sneers of those who consider him or affect to consider him as a puerile writer [who] attempts only little things. But it will draw on him the imputation of dullness possibly. Still it will, I trust, strengthen the zeal of his few friends. My anxiety is great to read it.

[*Travel Journal: Paris.*] SEPT. 22nd . . . While here, [in the Louvre] I learned that Mrs. Siddons was in the room. She was with Horace Twiss's mother. I am almost ashamed to own that the sight of her gave me a delight beyond almost any I have received in Paris. Yet at times her countenance pained me. I watched her closely and did not like to see her knit her brows to assist her view of the pictures. Nor was she becomingly dressed; Mrs. Siddons's head ought not to be in a small chipped hat. Yet when she spoke to her sister and Mr. Lock who was with her she had her own graceful and fascinating smile, which notwithstanding some coarse features about the mouth delighted me. I followed her to the door; it rained. I offered her my umbrella as no gentleman was with her; she did not accept it, but I received her smile and thanks. . . .

OCT. 4th . . . I had barely time to dress myself and walk to Clichy by dinner time. I, however, reached Madame de Staël's a little after five. Monsieur Benjamin Constant was there. He looked much older than when I saw him at Weimar. At table were a sort of secretary of Madame de Staël, and a gentleman at the bottom of the table who held a long and lively conversation with Benjamin Constant on the subject of Animal Magnetism, which I did not wholly comprehend, but in which I nevertheless discerned the man of *esprit* and address. It was not till after a considerable time that I found this stranger was Wilhelm Schlegel, whom I had dined with at Goethe's. I was very glad to see him, and when the stiffness of dinner was removed, I chatted with him on German literature and poetry with interest and pleasure. . . .

Schlegel conversed in English with me, and he was curious to inquire about our English poets. He had received a favourable impression of Lord

Byron from Madame de Staël, who considers him as the best of our poets. I objected to him the want of repose and an intellect calmly contemplating the passions it regulates, at least in the poetic representation of them. This Schlegel assented to. I repeated to him three of Wordsworth's sonnets, *Westminster Bridge*, *Switzerland*, and *The King*. He seemed to be pleased with them all, and took a list of his and Southey's works with evident interest. But he said he was more curious to know the general character of English literature than to be acquainted with any one work.

Rogers, he said, is the only poet of the *old* school now living. He thought that the English had gained by the new turn given to poetry, which has been taking a direction like that of the Germans, though there was no connection between them.

He expressed his regret that he had not seen Flaxman when in England. He was there only a fortnight! He seemed unacquainted with Flaxman's merits as a sculptor. . . .

OCT. 10th . . . We breakfasted at Boulogne. . . . I ascended a height from whence I saw with pleasure the white cliffs of England. . . . I observed some boats up a creek in the river, which I understood to be some of the formidable armada for the projected invasion of England by Buonaparte, and I observed also the scaffolding of a tower which was to be erected within sight of the English coast—a sign of terror, I suppose, and a threat. This would have added to the force of the expression 'frightful neighbourhood' which Wordsworth applies to the proximity of the French coast.

NOV. 2nd [*London.*] . . . Sat at home this evening from six to half-past eight reading Wordsworth's *Excursion*. I have yet read but little of this exquisite work. I have, however, already no doubt that it will be for other reasons as unpopular as his other works, and that it will be highly admired by his former admirers. . . .

And afterwards I called at the Godwins' and saw the young people, and then returned and read Wordsworth again till past midnight with high delight.

NOV. 4th I spent part of the morning at home and continued Wordsworth's poem. The fourth book I found by no means dull or uninteresting, though purely reasoning, and the book has hitherto had in my mind greater beauties and fewer faults than I anticipated. . . .

NOV. 17th . . . After nine, I went to Charles Lamb's, whose parties are now once a month only. I played a couple of rubbers pleasantly, and afterwards chatted with Hazlitt till one o'clock. He is become an *Edinburgh* reviewer through the recommendation of Lady Mackintosh, who had sent to the *Champion* office to know the author of the articles on Institutions. Hazlitt sent those other writings to Jeffrey, and has been in a very flattering manner enrolled in the corps. This has put Hazlitt in good spirits; he now again hopes that his talents will be appreciated, and become a subsistence to him. He complains bitterly of Perry's treatment of him, and I believe his statement, for he is too proud and high-minded to lie. He says that during the last six months he wrote seventy columns for the *Chronicle*, that Perry himself confessed to him that Hazlitt's had done more for the paper than all the other writings, and in consequence of his approbation of what Hazlitt had done, advanced him a £100, of which £50 are due. I had understood from the Colliers that Perry had not actually dismissed Hazlitt, but that he abstained from coming. Hazlitt states the fact thus: Perry said to him expressly that he wished Hazlitt to *look out for another* situation—the affronting language Hazlitt could not easily forget—as he was not fit for a reporter. Hazlitt said he thought he could do miscellaneous things. Perry said he would think of it. However, when Hazlitt afterwards went to the office for his salary he was told Mr. Perry wished to speak with him. He went to Perry's room. Perry was not alone, and desired Hazlitt to wait. Hazlitt went to another room. Perry then seeing Hazlitt there, went out of the house. Hazlitt, in consequence, never called again. As there [was] no express refusal either to pay or to accept his services in another way than as reporter, Perry has an excuse for saying he did not dismiss Hazlitt.

Hazlitt also mentions instances of Perry's insolent behaviour to him which must render dependence on such a man a galling servitude. He called on Hazlitt one evening to answer on the spot an article or speech about the liberty of the Press. Hazlitt wrote one, he says not a good one. Perry looked it over. 'This is the most pimping thing I ever read. If you cannot do a thing of this kind off-hand you won't do for me.' Yet on former occasions he had been vastly pleased with Hazlitt's articles, and had turned his letters into leading articles. Hazlitt says Perry's conduct is to be ascribed to the fall of Buonaparte, 'by which,' says he, 'my articles were made in the event very unfortunate. But it is hard to make me suffer for that.' Whether Hazlitt's offence was writing in other papers, I cannot tell, but certainly Perry, who has no delicacy or regard for the feelings of others, would not have scrupled to insist on Hazlitt's leaving off if such had been his real objection to him. It is quite painful to witness the painful exertions for a livelihood which Hazlitt is condemned to make. And how strongly it shows that a modicum of mechanical marketable talent outweighs an ample endowment of original thought, and the highest powers of intellect, when a man does not add to that endowment the other of making it turn to account. How many men are there connected with newspapers who live comfortably with not a tithe of Hazlitt's powers as a writer!

DEC. 8th . . . Barnes also related some particulars of his friend, Leigh Hunt. Hunt, it seems, is so exceedingly sensitive and impatient of censure or reproach that his wife is in the habit of opening all his letters and burning whatever she thinks would give him pain. Barnes has often abstained from giving him the advice he wished to give because he knew that it would put an end to their friendship, and, said Barnes, 'I cannot afford to lose Hunt's friendship, for there is hardly a man I love so much.'

This is a strange state of feeling in a man whose life consists in the wounding of other men's feelings. Barnes says Hunt has strong affections, but no general humanity. This account of him renders the coarseness of his attacks on other people more inexcusable. A callous man may be excused for dealing about severe blows, but not the man who smarts at the slightest infliction. Hunt has been so put out of sorts by Wordsworth's *Excursion* that it makes him uncomfortable to hear it mentioned in company, and his friends therefore avoid the subject out of tenderness to him. Hunt at first ridiculed Wordsworth as a contemptible writer; then he mingled warm praise with reproof, and now he dislikes his great poem so much that, probably because he is dissatisfied with his own sentiment and dares not avow it, he is made unwell by hearing it mentioned. How much of envy enters into this feeling I cannot tell. . . .

1815

JAN. 3rd . . . *The Excursion* on the second perusal gratified me still more than the first, and my own impressions were not removed by the various criticisms I about this time became acquainted with. . . .

Perhaps, after all, *The Excursion* will leave Mr. Wordsworth's admirers and contemners where they were. Each will be furnished with instances of excellence and deformity to strengthen his own persuasions. Certainly I could wish for a somewhat clearer development of the author's opinions, for the retrenchment of some of the uninteresting interlocutory matter, and for the exclusion of one tale, the angry and avaricious and unkind woman, and curtailments in most of the other narratives. But with these deductions from the worth of the poem, I do not hesitate to place the poem among the noblest works of the human intellect, and to me it is one of the most delightful. What is good, is of the best kind of goodness, and the passages are not few which place the author on a level with Milton. It is true, Wordsworth is not an epic poet. . . . Wordsworth is purely and exclusively a lyric poet, in the extended use of that term. . . .

Feb. 26th[1] . . . Dined with Alsager.[2] Charles and Mary Lamb and Barnes formed the party, and Barnes soon left us to a party at whist.

The afternoon was not so very pleasant, on account of Charles Lamb taking too much wine. He was not so far gone as to be outrageous, and he could even play whist; but he was flurried in his manner, so as to make me uncomfortable. However, we stayed till near twelve. Lamb was uncomfortable to himself as we came home. . . .

Feb. 28th . . . I concluded the evening by a call on Godwin. The Lambs were there. Mrs. Godwin ill in her room. I should not wonder if she were to sink under her afflictions, and her death would sink poor Godwin lower in calamity. They are, indeed, objects of great pity.

April 15th . . . I called at the Colliers', and finding that Miss Lamb was gone to Alsager's, from whom I had an invitation, I went *as a duty*. There was a largish party, and I stayed till near two, playing whist ill, for which I was scolded by Captain Burney—and vingt-et-un unfortunately—and debated with Hazlitt, in which I was also not successful, as far as the talent of the disputants was involved, though Hazlitt was wrong as well as offensive in almost all he said. When pressed, he does not deny what is bad in the character of Buonaparte. And yet he triumphs and rejoices in the late events. Hazlitt and myself once felt alike on politics, and now our hopes and fears are directly opposed. Hazlitt retains all his hatred of kings and bad governments, and believing them to be incorrigible, he from a principle of revenge, rejoices that they are punished. I am indignant to find the man who might have been their punisher become their imitator, and even surpassing them all in guilt. Hazlitt is angry with the friends of liberty for weakening their strength by going with the common foe against Buonaparte, by which the old governors are so much assisted, even in their attempts against the general liberty. I am not shaken by this consequence, because I think, after all, that should the governments succeed in the worst projects imputed to them, still the evil will be infinitely less than what would arise from Buonaparte's success. I say destroy him at any rate and take the consequences. Hazlitt says: 'Let the enemy of old tyrannical governments triumph, I am glad, and I do not much care how the new government turns out.' Not that either I am indifferent to the government which the successful kings of Europe may establish or that Hazlitt has lost all love for liberty. But his *hatred*, and my

[1] Dated March 3rd in the MS., but internal evidence proves this to be a mistake.
[2] T. M. Alsager (1779–1846), who became manager of *The Times*.

fears, predominate and absorb all weaker impressions. This I believe to be the great difference between us.

MAY 7th . . . I read some of Wordsworth's poems, particularly the extracts from his first published works, which are in so different a style from his subsequent works as not to be recognised as his; and I could not relish them though they appear to be full of those elaborately fine descriptions which have given reputation to other and inferior poets. . . .

On coming home I found a card from Wordsworth, and running to Lamb I found him and Mrs. Wordsworth there. After sitting half an hour with them I walked with them to their lodgings near Cavendish Square.

Mrs. Wordsworth appears to be a mild and amiable woman, not so lively or animated as Miss Wordsworth, but like her, devoted to the poet.

We chatted, of course, about the new edition, etc., of which hereafter.

MAY 9th . . . I took tea with the Lambs. Mr. and Mrs. Wordsworth were there. We had a long chat. I regret that I can relate but little. Wordsworth is, as he was before, most acutely sensible to a censure, however slight. I told him I did not like his supplementary preface against the reviewers because it betrayed anger. He denied that there is any expression of anger in the preface, though he has nothing but contempt, etc.

Wordsworth is by no means satisfied with Hunt's judgment of him, yet on the representation by Brougham that Hunt had been pleased with his poems he sent him a copy of them.

Wordsworth, in answer to the common reproach that his sensibility is excited by objects which produce no effect on others, admits the fact and is proud of it. He says that he cannot be accused of being insensible to the real concerns of life. He does not waste his feelings on unworthy objects. For he is alive to the actual interests of society. I think the justification complete. If Wordsworth expected immediate popularity, he would betray an ignorance of public taste reproachful to a man of observation.

Wordsworth spoke of the changes in his new poems. He has substituted 'ebullient' for 'fiery', speaking of the nightingale, and 'jocund' for 'laughing' applied to the daffodils; but he will probably restore the original epithets. We agreed in preferring the original reading. But on my gently alluding to the lines: 'Three feet long and two feet wide,' and confessing that I dared not read them out in company, he said 'they ought to be liked.'

Hazlitt said in his ferocious way at Alsager's that 'if Lamb in his criticism had found but one fault with Wordsworth he would never have forgiven him.' And some truth there is in the extravagant statement.

Wordsworth particularly recommended to me among his Poems of Imagination *Yew Trees* and a description of Night.[1] These, he says, are

[1] *A Night-piece.*

among the best for the imaginative power displayed in them. I have since read them. They are fine, but I believe I do not understand in what their excellence consists. Wordsworth himself, as Hazlitt has well observed, has a pride in deriving no aid from his subject. It is the mere power which he is conscious of exerting in which he delights, not the production of a work in which men rejoice on account of the sympathies and sensibilities it excites in them. Hence he does not much esteem his *Laodamia*, as it belongs to the inferior class of Poems Founded on the Affections. Yet in this, as in other peculiarities of Wordsworth, there is a *German* bent in his mind. Wordsworth gave me a pamphlet printed, but not published, against Lord Byron, by a Miss Barker, 'By one of the small fry of the Lakes,' founded on a letter by Lord Byron to Hogg, the Ettrick Shepherd, in which he talks of the *Pond* poets. Not a good satire, and far below the *Rejected Address*. . . .

JUNE 15th . . . I called on Wordsworth for the first time at his lodgings. He was luckily at home, and I spent the forenoon with him, walking. We talked about Hazlitt in consequence of a malignant attack on Wordsworth by him in Sunday's *Examiner*. Wordsworth that very day called on Hunt, who, in a manly way, asked whether Wordsworth had seen the paper of the morning, saying, if he had, he should consider his call as a higher honour. He disclaimed the article. The attack by Hazlitt was a note in which, after honouring Milton for being a consistent patriot, he sneered at Wordsworth as the author of 'paltry sonnets upon the royal fortitude,' etc. and insinuated that he had left out the *Female Vagrant*, a poem describing the miseries of war sustained by the poor. This led to Wordsworth's mentioning the cause of his coolness towards Hazlitt. It appears that Hazlitt, when at Keswick, narrowly escaped being ducked by the populace, and probably sent to prison for some gross attacks on women. He even whipped one woman, *more puerorum*, for not yielding to his wishes. The populace were incensed against him and pursued him, but he escaped to Wordsworth, who took him into his house at midnight, gave him clothes and money (from three to five pounds). Since that time Wordsworth, though he never refused to meet Hazlitt when by accident they came together, did not choose that with his knowledge he should be invited. In consequence, Lamb never asked Hazlitt while Wordsworth was in town, which probably provoked Hazlitt, and which Lamb himself disapproved of. But Lamb, who needs very little indulgence for himself, is very indulgent towards others, and rather reproaches Wordsworth for being inveterate against Hazlitt.

I called with Wordsworth, etc., on Daniel Stuart. He lives quite in splendour, the produce of newspaper writing and editing; but I cannot think the fair and mere mercantile produce of that trade. I thought of what Coleridge said: 'He is a Scotchman, glad to get rid of the itch now he can afford to wear clean linen.' Wordsworth spoke with interest of his *White Doe* as an imaginative poem. The ascription of more than human feelings to that animal in connection with the tragic story, which is purified and elevated by it. . . .

JUNE 16th I joined Wordsworth, etc., at the British Museum, and accompanied him round the museum, Mr. Alexander was our conductor. Wordsworth beheld the antiquities with great interest and feeling as objects of beauty, but with no great historical knowledge. . . .

NOV. 14th . . . After nine I called on Charles Lamb. He was much better in health and spirits than when I saw him last. Though *tête-à-tête*, he was able to pun. I was speaking of my first brief when he asked: 'Did not you exclaim when you had your first brief—"Thou great first cause, least understood"?' . . .

NOV. 17th . . . Called on Godwin. Godwin was in high spirits, but hardly in good spirits. He laughs long and loud without occasion, and mingles with this causeless hilarity great irritability. He is vehement and intolerant. He was this evening in particular abusive on Wordsworth, Coleridge, Southey, and Stoddart—for what he calls their political tergiversation, and he reproaches me with being guilty to some extent, but luckily without being paid for it. I fear every day hearing something painful of poor Godwin.

1816

FEB. 10th . . . After calling at the Colliers' I went to Alsager's, with whom I spent an agreeable [time] without conversation or music: the party, Burrell, Godwin, and Hazlitt. The conversation was very shrewd on Hazlitt's part, captious and minutely critical and even rude by Godwin. . . . Hazlitt was bitter, as he always is, against Wordsworth, who, he says, is satisfied with nothing short of indiscriminate eulogy, and who cannot forgive Hazlitt for having passed him off with a slight reserve of blame—so as to Southey, Hunt, etc. etc.; and if a man has ever disliked Wordsworth's poetry no subsequent love of it can ever atone for the offence. In this there is an *aliquid veri* only. Mandeville was praised. Hazlitt asserted, and on a reference to the book it appeared, that the leading ideas of Mandeville are contained in an essay by Montaigne entitled: 'One man's gain another's loss.' Both Godwin and Hazlitt expressed themselves very strongly in admiration of Montaigne.

Godwin, Burrell, and I left Alsager's at half-past twelve. As usual, Hazlitt stayed behind. Alsager had liquor behind which Hazlitt wished to drink, and Hazlitt's sense Alsager enjoys and appreciates.

FEB. 11th . . . I walked to Newington and dined with Mrs. Barbauld.[1] . . . As usual, we were very comfortable. Mrs. Barbauld can keep up a lively argumentative conversation as well as any one I know, and at her advanced age (she is turned of seventy) she is certainly the best specimen of female Presbyterian society in the country. . . .

MARCH 3rd . . . Read till near one the beginning of *Vathek*.[2] . . .

MARCH 4th . . . Continued till near one *Caliph Vathek*, a book which is quite original in its style. It is marvellous without surfeiting and, without falling into the ridiculous, is humorous. I know not when I have been so amused.

MARCH 5th . . . Read *Vathek* till past one—the tale increases in horror, perhaps it becomes disgusting as it advances. It is a powerful production. . . .

MARCH 10th . . . Finished *Vathek*. As I advanced in this book it pleased me less. There is a strange want of keeping in the style, Johnsonian parade being blended with colloquial familiarities, and an unsuccessful attempt to unite the description of horrid situations and incidents with strokes of humour. The finest part is the description of hell at the close. The immense and gorgeous hall surrounded by objects of magnificence and wealth, full of wretches each tormented by an incessantly burning heart and each bearing his torment in mournful seclusion from others, all crowded together and each bearing his own suffering and further tormented by his hatred of his former friends—this is a very fine picture certainly. But the philosophy of the tale is not better than the philosophy of other like tales. If all the sufferers like Vathek have been wrought on by the agency of the necromancer and Giaour who wrought the Caliph's downfall, the same objection will apply to all. Either such an agent was not wanted to effect the perdition of the individual, and then he is an impertinent intruder; or he was, and then why was he permitted to ruin those who otherwise would have remained innocent?

How glad I should be if such an objection never occurred to me but on the perusal of a fairy tale! . . .

MAY 15th . . . I forwarded to Miss H. M. Williams, Wordsworth's Thanksgiving Ode [*Ode. 1815*.] recently published.

[1] Anna Letitia Barbauld, *née* Aikin (1743–1825), poet and miscellaneous writer.

[2] *The History of the Caliph Vathek*, translated by the Rev. S. Henley from an unpublished MS. by William Beckford, 1786. The French original appeared in the following year.

I supped with Mrs. Thornthwaite and read Wordsworth's ode. It has heavy passages, but the commencement and conclusion are both fine indeed. His assertion that the great calamities of life are the instruments of Providence, though very trite, was never expressed with more force and beauty.

He puts the Earthquake on its[1] still design

deserves to pass into a proverb. The verses on the Russian Winter are, perhaps, the most delightful in the volume. There are beautiful sonnets on the Battle of Waterloo. The volume is worthy of Wordsworth, but it will have the fate of his other works. It was not relished by the party I had to read to this night. . . .

JULY 14th . . . I walked afterwards to Becher's and he accompanied me to Gillman's, an apothecary at Highgate with whom Coleridge is now staying under a sort of medical surveillance, and he seems to have profited already by the abstinence from opium, etc., on which he had lately lived, for I never saw him look so well. He talked sensibly but less eloquently and vehemently than usual. He asked me to lend him some books, etc., and related a history of the great injustice done him in the reports circulated about his losing books; and certainly I ought not to join in the reproach, for he gave me today Kant's *Works*, three volumes *Miscellanies*, and Lamb brought me my other books from Calne [Wiltshire]. Coleridge talked about Goethe's work on the theory of colours: said he had some years back discovered the same theory, and would certainly have reduced it to form and published it had not Southey diverted his attention from such studies to poetry. On my mentioning that I had heard that an English work had been published lately developing the same system, Coleridge answered with great naiveté that he was very free in communicating his thoughts on the subject wherever he went and among literary people. Becher was pleased with Coleridge. Lamb, who was to have joined me at Becher's, came to us here. He had not been long with us before Mr. Gillman entered the room very much with the air of a man who meant we should understand him to mean: 'Gentlemen, it is time for you to go!' We took the hint and Lamb said he would never call again. . . .

[*Travel Journal: Kendal*, '*White Hart*'.] SEPT. 3rd . . . The landlord . . . called himself the *friend* of Wordsworth, which somewhat amused the poet, who, with difficulty, recollected some service he had rendered the good man, for which he obtained the honourable appellation. . . .

SEPT. 5th . . . It was the plan of my companions [Torlonia[2] and Walter]

[1] Modern editions read *her* for *its*.

[2] Count Torlonia and his tutor, W. J. Walter. This was Crabb Robinson's first visit to Rydal.

to proceed from Ambleside immediately, but Mr. Walter expressed so strong a desire to see Wordsworth that I resolved to take him with me on a call for advice how we should proceed. . . . We met him in the road before the house. His salutation was most cordial. He received Mr. Walter, too, with great cordiality—whose plans were very soon overthrown by the conversation of the poet in such a spot. He at once agreed to protract his stay among the lakes, and to devote this day to Grasmere. Wordsworth accompanied us to Ambleside. There Torlonia was placed on a pony, which was a wild mountaineer. . . . Wordsworth then slowly accompanied us. I had before conversed a few minutes with the ladies of Wordsworth's family, his wife, sister, and Miss Hutchinson, and by their kindness and the expectation of spending the evening with them, was thrown into the best mood for enjoying the day. The day I did enjoy. Wordsworth accompanied us on the north-west side of Rydal Water and Grasmere Lake. . . . The most striking point from below Loughrigg is the bold and lofty, craggy projection called Helm Crag, to the right of which is a sort of gap in the mountain in which lies the Keswick road, and to the left of Helm Crag is Easedale, a recess in the valley altogether closed in. From a beautiful hillock Wordsworth showed us these objects and pointed out to us several houses in which he had lived in the village, none of which, however, appears remarkably well situated. . . . Having myself dined, I left my companions at the inn and called on Mr. De Quincey, my Temple Hall acquaintance. He has been very much an invalid, and his appearance bespoke ill-health. He was very dirty and even squalid. I had read a bad account of him from Wordsworth, whom he has not seen for a long time. It appears that he has taken to opium, and, like Coleridge, seriously injured his health. I understand, too, though Wordsworth was reserved on the subject, he has entangled himself in an unfortunate *acquaintance* with a woman. He seemed embarrassed when he saw me, and did not ask me to walk upstairs, but said he should have a bed for me tomorrow. He *apologised* for not having written on account of bad spirits, and said he was *unfit* to see company. On this I intimated I should be sorry to break on his retirement. However, afterwards he became better, and on my mentioning to Wordsworth and the ladies what I had seen, all wished me, for his sake, to accept his offer to walk out with me as *beneficial* to himself. Mr. De Quincey returned with me to the inn . . . and he accompanied us a considerable way on our road to Ambleside. . . . We reached Wordsworth's near seven o'clock. We found at his house Mr. Tillbrook of Cambridge, formerly Thomas Clarkson's tutor, and Mrs. Lloyd, poor Charles Lloyd's wife. Our evening was most delightfully spent. The conversation was general but highly interesting. The ladies were all pleased with my companions, and I had the satisfaction of giving satisfaction to all parties by the introduction. The evening, too, was very fine, and we, for the first time, perceived all the beauties (glories they might be called) of Rydal Mount. . . . The house, too, is convenient and large enough for a family man, and it was a serious gratification to behold so great and so good a man as Wordsworth in the bosom of his family enjoying these comforts which are apparent to the eye. He has two sons and a daughter surviving. They appear to be amiable children, if not of superior intellectual endowments. And adding to these external blessings the *mind* of the man, he may justly be considered as one of the most enviable of mankind. The injustice of the public towards him in the appreciation of his works, he is sensible of I know—not that he feels it too strongly, certainly not so as to interfere with the enjoyment of life. His place as stamp distributor relieves him from pressing cares for his family, though not from anxiety for their future welfare, and he is aware that though the great body of readers, the admirers of Lord Byron, for instance, cannot and ought not to be his admirers too, still, he is not without his fame. And he has the expectation of posthumous renown which has cheered many a poet before him, who has had less legitimate claims to it, and whose expectations have not been disappointed. . . . We did not leave Rydal Mount till late. My companions declare it will be to them a memorable evening. Wordsworth, too, was pleased with my companions.

Just as we were going to bed De Quincey called on me. He was in much better spirits than when I saw him in the morning, and expressed a wish to walk with me about the neighbourhood—an offer which when repeated I shall accept.

SEPT. 9th [*Keswick.*] . . . On our return to our inn we were gratified by receiving an invitation to take tea with the poet laureate. . . . The laureate lives in a large house in a nurseryman's grounds. It enjoys a panoramic view of the mountains around, and, as Southey spends so much of his time within doors, this lively and extensive [view] supplies the place of travelling beyond his own premises. We spent a highly agreeable evening with Southey. . . . The conversation was on various subjects. Southey's library is richly stored with Spanish and Portuguese books. These he showed to my Catholic friends, withholding some from them which he thought might give them uneasiness. On Spanish politics he spoke freely. . . . I found his opinions concerning the state and prospects of this country most gloomy. He considers the government seriously endangered by the weekly papers—by Cobbett[1] and still more by the *Examiner*. Jacobinism he deems more an object of terror than at the commencement of the

[1] William Cobbett.

French Revolution from the difficulties arising out of the financial embarrassments. He says that he thinks there will be a convulsion in three years! I was more scandalized by his opinions concerning the Press than be any other doctrine. He would have transportation the punishment for a seditious libel! I ought to add, however, that I am convinced Southey is an honest alarmist. I did not dispute any point with him. I did not like any of the three sisters. Mrs. Coleridge is a very unpleasant woman: she is not *handsome*, and her manners are obtrusive. She inquired about her husband with more *affectation* of feeling than real feeling.

Hartley Coleridge is one of the strangest boys or young men I ever saw. He has the features of a foreign Jew, with starched and affected manners. He is a prim boy pedant, exceedingly formal and I should suppose clever. Coleridge's daughter has a face of great sweetness and correct habits. Derwent Coleridge I saw at Wordsworth's. He is a hearty boy with a good-natured expression. He is no scholar. Of literature not much was said. Southey seems more independent of vulgar abuse and plausible, though fallacious, criticism than his friend Wordsworth. Literature is now, however, his trade, and the habit of composition as task-work must blunt all perceptions that are not connected with the trade of book-making. He is a manufacturer, and his workshop is his study, a very beautiful one certainly, but its beauty and the delightful environs subject him to interruptions as well as his own celebrity. His time is his wealth, and I shall, therefore, scrupulously abstain from stealing any portion of it. . . .

SEPT. 11th . . . Mr. Wordsworth came to me, and between three and four o'clock we set out on our journey, he on horseback, I on foot. We set out during a heavy shower, which thoroughly wetted me, and from which I did not entirely recover the whole evening. The rain continued with but little intermission during a great part of the afternoon. . . . In the close and interesting conversation we kept up, Mr. Wordsworth was not quite attentive to the road . . . and it was late before we reached the Globe at Cockermouth. . . . If this were the place, and if my memory were good, I could enrich my journal by one valuable page in retailing Wordsworth's conversation. He is an eloquent speaker, and he talked upon his own art and his own works very feelingly and very profoundly, but I cannot venture to state more than a few intelligible results, for I own that much of what he said was above my comprehension. He stated, what I had before taken for granted, that most of his *Lyrical Ballads* were founded on some incident he had witnessed or had heard of, and in order to illustrate how facts are turned into poetry he mentioned the origin of several poems; *Lucy Gray*, that tender and pathetic narrative of a child mysteriously lost on a common, was occasioned by the death of a child who fell into the lock of a canal. He removed from his poem all that pertained to art, and it being his object to exhibit poetically entire *solitude*, he represents his child as observing the day-*moon* which no town or village girl would ever notice.

The Leech Gatherer he did actually meet near Grasmere, except that he gave to his poetic character powers of mind which his original did not possess. The fable of the *Oak and Broom* proceeded from his beholding a rose in just such a situation as he has described the broom to be in. Perhaps, however, all poets have had their works excited in like manner. What I wish I could venture to state after Wordsworth is his conception of the manner in which the mere fact is converted into poetry by the power of imagination.

He represented, however, much as, unknown to him, the German philosophers have done—that by the imagination the mere fact is exhibited as connected with that infinity without which there is no poetry.

He spoke of his tale of the dog called *Fidelity*. He says he purposely made the narrative as prosaic as possible in order that no discredit might be thrown on the truth of the incident. In the description at the beginning and in the moral at the end he has alone indulged in a poetic vein—and these parts he thinks he has peculiarly succeeded in. He quoted some of the latter passage and also from *The Kitten and the Falling Leaves* to show how he had connected *even the kitten with the great*, *awful and mysterious powers of nature*. But neither now, nor in reading the preface to Wordsworth's new edition of his poems, have I been able to comprehend his ideas concerning poetic imagination. Further than this idea of imagination I have not been able to raise my mind to the subject, viz. that imagination is the faculty by which the poet conceives and produces—that is, images—individual forms in which are *embodied universal ideas* or *abstractions*. This I do comprehend too, and I find also clearly the most beautiful and striking illustrations of this faculty in the works of Wordsworth himself. The incomparable twelve lines: 'She dwelt among the untrodden ways,' ending 'the difference to me,' are finely imagined. They exhibit the powerful effect of the loss of a very obscure object upon one tenderly attached to it—the opposition between the apparent strength of the passion and the insignificance of the object is delightfully conceived and the object itself well imagined. . . .

SEPT. 12th . . . I accompanied Mr. Wordsworth . . . to look at some fields belonging to the late Mr. Wordsworth which were to be sold by auction this evening. . . .

SEPT. 13th . . . I was called to accompany Wordsworth. . . . The dreary walk [over Cold Fell in mist and storm] had been relieved by long and interesting conversation, sometimes on law subjects connected with the business arising out of the late Mr. Wordsworth's will and sometimes on poetry. We had, too, at the close of the walk a very great pleasure. We turned out of the road to look at the ruins of Calder Abbey. . . . At half a mile distance is Calderbridge. . . . We dined and took tea. Wordsworth was fatigued, and therefore after an hour's chat he took the *Quarterly Review* and I took to my journal. . . . I omitted to notice that I read yesterday Southey's article on the poor in the last *Quarterly Review*—a very benevolently conceived and well-written article abounding in excellent ideas and proving that though he may have changed his opinions concerning governments and demagogues he retains all his original love of mankind, and the same zeal to promote the best interests of humanity. . . .

SEPT. 14th [*Ravenglass.*] . . . I have been reading the *Quarterly* review by Southey of *Madame de la Rochejaquelein*, a very interesting article, like the *Edinburgh* review of the same book—an interesting epitome of the narrative. . . . I slept in a double-bedded room with Wordsworth, and I went early to bed and read till he came upstairs. . . .

SEPT. 15th [*Eskdale.*] . . . Mr. Wordsworth was satisfied with his journey, having sold better than he expected the Ravenglass property and part of the property at Cockermouth. . . . We had no rain all day, but the mist was on the mountains, and hid their summits so that Wordsworth determined not to go back by Wastdale. Eskdale, he said, would be agreeable even in this weather, while Wastdale mountains would be utterly lost. . . . Up Hardknot, one of the mountains at the upper end of the valley. . . . Here I parted from Wordsworth. . . .

SEPT. 22nd [*Keswick.*] . . . I carried a book to Southey and took leave of the ladies. He insisted on accompanying me, at least to the point where the Thirlmere road . . . turns off. I enjoyed the walk. He was both frank and cordial. We spoke freely on politics. I have no doubt of the perfect purity and integrity of his mind. I think that he is an alarmist, though what he fears is a reasonable cause of alarm, viz. a *bellum servile* stimulated by the press. . . . But he is still, and warmly, a friend to national education, and to the lower classes, and as humane as ever he was. He has convinced me of the perfect exemption of his mind from all dishonourable motives and views in the change of his practical politics and philosophy.

We conversed also on literature—on Wordsworth and his own works. He appreciates Wordsworth as he ought. Of his own works he thinks *Don Roderick* by far the best, though Wordsworth prefers, as I do, his *Kehama*. Neither of us spoke of his political poems. At a little past one, Southey left me. . . . I called at De Quincey's at the bottom of the lake, and left a note for him, he being from home. I then called at Wordsworth's and resisted their kind pressing to take a bed with them. I sat till past eight, and then walked to Ambleside. . . .

SEPT. 23rd . . . Before I rose, I received a letter from De Quincey, informing me that he had come past twelve last night to the inn, but could not get admission, and would call on me after one today. I therefore resolved to wait for him. . . . He very obligingly walked with us on the way we had planned to go, and crossing the river between Grasmere and Rydal Water, showed us the fine views of Grasmere which were the first scenes pointed out to me by Wordsworth. Here he left us. . . . I engaged to dine with him tomorrow. . . .

SEPT. 24th . . . I called on Wordsworth, who offered to accompany me up Nab's Scar, the lofty rocky fell immediately over his house. . . . Wordsworth conducted me over the fell and left me near De Quincey's house a little after one. He was in bed but rose on my arrival. I was gratified by the sight of a large collection of books which I lounged over. De Quincey, about two, set out on a short excursion with me which I did not so much enjoy as he seemed to expect. We crossed the sweet vale of Grasmere and ascended up the fell on the opposite corner of the valley to Easedale Tarn. The charm of this spot is the solemnity of the seclusion in which it lies. . . . We returned to dinner at half-past four, and in an hour De Quincey accompanied me on the mountain road to Rydal Mount, and left me at the gate of Wordsworth's garden terrace. . . . I took tea with Wordsworth, Mrs. Wordsworth, and Miss Hutchinson. I had four hours of conversation as various and delightful as I ever enjoyed, but the detail ought not to be introduced into a narrative like this.

Wordsworth accompanied me on the road, and I parted from him under the impression of thankfulness for personal attentions in addition to the high reverence I felt for his character before. I found De Quincey up and I chatted with him till past twelve. I went first to bed. He slept in the same room on the floor.

SEPT. 25th . . . Lounged over books till past ten, when De Quincey came down to breakfast. It was not till somewhat past twelve that we commenced our walk, which had been marked out by Wordsworth. [Dungeon Gill.] . . . We crossed a sort of chasm in the fell which led to a . . . scene marked by one house and one small piece of water, Bleatarn, which the late Bishop of Llandaff has not improved by planting firs along one of its sides. Wordsworth has, however, made it the residence of his Solitary,[1] and it is, indeed, the fitting abode of a man at war with society and nature, with himself and their common Creator. . . . This interesting

[1] *Excursion*, Book ii, l. 327.

day was happily terminated in a very agreeable inn (Coniston, Waterhead). . . . De Quincey took tea here and stayed till half-past ten. I wrote a little in my journal after he was gone. De Quincey completely tired me today, and I am very sorry that by accepting his attentions here, I cannot now *cut* him without exposing myself to imputations of ingratitude. De Quincey is a learned man; he says himself he is the second Greek scholar in the kingdom. He is certainly a man of talents and a *thinker*, but he is very *entêté* and *bores* more than any one I know. I believe him to be very *honourable* and *gentlemanly*, but these are not sufficient *qualities* in a companion. He spoke about himself and his situation with a frankness that I am far from disliking. 'Tis his misfortune, perhaps, that he has taken some disgust with the Wordsworths and has broken off all attentions with them. This, I suspect, arose from an attachment he has formed for a girl, the daughter of a statesman,[1] one Simpson. Mrs. Wordsworth has expressed her disapprobation of the connection, and I expect has affronted him. He asked me whether Wordsworth had spoken on the subject, which I denied and was forced to utter an untruth, that I might not violate confidence—I hope the most excusable of falsehoods. De Quincey still praises Wordsworth's poetry, but he speaks with no kindness of the man. He says he is incapable of friendship out of his own family, and that he is very secular in his feelings. Like myself, he has seen and mentioned Wordsworth's irritability about his poetry and the public opinion, and his inability to enjoy the works of others. He admires Coleridge, but speaks severely of him, and has a very low opinion of Southey. He is intimate with Wilson, but does not praise his poetry.

One of the most offensive qualities of De Quincey's is that he likes nothing, he is *poco curante*; he decides at once on the merits of Schiller, Goethe, etc., and maintains they have very little. We were seven hours on foot, etc.

Nov. 2nd . . . At ten o'clock I called on the Lambs. Burney was there, and we played a rubber and afterwards Talfourd stepped in. We had a long chat together. We talked of puns, wit, etc. Lamb has no respect for any wit which turns on serious thought. He positively declared that he thought his joke about my 'great first cause least understood' a bad one, as well as the 'luke-warm Christian' applied to Evans. 'On the other hand,' he says, 'if you will quote any one of my jokes, quote this which is really a good one. Hume[2] and his wife and several of his children were with me. Hume repeated the old saying, "One fool makes many." "Aye, Mr. Hume," said I, pointing to the children, "You have a fine family." '

[1] *Dialect*. A small landholder who farms his own estate.

[2] Joseph Hume, M.P.

Neither Talfourd nor I could see the excellence of this. However, he related a piece of wit by Coleridge which we all held to be capital. Lamb had written to Coleridge about one of their old Christ College masters who had been a severe disciplinarian, intimating that he hoped Coleridge had forgiven all injuries. Coleridge replied that he certainly had; he hoped his soul was in heaven, and that when he went there he was borne by a host of cherubs, all face and wing and without backsides to excite his whipping propensities! . . .

DEC. 21st . . . I proposed to Cargill, as the day was inviting, a walk to Highgate. We enjoyed the day out of town, though within was a thick mist. I read to Cargill a long note to Coleridge's *Lay Sermon* in which he compares religion and reason. In substance this is the same distinction which for years I have been in the habit of promulgating, but given with a beauty and force truly admirable. I was glad to find that Cargill soon and fully comprehended it.

We found Coleridge at home, and we enjoyed his conversation for an hour and half. He looked ill, and indeed Mr. Gillman says he has been very ill. His bowels have been diseased, which he says is a family disease; but Gillman gives the best account of Coleridge's submission to discipline. He drinks only three glasses of wine every day, and takes no spirits nor any opium but when prescribed by Mr. Gillman himself. Coleridge has been able to work a great deal of late and with success. His second and third *Lay Sermons* and his *Poems* and Memoirs of his life, etc., in two volumes are to appear. These exertions have been too great, Mr. Gillman says. Coleridge talked easily and well, with less than his usual declamation. He explained at our request, and as I anticipated, his idea of fancy, styling it memory without judgment, and, of course, not filling that place in a chart of the mind which imagination holds, and which in his *Lay Sermon* he has admirably described as the 'reconciling and mediatory power which, incorporating the reason in images of the sense, and organizing as it were the flux of the senses by the permanence and self-circling energies of the reason, gives birth to a system of symbols,' etc. . . . Wordsworth's obscure discrimination between fancy and imagination in his last preface is greatly illustrated by what Coleridge has here said and written. Coleridge read us some extracts from his new poems, etc., and spoke of his German reading. He praises Steffens, and complains of the Catholicism of Schlegel and Tieck, etc. He mentioned Hazlitt's attack [on him] with greater moderation than I expected. He complains, and with reason, I think, of Lamb, who, he says, ought not to admit a man into his house who abuses the confidence of private intercourse so scandalously. He denies Hazlitt, however, originality, and ascribes to Lamb the best ideas in Hazlitt's article. He was not displeased to hear of his being knocked down by John Lamb lately. . . .

DEC. 22nd . . . After tea went to Basil Montagu's.[1] Hazlitt was there. I could not abstain from adverting to a scandalous article in this morning's *Examiner* in which he attacks Wordsworth. Hazlitt, without confessing himself the author, spoke as if he were but did not vindicate himself boldly. He said: 'You know I am not in the habit of defending what I do. I do not say that all I have done is right.' In the same tone, and after I had said that I was indignant at certain articles I had read, and at the breach of private confidence in the detail of conversation, Hazlitt said: 'It may be indelicate, but I am forced to write an article every week, and I have not time to make one with so much delicacy as I otherwise should.' To this I replied by alluding to the anecdote of the French minister who answered the libeller who said he must live: 'I do not see the necessity.' Hazlitt then made a distinction. He said he would never take advantage of a slip in a man's conversation, and repeat what was not such person's real opinion; but where what he had said was his notorious opinion not said to one person only, but generally, he thought such things might without injustice be repeated. I said: 'One aggravation is wanting in such a case, and your distinction amounts to this: I won't lie, I will only violate the confidence of friendship.' Hazlitt then adverted to the tergiversation of these persons. He thought it, he said, useful to expose people who otherwise would gain credit by canting and hypocrisy. I admitted the attack on Southey's *Carmen Nuptiale* to be unexceptionable; but Hazlitt admitted that he believes Southey to be still a perfectly honest man. Wordsworth was not named. Coleridge he seemed very bitter against. Basil Montagu seemed inclined to take part with Hazlitt. He said: 'It is difficult to draw the line in such cases. If I were in the House of Commons, and I heard a man applaud a measure of government publicly which he had privately reprobated to me the day before, should I be censurable in rising up and declaring this?'

I carefully abstained from shaking hands with Hazlitt. We were, of course, stiff towards each other, and I having praised a picture by Domenichino, engraved by Müller, of St. John, he said to Mrs. Montagu, in a marked way: 'A very bad thing, ma'am.' . . .

[1] Basil Montagu (1770–1851), legal and miscellaneous writer, a college friend of Wordsworth.

1817

FEB. 13th . . . We then passed Palace Yard and heard Mr. Hunt,[1] the demagogue of the day. He speaks in a gentlemanly manner, though the substance of his speeches is as low as the people he addresses them to. One Walker spoke also—a coarse mob-orator with a stentorian voice. I saw young Cobbett, who also came forward. I could not [hear] him—I thought he looked chuckle-headed. They say he is *dignus filius dignioris patris*. . . .

MARCH 10th . . . I wrote today to Southey, merely putting in a very general way the question to him whether he would listen to proposals to undertake the management of a very profitable literary concern.[2]

JUNE 13th . . . I dined at Mr. Green's, No. 22 Lincoln's Inn Fields. Coleridge, Ludwig Tieck, Von Buch, and Schlichtegroll were our party. Mr. [blank in MS.], brother of Mrs. Green, joined us after dinner. It was an afternoon and evening of very high pleasure indeed.

Ludwig Tieck has not a prepossessing exterior. He has a shrewd, clever face, but I should rather [have] thought him an able man of the world than a romantic poet. He was not the greatest talker today. Indeed, the course of the conversation led others to give him information; but what he did say was sensible and judicious.

Coleridge was not in his element. His German was not good and his English was not free. He feared he should not be understood if he talked his best; his eloquence was, therefore, constrained.

Tieck's journey to England is undertaken with a view to the study of our old English dramatists, contemporaries of Shakespeare. He incidentally gave opinions of our elder poets more favourable than I expected; he estimates them highly, as it seems.

NOV. 2nd I breakfasted with Basil Montagu. . . .

Montagu was employed by Shelley lately on the application to have his children taken from him by his late wife's father, on the ground that Shelley avowed atheism and lived in adultery with Godwin's daughter. The application was granted. It appeared that Mrs. Shelley, being pregnant, threw herself into the river and was drowned. It is singular that it was not suggested to Basil Montagu by Shelley that he was not the father of his wife's child. Mrs. Godwin had stated this to me as a fact. Basil Montagu thinks it improbable. Basil Montagu says that Godwin

[1] Henry Hunt.

[2] He was, in fact, offering him, on John Walter's behalf, the editorship of *The Times*, which Southey declined.

borrowed money of Shelley after his daughter ran away with Shelley and before the marriage. This I am unwilling to believe. Though when integrity is so hard to preserve under poverty we ought not to expect moral delicacy and refinement. . . .

Nov. 6th . . . 10 [p.m.]. I then went to Godwin. Mr. Shelley was there. I had never seen him before. His youth and a resemblance to Southey, particularly in his voice, raised a pleasing impression, which was not altogether destroyed by his conversation, which is vehement and arrogant and intolerant. He was very abusive towards Southey, whom he spoke of as having sold himself to the Court, and this he maintained with the usual party slang. His pension and his laureateship, his early zeal and his recent virulence, are the proofs of gross corruption. On every topic but the last the friends of Southey are under no difficulty of defending him. Shelley spoke of Wordsworth with less bitterness, but with an insinuation of his insincerity, etc. The passage about baptism in *The Excursion*, it is not easy to defend. Mrs. Godwin, in Shelley's absence, took occasion to observe angrily that no one asked for Mrs. Shelley, and inquired whether I did not know she was married. Shelley's return prevented my reply, which would not have been agreeable.

Dec. 4th . . . I breakfasted early, and soon after nine walked to Doctor Wordsworth at Lambeth. I crossed for the first time Waterloo Bridge. The view of Somerset House is very fine indeed, and the bridge itself is highly beautiful; but the day was so bad that I could not see either of the other bridges, and, of course, scarcely any objects.

I found Mr. and Mrs. Wordsworth and the Doctor at breakfast, and I spent a couple of hours with them very agreeably. . . .

We talked about poetry. Wordsworth has brought manuscripts with him, and is inclined to print one or two poems, as it is the fashion to publish small volumes now. He means then to add them to the *Thanksgiving Ode*, etc., and form a third volume. He read to me some very beautiful passages.

Coleridge's book has given him no pleasure, and he finds just fault with Coleridge for professing to write about himself and writing merely about Southey and Wordsworth. With the criticism on the poetry too he is not satisfied. The praise is extravagant and the censure inconsiderate. I recollected hearing Hazlitt say that Wordsworth would not forgive a single censure mingled with however great a mass of eulogy. . . .

Dec. 27th . . . I called on Lamb and met Wordsworth with him and returned to Lamb's again, but Wordsworth did not meet me to go with me to Monkhouse's,[1] with whom I dined. The party was small—Mr.

[1] Thomas Monkhouse, a wealthy kinsman of Mrs. Wordsworth.

and Mrs. Wordsworth and Miss Hutchinson, Coleridge and his son Hartley, and Mr. Tillbrook. After dinner Charles Lamb and his sister joined the party. I was glad to hear Coleridge take the right side on Hone's trial. He eloquently expatiated on the necessity of saving Hone in order to save English law, and he derided the legal definition of a libel, whatever tends to produce certain consequences—without any regard to the intention of the publisher.

Among the light conversation at dinner Tillbrook related that Southey had received a letter from a person requesting him to make an acrostic on the name of a young lady in Essex whom he was addressing, but he had a rival who beat him in writing verses—the name Rebecca Rankin. Southey did not send the verses, and distributed the money in buying blankets for some poor women of Keswick. The party, however, was not well assorted, and the conversation not altogether as it ought to have been. I was for the first time in my life not pleased with Wordsworth, and Coleridge appeared to advantage in his presence. Coleridge spoke of painting in that style of mysticism which is now his habit of feeling. Wordsworth met this by dry, unfeeling contradiction. The manner of Coleridge towards Wordsworth was most respectful, but Wordsworth towards Coleridge was cold and scornful. Coleridge maintained that painting was not an art which could operate on the vulgar, and Wordsworth declared this opinion to be degrading to the art. Coleridge illustrated his assertions by reference to Raphael's Madonnas. Wordsworth could not think that a field for high intellect lay within such a subject as a mother and child, and when Coleridge talked of the divinity of those works, Wordsworth asked whether he thought he should have discerned those beauties if he had [not] known that Raphael was the artist; and when Coleridge said that was an unkind question, Wordsworth made no apology. Independently of the unfeeling manner, I thought Wordsworth substantially wrong. It was not so clear to me that Coleridge was right. Coming away I found the Lambs felt as I did.

Dec. 30th . . . I dined with the Colliers and spent the evening at Lamb's. I found a large party collected round the two poets, but Coleridge had the larger body. Talfourd only had fixed himself by Wordsworth and remained by his side all the evening. There was, however, scarcely any conversation beyond a whisper. Coleridge was philosophising in his rambling way to Monkhouse, who listened attentively; to Manning, who sometimes smiled as if he thought Coleridge had no right to metaphysicise on chemistry without any knowledge on the subject; to Martin Burney, who was eager to interpose, and Alsager, who was content to be a listener; while Wordsworth was for a great part of the time engaged *tête-à-tête* with

Talfourd. I could catch scarcely anything of the conversation; but I heard at one time Coleridge quoting Wordsworth's verses, and Wordsworth quoting—*not* Coleridge's but his own. I chatted with the ladies. Miss Lamb had gone through the fatigue of a dinner-party very well, and Charles Lamb was good-humoured. His object of attack was Martin Burney, who was in very good spirits. His uncle, Dr. Charles Burney, died on Sunday, and Charles Lamb protested Martin had eaten enormously on account of his grief. . . .

1818

JAN. 27th . . . I heard Hazlitt lecture on Shakespeare and Milton. He delighted me much by the talent he displayed, but I was equally disgusted with the malignant spirit that broke through in the covert attack on Wordsworth without naming him; he was very abusive, reproaching modern poets for their vanity and incapacity of admiring and loving anything but themselves. He was applauded at this part of his lecture, but I know not whether he was generally understood.

From hence I called at Collier's, and taking Mrs. Collier with me I went to a lecture by Coleridge in Fleur de Luce Court, Fleet Street. I was gratified unexpectedly by finding a large and respectable audience—generally of very superior looking persons—in physiognomy rather than dress. But the lecture was heavy. Coleridge treated of the origin of poetry and of Oriental works, but he was little animated, and an exceedingly bad cold rendered his voice scarcely audible. . . .

JAN. 30th . . . I then went to Coleridge's second lecture. It was much more brilliant than the first and seemed to give general satisfaction. . . . As soon as the lecture was over I went, though late, to Mr. C. Aikin's. The party was smaller than usual and perhaps on that account more pleasant. I chatted agreeably with Mrs. Barbauld and came home late.

FEB. 24th . . . Heard a part of a lecture by Hazlitt at the Surrey Institution. Hazlitt was so contemptuous towards Wordsworth, speaking of his letter about Burns, that I lost my temper and hissed; but I was on the outside of the room. I was led to burst out into declamations against Hazlitt which I afterwards regretted, though I uttered nothing but the truth. Hazlitt abused Wordsworth in a vulgar style, imputing to him the mere desire of representing himself as a superior man. I hurried away to attend Mrs. Smith to Coleridge's lecture. She accompanied me in a coach and I procured one for our return.

The lecture was on Wit and Humour, and the great writers of wit and humour. There was much obscurity and metaphysics in the long introduction and not a little cant and commonplace in the short criticisms. I fear that Coleridge will not on the whole add to his reputation by these lectures. . . .

APRIL 18th . . . Then called at Reid's, of whom I procured a copy of *Tales of my Landlord* which my sister [in-law] sent . . . as a present . . . and I sent her the *Elegant Extracts in Verse*.[1] I took tea with the Lambs and played two rubbers. I then returned to chambers. . . . I returned to Lamb's again. There was a large party—the greater part of those who are usually there, but also Hunt and his wife—she a very disgusting woman; he, though a man I very much dislike, did not displease me this evening. He has improved in manliness and healthfulness since I saw him last, some years ago. There was a glee about him which evinced high spirits, if not perfect health, and I envied his vivacity. He imitated Hazlitt capitally, Wordsworth not so well. Talfourd was there, and injudiciously loquacious, quoting verses without mercy. He threw away Wordsworth's fine lines on scorners.[2] Hunt, who did not sympathize with Talfourd, opposed him playfully, and that I liked him for. . . .

APRIL 30th . . . I called on Lamb and accompanied him to Mr. Monkhouse, St. Anne Street East. I had a pleasant evening there. Haydon and Allston, painters, were there, and two other gentlemen whose names I did not collect. The conversation was very lively and agreeable. Allston has a mild manner, a soft voice, and a sentimental air with him, not at all Yankyish; but his conversation does not indicate the talent displayed in his painting. There is a warmth and vigour about Haydon, indicating youthful confidence, which is often the concomitant of talents and genius, which he is said to possess. His conversation is certainly interesting. Monkhouse himself is a gentlemanly sensible man. Lamb, without talking much, talked his best. I enjoyed the evening.

MAY 29th . . . I read today Hazlitt's last lecture on the Poets, in which he flippantly and cavalierly, but with eloquence occasionally, breaks the staff over the heads of the living poets. He bepraises Coleridge with outrageous eulogy, at the same time that he reproaches him bitterly. Praises Wordsworth warmly but in a sentence or two, while he dwells with malignity on his real and imputed faults, and treats Southey absolutely with contempt. Rogers he passes over as if he were a lady whom he was not at liberty to abuse. Does not name Crabbe, and rather avoids meeting

[1] By Vicesimus Knox.

[2] '. . . That he, who feels contempt For any living thing . . .'—*Lines left upon a seat in a Yew Tree.*

public opinion on the merits of Lord Byron. Indeed, it is easy to give evasive judgment by dwelling on accidents only. Moore he seems desirous of favouring, and he is kind to Walter Scott.

DEC. 21st . . . Read Hazlitt's criticisms on the Stage. This is but a reprint of his newspaper criticisms which he has ventured to publish on the credit of his lectures on the Poets and his characters of Shakespeare's plays. A very inferior book, but it has still amused me and stolen more time from me than I ought to waste on such books. His manner of saying things is always amusing; but Amyot prefers the judgment itself to the style. Certainly Hazlitt's taste is not correct, and he is more desirous to say a smart than a true thing, and his political and personal antipathies and partialities peep out very unpleasantly every moment. . . .

DEC. 31st . . . I read, beginning of the week, *Headlong Hall*[1]—satirical dialogues—an account of a visit to a Welsh squire's seat. The interlocutors represent certain literary parties in the country. There is one who is an optimist, another a deteriorist, who obtrude their speculations on every occasion; there are reviewers, a picturesque gardener, etc.; but the commonplaces of the literators of the day are not preserved from being tiresome by original humour or wit, so that the book is very dull.

1819

JAN. 11th . . . Amused myself by reading *Pride and Prejudice*. . . .

JAN. 12th . . . I sat up till two, as I did last night, to finish *Pride and Prejudice*. This novel I consider as one of the most excellent of the works of our female novelists. Its merit lies in the characters, and in the perfectly colloquial style of the dialogue. Mrs. Bennet, the foolish mother, who cannot conceal her projects to get rid of her daughters, is capitally drawn. There is a thick-headed servile parson, also a masterly sketch. His stupid letters and her ridiculous speeches are as delightful as wit. The two daughters are well contrasted—the gentle and candid Jane and the lively but prejudiced Elizabeth, are both good portraits, and the development of the passion between Elizabeth and the proud Darcy, who at first hate each other, is executed with skill and effect.

JAN. 13th . . . After dinner Mrs. Opie came and I had a very pleasant evening with her, Mrs. Alderson and Miss Alderson (a niece), the gentlemen not coming upstairs. Mrs. Opie sang, told good stories, was in spirits, and at her ease. She spoke of literary men; of Rogers the poet she

[1] By T. L. Peacock.

spoke with great bitterness; she says he is made wretched by excess of envy at the success of the more popular poets. Fuseli said of him: 'When Rogers says, "Sir, I am glad to see you," he looks as if he said, "Go to Hell."' Fuseli, also expressing himself of Rogers's face, said: 'I met Rogers today, and he offered me his hand, but I declined it. I was not prepared to make one in death's dance.' A happy painter's image. Sydney Smith, in allusion to Rogers's character, said to Mrs. Opie: 'I saw Rogers today, and told him I never could read twenty lines together of Campbell, and he instantly asked me to dinner.' Smith is an admirer of Campbell.

FEB. 22nd . . . I borrowed . . . *Nightmare Abbey*, a satire by one [Peacock], sketches of character chiefly in dialogue. One Flosky is Coleridge. The others are less marked personages—geologists, metaphysicians, and sentimentalists are laughed at, but I could not laugh with the author. . . .

MAY 3rd . . . Calling on Walter (I dined also with Walter, Fraser and Barnes there), Fraser I attacked on a trimming article in yesterday's *Times* about Catholic Emancipation, and Barnes attacked me about *Peter Bell*. But this is a storm I must yield to. Wordsworth has set himself back ten years by the publication of this unfortunate work. . . .

I read also *Tom Cribb's Memorial to the Congress*, an amusing volume, but I would rather read than have written it. It is really surprising that a gentleman—for so Moore is, in station and connections—should so descend as to exhibit the Prince Regent and the Emperor of Russia at a boxing match under the names of Porpus and Long Sandy. The boxing cant language does not amuse me even in Moore's gravely burlesque lines.

MAY 4th . . . Having received fresh stone drawings from Frankfurt, carried Mr. Gurney his. Mrs. Barbauld was there. Showed my Piranesi to them. Mrs. Barbauld betrayed more symptoms of old age than I ever noticed before. Her judgment and taste remain, her activity of mind slowly declines. . . .

MAY 11th . . . I then went to Charles Lamb's. Mrs. Hazlitt and some old female friends of Lamb's there. I gossiped there till eleven. Lamb *ennuyé* with the good kind of people who had visited him, whom he had too much kindness of heart not to entertain to the best of his capacity, but who could not entertain him in return. Lamb spoke of *Peter Bell*, which he considers as one of the worst of Wordsworth's works. The lyric narrative Lamb has no taste for, he is disgusted by the introduction, which he deems puerile, and the story he thinks ill told, though he allows the idea to be good. . . .

JULY 8th . . . Read . . . an able criticism on *Peter Bell* in the *Eclectic Review*, which, though severe, I felt to be for the greater part just. It is written by one who understands, as well as feels, the excellence of Wordsworth as well as his great faults. I could not but feel the force of the remark that to dwell as Wordsworth does on the meanest of objects, exerting on them all the force of his intellect, evinces a sort of insanity. The author has too sarcastically reproached Wordsworth with conceit, and seems to impute as vice what is, I believe, mere peculiarity of taste; nor do I think he can be justly reproached with having lost the faculty of distinguishing great and small, noble and mean....

AUG. 30th ... Called on Miss Hays, who is removed to Pentonville. She wants society and I shall feel it a duty to be pretty frequent in my calls. But alone she rather *bores*, though she is a sensible as well as very excellent and worthy woman, and her improved health and spirits render her society less burdensome than when she was more sentimental. She tells me that poor [Fanny] Imlay, who it was said died in Ireland—and about whose death I never heard anything said—in fact, died, not in Ireland, but in England, and by her own hand! She hung herself! Poor Godwin! How sadly visited he has been in his own family for the errors in speculation which his early works may have disseminated! He is a man of deep sensibility, and must have suffered grievously from such a catastrophe. Mrs. Godwin, too, must have felt, for she is not without feeling! It is said she was never married, but was kept and abandoned by her keeper, or, rather, left destitute at his death. She was relieved by a charitable subscription, and taken out of a prison; on which she came up to town with her young children, met with Godwin at Somers Town and became certainly towards him a meritorious wife, though towards others I doubt both her sincerity and her integrity....

SEPT. 10th ... I also read and with interest the third volume of Disraeli's[1] *Curiosities of Literature*, though this volume is as much historical as literary.... Disraeli is certainly one of the best gossiping writers I am acquainted with. He chooses his subjects well. They all interest....

OCT. 6th ... I read during this week Hazlitt's political essays. None pleased me more than his critique on Burke, which he now calls a piece of extravagant candour. Hazlitt's last writings are more ferocious and malignant, more laboured and stuffed with ornament than his earlier writings. He is on the decline, I think.

NOV. 19th ... I dined again in Wardour Street and met Hogg there—a man whom I do not like, though he is a person of talent certainly. He is a contemptuous polemic, and offensive by his scorn of those I most reverence and love. But he is the friend of Shelley and an avowed atheist....

[1] Isaac Disraeli.

DEC. 16th . . . I went after nine to Lamb's. The party there, Hazlitt, too. He and I exchanged a few words. I was the first to speak, and he only answered me. Played whist. . . .

1820

JAN. 21st . . . Read this week *Ivanhoe*. As a tale it interests much less than the Scottish romances, but this is hardly the author's fault. He has thrown more interest than could have been reasonably expected into a tale the manners of whose characters are so little known to us. He has contrived to work into his work a great deal of antiquarian and curious knowledge. He has, however, failed in rendering Robin Hood acceptable —the delightful hero of the old popular ballad is degraded in the modern romance into a sturdy vagrant. . . .

MAY 11th This was a day of agreeable dissipation. I called on the Nashes early and accompanied them into Piccadilly. We saw Haydon's picture of the entrance of Christ into Jerusalem. It does not please me. Our Saviour has a face not of divine meekness but of sheer human lowliness—a sort of dreamy meditation, not of superhuman foreknowledge. There are a few fine groups. Jairus and his daughter and a penitent girl brought to him; but the mass, though composed of many figures, does not impose, nor are the Apostles characteristic. The group of Wordsworth, Newton, and Voltaire is ill executed. The poet is a forlorn and haggard old man, the philosopher is a sleek, well-dressed citizen of London, and Voltaire is merely an ugly Frenchman. . . .

JUNE 11th This was a very agreeable day. I rose early and by appointment breakfasted with Mr. Monkhouse. Wordsworth and Mrs. Wordsworth, a Mr. Kenyon[1] were there. Haydon came in for a few minutes only. We talked of our expected journey, and Wordsworth still lets me hope that I may have the opportunity of travelling with him. He was, however, more occupied about the new edition of *Peter Bell*. He has resolved to make some concessions to public taste, and has resolved to strike out several offensive passages, such as 'Is it a party in a parlour, etc.,' which I had implored him to leave out before the book first appeared. So the over-coarse expressions: 'But I will bang your bones,' etc. I never before saw Wordsworth so little opinionated, so willing to make sacrifices for the

[1] John Kenyon (1784–1856), poet and philanthropist, who, with his brother Edward, became an intimate friend of Crabb Robinson. It was Kenyon who introduced his cousin Elizabeth Barrett to Robert Browning.

sake of popularity as now. He is improved not a little by this, in my mind. We talked of Haydon. Wordsworth wants to have a large sum raised to enable him to continue in his profession. He wants £2,000 for his great picture (the produce of the Exhibition—the gross produce is £1,200) and he has suggested that part of this could be raised by subscription, so that the remainder could be advanced by way of purchase money for it, as an altar-piece to one of the new chambers [*sic*]. Sir George Beaumont will give £50, but will not otherwise interfere. . . .

JUNE 21st . . . After taking tea at home I called at Monkhouse's and there spent an agreeable evening. Wordsworth was very pleasant; indeed, he is uniformly so now, and there is absolutely no pretence for what was always an exaggerated charge against him, that he can talk only of his own poetry and loves only his own works. He is more indulgent than he used to be of the works of others, even rivals and contemporaries, and is more open to argument in favour of changes in his own works. Lamb was in excellent spirits. Talfourd came in late, and we stayed till past twelve. Lamb was at last rather overcome, but it produced nothing but humorous expressions of his desire to go on the Continent—in which I should delight to accompany him.

JULY 5th . . . I called on Wordsworth to take leave, etc. He has left me memoranda of the places where I am to inquire for letters from him in Switzerland. I, on my part, left letters for him and memoranda, but his plans are so unfixed that I am really afraid of losing him after all. If I do I shall suffer from the loss of his society, but I shall perhaps gain as to the mere journey itself, seeing more objects and more easily. . . .

JULY 18th . . . I was agreeably surprised by a call from Miss Lamb [at Cambridge, where he was on Circuit]. I was heartily glad to see her, and, accompanying her to her brother's lodgings, I had a very pleasant rubber of whist with them and a Mrs. Smith, a widow—an acceptable relief from Circuit society.

JULY 20th I had nothing to do today, and therefore had leisure to accompany Lamb and his sister on a walk behind the colleges. All Lamb's enjoyments are so pure and so hearty that it is an enjoyment to see him enjoy. We walked about the exquisite chapel and gardens of Trinity. . . .

[*Travel journal: Switzerland; Italy.*] AUG. 16th . . . It was dark when we entered Lucerne. . . . I ran to the Cheval Blanc, and the supper being on the table I went into the dining-room in search of my friends. I heard my name pronounced before I could get an answer to my question, and I received a flattering welcome from Mr., Mrs., and Miss Wordsworth and Mr. Monkhouse. I took supper with my companions, who shared to some degree the satisfaction I expressed. . . . My first object was now happily obtained. I had reached the friends with whom I was to survey Switzerland and until I had joined them I felt myself not at liberty to indulge in any sights which occupied time.

AUG. 17th Wordsworth's stay at Lucerne had been lengthened by an impudent imposition practised on him by the owner of a char-à-banc who had seized his greatcoat, etc., because Wordsworth would not pay him for three days' hire of his car contrary to the agreement for two. Wordsworth had resolved to apply to a magistrate and I arrived at the lucky minute. By a singular good fortune one of my travelling companions yesterday was the Statthalter of Sarnen where the man lived. We spoke to him last night. He was to go on foot this morning to his town, and we therefore gladly accompanied him. This, therefore, was an excursion on business, but I was amply rewarded by the delightful scenes I saw.

We rose at four and walked to Winkelbrunnen where we embarked on the lake. . . . It is, Wordsworth says, incomparably the finest of the lakes for variety of excellence and especially for the sublimity of its rocks round the great number [*sic*] of its shores. . . . We landed at Alpnach and then proceeded to Sarnen. We found the landlord on the road, who confirmed Wordsworth's statement to the Statthalter, and this magistrate . . . was so satisfied with the innkeeper's testimony that he promised Mr. Wordsworth should have the clothes back and that the offender should be punished. . . .

AUG. 29th . . . This day has been spent on the lake [Como], and so much exquisite pleasure I never had on water. The tour or rather excursion we have been making surpasses certainly all I have ever seen, and Wordsworth asserts the same. . . . But the pleasure can hardly be recorded, it consisting in the contemplation of scenes absolutely indescribable by words, and in sensations for which no words have been even invented. . . .

SEPT. 1st [*Milan. Hotel Reichmann.*] At four we went to the table d'hôte. . . . The English were placed together. There were several gentlemanly young men. One took the lead in conversation and it was apparent at once that he had been used to much and good company. . . . He spoke with warmth in favour of German literature, and that was the point of approximation between him and me. He asserted the superiority of the German to the living English poets. I said, in German: 'The present company is excepted.' Wordsworth took up the argument with warmth, and spoke of his knowledge of Schiller whom the stranger had extravagantly praised, as derived from his friend Coleridge. In almost an instant afterwards the stranger said: 'There is, indeed, but one poet in England that is to be compared with Schiller, and he is a greater poet—Wordsworth.' Miss Wordsworth laughed and said: 'This is too ridiculous,' and Wordsworth gravely said: 'It is singular that I should be that very Wordsworth.' The expression of surprise and pleasure on the part of the stranger was at least well acted. The ladies are quite convinced that he knew Wordsworth when he said this. I am unwilling to suppose that there was a distinct, conscious knowledge on his part, for such gross flattery is hardly compatible with the turn of mind which renders Mr. Graham certainly an admirer of Wordsworth. Be that as it may, the ice was broken, a rapid acquaintance was formed. He became our cicerone, and is now the companion of Wordsworth and the ladies on a separate excursion. He soon made himself known as a Mr. Graham who has been travelling for some years. . . . He is a very lively, pleasant companion certainly, and I suspect a disciple of St. Paul in being 'all things to all men,' though for a very different purpose. He has associated with Shelley and Lord Byron, corresponded with Leigh Hunt, and knows Lamb and Hazlitt. . . .

SEPT. 20th [*Lausanne.*] . . . A stranger hearing my name pronounced on the walk made himself known to us as a Mr. Mulock, a lecturer on English Literature at Geneva and Lausanne. He had letters to Mr. Monkhouse, to whose lady he had rendered services. Before he had been with us five minutes he took Mr. Monkhouse aside, and without any apology intimated to him that the world made comments on his having left Mrs. Monkhouse and Miss Horrocks at Geneva, and very seriously advised him as to his duty as a married man. His conversation began with me by saying that he considered all Mr. Wordsworth's religious poetry as atheism—whose school of poetry he had been 'castigating'. On my remonstrating on this harsh position, he burst out into a furious ultra-Calvinistic rant that all religion was founded on a recognition of the fall of man—that all declamations about God as recognised in the beauties and wonders of nature were mystical nonsense. In perfect consistency with his contempt for Wordsworth he avowed the highest admiration of Lord Byron, a greater poet than Shakespeare; he saw in his works the profoundest views of the depravity of human nature—not indeed spiritual views, but though not spiritually-minded, Lord Byron has developed the human heart, and the intense truth of all his poetry is its great excellence. I admitted that Lord Byron's works do exhibit a most depraved and corrupt heart, but observed that he shares this merit with Voltaire, Lord Rochester, and all the obscene and profligate writers of Italy and France. Mr. Mulock did not feel the observation. Of course, these speculative opinions could not offend Mr. Monkhouse or me, but that seeing us with Mr. Wordsworth, and knowing us to be his friends, he should express his contempt of his writings to us in the grossest terms, and at the same time obtrude himself into his company, appeared to us an instance of indelicacy quite unexampled. I did not conceal my opinion of him. In the evening he forced Mr. Wordsworth into an argument, and on coming up I heard him utter such impertinences to Mr. Wordsworth that I could not help interfering, and assisted in putting an end to the unpleasant conversation. I said: 'Mr. Wordsworth, you are not aware that this gentleman is a lecturer by profession. He has been lecturing Mr. Monkhouse on the duties of a husband, you on poetry, and I dare say will soon instruct me in law, and Mrs. Wordsworth how a lady should conduct herself.' This served to divert the lecturer's attention from Wordsworth to me, and the controversy ended. . . .

SEPT. 26th [*Posthouse at Morez.*] . . . We reduced the bill from thirty-three to twenty-four francs through Wordsworth's laudable perseverance.

SEPT. 28th Miss Wordsworth got into conversation with Miss Baudouin, whose brother married a natural child of Wordsworth.

OCT. 2nd [*Paris.*] The Wordsworths having removed to Rue Charlot, Boulevard du Temple, I dined alone in the Rue Montmartre.

OCT. 3rd . . . I repaired to Rue Charlot and was introduced to Mrs. Baudouin, a mild, amiable little woman in appearance. I liked everything about her except that she called Wordsworth 'father', which I thought indelicate. The mother is said to be a clever woman and she seems so.

NOV. 20th [*London.*] . . . I was glad to accompany the Wordsworths to the British Museum. I had to wait for them in the ante-room, and we had at last but a hurried survey of the antiquities. I did not perceive that Wordsworth enjoyed much the Elgin Marbles, but he is a still man when he does enjoy himself and by no means ready to talk of his pleasure except to Miss Wordsworth. But we could hardly see the statues. The Memnon, however, seemed to interest him very much. I have thought that Wordsworth's enjoyment of works of art is very much in proportion to their subserviency to poetical illustration. I doubt whether he feels the beauty of mere form. . . .

DEC. 5th . . . I went to B[ancus] R[egius][1] hearing that Cobbett was to be seen there. He had finished his defence in a libel case already. I could, therefore, only look at him. His countenance rather softens my dislike to him. He has small eyes with a slight cast apparently and an air of simplicity disarming to an adversary, but a noble forehead. His dress very plain. . . .

DEC. 8th . . . I met Coleridge; he was looking well. 'I hope you are a Queenite,' said he. 'No,' said I, 'only an anti-Kingite.' 'Aye, that's all I mean.' We soon after parted. . . . I read a little of Keats's poems to the Aders. The beginning of the *Hyperion*—really a piece of great promise.

[1] i.e. King's Bench.

There is a force, wildness, and originality in the works of this young poet which, if his perilous journey to Italy does not destroy him, promise to place him at the head of the next generation of poets. Lamb places him next to Wordsworth—not meaning any comparison, for they are dissimilar.

DEC. 11th I was at the King's Bench early and was soon met by Mr. and Mrs. Aders. I procured a place for Mrs. Aders among the barristers, and she stayed several hours. The case of Wright *v.* Cobbett was heard, and it produced considerable interest. Scarlett took great pains in his opening speech. Cobbett was cool and impudent, with affected ease. His examination of witnesses was not at all able or judicious and his speech to the jury chiefly remarkable for assurance. He abandoned the justification of his libel, which charged Wright with forgery, cheating, etc., but in his speech by no means abandoned the charge. He was acute and bitter, and able too, on extraneous matters; attacked Scarlett and Brougham, etc. He was forced to call his sons to prove that it was not himself but one of them who was the author of the libel. I understand that on cross-examination they proved plaintiff's case, and £1,000 were given against Cobbett, to my great pleasure, for he is a superlative scoundrel. But though my opinion of him is so bad, yet while he was speaking his good-humoured manner nearly disarmed me. His manner is almost puerile occasionally, and at times he has a simple air, the effect of which is heightened by a cast of the eye. His voice and manner vary much, indications of insincerity and falsehood, which certainly do not fail here. He lied egregiously during his speech, and even of his speech.

This occupied me all day, though I left Cobbett speaking. . . .

DEC. 15th . . . I read Keats's *Pot of Basil*—a pathetic tale delightfully told. I afterwards read the story in Boccaccio, each in his way excellent. I am greatly mistaken if Keats do not very soon take a high place among our poets. There is great feeling and a powerful imagination in this little volume.

DEC. 27th . . . Took tea, etc., at Lamb's. One of his monthly parties; less agreeable than usual. His vulgar brother there whose manners are intolerable, and Phillips, and, late, Ayrton; also Talfourd stepped in, smartly dressed for a party. Talfourd does not gain by personal decoration. I begin to think him personally vain. I have read his article on Wordsworth in the *New Monthly Magazine*. It is all praise and luscious, though not mawkish. John Scott, on the other hand, has in Baldwin's *London Magazine* eulogised with discrimination as well as with eloquence. It is an article that may convert a scorner. Talfourd can only delight a disciple and partisan. Talfourd has so much to write for the periodical works that he can hardly allow himself time to think; he is in danger of becoming a commonplace declaimer. He is to succeed Hazlitt as dramatic critic in the *London*. It will be, I fear, a falling off, for Hazlitt, though a mannerist in style, is a thinker at least. Hazlitt's *Table Talk* in the *London* is full of acute observation. If spleen did not throw an offensive hue over all he writes, and were not his style spoiled by an ambition of ornament, he would be a very first-rate writer. As it is, I read all he writes with zest.

1821

JAN. 16th . . . Reading for the greater part the *Sketch Book* by the American (Irving). The articles are very unequal indeed. In general I prefer the pieces of humour—*The Legend of Sleepy Hollow* and *Van Winkle*, the one relating how a henpecked husband was charmed away and slept twenty years in the mountains near the Hudson, and the other how a village schoolmaster lost his life in a conflict with a ghost, are both delightfully written. So *Little Britain*, a piece of mock antiquarianism, is very pleasing. The author's pathos is less successful and his preaching is dry. He has elaborately described Christmas frolics, but he has taken his materials from books of more than a century ago, not from the just vanished customs. No country squire has of late years sung songs written by Herrick. *Westminster Abbey* gives occasion to an interesting article and the *Boar's Head*, Eastcheap, to one rather better; but the author's journey to Stratford-on-Avon was a lost labour. He does not attempt to describe the subsisting manners of the Americans, and therein is wise; but the best thing I yet know of America is that it should have produced so good a writer. The picture of John Bull is well preserved, but he has many poor articles in both volumes. . . .

JAN. 21st . . . Went to Mrs. Barbauld's. She was in good spirits, but she is now the confirmed old woman. Independently of her fine understanding and literary reputation she would pass for an interesting old lady. Her white locks, fair and wrinkled skin, brilliant starched linen, and rich silk gown make her a fit object for a painter. Her conversation is lively, her remarks judicious, and always pertinent, though she has not gone with the age in matters of taste and poetry, and has gone too exclusively with a sect in religion and morals; yet of that sect, Unitarian Christians, she is the chief boast and ornament. . . .

FEB. 21st . . . Hazlitt and I now speak again, but he does not omit the 'Sir' when he talks to me. I think he behaves with propriety and dignity towards me; considering the severity of my attack on him, which, though warranted by my friendship with Wordsworth, was not justified according to the customs of society. Stayed at Lamb's and played whist till very late.

MARCH 3rd Another morning of calls, the only one interesting on Miss Lamb. Lamb seems to have felt acutely poor Scott's death.[1] Talfourd was thinking of applying for the editorship, but Lamb agreed with me in thinking it incompatible with his profession. . . . I spent the evening at Lamb's chiefly playing piquet with Miss Lamb while Charles Lamb read. . . .

APRIL 16th . . . I walked to Hatfield . . . looked into the church. The vicar, Bennett, was our cicerone. He spoke of Goldsmith as a man he had seen. Goldsmith had lodgings at Springfield, where he lodged with some farmers. He spent his forenoons in his room writing; breakfasted off water-gruel without bread. In his manners he was a *bear*. A tame one, I observed, and it was assented to. He dressed shabbily, and was an odd man. No further particulars could I get, except that while Goldsmith was there a gentleman took down some cottages, which Bennett supposes gave rise to *The Deserted Village*. . . .

JULY 15th I had an idle lounge over *The Lady of the Lake* today—I read it through. A book which leaves no impression on a second perusal can deserve no place in the permanent literature of a nation. This is certainly the case with this, the first of Walter Scott's poems. I suspect the others are not substantially different. A want of import in the characters, of depth in the sentiments, of originality in the conception of his poems, will never permit him to hold high rank among poets, though the vivacity of his description and facility in his narratives make him an entertaining writer. . . .

[*Travel Journal.*] SEPT. 28th [*Lanark.*] . . . My cicerone led me through the grounds of Mr. Owen,[2] the celebrated philanthropist. . . . His works . . . consist of a great number of large buildings, too large for ornament, yet their neatness and the exquisitely picturesque situation prevent their being unpleasant. Great neatness is apparent in the dwelling-houses, and as I passed some large rooms I saw numbers of children dancing. . . . I should have had great pleasure in observing what is certainly a novel experiment, an institution of which the leading idea is that the labourer is himself to be the gainer by his own labour. Most manufacturers consider their workmen as they do their other tools and instruments. Provided they answer their purpose, it matters not what becomes of them.

[1] John Scott, editor of the *London Magazine*, was killed by Christie in a duel in 1821.
[2] Robert Owen.

Owen's object is to show that labourers may have every rational enjoyment even of literature, taste, and imagination and on that principle he has combined with his workhouses, schools of every kind. His children, the future workmen, are taught dancing, music, mathematics, etc. . . . Owen's books I have not read. He is an enthusiast. Barnes[1] observes that he is an exception to what one commonly sees, for all his theory and general ideas are excessively absurd, while all his detail is excellent. . . .

. . . I took Barnes with me a mile below the town to see a deservedly famous spot—Cartland Crags . . . a deep ravine or glen, clothed with wood on both sides, and occasionally displaying lofty precipices of rock. . . . A bridge is now erecting across this glen. . . . The union of elaborate works of art and of mighty and strange forms of nature is to me peculiarly interesting. Hence I prefer the passage of the Simplon to that of St. Gotthard on account of the road. Wordsworth, and I believe the majority of men of taste, think that the intermingling of art destroys the effect of natural scenery. I think otherwise.

Oct. 3rd [*Keswick.*] . . . Notwithstanding Southey's absence, I had a very agreeable chat with the ladies of his family till past nine. It is a charming family. Sara Coleridge I admired beyond any of Southey's children. She has a very fine face with some resemblance to her father, and her manner in conversation has the grave considerateness rather of a Scotch than English girl. She is, I believe, seventeen, perhaps eighteen. I understand she has made a translation which is about to be published. She has taught herself modern languages, and is said to have great talent. There was nothing forward in her behaviour, nor anything assuming, except that she had formed and intimated an opinion of her own upon the literary questions of the day. . . .

Oct. 31st [*London.*] . . . I then called on De Quincey—a visit of duty. De Quincey is a tiresome man, though certainly of great talent; he is necessitous and will be in great distress soon, for his talents are not marketable. He is in ill-health, is querulous, very strongly impressed with his own excellence, and prone to despise others. But I cannot shun him, situated as he is—he is in search of and has a prospect of literary employ. . . .

Nov. 6th . . . I called on Valpy early. We spoke about the translator wanted for the *Star*. As already stated, I took occasion to recommend De Quincey for the classical journal and Valpy will be glad of his assistance. . . .

[1] Thomas Barnes was Crabb Robinson's travelling companion at the moment. They had recently met, as they had done the year before at Geneva, quite by chance, and were spending the day together.

Nov. 7th . . . I called afterwards on De Quincey to speak about the classical journal. He speaks highly of the liberality of Taylor and Hessey, who had paid him forty guineas for his article on the Opium Eating. . . .

Nov. 10th . . . I came home early to receive De Quincey, whom I wish rather to serve than much associate with. Yet he was [not] unpleasant this evening. He is less offensively arrogant than he was, and is fully sensible of every intended kindness. Talfourd came and sat with him. . . .

Nov. 18th . . . I stepped into the Lambs' cottage at Dalston. Mary pale and thin, just recovered from one of her attacks. They have lost their brother John and feel their loss. They seemed softened by affliction and to wish for society. . . .

Nov. 20th . . . Read Hazlitt's *Table Talk*—a delightful volume, though it frequently annoys and disgusts me. But it was with mere pain and with no disapprobation that I read a sentence this morning which goes home to my feeling: 'A lounger who is ordinarily seen with a book in his hand is (we may be almost sure) equally without the power or inclination to attend to what passes around him or in his own mind.' But having dismissed, though with a struggle, all hopes of reputation, I can with tranquillity read such a damning sentence. I find other truths equally striking and equally painful in the course of reading the volume. . . .

Dec. 2nd . . . I have finished *Waverley*. As a novel it cannot be said to be very interesting. It is better on reflection than on perusal. Its merit lies in portrait and scene painting. . . .

Dec. 28th . . . In the evening reading at home. I began Shelley's *Prometheus*, which I could not get on with. I was quickened in my purpose of throwing it aside by the *Quarterly Review*, which exposes the want of meaning in his poems with considerable effect. It is good to be now and then withheld from reading bad books. Shelley's polemical hatred of Christianity is as unpoetical as it is irrational. He says in an address to Liberty:

> What if the tears rained through thy shattered locks
> Were quickly dried? For thou didst groan, not weep,
> When from its sea of death to kill and burn
> The Galilean Serpent forth did creep,
> And made thy world an undistinguishable heap.

This is part of an ode in which he traces the history of the world as regarding Liberty. He afterwards exclaims:

> Oh that the free would stamp the impious name
> Of * * * * into the dust, etc.
> Disdain not thou, at thy appointed term,
> To set thine armed heel on this reluctant worm.

The *Quarterly Review* unfairly puts six instead of four stars. However, the context shows that Christ was meant. This is miserable rant, and would be so were it as true as it is false. I shall send Shelley back to Godwin unread. Godwin himself is unable to read his works.

1822

JAN. 10th . . . At twelve Monkhouse called. I walked with him and had a high treat in a call at Chantrey's, having to speak with him about Wordsworth's bust. We saw Chantrey. He is a florid well looking man, with the face rather of a man of business than of an artist. But he talks with the ease of one who is now familiar with good company and with the confidence of one who is conscious of his fame. His study is rich in works of art. His busts are admirable. His compositions do not in general please me; he wants imagination and taste for ideal beauty. He has in hand a fine monument of Ellenborough—a good likeness too. . . .

JAN. 31st . . . At six went to Lamb's by appointment. Hartley Coleridge was there (an unpleasant youth but a clever man who will probably one day obtain distinction). Mrs. John Lamb and a Frenchman, Miss Lamb's master, were there. I had a game of whist and came home early to read.

APRIL 9th . . . I called on Miss Lamb. She accompanied me to Mrs. Aders, whom I found improved in appearance. Miss Lamb tells me that Hazlitt and his wife are gone to Scotland for the express purpose of obtaining divorce by the commission of adultery by Hazlitt, who is then to marry the servant girl of a house where he lodges! and this though she must swear that there is no collusion! This was mentioned without any injunction of secrecy. Miss Lamb spoke with becoming disgust of this scandalous proceeding, yet I doubt if she will have strength to break off the connection.

JUNE 15th . . . Monkhouse called and chatted some time about the Wordsworths. He assures me that Wordsworth's late accident[1] has had no serious consequences whatever. Godwin also called. He related to me his late lawsuits which ended in his being turned out of his house. He has lived some years without paying any rent, availing himself of points of law which rendered it difficult for any person to make a title, and the complacency with which he was content to profit by this has lessened him in my opinion. However, he suffers now by being obliged to go into a

[1] Wordsworth was thrown from his horse in May 1822 and his head was badly injured. But he recovered quickly and there were no after ill-effects.

new house; he has a large arrear of rent to discharge and the costs of actions to pay, and he has been in great distress. Lamb has lent him £50. I could not refuse him £30; I doubt whether I shall ever be repaid. . . .

Nov. 17th . . . From Ayrton I learned that Godwin's affairs are going on wretchedly. I have I fear given my £30 for no purpose. Godwin probably is not sensible of a kindness which is not effectual relief. He has not called on or written to me, and when the catastrophe comes will be ready to require further assistance!

Dec. 8th . . . I was gratified by learning from her [Mrs. Monkhouse], as well as from a letter of Mrs. Clarkson's, that I stand in high favour at Rydal Mount. Wordsworth says he 'will write anything to please me'—a great compliment! . . .

1823

Jan. 8th . . . I then went to Lamb. I have seldom spent a more agreeable few hours with him—he was serious and kind; his wit was subordinate to his judgment, as is usual in *tête-à-tête* parties. He spoke respectfully of an allegoric poem John Collier has written, says the style is remarkably good, adding: 'It is like a collection of the duller parts of Spenser, and not quite so good.' Speaking of Coleridge, he said: 'He ought not to have a wife or children; he should have a sort of diocesan care of the world, no parish duty.' He reprobated the persecution of *The Vision of Judgment*, by Lord Byron. Southey's *Vision of Judgment* is more worthy of punishment—for his is an arrogance beyond endurance. Lord Byron's satire is one of the most good-natured description—no malevolence! . . .

April 2nd An interesting day, which alone compensated for my journey to London. I breakfasted at Monkhouse's and after breakfast walked out with Wordsworth, his son John, [and] Monkhouse. We called at Sir George Beaumont's to see his fragment of Michael Angelo, a piece of sculpture in bas- and haut-relief, a Holy Family.[1] The Virgin has the child in her lap; he clings to her, alarmed by something St. John holds towards him, probably intended for a bird. The expression of the Infant's face and the beauty of his limbs cannot well be surpassed. Sir George supposes that Michael Angelo was so persuaded he could not heighten the effect by completing it, that he never finished it. There is also

[1] The tondo had just been acquired by Sir George Beaumont for about £1,500. He bequeathed it to the Royal Academy, who insured it in 1966 for three million pounds.

a very fine landscape by Rubens full of power and striking effect, highly praised by Sir George for its execution, the management of the lights, its gradation, etc. Sir George is himself a very elegant man and talks well on matters of art. Lady Beaumont is also a gentlewoman of great sweetness and dignity, I should think among the most interesting by far of persons of quality in the country. I should have thought this even had I not known of their great attachment to Wordsworth.

We then called on Moore and had a very pleasant hour's chat with him. Politics were a safer topic than poetry, though the opinions of Moore and Wordsworth are as adverse nearly as their poetic character. Moore spoke freely and in a tone I cordially sympathised with about France and the Bourbons. He considers it quite uncertain how the French will feel at any time on any occasion, so volatile and vehement are they at the same time; yet he is of opinion that, as far as they have any [feeling], it is entirely in favour of the Spaniards and liberal opinions. Notwithstanding this, he says that he is disposed to assent to the notion that, of all the people in Europe, the French alone are unfit for liberty. Wordsworth freely resisted some of Moore's assertions, but assented to the last. Of French poetry Moore did not speak highly, and he thinks that Chenier has overrated the living poets in his late articles in the *Edinburgh Review*. Moore's person is very small, his countenance lively rather than intellectual. He resembles Hill greatly. I should judge him to be kind-hearted and friendly.

Afterwards we walked towards the city and Wordsworth and I went to the Society of Arts. Arthur Aikin was not at home. We took shelter during a heavy rain in the great room. Wordsworth's curiosity was raised, and soon satisfied, by Barry's pictures. It requires no connoisseurship to perceive the utter want of all skill in colouring and the mediocrity of his drawing.[1] . . .

APRIL 4th . . . I had barely time to return home to dress for dinner. Then I called on my way upon Masquerier[2] and afterwards proceeded to Monkhouse's. Our party consisted of Wordsworth, Coleridge, and Lamb, Moore and Rogers, five poets of very unequal worth and most disproportionate popularity whom the public probably would arrange in the very inverse order, except that it would place Moore above Rogers. During this afternoon Coleridge alone displayed any of his peculiar talent. He talked much and well. I have not for years seen him in such excellent health and spirits. His subjects, metaphysical criticism. Wordsworth he

[1] The verdict is much too harsh, but the pictures have not been improved by subsequent cleaning.

[2] John James Masquerier (1778–1855), portrait-painter. He made at least two drawings of H.C.R., who in later years was to stay with him frequently at Brighton.

chiefly talked to. Rogers occasionally let fall a remark. Moore seemed conscious of his inferiority. He was very attentive to Coleridge, but seemed to relish Lamb whom he sat next. Lamb was in a good frame, kept himself within bounds, and was only cheerful at last. Besides these five other wandering bards, were no one but Mrs. Wordsworth, Miss Hutchinson, and Mr. Gillman. I was at the bottom of the table, where I very ill performed my part. We adjourned soon to the drawing-room, where Mrs. Monkhouse was an invalid on the sofa (a disease of the spine which leaves her as beautiful and charming as ever). I walked home late with Lamb.

APRIL 5th . . . Went to a musical party and supper at Aders's. This party I had made for them. Wordsworth, Monkhouse, and the ladies, the Flaxmans, Rogers, Coleridge, Mr. and Mrs. Gillman were *my* friends. Besides, the Reeces and other musical party. Everybody seemed to enjoy themselves. Wordsworth refused other engagements and then accepted this, being promised first-rate music. He declared himself perfectly delighted and satisfied; but he sat alone, covering his face, and—as was generally supposed—asleep. Flaxman, too, confessed his inability to endure fine music long; but Coleridge's enjoyment was very great indeed, and I never had more pleasure from music. Our supper, too, was very elegant, and we sat a reasonable time afterwards. Our hosts were delighted with the pleasure they had given, and I believe everybody was satisfied.

MAY 21st . . . Arrived Naylor's at three. The great man whom we were met to admire came soon after. It was the famous Scotch preacher, the associate of Dr. Chalmers at Glasgow—Mr. Irving.[1] He was brought by his admirer, . . . a Mr. Laurie, a worthy Scotchman who today was in the background, but speaks at religious meetings. . . . Irving on the whole pleased me. Little or no assumption, easy and seemingly kindhearted, talking not more of his labours in attending public [meetings] (he was come from one) than might be excused. He did not obtrude any religious talk and was not dogmatical. He is a very ugly man. Looks more like an Italian assassin than a Gospel preacher; has a powerful voice, feels always warmly, is prompt in his expression, and not very careful of his words. His opinions I liked. . . .

MAY 25th . . . Went to the Caledonian Chapel to hear Mr. Irving. Very mixed impressions. I do not wonder that his preaching should be thought to be acting, or at least as indicative of vanity as devotion. . . . Abrupt changes of style as if written (and it was written) at a dozen different sittings, his tone equally variable, no master-feeling running through the whole like the red string through the Royal Marine ropes, to borrow an

[1] Edward Irving (1792–1834), founder of the Catholic Apostolic Church.

image from Goethe. Yet his sermon was very impressive. I caught myself but once a-wandering. . . . He was very vehement in gesticulation and declamation, but his vehemence was not the earnest warmth of piety. . . .

June 8th I . . . , [went] to hear Mr. Irving, and was better pleased with him than before. There was an air of greater sincerity in him than when I heard him before, and his peculiarities were less offensive. The discourse was a continuation of last week's on the Intellectual Man as opposed to the Spiritual Man. . . .

June 23rd Finished early Hazlitt's disgusting *New Pygmalion*. One can tolerate the passion of a St. Preux or a Werther, as it is set off by the eloquence of Rousseau or Goethe, but such a story as this is nauseous and revolting. The raving of a married man who goes to Scotland to be divorced in the hope that the daughter of the keeper of a lodging-house will marry him, and finds himself disappointed on his return, is the matter of this book, which is low and gross and tedious and every way offensive. It ought to exclude the author from all decent society. He has been exposed in *John Bull*, and I should think will feel the effects of his exposure of himself in being slighted by many who tolerated him before. . . .

Oct. 26th . . . I met with Talfourd and heard from him much of the literary gossip of the last quarter. Sutton Sharpe, whom I called on, gave me a second edition. He lent me the last *London Magazine*, containing Lamb's delightful letter to Southey, which Southey must feel. His remarks on religion are full of deep feeling, and his eulogy on Hazlitt and Leigh Hunt most generous. Lamb must be aware that he would expose himself to obloquy by such declarations. It seems that he and Hazlitt are no longer on friendly terms. I do not wish them to be reconciled. Lamb has introduced the names or initials of his friends. I was gratified by finding in the catalogue: 'H.C.R., unwearied in every office of a friend.' Nothing that Lamb has ever written has impressed me more strongly with the sweetness of his disposition, the strength of his affections. . . .

Nov. 8th . . . A letter from Godwin informing me that Read, his creditor, had settled with him. His total claim was £430, of which Murray had paid him £250, and for the remainder Godwin had given four notes for £45, each at six, twelve, eighteen, twenty-four months, and Murray has in hand £41 5*s*., so that there is a delay of a year before any fresh demand will be made. Unfortunately, after the first burst of generosity or good-nature, it is difficult to obtain money from any one. Godwin expresses his obligations to me in more thankful terms than I ever knew him employ before, the effect of which I feel to be that I am already disposed to give a new subscription. . . .

Nov. 10th An interesting day. I breakfasted with Flaxman, by invitation to meet [A. W.] Schlegel. Had I as much esteem for Schlegel's personal character as I have admiration of his literary powers I should have been gratified by his telling Flaxman that it was I who first named him to Madame de Staël and who gave Madame de Staël her first ideas of German literature. Schlegel is now devoting himself to Indian learning, and hardly attends to anything else, and our conversation during a short breakfast was chiefly on Oriental subjects. . . .

Nov. 26th . . . Took tea and supped at Godwin's. The Lambs there and some young men. We played whist, etc. Mrs. Shelley there; she is unaltered, yet I did not know her at first; she looks elegant and sickly and young. One would not suppose she was the author. . . .

1824

Jan. 10th . . . Called on Miss Lamb. I looked over Lamb's library in part. He has the finest collection of shabby books I ever saw. Such a number of first-rate works of genius, but filthy copies, which a delicate man would really hesitate touching, is, I think, nowhere to be found. . . .

Feb. 27th . . . Engaged looking over the *Retrospective Review*. Hardly worth the while. I despair of ever laying aside the reading of trifling books. What I begin I must end. I am in reading what others are in morals—an errant formalist. Read lately a *Table Talk* by Hazlitt, *On Study*. 'Why,' says he, 'do men do nothing? Because they cannot do anything.' A mere trivial truism, yet in combination with better things it pleased and comforted me.

March 5th . . . Walked over to Lamb. Meant a short visit, but Monkhouse was there as well as Manning, so I took tea and stayed the whole evening and played whist. Besides, the talk was agreeable. . . . Charles Lamb's impressions against religion are unaccountably strong, and yet he is by nature pious. It is the dogmatism of theology which has disgusted him and which alone he opposes. He has the organ of theosophy.

April 19th . . . I went after breakfast to Monkhouse. Found Mr. Irving there; he was very courteous. Listened with interest to a serious conversation between the poet and the pulpit orator, and took a share in it. Wordsworth stated that the great difficulty which had always pressed on his mind in religion is the inability to reconcile the divine [foreknowledge] with accountability in men. I stated mine to be the incompatibility of the existence of evil as final and absolute with the divine attributes. Irving did not attempt to solve either. He declared that he is no metaphysician, and that he did not pretend to know more of God than was revealed to him. He did not, however, seem to take any offence at the implied scepticism or the difficulties suggested as being unsolved. On the whole an interesting hour's conversation. . . .

April 22nd . . . I went to Monkhouse to take leave of the Wordsworths. Wordsworth was unusually communicative and spoke at large of politics. He thinks less favourably of Canning's abilities than most men and apprehends that he has undertaken more than he can perform. Canning, he says, has intrigued to bring in a portion of the Whigs. Marquis of Lansdowne has rejected the overtures made him, and will not accept of place without Lord Grey and Lord Holland. It is Lord Liverpool who has forced Canning on the King and Chancellor. To gain the Whigs and popularity Canning has declared against the Holy Alliance and has been most rash in language which is insulting to the great potentates. A war will certainly take place in a few years, and probably Hanover will be seized, in hostility to this country. France, Prussia, Russia, and Austria will probably dismember Holland, and the absolute sovereigns will make a further attack on representative governments. In such a state of things Canning is not the man who will be competent to the great task of defending this country! These were Wordsworth's chief declarations. I was less inclined to doubt the facts than to be surprised at the feeling with which they were contemplated. . . .

May 9th . . . Read Lord Byron's *Deformed Transformed*—a poem, offensive, as all he has written, but with striking passages. The Evil Spirit has the character of Mephistopheles, and the deformed man who performs the part of Faust will be more interesting to the general reader than his prototype, though his character has neither the profundity nor the significance of the original. The songs are the best things in the poem. The death of Lord Byron, since announced, has probably interrupted the course of a fiction which would have been as unsatisfactory to the contemplative critic and as useless to the moral world as all the other works of the author. I do not join in the cant of lamentation which will sicken us for the next month from every quarter.

May 22nd . . . Dined with Captain Franklin, after a call on Flaxman. A small but interesting party. Several friends of Captain Franklin, travellers or persons interested in his journeys. . . . They talked of the Captain's travels with vivacity, and he was in good spirits. He appeared today quite the man for the perilous enterprise he has undertaken. . . .

May 25th . . . Began *Hajji Baba*[1]—an amusing tale, the tone as unlike

[1] By J. J. Morier.

Anastasius as possible. It sustains the character of the Persian Gil Blas with respectable ability. . . .

JUNE 1st . . . Call at home from Godwin. I was induced to engage myself to dine with Charles Lamb. After dinner he and I took a walk to Newington. I sat an hour with Mrs. Barbauld; she was looking tolerably, but Charles Lamb (not his habit) was disputatious with her and not in his best way. He reasons from feelings, and those often idiosyncrasies; she from dry abstractions and verbal definitions. Such people cannot agree and infallibly dislike each other. We came back to a late dish of tea. Godwin, etc., there. I had whist with Mary Lamb, Godwin, and his ill-bred son, William. The loud laugh of the father and the noisy knock on the table of the son together put me out of humour and I came away early, though there came in some agreeable people. . . .

JUNE 5th . . . Finished *Hajji Baba*—the most pleasant book written in imitation of the Eastern style I ever met with. Humour and gaiety throughout, and no Oriental bombast; only enough of Orientalism to be comic and humorous and yet sufficiently characteristic. The incidents bear a resemblance to those of *Gil Blas*, and are unconnected adventures of an unprincipled knave whom the reader does not care about but does not hate. . . .

JUNE 10th . . . I dined at Lamb's and then walked with him to Highgate self-invited. There we found a large party: Mr. and Mrs. Green, the Aders, Irving, Collins, R.A., a Mr. Taylor, a young man of talents in the Colonial Office, Basil Montagu, a Mr. Chance, and one or two others. It was a *rich* evening. Coleridge talked his best, and it appeared better because he and Irving supported the same doctrines. His superiority was striking. The idea dwelt upon was the higher character of the internal evidence of Christianity as addressed to our immediate consciousness of our own wants and the necessity of religion and a revelation. In a style not to me clear or intelligible Irving and Coleridge both declaimed. The *advocatus diaboli* for the evening was Mr. Taylor, in a way very creditable to his manners as a gentleman, but with little more than verbal cleverness and an ordinary logic and the confidence of a young man who has no suspicion of his own deficiencies. He affirmed that those evidences which the Christian thinks he finds in his internal convictions the Mahometan also thinks he has, and he affirmed that Mahomet had improved the condition of mankind. Lamb asked him whether he came in a turban or a hat. There was also a Mr. Chance, who broke out at last by an opposition to Mr. Irving which made the good man so angry that he exclaimed: 'Sir, I reject the whole bundle of your opinions.' Now it seemed to me that Mr. Chance had no opinions, only words, for his assertions seemed a mere galimatias; but Irving, I believe, smelt antinomianism in them. The least agreeable part of Coleridge's talk was about German literature. He called Herder a coxcomb, and set Goethe far below Schiller, allowing no other merit than that of exquisite taste, repeating his favourite reproach that Goethe wrote from an idea that a certain thing was to be done in a certain style, not from the fullness of sentiment on a certain subject. He treats Goethe with more plausibility as utterly unprincipled. Basil Montagu, Irving, and Taylor and myself walked back together. . . . My talk with Irving alone was more satisfactory. He spoke of a friend (Mr. Carlyle) who has translated *Wilhelm Meister*—said: 'You will find we do not sympathise on religious matters, but that is nothing; where I find that there is a sincere searching after truth I think I like a person the better for not having found it.' 'At least,' I replied, 'you have an additional interest in him.' Whether Irving said this, suspecting me to be a doubter, I do not know. Probably he did. . . .

JUNE 22nd . . . Being engaged at Highbury, in my way I called on Mr. Irving. Mr. Carlyle, the translator of *Wilhelm Meister*, was there.[1] He had the appearance of a sensible man, but his translation, from what I have seen, appears bad. He renders the Confessions of *einer schönen Seele* a 'Fair Saint', and his version of Mignon's song is as bad as possible. . . .

JUNE 23rd . . . I was all this morning at home waiting for Mr. Carlyle, who promised to breakfast with me, till near twelve. . . .

JULY 5th . . . Took tea at Lamb's. Mr. Irving there and his friend Mr. Carlyle. An agreeable evening enough, but there is so little sympathy between Lamb and Irving that I do not think they can or ought to be intimate. Lamb has no respect for Irving's opinions—perhaps not for his mind. Irving ought not to like Lamb, whose levity and want of serious thought is incurable. . . .

JULY 6th . . . Took tea with Lamb. There were Hessey and Taylor, Clare the shepherd poet, Bowring, and Elton, the translator from the classics. Clare looks like a weak man, but he was ill. Elton a sturdy fellow, more like a huntsman than a scholar. But little conversation. Bowring gave an account of Bentham's body. Perhaps had I asked I might have obtained a sight of it, but I would not affect admiration for him, and mere curiosity without love has no right to be gratified. Hessey gave an account of De Quincey's description of his own bodily sufferings. 'He should have employed as his publishers,' said Lamb, 'Payne & Foss (fuss).' . . .

AUG. 12th [*On Circuit.*] . . . I held a brief under H. Cooper, the attorney. A stranger, Garwood of Wells, told me that he was informed by his friend Evans (son of Joseph Evans, my old friend) that I was the H.C.R. men-

[1] Crabb Robinson's first meeting with Thomas Carlyle.

tioned in the *London Magazine* as the friend of Elia. 'I love Elia,' said Mr. Garwood, 'and that was enough to make me come to you!' A singular occurrence. I have no doubt Mr. Garwood will remain my client. . . .

AUG. 26th . . . Returned to Masquerier's to attend a party at his house. . . . It was an evening of lively conversation, and Masquerier's collection of prints rendered cards almost superfluous. Poetry, art, etc., were talked of. A Mrs. Sparrow, a fine old lady, took an interest in Coleridge, with whose family she is connected. Of the party [was] Mr. Constable, a landscape painter of great merit, Masquerier says: he knew Wordsworth formerly, took an interest in his conversation, and preserved some memorials of his composition when they met at Sir George Beaumont's. He furnished me with the (not very characteristic lines) which are at the other end of the book.[1]

NOV. 26th . . . Took tea at home—a pleasant evening—Barron Field[2] and Carlyle. Afterwards Joseph Wedd, and also Southern,[3] stepped in, so I was kept at home till late—but pleasantly. Barron Field talks amusingly, though there is something of grand ha! about him. Southern left the party because he could not endure Carlyle, and he certainly pleases me little enough.

DEC. 5th . . . Walked back by Islington and met there with Mr. and Mrs. Talfourd and Miss Mitford, the dramatist and poet, a squat person but with a benevolent and intelligent smile; scarcely any conversation. Lamb merry.

DEC. 10th . . . Took tea at home, Mr. Carlyle with me. He presses me to write an account of my recollections of Schiller for his book. I was amused by looking over my manuscripts, autographs, etc., but it has since given me pain to observe the weakness and incorrectness of my memory. I find I recollected nothing of Schiller worth recording. . . .

1825

JAN. 3rd . . . Went to a party at Field's in Berners Street. . . . The only new and interesting person Horace Smith, one of the authors of *Rejected*

[1] i.e. of the diary in which he is writing. Wordsworth's lines, in praise of Sir Joshua Reynolds, are taken from the third of the *Inscriptions in the Grounds of Coleorton*, viz.: 'Ye Lime-trees, ranged before this hallowed Urn,' etc.

[2] An intimate and correspondent of Lamb as well as of Crabb Robinson. He was a miscellaneous writer and dramatic critic to *The Times*, and also served first as a judge in New South Wales and subsequently as Chief Justice at Gibraltar.

[3] Henry Southern (1799–1853); a journalist friend of H.C.R., he had founded and was at this time editing the *Retrospective Review*. He later joined the diplomatic service.

Addresses, a grave but sensible and intelligent man. His brother James is the joker who is invited to great parties to make sport by puns and songs, etc. Horace has £200 per annum for writing what he likes in the *New Monthly Magazine*. We talked of Hazlitt—his *Spirit of the Age*, . . . a piquant book very eulogistic of Godwin, but with bitter ingredients notwithstanding—violent praise and very ill-natured sneers strangely jumbled together. . . .

FEB. 18th . . . My morning was spent partly in a long gossip with Carlyle, who had sent me his *Life of Schiller* and was about to leave London. . . .

FEB. 25th . . . Called on Mr. Irving and took tea with him. Carlyle there, who leaves tomorrow. I had a pleasant chat with him. . . .

APRIL 22nd . . . I called . . . on Charles Lamb. He and his sister in excellent spirits. Lamb has obtained his discharge from the India House with the sacrifice of rather more than a third of his income, but he gave away more than a third of what he had so that he will still have an ample income, and that with entire leisure. He says he would not be condemned to return to his office for seven years . . . for a hundred thousand pounds. I never saw him so calmly cheerful as he seems now to be.

MAY 8th . . . I called on Sieveking and stayed late with him, making inquiries about German novels for Mr. Carlyle. . . .

MAY 19th . . . Wrote a letter to Carlyle in Scotland giving him advice about the selection of German novels for translation. . . .

JUNE 16th . . . Went to Basil Montagu by appointment. Mr. Irving was there and Mr. Wrangham, whom I saw for a few minutes; his person and manners are prepossessing. Mr. Irving and his brother-in-law Mr. Martin and myself placed ourselves in a chariot and Basil Montagu took a seat without and we rode to Highgate, where we took tea at Mr. Gillman's. I think I never heard Coleridge so very eloquent, and yet it was painful to find myself unable to recall anything of what had so delighted me, that is, anything that seemed worthy to be noted, so that I could not but suspect some illusion arising out of the impressive tone and the mystical language of the orator. He talked on for several hours without intermission, his subject the ever recurring one, religion, but so blended with mythology, metaphysics and psychology that it required great attention to find really the religious element. I observed that when Coleridge quoted Scripture or used well-known religious phrases Irving was constant in his exclamations of delight, but that he was silent at other times. . . .

JULY 11th . . . During the day I read Lucy Aikin's *Memoir of Mrs. Barbauld*—but an inferior performance. I met with some new poems which I thought pleasing. I was also greatly amused by Hazlitt's *Spirit of the Age*. In spite of his malice, his eternal repetitions, his laboured expansion of his matter *lucri causa* and the occasional bombast, with the bad taste and overloaded ornaments, all which faults proceed from one source (that he is always thinking as much of his honorarium as of his honour)—in spite of these great drawbacks his works always interest me. In this book he is generally mild and even now and then makes the *amende honorable*. . . .

OCT. 9th . . . I walked out and called on Charles Lamb. I found him recovering from a severe illness and looking wretchedly. His sister too, overpowered by her attentions to him, had been visited by one of her periodical attacks. I borrowed from Lamb one of the *London Magazines*, which I read in bed. . . .

OCT. 11th . . . I then went to Lamb's; he seemed to me in better health and spirits. But Hone, the parodist, was with him, and society relieves Lamb. Hone's conversation, or, rather, his manners, pleased me: he is a modest unassuming man.

OCT. 28th . . . I went to Lamb's—he is finely improved in health. Rejoiced to hear that in case of his death his sister will be, if not legally entitled to, yet morally assured of, a pension discretionary with the trustees, not exceeding £300 per annum! . . .

NOV. 5th . . . Concluded the evening with Lamb and playing piquet—a resource with him, for he wants occupation with every one, and I want to be relieved from the sense of being tiresome to him. . . .

DEC. 10th Dined with Aders, a very remarkable and interesting evening. The party Blake the painter and Linnell, also a painter and engraver. . . .

BLAKE

I will put down as they occur to me without method all I can recollect of the conversation of this remarkable man. Shall I call him artist or genius—or mystic—or madman? Probably he is all. He has a most interesting appearance. He is now old—pale, with a Socratic countenance and an expression of great sweetness, but bordering on weakness except when his features are animated by expression, and then he has an air of inspiration about him. The conversation was on art and on poetry and on religion; but it was my object—and I was successful—in drawing him out and in so getting from him an avowal of his *peculiar* sentiments. I was aware before of the nature of his impressions or I should at times have been at a loss to understand him. He was shown soon after he entered the room some compositions of Mrs. Aders, which he cordially praised, and he brought with him an engraving of his 'Canterbury Pilgrims' for Aders. One of the figures resembled one in one of Aders's pictures. 'They say I stole it from this picture, but I did it twenty years before I knew of the picture. However, in my youth I was always studying this kind of painting; no wonder there is a resemblance.' In this he seemed to explain *humanly* what he had done; but he at another time spoke of his paintings as being what he had seen in his visions, and when he said '*my visions*' it was in the ordinary unemphatic tone in which we speak of trivial matters that every one understands and cares nothing about. In the same tone he said repeatedly: 'The Spirit told me.' I took occasion to say: 'You use the same word as Socrates used. What resemblance do you suppose is there between your spirit and the spirit of Socrates?' 'The same as between our countenances.' He paused and added: 'I *was* Socrates,' and then, as if correcting himself, 'a sort of brother. I must have had conversations with him, so I had with Jesus Christ. I have an obscure recollection of having been with both of them.' It was before this that I had suggested on very obvious philosophical grounds the *impossibility* of supposing an immortal being created—an eternity *a parte post* without an eternity *a parte ante*. This is an obvious truth I have been many (perhaps thirty) years fully aware of. His eye brightened on my saying this, and he eagerly concurred: 'To be sure it is impossible; we are all co-existent with God, members of the divine body; we are all partakers of the divine nature.' In this, by the bye, Blake has but adopted an ancient Greek idea, Query of Plato? As connected with this idea I will mention here (though it formed part of our talk walking homeward), that on my asking in what light he viewed the great question concerning the divinity of Jesus Christ, he said: 'He is the only God'; but then he added: 'and so am I and so are you.' Now he had just before (and that occasioned my question) been speaking of the errors of Jesus Christ: 'He was wrong in suffering himself to be crucified, he should not have attacked the government, he had no business with such matters.' On my inquiring how he reconciled this with the sanctity and divine qualities of Jesus, he said: 'He was not then become the Father.' Connecting as well as one can these fragmentary sentiments it would be hard to fix Blake's station between Christianity, Platonism, and Spinozaism, yet he professes to be very hostile to Plato and reproaches Wordsworth with being not a Christian but a Platonist.

It is one of the subtle remarks of Hume on certain religious speculations that the tendency of them is to make men indifferent to whatever takes place by destroying all ideas of good and evil. I took occasion to apply this remark to something Blake said. 'If so,' I said, 'there is no use in discipline or education, no difference between good and evil.' He hastily broke in on me: 'There is no use in education—I hold it wrong—it is the great sin—it is eating of the tree of knowledge of good and evil. That was the fault of Plato: he knew of nothing but of the Virtues and Vices and Good and Evil. There is nothing in all that. Everything is good in God's eyes.' On my putting the obvious question, 'Is there nothing absolutely evil in what men do.' 'I am no judge of that—perhaps not in God's eyes.' Though on this and other occasions he spoke as if he denied altogether the existence of evil and as if we had nothing to do with right and wrong, it being sufficient to consider all things as alike the work of God. I interposed with the German word objectivity, which he approved of, yet at other times he spoke of error as being in heaven. I asked about the *moral* character of Dante in writing his *Vision*—was he *pure*?—'*Pure?*' said Blake. 'Do you think there is any purity in God's eyes; the angels in heaven are no more so than we. He chargeth his angels with folly.' He afterwards extended this to the Supreme Being. 'Did he not repent him that he had made Nineveh?' It is easier to repeat the personal remarks of Blake than these metaphysical speculations so nearly allied to the most opposite systems. He spoke with seeming complacency of himself, said he acted by command; the Spirit said to him: 'Blake, be an artist and nothing else. In this there is felicity.' His eye glistened when he spoke of the joy of devoting himself solely to divine art. Art is inspiration—When Michael Angelo or Raphael or Mr. Flaxman does any of his fine things he does them in the spirit. Blake said: 'I should be sorry if I had any earthly fame, for whatever natural glory a man has is so much detracted from his spiritual glory. I wish to do nothing for profit. I wish to live for art. I want nothing whatever. I am quite happy.'

Among the unintelligible sentiments which he was continually expressing is his distinction between the natural and spiritual world. The natural world must be consumed. Incidentally Swedenborg was spoken of. 'He was a divine teacher; he has done much and will do much good; he has corrected many errors of Popery, and also of Luther and Calvin.' Yet he also said that Swedenborg was wrong in endeavouring to explain to the *rational* faculty what the reason cannot comprehend; he should have left that. As Blake mentioned Swedenborg and Dante together I wished to know whether he considered their visions of the same kind. As far as I could recollect he does. Dante, he said, was the greater poet—he had political objects; yet this, though wrong, does not appear in Blake's mind to affect the truth of the vision. Strangely inconsistent with this was the language of Blake about Wordsworth. Wordsworth, he thinks, is no Christian, but a Platonist. He asked me: 'Does he believe in the Scriptures?' On my answering in the affirmative he said he had been much pained by reading the introduction to *The Excursion*—it brought on a fit of illness. The passage was produced and read:

> Jehovah—with his thunder and the choir
> Of shouting angels, and the empyreal thrones—
> I pass them unalarmed.

This '*pass them unalarmed*' greatly offended Blake. 'Does Mr. Wordsworth think his mind can surpass Jehovah?' I tried to twist this passage into a sense corresponding with Blake's own theories, but failed, and Wordsworth was finally set down as a Pagan, but still with great praise as the greatest poet of the age.

Jacob Boehmen was spoken of as a divinely inspired man. Blake praised, too, the figures in Law's translation as being very beautiful, and Michael Angelo could not have done better. Though he spoke of his happiness he spoke of past sufferings and of sufferings as necessary. 'There is suffering in heaven, for where there is the capacity of enjoyment there is the capacity of pain.'

I have been interrupted by a call from Talfourd in writing this account, and I cannot now recollect any distinct remarks; but as Blake has invited me to go and see him I shall possibly have an opportunity again of noting what he says and I may be able hereafter to throw connection, if not system, into what I have written above. I feel great admiration and respect for him; he is certainly a most amiable man, a good creature, and of his poetical and pictorial genius there is no doubt, I believe, in the minds of judges. Wordsworth and Lamb like his poems, and the Aders his paintings.

A few other detached thoughts occur to me:

Bacon, *Locke*, and *Newton* are the three great teachers of atheism or of Satan's doctrine.

Everything is atheism which assumes the reality of the natural and unspiritual world.

Irving. He is a highly gifted man; he is a sent man, but they who are sent sometimes go further than they ought.

Dante saw devils where I see none—I see only good. I saw nothing but good in *Calvin's* house; better than in Luther's—he had harlots.

Swedenborg. Parts of his scheme are dangerous. His sexual religion is dangerous.

'I do not believe that the world is round, I believe it is quite flat.' I objected the circumnavigation. We were called to dinner at the moment and I lost the reply.

The Sun. 'I have conversed with the spiritual Sun—I saw him on Primrose Hill. He said: "Do you take me for the Greek Apollo?" "No," I said. "That (and Blake pointed to the sky)—that is the Greek Apollo. He is Satan."

'I know now what is true by internal conviction. A doctrine is told me. My heart says it must be true.' I corroborated this by remarking on the impossibility of the unlearned man judging of what are called the *external* evidences of religion, in which he heartily concurred.

I regret that I have been unable to do more than set down these seeming idle and rambling sentences. The tone and manner are incommunicable. There is a natural sweetness and gentility about Blake which are delightful, and when he is not referring to his visions he talks sensibly and acutely.

His friend Linnell seems a great admirer. Perhaps the best thing he said was his comparison of moral with natural evil. 'Who shall say what God thinks evil? That is a wise tale of the Mahometans, of the Angel of the Lord that murdered the infant (alluding to *The Hermit* of Parnell, I suppose). Is not every infant that dies of disease in effect murdered by an Angel?'

DEC. 17th For the sake of connection I will here insert a minute of a short call I this morning made on Blake. He dwells in Fountain Court in the Strand. I found him in a small room which seems to be both a working-room and a bed-room. Nothing could exceed the squalid air both of the apartment and his dress; but in spite of dirt—I might say filth—an air of natural gentility is diffused over him; and his wife, notwithstanding the same offensive character of her dress and appearance, has a good expression of countenance, so that I shall have a pleasure in calling on and conversing with these worthy people. But I fear I shall not make any progress in ascertaining his opinions and feelings,—that there being really no system or connection in his mind, all his future conversation will be but varieties of wildness and incongruity.

I found him at work on Dante, the book (Cary) and his sketches both before him. He showed me his designs, of which I have nothing to say but that they evince a power of grouping and of throwing grace and interest over conceptions most monstrous and disgusting, which I should not have anticipated.

Our conversation began about Dante. 'He was an atheist—a mere politician busied about this world as Milton was till in his old age he returned back to God whom he had had in his childhood.' I tried to get out from Blake that he meant this charge only in a higher sense and not using the word atheism in its popular meaning. But he would not allow this, though when he in like manner charged Locke with atheism, and I remarked that Locke wrote on the evidences of Christianity and lived a virtuous life, he had nothing to reply to me, nor reiterated the charge of wilful deception. I admitted that Locke's doctrine leads to atheism, and this seemed to satisfy him. From this subject we passed over to that of good and evil, on which he repeated his former assertions more decidedly. He allowed, indeed, that there is error, mistake, etc., and if these be evil then there is evil, but these are only negations. Nor would he admit that any education should be attempted except that of cultivation of the imagination and fine arts. 'What are called the vices in the natural world, are the highest sublimities in the spiritual world.' When I asked whether if he had been a father he would not have grieved if his child had become vicious or a great criminal, he answered: 'I must not regard when I am endeavouring to think rightly my own any more than other people's weaknesses.' And when I again remarked that this doctrine puts an end to all exertion or even wish to change anything, he had no reply. We spoke of the Devil, and I observed that when a child I thought the Manichaean doctrine, or that of two principles, a rational one. He assented to this and in confirmation asserted that he did not believe in the omnipotence of God—the language of the Bible on that subject is only poetical or allegorical. Yet soon after he denied that the natural world is anything. 'It is all nothing, and Satan's empire is the empire of nothing.' He reverted soon to his favourite expression 'my visions'. 'I saw Milton in imagination and he told me to beware of being misled by his *Paradise Lost*. In particular he wished me to show the falsehood of his doctrine that the pleasures of sex arose from the Fall. The Fall could not produce any pleasure.' I answered the Fall produced a state of evil in which there was a mixture of good or pleasure, and in that sense the Fall may be said to produce the pleasure. But he replied that the Fall produced only generation and death and then he went off upon a rambling state[-ment?] of a union of sexes in man as in God—an androgynous state in which I could not follow him. As he spoke of Milton's appearing to him I asked whether he resembled the prints of him. He answered: 'All.' 'Of what age did he appear to be?' 'Various ages; sometimes a very old man.' He spoke of Milton as being at one time a sort of classical atheist, and of Dante as being now with God.

Of the faculty of vision he spoke as one he had had from early infancy. He thinks all men partake of it, but it is lost by not being cultivated, and he eagerly assented to a remark I made that all men have all faculties to a greater or less degree. I am to renew my visits and to read Wordsworth to him, of whom he seems to entertain a high idea.

DEC. 24th A call on Blake—my third interview. I read him Wordsworth's incomparable *Ode*, which he heartily enjoyed. The same half-crazy crotchets about the two worlds, the eternal repetition of which must in time become tiresome. Again he repeated today: 'I fear Wordsworth loves Nature, and Nature is the work of the Devil. The Devil is in us, as far as we are Nature.' On my inquiring whether the Devil would not be destroyed by God as being of less power, he denied that God has any power, asserted that the Devil is eternally created not *by* God but by God's permission, and when I objected that permission implies power to prevent, he did not seem to understand me. It was remarkable that the parts of Wordsworth's *Ode* which he most enjoyed were the most obscure and those I the least like and comprehend. . . .

1826

JAN. 6th A call on Blake. I hardly feel it worth while to write down his conversation, it is so much a repetition of his former talk. He was very cordial today. I had procured him two subscriptions for his *Job* from George Proctor and Basil Montagu. I paid £1 on each. This probably put him in spirits more than he was aware of. He spoke of his being richer than ever in having learned to know me, and he told Mrs. Aders he and I were nearly of an opinion; yet I have practised no deception intentionally, unless silence be so. He renewed his complaints, blended with his admiration of Wordsworth. The oddest thing he said was that he had been commanded to do certain things—that is, to write about Milton—and that he was applauded for refusing. He struggled with the Angels and was victor. His wife joined in the conversation. . . .

FEB. 18th . . . Then called on Blake—an amusing chat with him, but still no novelty. The same round of extravagant and mad doctrines, which I shall not now repeat but merely notice their application. He gave me copied out by himself Wordsworth's preface to his *Excursion*. At the end he has added this note:

Solomon when he married Pharaoh's daughter and became a convert to the Heathen Mythology talked exactly in this way of Jehovah as a very inferior object of man's contemplation, he also passed him by unalarmed and was permitted. Jehovah dropped a tear and followed him by his Spirit into the abstract void. It is called the Divine Mercy. Satan dwells in it, but mercy does not dwell in him.

Of Wordsworth he talked as before. Some of his writings proceed from the Holy Ghost, but then others are the work of the Devil. However, I found on this subject Blake's language more in conformity with orthodox Christianity than before. He talked of the being under the direction of Self, and [of] Reason as the creature of man and opposed to God's grace, and warmly declared that all he knew was in the Bible; but then he understands by the Bible the spiritual sense. For as to the natural sense, *that* Voltaire was commissioned by God to expose. 'I have had much intercourse with Voltaire, and he said to me: "I blasphemed the Son of Man, and it shall be forgiven me; but they (the enemies of Voltaire) blasphemed the Holy Ghost in me, and it shall not be forgiven them." I asked in what language Voltaire spoke. He gave an ingenious answer: 'To my sensations it was English—it was like the touch of a musical key. He touched it probably French, but to my ear it became English.' I spoke again of the *form* of the persons who appear to him; asked why he did not draw them. 'It is not worth while; there are so many, the labour would be too great. Besides, there would be no use. As to Shakespeare, he is exactly like the *old* engraving, which is called a bad one. I think it very good.'

I inquired about his writings. 'I have written more than Voltaire or Rousseau—six or seven epic poems as long as Homer and twenty tragedies as long as *Macbeth*.' He showed me his version (for so it may be called) of Genesis: 'as understood by a Christian Visionary'—in which, in a style resembling the Bible, the spirit is given. He read a passage at random; it was striking. He will not print any more. 'I write,' he says, 'when commanded by the spirits, and the moment I have written I see the words fly about the room in all directions. It is then published and the spirits can read,—my manuscripts [are] of no further use. I have been tempted to burn my manuscripts, but my wife won't let me.' 'She is right,' said I. 'You have written these, not from yourself, but by a higher order; the manuscripts are theirs, not your property. You cannot tell what purpose they may answer, unforeseen to you.' He liked this, and said he would not destroy them. His philosophy he repeated—denying causation, asserting everything to be the work of God or the Devil,—that there is a constant falling off from God, angels becoming devils. Every man has a devil in him, and the conflict is eternal between a man's self and God, etc. He told me my copy of his Songs would be five guineas, and was pleased by my manner of receiving this information. He spoke of his horror of money, of his turning pale when money had been offered him, etc. . . .

MAY 12th . . . Tea and supper at home. The Flaxmans, Masqueriers, a Miss Forbes, Blake, and Sutton Sharpe. On the whole the evening went off tolerably. Masquerier not precisely the man to enjoy Blake, who was, however, not in an exalted state. Allusions only to his particular notions, while Masquerier commented on his opinions as if they were those of a man of ordinary notions—Blake asserted that the oldest painters, poets, were the best. 'Do you deny all progression?' says Masquerier. 'Oh yes!' I doubt whether Flaxman sufficiently tolerates Blake. But Blake appreciates Flaxman as he ought. Blake relished my stone drawings. They stayed till eleven. Blake more and more convinced that Wordsworth worships Nature and is not a Bible Christian. I have sent him the *Sketches*. We shall see whether they convert him.

MAY 15th . . . Wrote to Carlyle about German books on which he gave me a commission. I spoke with Tait [a bookseller in Fleet Street] on the business, and wrote at length translating extracts from *Konversations Lexikon*. . . .

MAY 26th . . . Called on Meyer of Red Lion Square where Lamb was sitting for his portrait—a strong likeness. It is to be engraved, perhaps; it gives Lamb the air of a thinking man more like the framer of a system of philosophy than of the genial and gay effusions of Elia. . . .

JUNE 5th . . . Attended a party at Miss Benger's. . . . Miss Landon, a young poetess—a *starling*—the 'L.E.L.' of the *Gazette*. A good-humoured face gave me a favourable opinion of her. Hervey,[1] a poet, author of *Australia*, with the face of a frog; Miss Porter (Jane) grown old and scraggy and old-maidish since I saw her. These were the authors. . . .

JUNE 9th Alaric Watts breakfasted with me; a young man of very agreeable manners said to have poetic talents, and having business sense as it seems to me. He came about Wordsworth's poems, of which he had undertaken to negotiate an edition, and it is a great relief to me that he, being in town, will still undertake a business for which he is so much better qualified than I am. But he has no expectation of succeeding to his wish or Wordsworth's expectations. The booksellers are in a deplorable condition: Watts says that with the possible exception of Colburn and Longman, he doubts whether any of them are solvent. He thinks Baldwin's poor, very poor, and even Murray too. Watts is a business man and is editor and publisher on his own account. He seems desirous to cultivate an acquaintance with me. . . .

[1] Thomas Kibble Hervey published *Australia*, a poem, in 1824.

June 13th . . . Called early on Blake. He was as *wild* as ever with no great novelty, except that he confessed a practical notion which would do him more injury than any other I have heard from him. He says that from the Bible he has learned that *Eine Gemeinschaft der Frauen Statt finden sollte*. When I objected that *Ehestand* seems to be a divine institution he referred to the Bible: 'that from the beginning it was not so.' He talked, as usual, of the spirits—asserted that he had committed many murders, that reason is the only evil or sin, and that careless gay people are better than those who think, etc. . . .

[*Travel Journal.*] Oct. 5th [*Keswick.*] . . . I made a call at Mr. Southey's. He was from home, but I had a long chat with the ladies. From them I learned that I should find the house of my Rydal friends in trouble, Miss Dorothy Wordsworth being alarmingly ill. I was on this account glad I had not walked to Rydal by way of Ullswater, as I should then have gone to Mr. Wordsworth's house as my home, which I now resolved not to do. . . . Walked back to Rydal. I found my friends comfortable, for Miss Dorothy Wordsworth was in better health. I took tea with them, had an interesting conversation and returned to my inn. . . .

Oct. 6th After breakfast I walked to Rydal Mount and remained with the Wordsworths the rest of the day. . . . The weather allowed of very little walking. . . . One walk, however, Mr. Wordsworth and I did take. It was over Loughrigg Fell by Loughrigg Tarn down to Grasmere lake and back by Rydal Water. It was a delightful walk. . . . Mr. Wordsworth showed me the field he has purchased on which he means to build should he be compelled to leave the Mount. He took me over Mr. Tillbrook's knacky [?] cottage, the *Rydal Wife-Trap*, really a very pretty toy. He also pointed out to my notice the beautiful spring, a description of which is to be an introduction to a portion of his great poem—containing a poetical view of water as an *element* in the composition of our globe. The passages he read me appear to be of the very highest excellence. The anxiety of the whole family about Miss Dorothy Wordsworth threw a shade over the enjoyment of the day. At nine I left my friends. . . .

Oct. 7th . . . It rained incessantly . . . did not reach Rydal till late. We had no resource but books and conversation, of which there was no want. Poetry the staple commodity, of course, but of this there is nothing to be said here. . . . The pleasure of the day is not to be measured by the small space it occupies in this journal. . . . Read the first part of Osborne's *Advice to his Son*, a book Wordsworth gave to Monkhouse, and which I supposed, therefore, a favourite. This I wondered at, but I found on inquiry that Wordsworth only respected the sagacity of detached remarks, for Osborne is like Lord Burleigh, a mere counsellor of selfish prudence and caution. Surely it need not be printed: 'Beware lest in trying to save your friend, you do not get drowned yourself'!

Oct. 8th . . . Did not reach Rydal till late. The family at church. We took an early dinner, and afterwards Wordsworth and I attempted a walk, for the day had brightened a little, but we were forced to take refuge in a cottage beyond Rydal Water and were still severely drenched. . . .

Nov. 29th . . . At four I went to James Stephen's and drove down with him to his house at Hendon—a genteel dinner party by Stephen, but the company were by no means interesting. On the other hand I had a most interesting companion in young Macaulay—one of the most promising of the rising generation I have seen for a long time. Macaulay is the author of several much admired articles in the *Edinburgh Review*. A review of Milton's poetical and political character in an article on the lately discovered work of Milton on the Christian doctrine—and an article on the London University. In the former I was better pleased with the political than the critical part. In the latter the low estimate given of Greek and Latin learning and of the advantages and prerogatives of college men is the more remarkable coming from an accomplished scholar and from a man who as a Fellow has drawn the greatest advantages from his university. Macaulay has a good face, not the delicate and expressive features of a man of sensibility and genius but the strong lines and well-knit limbs of a man sturdy both of body and mind. He is very cheerful and eloquent and overflowing with expression and not poor in thought. His opinions are quite liberal and yet he is by no means a vulgar radical. He seems a correct as well as a full man and on subjects not introduced by himself showed a minute knowledge of petty particulars. We talked on all subjects literary and political. Macaulay is just called to the Bar and goes the Northern Circuit.

Dec. 7th I sent Brittain [his clerk] to inquire after Mr. Flaxman's health, etc., and was engaged looking over the Term Reports while he was gone. On his return he brought the melancholy intelligence of his death early in the morning. The country has lost one of the greatest and best of men. As an artist he has spread the fame of the country beyond any other of his age—as a man he exhibited a rare specimen of Christian and moral excellence.

I walked out and called at [Sir John] Soane's—he was from home. I then called on Blake, desirous to see how, with his peculiar feelings and opinions, he would receive the intelligence. It was much as I expected. He had himself been very ill during the summer, and his first observation was with a smile: 'I thought I should have gone first.' He then said: 'I cannot consider death as anything but a removing from one room to another.' One thing led to another and he fell into his wild, rambling way of talk. Men are born with a devil and an angel, but this he himself interpreted body and soul. Of the Old Testament he seemed to think not favourably: 'Christ,' said he, 'took much after his mother (the law), and in that respect was one of the worst of men.' On my requiring an explanation he said: 'There was his turning the money-changers out of the Temple; he had no right to do that.' Blake then declaimed against those who sat in judgment on others. 'I have never known a very bad man who had not something very good about him.' He spoke of the Atonement, said: 'It is a horrible doctrine. If another man pay your debt I do not forgive it,' etc. He produced *Sintram* by Fouqué: 'This is better than my things!' . . .

1827

JAN. 25th . . . With [Murray] I had a conversation about Wordsworth which ended in his authorising me to write to Wordsworth that he acceded to a proposal by Wordsworth for the publication of his poems. This I informed Wordsworth of the following day, but in answer found that Wordsworth had, in consequence of Murray's silence, contracted with Longman for the publication on similar terms. . . .

FEB. 2nd Götzenberger, the young painter from Germany, called on me and I accompanied him to Blake. We looked over Blake's *Dante*. Götzenberger seemed highly gratified by the designs, and Mrs. Aders says Götzenberger considers Blake as the first and Flaxman as the second man he has seen in England. The conversation was slight—I was interpreter between them, and nothing remarkable was said by Blake—he was interested apparently by Götzenberger. . . .

At nine went to Lamb's—found Godwin there. I had not seen him for years; he reproached me in a high tone for not having called on him. I did not promise nor do I intend to do so. It is a relief to be disburthened of his acquaintance. Came home late.

MAY 20th . . . Went to Lamb's—not an agreeable visit. I foolishly told Lamb that he had been seen drunk on the Enfield road by the Procters . . . who were in a gig and passed him. Lamb was very angry and said it was brutal on their part, he will never forgive them. I was angry with myself for mentioning the matter.

JUNE 30th . . . Having taken a cold dinner at the Athenaeum I went down to Lamb at Enfield Chase. I rode to Edmonton—a sad wet ride, but

I was recovered from the ride by the later walk. Found Lamb and his sister in good spirits and I played some agreeable rubbers of dummy whist with them. I had a fine walk afterwards and the nine miles went off rapidly enough, nor was I by any means uncomfortably tired when I came home. Read this afternoon Carlyle's prefaces about Tieck, Hoffmann, Musaeus, and Fouqué. He had in the first article availed himself of hints from me, and his other prefaces read more like translations than compositions. Carlyle sent me his four volumes of *German Romance*—a present I did not want and do not much value, but I respect him and am pleased with his attention.

Nov. 10th . . . Dined with James Stephen today—a party of superior people, but on the whole a dull day. . . . Macaulay was the only talker. He speaks with the ease and assurance of a man conscious of abilities, and that they are appreciated, but he said nothing out of the line of well-delivered commonplace. . . .

Nov. 25th I was engaged today from half-past eight to half-past five, and from eleven till one reading Hallam's *History*. If I did not feel that my eyes begin to fail me, I should find in the undiminished pleasures of reading an assurance of never-ceasing or declining enjoyment in old age. This book kept me employed about eleven hours today. I read it with the interest of a novel. Hallam is a most impartial historian, and his opinions are urged with a convincing plausibility. . . .

Dec. 17th Finished Walter Scott's *Napoleon*—the last volume alone tiresome. The fact is that it is only the station and position in which the emperor was placed that rendered him an object of interest. The man I care nothing about. His was not a mind which at all interested me. A vulgar nature though of tremendous power. A sort of Hercules, by no means one of the *dii majores*. . . .

Dec. 20th . . . Began this evening to look into Shelley's poems. His *Lines written among the Euganean Hills* and his *Sensitive Plant* are very pleasing poems. Fancy seems to be his best quality; he is rich and exuberant. When he endeavours to turn the abstractions of metaphysics into poetry he probably fails—as who does not? But even in his worst works, I have no doubt there is the enthusiasm of virtue and benevolence. I think him worth studying and understanding if possible. I recollect Wordsworth places him above Lord Byron. . . .

Dec. 26th Having heard from Charles Lamb that his sister was again well I lost no time in going to see them, and accordingly as soon as breakfast was over I walked into the city and took the Edmonton stage and walked thence to Enfield. A fine ride. I found them in their new house, a small but comfortable place, and Charles Lamb quite delighted with his retirement. He fears not the solitude of his situation, though he seems to be almost without an acquaintance, and dreads rather than seeks visitors. I spent the day both before and after dinner at cards, which both he and his sister enjoyed. . . . I took a bed at the near public-house and was comfortable there.

1828

JAN. 8th . . . Walked with Field to Mrs. Blake. The poor old lady was more affected than I expected, yet she spoke of her husband as dying like an angel.[1] She is the housekeeper of Linnell the painter and engraver and at present her services must well pay for her board. A few of her husband's works are all her property. We found that the *Job* is Linnell's property, and the print of Chaucer's pilgrimage hers. Therefore, Field bought a proof and I two prints at two and a half guineas each. I mean one for Lamb. Mrs. Blake is to look out some engravings for me hereafter. . . .

FEB. 5th . . . I went to the Athenaeum, where I finished Hunt's *Lord Byron*.[2] This book contains an able apology for the opinions and character of Shelley—his supposed atheism seems to be the result of an excessive sensibility to the wrongs committed by the great and powerful who are the noisy asserters of the doctrines of religion, and an excessive refinement of thought. The extracts from his poems are delightful. Justice is also done to the genius of poor Keats; but Hunt, who is glad of an opportunity of attacking Wordsworth, insinuates a jealousy and damning by faint praise on his part. . . .

APRIL 4th . . . As soon as breakfast was over I set out on a walk to Lamb's, whom I reached in three and a half hours at one. . . . At Lamb's I found Moxon and Miss Kelly;[3] Miss Kelly is an unaffected, sensible, clear-headed, warm-hearted woman; she has none of the vanities or arrogance of the actress; no one would suspect her profession from her conversation or manners. We talked about the French Theatre and dramatic matters in general. Miss Lamb and Charles were glad to have a dummy rubber and also piquet with me. Moxon and I left at ten and I was in chambers at half past one. A chatty walk. Moxon is a respectable man—one of Longman's journeymen and I believe a very mediocre poet,

[1] William Blake died on 12 August 1827.

[2] *Lord Byron and Some of his Contemporaries, with Recollections of the Author's Life, and of his Visit to Italy*, by Leigh Hunt, 1828.

[3] Frances Maria Kelly, the actress to whom Lamb proposed marriage.

but he takes nothing on himself in the latter character and is as humble as Shoberl. . . .

MAY 14th Wordsworth and the Masqueriers breakfasted with me by appointment. They had a subject in common to talk upon. The Masqueriers delighted with the poet and he glad to obtain information from them about travelling economically, so that the rencontre though casual was very agreeable. Wordsworth brought a young man with him, a Mr. Hall, a sensible man, judging by appearances. I afterwards accompanied Wordsworth on several calls—upon Longman, upon Johnson at the National Schools, and to several other places. A chat with Wordsworth about myself—he consents to my leaving the Bar, giving credit to my assurance that in all probability if I stay I shall lose the business I now have. As to my own conviction that I do not deserve business and am inferior to others, that is a subject, he says, on which he will not take my opinion. He seems bent on a journey to Italy next year and fully expects me to be of the party. . . .

MAY 26th An interesting day. Rode after breakfast to Edmonton and thence walked to Enfield. Found Miss Lamb at home, but Charles Lamb was gone for a walk. I therefore proposed making then my call on Mr. Relph. I did so and had a delightful walk to Cheshunt. . . . Returned to the Lambs in time for their tea and then I spent the rest of the evening with them at dummy whist, to them a great enjoyment, and to me also, especially in their society. I found both of them in good health and as cordial as possible. I sat up late lounging over Lamb's books—a motley collection of old English classics, his favourite writers, and of modern books, chiefly presentation copies.

MAY 28th . . . I then proceeded to a dinner party at Mr. Quillinan's.[1] Thirteen of us were crowded to a table fit for ten. Rather a heterogeneous party. Quillinan was once in the army, and among his military friends were a few who had just curiosity enough to be desirous to see two poets. The *civil* portion of the guests were the three Wordsworths, Southey, Kenyon, the friend of Southey and Wordsworth, a young barrister (Dawson), a gentlemanly man, Lodge, the antiquary and author, with me and our host, nine. . . . In the drawing-room were the younger Coleridge (the author of *West Indies*[2]), an American lady, who, as Wordsworth says, is anxious to see great people and talk herself. . . . Of the conversation not much to say. Southey was civil but no more to me. He would have burst out on the Catholic Question if he had not been at a Catholic's

[1] Edward Quillinan (1791–1851), a poet who, as a widower, was to marry Wordsworth's daughter Dora. See *infra*, May 11th, 1841.

[2] *Six Months in the West Indies*, 1825, by Henry Nelson Coleridge.

table. He abstained from talking offensively, but *looked* delighted at the change of the Ministry. . . .

MAY 29th An interesting morning. Met by appointment Wordsworth, etc., at the National Gallery. Benson came on a hint from me. The Rogers were also there. A long lounge over the pictures. Wordsworth is a fine judge of paintings and his remarks are full of feeling and truth. We afterwards went to the British Institution, where we also lounged a long time over a glorious collection of the Old Masters—a very fine collection.

JUNE 3rd Wordsworth came early, having seen Mrs. Wordsworth into a stage. He and T. Clarkson and Benson and Mr. Hills breakfasted with me, and I spent the rest of the morning with Wordsworth. I joined him at Longman's. . . . I then made several calls with Wordsworth, *inter alia* on Montagu, and went with him to a book auction. Wordsworth was very communicative about his affairs. It seems that, including £100 annuity given him by Sir G. Beaumont, he has about £400 a year income without his place, but he has to maintain his sister out of this. Wordsworth is so little pleased with his place that he would give it up had he £700 a year. Our journey in Italy will depend on family arrangements, and on his power of obtaining permission to go from the Government. . . .

JUNE 11th At half-past nine Wordsworth came to breakfast with me. I did not know of his coming in time to invite Mr. Green, but I ran to Paynter and he came, and just as we sat down to breakfast Alfred Becher came, bringing with him Professor Friedlander from Halle. Wordsworth was in excellent spirits, and conversed well on language; he remarked on the advantage which a mixed language like English has over one that is *single* like the German—in this, that the expressions do not so closely and palpably give the sensual image and direct sense, but convey indirect meanings and, faintly, allusions, by which poetry is favoured though philosophy may be injured. I am too lazy now to develop this thought; I had obscurely perceived it before. . . .

JUNE 18th An interesting day. Breakfasted with Aders. Wordsworth and Coleridge were there, Alfred Becher also. Wordsworth was chiefly busied about making arrangements for his journey into Holland. Coleridge was, as usual, very eloquent in his dreamy monologues, but he spoke intelligibly enough on some interesting subjects. It seems that of late he has been little acquainted with Irving; he says he silenced Irving by showing how completely he had mistaken the sense of the revelations and prophecies, and then Irving kept away for more than a year. Coleridge says: 'I consider Irving as a man of great power, and I have an affection for him; he is an excellent man, but his brain has been turned by the shoutings of the mob. I think him *mad*—literally mad.' He expressed strong indignation at the intolerance of Irving. He also expressed himself strongly about Southey. He said: 'He suffers himself to be flattered into servility by that one-testicled fellow Peel. He writes most servilely though very honestly.' I confounded their names together. 'Pray do not make such a blunder again. I should have no objection to your doing it with him.' (Pointing to Wordsworth.)...

JULY 8th . . . Walked to the Lambs. Found there Louisa Holcroft, a fine and interesting young woman, seemingly a girl of talents and sweet disposition. Also Mr. and Mrs. Hood. Charles was gone a-walking. Miss Lamb proposed a rubber before dinner to the Hoods. After tea played with the Lambs a dummy. The Hoods would not play. She seems a bad temper; he a good-humoured man, and his company as agreeable as that of so decided a punster can be. I was forced to leave early as I slept at the inn and they shut up at half-past ten. I sat up reading Goethe's *Kunst und Alterthum.*

JULY 23rd . . . I walked to Fornham to call on Lamb's protégée, Miss Isola,[1] governess at the Rev. Mr. Williams's. She is already much improved, has a gentlewomanly appearance and seems happy. She is duly grateful to Lamb and his sister, to whom she owes the attainments which qualify her for her situation. . . .

DEC. 2nd . . . Dined with Mrs. Shutt and her daughters and Shutt. Horace Smith was invited to meet me. I had seen him before at Barron Field's. His talk is that of a well-informed and sensible man, and no one would suspect in him either the witty author of the *Rejected Addresses* (he is *one* only) or the laborious author of the historical novels which he has encumbered the circulating libraries with. However, he made the evening pleasant enough.

1829

FEB. 14th After breakfast set out and had a very agreeable walk to Enfield by the Green Lanes with no other book than Wordsworth's poems—quite sufficient for the walk. I found my friends as usual. Mary Lamb eager for whist as soon as I arrived, and we did in fact play till dinner at four. After dinner we were interrupted by calls—a widow Leishman and a tailor; both were inclined to stay: I therefore stole out

[1] Emma Isola, the Lambs's adopted daughter, who was married to Edward Moxon in 1833.

with Wordsworth's poems till tea-time, and the intruders having gone we renewed our whist till supper. Lamb not quite comfortable, having taken wine, but his benevolence is as active as ever. He read me some feeling lines to Miss Isola on her coming of age next April. . . .

MAY 8th . . . Went by the early coach to Enfield, being on the road from half past eight to half past ten—nearly eleven. Lamb was from home great part of the morning. I spent the whole of the day with Lamb and his sister without going out of the house, except for a mile before dinner with Miss Lamb, and the greater part of the day was as usual spent over whist. I had plenty of books to lounge over. I read Brougham's *Introduction to the Library of Useful Knowledge*, remarkable only as coming from the busiest man living—a lawyer in full practice, a partisan in Parliament, an *Edinburgh* reviewer, and a participator in all public and party matters. Otherwise there is nothing remarkable in any of the thoughts, and the sort of encyclopaedic universal knowledge is what many a shallow fellow possesses. But little to interest, but much to mortify me in the book. Sat up late as usual.

MAY 9th Nearly the whole of the day within doors; I merely sunned myself at noon on the beautiful Enfield Green. . . . Of course great part of the time we were at dummy whist, and the rest of the day I was looking over a great number of Lamb's [books], of which no small number are curious. He throws away, indeed, all modern books, but retains the trash he liked when a boy. Looked over a *Life of Congreve*, one of Curll's infamous publications containing nothing: the first edition of the *Rape of the Lock* with the machinery—it is curious to observe the improvements in the versification:—Colley Cibber pamphlets against Pope—only flippant and disgusting—nothing worth notice. Read the beginnings of two wretched novels. Lamb and his sister were both in a fidget today by the departure of their old servant Becky, who had been with them many years, but being ill-tempered had been a plague and a tyrant to them. Yet Miss Lamb was frightened at the idea of a *new* servant, Becky's sister and aunt having long [been] with her. However, their new maid, a cheerful, healthy girl, gave them spirits, and next day Lamb was all day rejoicing in the change. Moxon came very late.

MAY 10th All the forenoon in the back room with the Lambs, except that I went out to take a place in the evening stage. About noon Talfourd came; he had walked. Moxon, after a long walk, returned also to dinner, and we had an agreeable chat between dinner and tea. At six I went back to London on the stage—a delightful evening. . . .

JUNE 5th . . . We had an agreeable dinner party [at Bear Wood[1] with

[1] John Walter's country house near Reading.

John Walter]. . . . Dr. and Miss Mitford, the Doctor an old Whig of more than seventy whose magisterial propensities are counteracted by very liberal opinions, so that he is a protector of village sports on the Sunday in opposition to the religious party. He likes his bottle, laughs and talks loud, but is on the whole a pleasant man. His daughter, Miss Mitford, in spite of her rotundity and literary pretensions, seems to be an amiable woman. I was pleased with her. Her conversation lively, but with no arrogance or pretence.

[*Travel Journal.*] AUG. 2nd [*Weimar.*] A golden day! But I feel ashamed at my inability to leave a memorial at all worthy of it. . . . It was between ten and eleven when I left my card at Goethe's house for his daughter-in-law, and we proceeded then to the small house in the park, where we were at once admitted to the Great Man. I was oppressed by the cordial reception, and as the cordiality increased during two most interesting conversations, the sense of unworthiness is but increased and now disturbs the otherwise delightful feelings which several hours' conversation has produced. . . . We spoke of Lord Byron and I mentioned the *Vision of Judgment.* He called it sublime and laughed while he referred to the summoning of Junius and Wilkes as witnesses and to the letting the king slip into heaven, etc., as admirable hits. He said: '*Es sind keine Flickwörter im Gedichte*,' and he compared the brilliancy and clearness of his style to a metal wire drawn through a steel plate! I informed him of my having brought Flaxman's lectures, which he politely accepted, and spoke of Flaxman's 'Homer' with great respect. . . . Returned to Goethe at six. I feared to stay too long, and we remained but an hour and half. He was friendly to a degree I cannot account for. . . . I inquired concerning his knowledge of Burns. He has no knowledge of the *Vision.* A most remarkable coincidence between that poem and the *Zueignung.* Goethe made inquiries of the taste for German literature in England, and I informed him of the several translations as well as of the sudden turn in the *Edinburgh Review.* He evidently enjoyed the prospect of his own extended reputation. He spoke of *Ossian* with contempt and said: 'No one remarked that while Werther is in his senses he talks about Homer, and only after he grows mad, is in love with *Ossian.*' I reminded him of Napoleon's love of *Ossian.* He said it was on account of the contrast between Ossian and his own nature. Napoleon loved only melancholy and soft music. *Werther* was among his books at St. Helena. . . .

AUG. 13th . . . I met Madame de Goethe going to the poet . . . and at twelve renewed my visit. . . . I read to her parts of Burns's *Vision*, of which she felt all the beauty and the resemblance to the *Zueignung.* I began also *The Vision of Judgment*, and gave an account of Wordsworth.

She will let me try to convince her (but it will be hard) that Wordsworth is a greater poet than Lord Byron. . . .

[Goethe] repeated the remark which is one of his fixed ideas that it is by the most laborious collection of facts that even a poetical view of nature is to be corrected, and, as it were, authenticated. He remarked in the same spirit that *occasional* poems are among the best poems when the poet takes care to retain all the spirit of the occasion. It is this which had made Goethe a *realistic* poet, as opposed to the idealism of such poetry as Wordsworth's. . . .

On my mentioning Marlowe's *Faust* he burst out into exclamations of wonder. '*Wie gross ist alles angelegt!*' He said he had some thought of translating it. He gave an account of the story to Frau von Goethe. He was fully aware that Shakespeare stood by no means alone in that age. He reverted again to Lord Byron. Knebel had shown me a lithographed manuscript to Goethe which was sent by Byron. It was a sketch of a dedication of *Sardanapalus* which, being approved of by Goethe, was sent back and Frau von Goethe says appeared before the second edition. It certainly is not before the new edition, nor, I believe, before the pirated German and French editions. I will try to get a copy. Goethe conceded to me that there is not character in Lord Byron, and that the idea of selling one's soul in order to gratify such an appetite as Manfred's is not poetical; but he praised the death of Manfred after the Devil could not carry him away as very fine.

I was glad to find that Goethe particularly admired Byron's *Heaven and Earth* and the first two acts of *The Deformed Transformed*. These are precisely my favourites. We spoke of Schiller. Goethe admitted that he detested Schiller's witch-scenes in *Macbeth*,[1] but said: 'It was *his* way. One must leave every one *his character*. I was always very tolerant of others.' . . .

AUG. 14th . . . I spent a delightful three hours nearly with Frau von Goethe. I was employed reading to her out of the Annuals, and from Lord Byron's *Vision of Judgment*. Frau von Goethe relished the wit and poetry and showed a quick perception of the beauties of every kind. . . .

Of Goethe's conversation I have chiefly to notice that on my mentioning Charles Lamb, he instantly said: 'Did he not write some pretty verses about his own name?' He quoted with great pleasure as being vastly clever, *King Coal's Levée*[2] and said the notes contain all the knowledge of geology a man wants. . . .

AUG. 15th . . . I went to Frau von Goethe. I spent from eleven to two

[1] Schiller translated *Macbeth* in 1787–8.

[2] *King Coal's Levée: or Geological Etiquette, with Explanatory Notes; and the Council of Metals*, by John Scafe.

with her. I read to her *The Vision* by Burns, and then I read a number of Wordsworth's finest philosophical sonnets and *Yew Trees* and I gave Frau von Goethe a manuscript sonnet—an autograph by Wordsworth, also an interesting letter from Coleridge and one from Lamb, and a note from Rogers. I was gratified by finding that my reading had produced the hoped-for effect. Wordsworth will not put the nose of Byron out of joint with Frau von Goethe, but he will be appreciated by her—I am afraid of the experiment with the great poet himself. . . . I read to him *The Vision of Judgment*. He enjoyed it like a child, but his criticism went little beyond the exclamatory: '*Toll! Gar zu gross! Himmlisch! Unübertrefflich!*' etc. In general, the most strongly peppered passages pleased the best. Stanza 9 he praised for the clear and distinct painting. [Stanza] 10. He repeated with emphasis the last two lines,[1] conscious that his own age was eighty. [Stanzas] 13, 14, 15 are favourites with me. Goethe concurred in the suggested praise. The stanza 24 he declared to be sublime. The characteristic speeches of Wilkes and Junius he thought most admirable: 'Byron *hat sich selbst übertroffen*,' and the introduction of Southey made him laugh heartily. . . .

AUG. 16th . . . At six Frau von Goethe and I drove to Goethe. I read to him Coleridge's *Love* and *Fire, Famine and Slaughter*. Goethe damned them with faint praise. On the contrary, he was very warm indeed in his praise of the first part of *Heaven and Earth*, which I read to him. He admired excessively the *devilish* parts, called Noah a Philistine and Abel a *Landprediger*. He said that Byron, had he lived, would have dramatised the Bible. The Tower of Babel would have been a capital theme. Lord Byron he declared to be inimitable. Such a one never existed before, nor ever will again. Ariosto was not so *keck* as Lord Byron in *The Vision of Judgment*. . . .

AUG. 17th I rose at 5. Was occupied . . . in translating an article by Goethe in the German edition of Lord Byron giving an account of the connection between them. I shall send this to Murray for Moore, but I doubt whether I shall make an article of any use to the biographer. . . . I read a little of Wordsworth to Frau von Goethe. . . . I spent another two hours with Goethe and read to him *Heaven and Earth*. His admiration was excessive, his remarks all eulogistic. He said Byron had not 'like myself devoted a long life to the study of nature, and yet I found only once or twice in all his works passages which I would have altered. His views of nature were equally profound and poetical. You must not take it evil [*Sie dürfen es nicht übel nehmen*], but Byron owes these fine views of

[1] It seem'd the mockery of hell to fold
The rottenness of eighty years in gold.

the Old Testament to the ennui he suffered at school. He must have been terribly annoyed (*ennuyéd?*] at the absurdities, and in his own mind he ruminated over them and turned them to account.'

He gave me a couple of medals of the Grand Duke, and was very kind. . . .

AUG. 18th . . . I wrote . . . to T. Moore with note to Murray. I had translated the account of connection between Goethe and Lord Byron. I copied Lord Byron's letter to Goethe and I gave an account of my conversation with Goethe about Lord Byron. . . . I read a very little of Lamb to Madame de Goethe. . . . I went for the last time to Goethe's cottage. . . . I read to him the first part of *Samson Agonistes* down to the end of the scene with Dalila. He did not praise with the warmth with which he praised Lord Byron, but still he thanked me for having made the poem known to him. He said: 'The whole is finely reasoned, and Samson's confession of his guilt is in a better spirit than anything in Lord Byron. There is a fine logic and keeping in all the speeches and Dalila is nobly conceived. The picture is complete. It gives me a higher opinion of Milton than I had before. It shows more of his mind than any other.' . . .

AUG. 22nd [*Dresden.*] . . . I was delighted to find that Tieck does not join in the love of Lord Byron by Goethe, which he calls infatuation. He hates *Manfred*, but likes the *Hebrew Melodies*. I have never read them. He also hates Hazlitt, but considers him a man of talents. . . .

AUG. 23rd . . . Tieck's literary opinions appear to me correct. He appreciates as they merit all *our* classics, Richardson and Fielding, but he likes even Smollett's *Peregrine Pickle*. He loves Sterne. . . . He is by no means narrow in his taste. Lord Byron will be disgraced by his jealous hatred of Shakespeare and Milton. His *Sardanapalus* alone of his dramas is readable; *Werner* is as bad as Kotzebue. . . .

1830

AUG. 16th [*Florence.*] . . . Mr. Landor[1] stepped in [to whom I was] introduced as a friend of Wordsworth and after a long talk Landor intimated a wish to be further acquainted. . . . Landor is altogether different from what I had imagined him to be. He is a florid man with large eyes, an animated air, having the look of a country gentleman and an officer. He talks decisively and freely, even cynically. He is said to be a man whom it is difficult to keep on good terms with, being apt to take

[1] Walter Savage Landor (1775–1864), author of *Imaginary Conversations*.

offence. In our first conversation we went over much ground. He spoke of Southey in terms of the warmest affection, as one of the best of men—hostile as he is to his politics. . . . Of poetry we also spoke. He incidentally said the greater part of Homer is trash—and so of Dante. This led me to explain Schlegel's theory of epic poetry, which Landor seemed both to comprehend and like. I also explained the first elements of Kantian philosophy. He was a good listener, and I tried him somewhat severely. . . . He was when we parted very civil indeed.

AUG. 20th . . . In the afternoon I walked to Landor's villa under Fiesole. I found him at home with his family—his wife a beautiful woman still, though the mother of four very fine children. Landor seems attached to his family and I left him with a favourable opinion of his heart and moral character. He told me something of his life. He was at Oxford. His father wished him to follow a profession and said: 'If you will go to London and study the law, I will give you £350, perhaps £400. If not, you shall have £120 and no more, and I do not wish to see your face again.' 'I thanked my father for his offer, saying: "I could take your £350 and deceive you by never studying, but I never did deceive you and never will. I will thank you for the £120." ' Landor then lived with great economy, refusing to dine out that he might not lose his independence. He was very young when he wrote *Gebir* both in English and Latin (twenty-one). He has probably now inherited his paternal estate. His establishment seems that of a man of fortune. His villa has a hundred acres of land and lies most delightfully. It grows olives and grapes. The house, too, is large and handsome—just two miles from the Porta San Gallo. We had a long and desultory chat *de omni scibili et quibusdam aliis.* And on all, Landor talks like a man of feeling rather than study. He seems to have of late even left off reading. He has long seen very few people. He says he shall never leave Italy, and does not wish to go north of Florence, yet he is not fond of the Italian character. He speaks ill even of the liberals here, with the exception of Niccolini[1] who, he says, is an honourable man. They want courage to assert their opinions: they might, without exposing themselves to any resentment, demand a representative government, but dare not. Not one of them will subscribe a shilling for the Parisians.[2] . . . Landor spoke of Lord Byron as utterly heartless: he loved no one. Rogers came in one day. Byron was excessively civil and flattering. On his going out, someone said to him: 'I did not know you had so much respect for him.' 'Respect! I forced him down upon the sofa and made him sit on a satire I wrote against him the other day.' 'But he can't help

[1] The poet, a constant visitor at the house where Crabb Robinson lodged.

[2] This was written while the French Revolution of 1830 was in progress.

it. It lies in the blood. All the family have been scoundrels; they are not to blame. . . .' I was glad to find Landor so warm an admirer of Wordsworth. He came up to my ideas, except that he would not decide on the relative worth of him and Southey! Milton he praised as the most harmonious of all poets. . . . He accompanied me part of the way home. Back late.

AUG. 21st . . . Before one, Landor called and he stayed till after three. Our chat this morning was like that of yesterday evening, very various. Personal and literary. He very warmly commended me for leaving the law. He said that no one need have more than £200 a year and that, therefore, he should bring up his children to no profession. He should have enough for all of them. Though he meant to die in Italy, he had no intention or wish that his children should live there. He would rather follow his daughter to the grave than to church with an Italian. Indeed, he visits but a single Italian here at Florence. Landor is a man of very decided tastes, and his dislikings, personal and literary, are expressed with offensive force, so that not to do him wrong, one must make allowances and say with Hamlet: 'I would not hear your enemy say so.' Of Dante, he said there is only about a seventieth part good; of Ariosto a sixth. 'But little of Tasso,' I interposed. 'Not a line worth anything—yes, one line,' which he repeated. Of Wordsworth, however, he thought very nearly all good. He did allow that few poems had been wisely altered, and in the detail concurred with me. . . .

AUG. 29th . . . After five I walked out and paid a second visit to Landor. I was quite as much pleased with this as with my former conversations. He showed me his pictures. Of painters he speaks as dogmatically as of poets. He considers Fra Bartolommeo as equal, or, at least, second to Raphael. Were he a very rich man he would not give £1,000 for the 'Transfiguration'. But he would give ten times that sum for the 'St. Mark'. Michael Angelo he thinks nothing of as a painter. Had he gone on in heaven improving as he did on earth, he could not now equal 'St. Mark' by Fra Bartolommeo. He also speaks slightingly of Leonardo da Vinci. Next to Raphael and Fra Bartolommeo, Perugino is his great favourite. In expression, even Raphael did not equal him. Landor has spent a deal of money on pictures in Italy and lost a deal by pictures in England. He accompanied me part of the way home. Mrs. Landor was a Somersetshire lady. In spite of the extravagancies in expression of Landor, I somehow almost always agree with him in opinion.

AUG. 31st . . . A call from Landor, whose dialogues (*Imaginary Conversations*] I have begun. In the fourth volume I have read a pleasing dialogue between Boccaccio and Petrarch. The novelist tells [talks?] in the spirit, but not in the style of the *Decameron*. The want of a colloquial tone is the greatest fault in the book I have yet remarked. People do not talk as Landor supposes. I have read but two yet—that between Plato and Diogenes is a severe but, I suspect, a just attack on the famous philosopher. Landor on Sunday evening expressed his contempt of Plato in unmeasured language, and he said what I had half thought when a young man, but did not dare to think fully. By the bye, a word which incidentally fell from Landor has rendered the famous beginning of St. John's gospel very clear and very harmless. Λόγος, he said, means in Plato *thought* or *idea*, and in that sense words are realities. If so, then this famous text is but an assertion that God is essentially an active or thinking being—that thought was with Him from the beginning and He had been eternally thought. Such verbose and tautological assertions are common to Oriental and Greek writers. Diogenes in this dialogue says many acute and striking things, but Plato is too insignificant by far. He is a feeble and inane objector without any power of reply. Landor would say: Such I believe [him] to have been in his famous dialogues, and I could not give him a *sense* which I meant by my dialogue to prove he *never had*. . . .

SEPT. 5th . . . Read . . . Landor's dialogues. That of Trelawny and Odysseus is even poetical. The scene—the cave where the hero and his young friend were so long concealed—is well described, and the girl Tersitza is both dramatically true and has the charm of an idyll. The finest I have yet read. At ten Mr. Landor came. We drove to an English painter's lodgings—a Mr. Kirkup, a very lively and pleasant talker. . . . The day was spent in all sorts of desultory chat, with less effort and less fatigue than I recollect for a long time. Both Mr. and Mrs. Landor appeared most amiable towards their fine boy, Arnold, who had been burnt in the face from spirits of wine, and narrowly escaped losing his eyesight. Landor and Kirkup talked about painting with a knowledge I envied and a promptitude of decision which I should also have envied if I had been certain the judgment was just. . . . We also talked on politics—our opinions not always but our feelings ever agreeing, Kirkup with playful extravagance, and Landor with honest vehemence, uttering sentiments that would have frightened a timid philanthropist. A disposition to ascribe to malice what is only weakness, and a want of indulgence for the frailties of others, are the only great objection I can make to Landor's judgments of persons.

Yet I have been this morning reading his little dialogue between Lady Lisle and Elizabeth Gaunt. Never was greater justice done to the pious character than in this beautiful composition.

SEPT. 17th . . . I walked in the afternoon to Mr. Landor's. . . . A two hours' chat. Were Mr. Landor's house nearer I should be a frequent visitor. The family give me pleasure. There is but one thing in Landor that disturbs me—his vehement abuse of almost every one, Englishmen in particular. Yet he says he is glad to see any one who calls on him who knew his friends in England. Nothing can be more kind than his conduct to me. Yet he talks of hating all society. I told him that he reminded me of what I used to say—that I hated all Frenchwomen except all I had ever seen. As I go on reading his dialogues, they please me more. . . .

SEPT. 30th . . . A call from Landor. As usual a pleasant chat—on character. He expressed himself more mildly than one might have expected. . . . He related his own quarrel with the head of the police. He was, for a bold word in reply to an insult, ordered out of the country in three days. He wrote a letter to the Grand Duke—after declaring to the officer who brought him the order, that he *would not* go in three days—in which, without asking any favour, he explained his reasons. He went away in about ten days. But without asking for such a thing, an intimation was given him that he might return. Today Mr. Landor spoke with perfect freedom concerning his own affairs. He says that his own estate is entailed and that his son will have four thousand a year, but that his other children will have nothing or little and his debts to pay, and that the estate now produces only three thousand and that he has put the estate in the hands of trustees who allow him six hundred to live on. This he said without the least hint of secrecy.

OCT. 2nd . . . I found Landor at my lodgings. He told me . . . of the death of William Hazlitt, a man for whom I once had kindness, and whom I have served as a friend. But for many years I have ceased to feel any respect for him and even to speak with him. I resented his ill-treatment of Wordsworth, etc. He was a very able man. He had a certain honesty about him in politics, but it was the honest hatred of the tyranny of the powerful in which so much of envy is blended with better feelings. He was precisely the *Jacobin* so admirably described by Burke in his *Reflections*. He was a gross sensualist, and was always in great poverty. He therefore was indelicate in money matters. His prose writings I have always read with great delight. It is more than thirty years since I assisted him to find a publisher for his first book. He used to say to Miss Lamb that he should always feel a kindness towards me, for I was the first man who found out that there was anything in him. . . .

OCT. 6th . . . Mr. Brown[1] . . . knew Hazlitt, of whom he speaks as *all* do.

[1] Charles Armitage Brown.

Congeniality of opinion made them intimate. Hazlitt left his books with Brown. They are of no value. . . .

Oct. 7th . . . We talked about Hazlitt. Brown spoke highly of Hazlitt's wife as a gentlewoman. She fell in love with him on account of his writings. She parted on account of the ill-conduct of the boy. Brown related anecdotes of Hazlitt's personal cowardice, as well as of his slovenliness, and says he was the worst-tempered man he ever knew. . . .

Oct. 12th . . . Mr. Landor came to me at twelve. . . . Mr. Landor accompanied me to the gallery. It was very amusing to hear his opinions, often running counter to popular judgment, but also instructive, as he gives his reasons for his opinions. Among the paintings in the corridor many by the elder masters, were praised by him—especially by Laurent Credi and Dom. Ghirlandajo and Pollajuolo, etc. In the Salle de l'École Toscane he gives the preference to the painting in chiaroscuro by Fra Bartolommeo over almost every other painting in the world. The *Christ in the Limbo* by Allori the Bronzino, he praised, but it has been spoiled in the cleaning. The two Rodolphi Ghirlandajos I have mentioned before. He *justified* my prior admiration. On the other hand, the Guido in the Tribune he declared to be not worth a guinea. On my inquiring why, he found great fault with the drawing. I took leave of Landor with a feeling of great regard. He will be by far my chief inducement to stay here on my return. . . .

1831

Jan. 22nd [*Rome.*] . . . The small and insignificant stones raised to Shelley and Keats will excite more general interest and deservedly. . . . Keats was a promising young man, but a great deal of fuss was made about his death which Lord Byron not unjustly ridiculed as if he were killed by 'an article.' Keats had probably as few enemies as any young poet. Through bad taste his genius was not appreciated, and from party spirit, he being a friend of persons who were proud in rendering themselves odious, his works were treated with unjust and stupid contempt in the *Quarterly Review. Voilà tout.*

May 24th [*Florence.*] . . . Walked to Mr. Landor's . . . a most hearty reception from the family. . . . I had several hours as agreeable gossip—political as well as literary—as can be imagined, Landor being full of sense, however extravagantly and sometimes whimsically expressed. . .

May 25th . . . Read a little in Landor's dialogues. That between Cicero and his brother did not please me. . . . On my return to my lodgings came Landor. As usual, a very amusing chat. He gave me an account of Hazlitt's awkward attempts to apologise for his scurrilous review of Landor's dialogues, confessing he had written for knaves and fools. We talked of Mandeville, Mrs. Barbauld, etc.

JUNE 24th . . . On Wednesday I had read with sorrow of the death of Mrs. Siddons, the most glorious female I ever beheld. . . .

JUNE 27th . . . I found Landor not ill-humoured but silent. Perhaps my visit was untimely, perhaps too soon repeated. . . .

JULY 11th In the evening an agreeable walk to Landor's, and I found him friendly and chatty. Of late, I have found him silent and reserved, and he has left off calling on me, so that I feared I was becoming as uninteresting to him as he declares all persons are—a circumstance that could not surprise and would not mortify me, as I am too reasonable to expect that I should be a permanent exception, and excite feelings of sociality in his mind which no one else can do. . . .

JULY 20th . . . In the evening walked to Landor's. I read to him some of Thomas Moore's political squibs. He felt their excellence. A very agreeable evening and delightful walk home.

OCT. 16th [*London.*] Breakfasted at home and late, so that it was between one and two when I reached Lamb, having rode on the stage to Edmonton and walked thence to Enfield. I found Lamb and his sister boarding with the Westwoods—good people, who I dare say take care of them—at least the women, for Westwood is an old man and invalid and seems nearly in his dotage. Mrs. Westwood seems active and kind. Lamb has rendered himself their benefactor by getting a place for their son in Aders's counting-house. They return his services by attentions which he and his sister want; but it is deplorable that he should be reduced to such a state that he has none to associate with but the very lowest of people in attainments. No wonder that he seems very discontented. Both he and Miss Lamb looked somewhat older, but not more than all do almost whom I have closely noticed since my return. They were heartily glad to see me, as it seemed. After dinner I was anxious to leave them before it was dark, and the Lambs accompanied me between four and five o'clock, but they walked only a short time with me. Lamb lame and rendered unable to walk by the little wine he drank with me. He has begged me to come next [time] after dinner and take a bed at his house, and so I must. . . .

NOV. 30th . . . I was engaged reading the *Lives* by Cunningham of Blake, Fuseli, etc., the book of no merit perhaps, but the subjects so interesting that any life whatever of such men must be attractive. He has softened down the more offensive parts in the biography of both as well as in the Life of Barry, to whom however he is less charitable. I felt some mortification in finding Fuseli represented to be a great painter, when in fact I could never relish one of his pictures. I have a strong impression in favour of Blake as a man, but as a painter his works are to me unattractive. Less important are the Lives of Morland and Opie; Bird merely insignificant, both as man and artist. . . .

DEC. 1st . . . Reading in Cunningham—his introduction to the *Lives of the Painters* is ambitiously written, with an attention to style which he would not give in writing the *Lives*, and in consequence this part of the work I read with interest. His sketches of Wilson and Gainsborough are shallow and unsatisfactory and on the whole the book is a made-up thing altogether.

DEC. 2nd . . . I read the Life of Hogarth by Cunningham and accompanied this with references to Ireland's illustrations; but how inferior all this to Charles Lamb's golden words on Hogarth! how vapid and unmeaning what common men have said! Genius only can comment on genius with propriety. . . .

DEC. 4th . . . Sat up as usual till one reading and finishing the Life of Reynolds, having finished the *Lives of the Painters* by Cunningham. The class to which Reynolds belongs is high, but he has no higher place in it than that of the first of his country; but Hogarth is the greatest artist in his way that ever lived. Were Reynolds's works taken from the world by a miracle they would not be missed, but the loss of Hogarth would leave a chasm, if not in fine art strictly speaking, but in pictorial wisdom. He was the greatest of moral painters that ever lived.

DEC. 5th [*Brighton.*] . . . My morning was broken in upon . . . by . . . Mr. Rogers, who stayed long. Rogers spoke of two artists whom he knew in great poverty—Gibson, now in Rome, a rich man and sculptor of fame, my acquaintance there, and Chantrey, still richer and of higher fame in the same art. Chantrey, not long since, being at Rogers's, said, pointing to a sideboard: 'You probably do not recollect that being brought to you by the cabinet-maker's man?' 'Certainly not.' 'It was I who brought it and it was in a great measure my work!' . . .

DEC. 31st [*London.*] I stayed at home reading Italian, etc., till half-past one when by appointment I went to see Jeremy Bentham with whom I walked for about half an hour in his garden—when he dismissed me to take his breakfast and have the paper read to him. I have but little to report concerning him; his person is not what I expected; he is a small man and stoops very much (he is eighty-four) and shuffles in his gait. His hearing is not good, yet excellent considering his age; his eye is restless and there is a fidgety activity about him, increased probably by the habit of having all around fly at his command. He began by referring to my late journey in Italy and, by putting questions to me, made me of necessity the talker. He seemed to have made Italian matters not at all his study and I suspect considers other countries only with reference to the influence his books and opinions may have had or have there. He mentioned Filangieri as a contemptible writer who wrote *after* himself, and said he had the mortification of finding Filangieri praised while himself was overlooked. I gave him my opinion as to the *political* character of the French Ministry and their purely selfish policy towards Italy—which he did not seem to comprehend. He said the most intimate friend he had, Dr. Bowring, was in France, an intimate friend with all the French Ministry. To which I answered that ministers had *no* friends. They would use the Doctor as a tool, but give him no other real confidence. This remark put him in a dilemma—he could not consistently with all his habits of feeling towards ministers deny this to be a just character of the class and yet he was unwilling to think his friend the Doctor of so small importance. He inquired about my professional life—he knew I had been of the Norfolk Circuit and spoke of the late Mr. Wilson (whom I recollect as a boy only) as the first of his disciples—he inquired how I became acquainted with Fonblanque—and though he dismissed me rather abruptly he shook me by the hand and said: 'I congratulate myself with having made your acquaintance.' I find that Bowring lives in an adjoining house which belongs to Jeremy Bentham. As Bowring must owe me a grudge for my having *cut* him, it is probable that he will take care to destroy any favourable impression if I have made any on Bentham and prevent his forming an acquaintance with me. . . .

1832

JAN. 5th . . . Mr. T. Wallis from Florence called and brought MSS. from Mr. Landor which will require some exertion on my part to dispose of—a business I am little fit for. . . .

JAN. 6th . . . I wrote to Julius Hare at Cambridge requesting his advice how to proceed with Mr. Landor's manuscript, in particular inquiring about Colburn and the success of the Dialogues. . . .

JAN. 9th . . . I had a letter from Julius Hare today in answer to mine of Saturday—he gives a sad account of the sale of Landor's last Dialogues—not forty copies, of the poems not more! he advises not to send the manuscript to Colburn. I therefore sent the manuscript . . . to Baldwin, but I expect a refusal.

JAN. 12th . . . Met Kenny at the Athenaeum. He gave me a very melancholy account of Charles Lamb, which looks like the approach of that catastrophe which every one must fear. His anti-social feeling is quite disease. I am afraid of going down to him. . . .

JAN. 29th . . . I saw Baldwin, who will perhaps take Landor's book. He speaks very favourably of it and only objects that it does not belong to his class of publication. . . .

FEB. 11th . . . I had a longer chat with Carlyle, my Scotch acquaintance —a deep-thinking German who contrives to unite his almost idolatrous admiration of Goethe with the profession of a sort of religion though mixed with sentimental metaphysics. We spoke of his friend Edward Irving. Carlyle says that Irving is quite mad on the subject of the Unknown Tongues, and therefore incurable. He has so connected this miraculous manifestation of the Spirit with Christianity that he cannot separate the one from the other. Irving has been by this extravagance estranged from nearly all his friends. Even Carlyle sees little of him, nor does Coleridge or Basil Montagu. Yet Irving was able to see the wisdom of Goethe's insight into the nature of Christianity in the *Wilhelm Meisters Wanderjahre*. . . .

FEB. 12th . . . Carlyle breakfasted with me and I had an interesting morning with him. He is a character and a singular compound. His voice and manner and even the style of his conversation are that of a religious zealot—and he keeps up that character in his declamations against the anti-religious. But then—if not the God of his idolatry—at least he has a priest and prophet of his church in Goethe, of whose profound wisdom he speaks like an enthusiast. But for him Carlyle says he should not now be alive. He owes everything to him! But in strange union with such idolatry is his admiration of Buonaparte. Another object of his eulogy is Cobbett, whom he praises for his humanity and love of the poor! Singular and even whimsical combinations of love and reverence these. He left me at one. . . .

FEB. 16th . . . I wrote a letter to Landor informing him that I had sent his manuscript to Murray, etc., and giving him an account of Moxon the publisher of his poems. By the bye, I went to Moxon this morning—bought of him the *Selections* from Wordsworth and Southey and also *Tales from Tieck*, which I sent to Walter Landor. Moxon I found a warm-hearted, zealous man. I must go with him to Lamb.

FEB. 17th . . . I took tea with Carlyle; he delighted me while he excited my envy by showing me the most charming verses accompanying little presents from Goethe to him and his wife. Goethe seems to hold Carlyle in high esteem. . . .

FEB. 18th . . . I went about to buy seeds for Landor. . . .

FEB. 19th . . . Carlyle came and breakfasted with me, and before breakfast was over Lowndes called. An agreeable chat. Carlyle rather less intolerant in his conversation than before, but his peculiar notions and a certain exclusiveness in his taste render him often an uncomfortable companion. . . .

MARCH 3rd . . . I had received an invitation to dine with Fonblanque, Romilly being of the party, so I agreed to walk with him, and we were joined by the much prone [*sic*] John Mill—certainly a young man of great talent; he is deeply read in French politics, and bating his—to me—unmeaning praise of Robespierre, for his incomparable talents as a speaker—being an irresistible orator—and for the respect he avowed for the virtues of Mirabeau, he spoke judiciously enough about French matters. . . .

MARCH 8th . . . I found the Lambs in excellent state—not in high health but, which is far better, quiet and cheerful—Miss Isola being there I could not sleep in the house, but I had a comfortable bed in the inn and I had a very pleasant evening playing whist. I found Lamb very chatty and altogether as I could wish. I looked over his articles in Moxon's short-lived *Magazine*.[1] One about Dawe in which the meanness of that man is exposed to a degree that displeased me. A man capable of feeling so strongly the radical worthlessness of Dawe's character ought not to have kept up an acquaintance with him. Infirmities that become known in the unreservedness of intimacy ought never to be exposed to public derision. It is a sort of betraying secrets.

MARCH 12th . . . Leaving Rolfe's I went to Aders. I found several persons there, and amongst others Thomas Campbell the poet. I was not prepossessed in his favour and he did not gain upon me during the hour we chatted, not that he was discourteous—on the contrary he was very civil—or assuming. But I did not like his face or the style or tone of his conversation. He has enlisted me to form one of a Society in favour of the Poles—about whom he talked with generous warmth but with no discrimination. I should not have suspected him of being in any way an eminent man. . . .

MARCH 24th . . . I forgot to say that yesterday I had a melancholy letter from Wordsworth. He gives a sad account of his sister and talks of leaving the country on account of the impending ruin to be apprehended from the Reform Bill! . . .

[1] *The Englishman's Magazine.*

MARCH 27th . . . At the same [breakfast] time Charles Lamb came and took some tea with me. . . . I accompanied Lamb to Cary[1] at the British Museum—he seemed a quiet and sensible man: I was pleased with him. We talked of his Dante, which however, Lamb thinks inferior to his translations from the old French poets. Cary is by no means a convert to the opinions of Rossetti. . . .

APRIL 2nd . . . My nephew called and brought the news of Goethe's death, an event that at his age is of no great moment, but the departure of the mightiest spirit that has lived for many centuries is an incident that awakens most serious thought. . . .

APRIL 12th . . . I had an interesting morning with Mrs. Aders, having driven with her to Mr. Gillman's. We saw Coleridge in bed—he looked beautifully; his eye remarkably brilliant and he talked as eloquently as ever. His declamation was against the Bill: he took strong ground, resting himself on the deplorable state to which a country is reduced when a measure of vital importance is acceded to merely from the danger of resistance to the popular opinion. A yielding to a government by the people for fear of the mob is a desperate remedy. . . .

MAY 2nd . . . At the Athenaeum was Julius Hare, who informed me that Landor is expected immediately in London—if not already here. This will relieve me from all embarrassment about the manuscripts.

MAY 13th . . . Landor called. He arrived from Florence yesterday: gratified by his early visit. A long and interesting chat on English politics. He had nothing to communicate on foreign matters. . . .

MAY 17th . . . There was a Galt,[2] also, the author,—in his manner quiet and well-behaved: neither rude nor servile, though a Scotchman. . . .

MAY 20th . . . Landor came and breakfasted with me and a most agreeable morning I had. After a long chat with him I walked out with Landor. . . .

MAY 21st This day also nearly devoted to Landor. He came to breakfast with me and also Hogg, and they stayed with me till past one. I then walked out with Landor. We went first to Mrs. Aders and had the good luck to find her going to the gallery and we accompanied her. Landor was exceedingly delighted with their pictures—some of which he declared with his usual exaggeration to be *finer than Raphael*, etc. However, his judgment seemed in substance to be that of Mrs. Aders, and I dare say they were pleased with each other. We afterwards walked to Leigh Hunt's, whom we saw living apparently in more comfort than I had supposed. Landor has given him his manuscript, which will probably be

[1] Henry Francis Cary (1772–1844).
[2] John Galt, author of *Annals of the Parish*.

profitable to him though Landor might not easily have disposed of it. I obtained it with difficulty from Murray only on Saturday. I was thus with Landor till past five, when we parted. He is to go on Wednesday to Wales, etc., and will not return till August, so I shall probably not see him again as he will return to Florence after a few weeks here. I have been gratified by his spending so much of his time with me. . . .

MAY 26th . . . I went to Talfourd to dine. I unwisely consented to dine with Lamb at his house. There was no one there except Price and Miss Isola. Lamb was very soon, as he always is, tipsy, and thoroughly uncomfortable, so that the visit was as little agreeable as possible. . . .

MAY 27th Before I arose Charles Lamb was thundering at my door. He had slept with his clothes on all night and came out not knowing what to do with himself. I persuaded him to breakfast with me, thinking that at least as an object of curiosity my friends would be glad of the incident. Quayle, Paynter, and Prandi[1] breakfasted with me and Shutt also stepped down and we had a desultory chat till past eleven with Lamb, who made himself as agreeable as he could—but I suspect he disappointed my party. The rest stayed till late. . . .

MAY 28th I was reading Boccaccio when Lamb was again at my door. He however did not stay, but I made a cup of coffee for him. He had slept at Talfourd's again with his clothes on. Yet in the midst of this half-crazy irregularity, he was so full of sensibility that speaking of his sister he had tears in his eyes—and he talked about his favourite poems with his usual warmth, praising Andrew Marvell extravagantly. . . .

JULY 23rd . . . I set off and walked to Enfield to see Charles Lamb; I had a delightful walk reading Goethe's *Winckelmann*. I reached Lamb at the lucky moment before tea; he was with Miss Isola; after tea he and I took a pleasant walk together. He was in excellent health and in tolerable spirits; he spoke of his sister with composure. She is now in confinement, but he says she suffers nothing. It is only before and after she entirely loses her mind that she is very wretched and suffers grievously. Lamb was tonight quite eloquent in praise of Miss Isola: he says she is the most sensible girl and best female talker he knows. He wants to see her well married, great as the loss would be to him. I sat up chatting with Lamb till past eleven o'clock and I slept at his house, or rather at the Westwoods'. By the bye, I find he does not like either the old man or his wife, a circumstance very annoying in his dependent state.

JULY 24th I read Goethe in bed; I was, however, summoned to breakfast at eight, and after breakfast I read some Italian with Miss Isola,

[1] Fortunato Prandi, a political refugee, whom Crabb Robinson assisted by taking a prolonged course of Italian lessons with him.

whom Lamb is teaching Italian without knowing the language himself. I then walked with Charles Lamb and Miss Isola. . . .

SEPT. 24th . . . I was interrupted by the arrival of Landor, which of course altered the occupation of the whole day. He is going directly to Brighton and I with difficulty excused myself for not going with him. I called with him on Trelawny; he looks quite human. Indeed, his countenance is amiable as well as handsome; we chatted but a few minutes; he spoke of Italy as a country for *poor* men only. I went with Landor to Flaxman's. He was most extravagant in his praise—would rather have one of Flaxman's drawings than the whole of 'Niobe'; indeed most of these figures, all but three, are worthless; and Winckelmann he abuses for praising [blank], and Goethe must be an ignoramus for praising Winckelmann. . . . In the evening went to Mrs. Dashwood's, where was Landor and with him Hare. . . . We had a short and agreeable chat about Goethe, etc. . . .

SEPT. 25th . . . Then drove to Edmonton on stage and walked to Lamb's. I found them on the whole comfortable, but Miss Lamb bore sad marks of her late illness, looked very low indeed and thin, but when she spoke her voice was strong and the rubbers that we played gave her pleasure. I walked out with Lamb to see the fair at Enfield—many shows and a number of people. . . .

SEPT. 28th Landor breakfasted with me and also Worsley, who came to supply Hare's place. After an agreeable chat we drove down to Edmonton and walked over the fields to Enfield, where Charles Lamb and his sister were ready dressed to receive us. We had scarcely an hour to chat with them, but it was enough to make both Landor and Worsley express themselves afterwards delighted with the person of Mary Lamb and pleased with the conversation of Lamb, though I thought Lamb by no means at his ease, Miss Lamb quite silent—nothing in the conversation recollectable. Lamb gave Landor White's *Falstaff's Letters*. Emma Isola just showed herself. Landor pleased with her and has since written verses on her. We were taken back by the Enfield stage. . . .

Between nine and ten I went by Landor's desire to Lady Blessington's, to whom he had named me. She is a charming and very remarkable person—and though I am by no means certain that I have formed a lasting acquaintance, yet my two interviews have left a delightful impression. How I wish for Boswell's memory! Lady Blessington is much more handsome than Countess Egloffstein, but their countenance and manners, particularly tone of voice, belong to the same class. Her dress rich and her library most splendid, and her servants numerous so that her appearance is imposing. Besides, her connection with Lord Byron—the book about him which is now publishing by driblets in the *New Monthly Magazine* and some other writings give her in addition the character of a *bel esprit*. Landor, too, in addition says that she was the most devoted wife to Lord Blessington he ever knew—and she writes about him with great warmth. She several times spoke of him with great earnestness—so that though the sister of the Speaker's wife I suppose she is in all points a most respectable woman; but Landor says she was by far the most beautiful woman he ever saw and so was deemed at the court of George IV. This is no slight glory: she is now, Landor says, about thirty; but I should have thought her older.[1] She is a great talker, but her talk is rather narrative than declamatory and very pleasant. She and Landor were both intimate with Dr. Parr, but they had neither of them any *mot* of the Doctor's to relate to match several that I told them of him, nor in the way of *bons mot* did I hear but one in the evening worth copying. I should have said there were with Lady Blessington her sister, a Countess St. Marsault, a small over-painted and sour-looking woman, and a handsome Frenchman of stately person who speaks English well, Count D'Orsay, and he related of Madame de Staël, whose character was discussed, that one day being on a sofa with Madame de Récamier, someone placing himself between them exclaimed: '*Me voilà entre la beauté et l'esprit.*' On which Madame Staël exclaimed: 'That is the first time I was ever complimented for beauty.' Madame de Récamier was thought the handsomest woman in Paris, but by no means famed for *esprit*. This was praised for its delicacy and not considered as offensive irony; surely it would have been in England! Nearly the whole conversation was about Lord Byron, to whose name perhaps Lady Blessington's will be attached when her beauty survives only in Sir Thomas Lawrence's painting and in the engravings. She is, however, by no means an extravagant admirer of Lord Byron, at least not of his character, and makes such admissions concerning him as will satisfy the enemies of Lord Byron. She went so far as to say that she thinks Leigh Hunt gave in the main a fair account of Lord Byron—not that she knows Leigh Hunt: she keeps aloof from all the literary connections of Lord Byron and spoke with great bitterness of Moore, against whom she is incensed. She mentioned among the causes of offence a note in the tenth volume to a poem copied from Lady Blessington's *Conversations* implying that it was not intended for the public—Moore having himself printed so many much worse of which the same may be said. Lady Blessington threatens to expose him, which she could do by

[1] She was 43. Born Marguerite Power in County Tipperary, of Irish parents, in 1789, she was married to the Earl of Blessington, 1818; was left a widow, 1829; and died in Paris, 1849.

repeating Lord Byron's contemptuous words and epigrams against him. One she mentioned. Lord Byron used to say: 'Tommy makes pretty *sweet* verses—sweet indeed, no wonder—he was fed on plums and sugar-candy by his father, the Dublin grocer.' It seems, according to Lady Blessington, that Lord Byron was incapable of loving any one with constancy. She repeated a most ferocious and scornful epigram against Rogers by Lord Byron, and he did not conceal his dislike of Hobhouse even while he confessed that Hobhouse had been a sincere friend. If, therefore, Lord Byron could attack his friends as he did, there is nothing remarkable in his hatred of Southey, against whom there exists an unpublished satire. Lady Blessington says that Byron's hatred of Southey originated in Southey's saying that Lord Byron was *the lover of two sisters*, Mrs. Shelley and Miss Clairmont—not that he was offended by the immorality imputed to him, but the bad taste of loving so vulgar a woman as Mrs. Shelley. By the bye, on my denying the vulgarity of Mrs. Shelley, Landor concurred in Lord Byron's judgment: I am more likely to be convinced of the justness of other imputations on Mrs. Shelley. She was hated intensely by Lord Byron; indeed, he also could not endure Miss Clairmont though she had a child by him—she forced herself on him, and declared she would have a child by the greatest poet of the age! Mrs. Shelley is said to be a great liar. This was Lord Byron's opinion of her, and she is accused of treachery in having opened a packet of letters from Lord Byron to Countess Guiccioli entrusted to her by Count Gamba, from which she supplied extracts to Moore. With difficulty the Guiccioli has got back the letters and means now, at some future time, to publish them and take her revenge on Mrs. Shelley. Mrs. Shelley sent to Lady Blessington to request her forbearance towards herself, and still more her sister, who would be ruined were an exposure to take place. 'This,' said Lady Blessington, 'I replied I should do out of regard to my sex.' Lord Byron was enraged that to the very last Shelley could never be made conscious of the artificial character and worthlessness of his wife. The best thing left by Lord Byron with Lady Blessington is a copy of a letter written by him in the name of Fletcher giving an account of his own death and of his abuse of his friends—humour and irony seemingly unusually graceful. Lady Blessington does not scruple to speak of the habitual insincerity of Lord Byron and of the immorality of his habits; I shall be very curious now to read what she has printed. She says Lord Byron was aware that Medwin meant to print what he said and purposely *hummed* him. She spoke of a novel I have somewhere read about in some magazine, called *The Three Brothers*, from which, if it were not written by Lord Byron, he has stolen the stories and many a detail of his works. Speaking of general literature, she praised excessively and everybody praised excessively, *Anastasius*[1]—a book I must therefore read again—though Julius Hare speaks of it, as I feel concerning it, that it is an odious book. Lady Blessington seems to be intimate with Bulwer; she is also acquainted with Dr. Maginn, the editor of *Fraser's Magazine*, and had influence enough to prevent her name appearing in *Fraser* invidiously against Bulwer.

These are all the memoranda, not of this evening only, but of the next.

SEPT. 29th . . . I went to Mrs. Dashwood's, where were Landor and Julius Hare; I then walked out with Landor in search of a conveyance to Highgate. We came eastward, took soup at Groom's and then hired a cab which took us to Coleridge's. We sat not much more than an hour with him; he was horribly bent and looked seventy years of age—nor did he talk with his usual fire but quite in his usual style. A great part of his conversation was a repetition of what I had heard him say before—an abuse of the Ministry for taking away his pension, he speaking of himself as having devoted himself not to the writing for the people, whom the public could reward, but for the nation, of which the King is the representative. The stay was too short to allow of our entering upon literary matters. He spoke only of Oriental poetry with contempt, and he showed his memory by alluding to Landor's juvenile poems in which were some said to be by: [?] but which were in fact original. Landor and he seemed to like each other. Landor spoke in his dashing way, which Coleridge could understand and he concurred with him. Indeed, I found Landor both with Coleridge and Lady Blessington more of an assentor than I should have expected. After a too short chat, we drove back. Then we called for a few minutes on Miss Flaxman, and I exchanged some volumes of Goethe at Stumpf's. I then came home to dress and at half-past seven I was again at Lady Blessington's. We had Count D'Orsay and Countess St. Marsault, Colonel Lister—a man of fashion, the look and manner of a sensible man. Our conversation a continuation of yesterday's. All included under the above notes. In addition I may say that Lady Blessington was very indignant because Brougham on occasion of Colburn applying for an injunction against a threatened piracy intimated there might be a libel in the book and if so there could be no protection for it. On this she wrote the Chancellor a very severe letter of which she read us a copy. She gave us an account of the suit to establish the marriage at Rome of Mr. Swift with Miss Kelly as represented to her by her attorney Mr. Powell. This evening her ladyship spoke with great indignation of the Duke of Sussex and told stories of him which betray very great meanness

[1] By Thomas Hope.

such as a mere ordinary peer of unroyal blood could hardly dare to be guilty of, such as accepting presents of a diamond cross and returning for it a Tunbridge Wells box, not worth forty shillings, and even fishing for a present of curious ebony chairs, a dozen worth twenty guineas apiece! I was surprised at the freedom with which she related these stories. The chairs I saw at Kensington Palace.

SEPT. 30th My brother Hab came to breakfast with me at nine. Landor promised to be with me at the same time and he came quarter before eleven! However, in return he stayed with me till past three. We were occupied reading from the *Tatler* Hunt's answer to Moore's *Life of Byron*. Hunt has published Moore's letters to him, which certainly prove Moore's duplicity and insincerity to a degree unusual, I hope, even among the literary companions of the great. We also read odd manuscript things which Landor had never seen, by Lamb, etc. When Landor went I continued writing the preceding memoranda of my visits to Lady Blessington and then I went to the Athenaeum, where I took coffee and chatted with Worsley. I wished him to go to Miss Flaxman's with Mr. Landor, but he did not come. However, with Landor came Mrs. Dashwood, Julius Hare, and a Mr. Cholmondeley: as all the Denmans were there the room was full. We stayed till past ten and Landor and the rest seemed all delighted with their visit. The drawings of Flaxman were admired and eulogised by all the party. . . .

OCT. 2nd . . . Today I left a card at Lady Blessington's, which I ought to have done before. Ayrton gives a very different account indeed of Lady Blessington from what Landor had done, and I fear the true one. Tonight I looked over the first three articles of her *Conversations with Lord Byron*. There is nothing remarkable in them—not even interesting except what interest the name of Lord Byron gives. . . .

OCT. 11th . . . The rest of the day was spent over Lord Byron's *Life*. The more I read of the book the less I like both writer and subject of it, though certainly Lord Byron rises in my estimation of his talents. . . .

OCT. 20th . . . Could settle to nothing, Lord Byron's *Life* had so completely taken possession of me. His letters are at least a psychological phenomenon. There were bursts of generous feeling throughout his life in behalf of oppressed humanity. This I believe has been found in many men who were nevertheless the slaves of their appetites, in the way of which they suffered no principle to influence them. . . .

OCT. 22nd . . . Reading Moore's *Byron*, especially the pamphlets about Pope; Byron's strange judgment about Pope was merely given to the world out of spite and affectation. It is, I think, impossible that his love for Pope could have been genuine. It would have produced fruits. . . .

OCT. 25th Today I read the *Hill and Valley*—Miss Martineau's[1] political economy tale. A book over-praised from party feelings but not so bad as one might have expected from the pedantic annunciation [*sic*] of the object. It teaches a useful doctrine—the evil of destroying machinery. Old Armstrong, the recluse, and the hardworking beggar-miser, Paul, are good characters at least. . . .

OCT. 27th Read this morning early *Brook Farm*, by Miss Martineau, intended to illustrate the advantage of small over large farms and to show the prosperity of Brook produced by the enclosure of a common. I fear Youngman's remark is true—that the Man, not the Lion, has been the painter, and he justly says that such tales ought to be founded on real facts and a faithful representation of the state of things, and he denies, I dare say truly, that labourers can be as well off as here represented. After breakfast I made a call on Bakewell and he took me to the house of the Martineaus and I was introduced to the authoress—who pleased me quite as well as her books. She is agreeable in her person and her manners (*circa* 30); not old-maidish and not offensively blue in the colour of her conversation. We talked of her books—I presuming to censure the title-page and she modestly ascribing to the title-page her success—not recollecting that party spirit had done as much for her as a good and attractive title usually does. She will go on to the extent of twenty-four tales. She spoke to me about my Goethe articles, not in compliment, but civilly, and says they are much inquired about and read. . . .

OCT. 30th Finished Moore's *Life of Byron*—a book of great interest, but giving little satisfaction. The power of Lord Byron cannot be denied; his strength of passion was, however, not accompanied by corresponding *art*; he had neither a sense of moral beauty to attract him to real excellence nor was he under the influence of a sense of duty. His works give me little pleasure. Nor was his poetical imagination strong, but he was a man of wit and an admirable satirist, and occasionally in his noisy expression of his misanthropy, when it seemed to proceed from a consciousness of his own worthlessness, one could feel respect for the truth of the sentiment. . . .

DEC. 28th . . . I also made a call of a different character indeed on Countess Blessington. Old Jekyll was with her—he recognised me and I stayed in consequence a considerable time and am invited generally to go in the evening—which I shall do but not soon or frequently. The conversation was various and anecdotic and several matters were related worth recollecting, but I made other calls afterwards so that all has escaped me. Lady Blessington spoke of Lord Byron's poem on Rogers,

[1] Harriet Martineau, author of *Illustrations of Political Economy*.

which is announced.[1] It will kill Rogers, she says. It begins: 'With nose and chin that make a knocker. With wrinkles that defy old Cocker', and his whole person is most malignantly portrayed. It concludes with a sneer; it being asked by what he is known: 'Why, he made a pretty poem.' Lady Blessington says Lord Byron spared no one, mother, wife, or friend; it was enough to raise his bile to praise any one in his presence; he would instantly fall abusing the friend that left him. . . .

1833

JAN. 13th . . . I concluded the night at the Athenaeum, where I met with Disraeli,[2] with whom I talked for a long time. He is more of a philosopher than I had any idea—it seems an *anti*-supernaturalist—at least not alarmed at any freedom of speculation. . . .

JAN. 14th . . . I finished the *Memoirs of Dr. Burney*. I know not when I have read so ill-written a book. It is not destitute of interesting matter, yet the proper names which so frequently occur raise disappointment continually. The reverence which Madame D'Arblay manifests for the Royal Family is even provoking: even that for Johnson and Burke is beyond bounds, but it excites no displeasure. The worse fact after all is that the book shows none of the talent for which in her youth she was famous. It tends to favour the extravagant remark cited by Hazlitt—that authors spend their life after twenty in teaching what they had learned and thought before.

JAN. 21st . . . At the Athenaeum . . . there was a stranger whose jokes I found very attractive to Ayrton, Amyot, etc., before I found he was James Smith, the brother of Horace. He has a genteel air with him, but after all the company of a man who is continually repeating his own epigrams and *bons mots* would be agreeable only every now and then.

JAN. 31st . . . I had a pleasant few hours in the Strand Theatre—Miss Kelly gave a performance alone, of Dramatic Recollections and Imitations, not of individuals, but of general nature. She looked old and almost ugly, and her singing was unpleasant, but some parts of the performance were very agreeable indeed; I am sure that the Prologue and a great part of the text is written by Charles Lamb—other parts, especially a song, I believe to be by Hood. What I particularly enjoyed were the anecdotes of John Kemble and his kindness to her when a child; her eulogy of Kemble was

[1] *Question and Answer*, first published in *Fraser's Magazine*, 1833.
[2] Isaac Disraeli.

affecting; her admiring praise of Mrs. Jordan also delightful; less cordial and satisfactory her mention of Mrs. Siddons. She related what I think incredible, that when as Constance Mrs. Siddons wept over her, her collar was wet with Mrs. Siddons's tears. The comic scenes were better, I thought, than the sentimental: I liked particularly an old woman, a Mrs. Parthian, who had lost her memory and makes *Gentleman* Smith *Adam* Smith, who wrote some pretty songs on political economy, and [speaks] of a person whose addresses were rejected at Drury Lane. This joke also I suspect to be Lamb's. Also a capital character, the keeper of a caravan of wild beasts, who asks for orders as belonging to one of the profession; she condescends to notice Miss Kelly as the best in her line, but makes a comparison of her 'beasteses' with actors, naturally in favour of her own. Is not this Lamb's?

MARCH 26th . . . I had (a rare occurrence) an open evening. I availed myself of it to do what I had so long put off, call on Lady Blessington, and enjoyed my two hours' chat with her so much that I wonder at my reluctance to go. I found her alone, and we talked on the old topics, Landor and Lord Byron. She lent me a letter from Landor—it contains merely that he has lost £700, adding that to a debt of £25,000, by his poems, since he would not suffer Moxon to lose by an improvident bargain. Hare is gone to Naples; Lady Blessington says he wrote about me, but that letter she did not give me. He complains of Arnold, who will neither study nor fence with him: 'He will dance worse than I do, and I have suffered more from bad dancing than from all the other misfortunes and miseries of my life.' Lady Blessington spoke with bitterness of Rogers; she says he is most malignant; she has seen both Rogers and Moore. . . . We talked about Madame de Staël—I related some anecdotes about her, and my stories were well received, but the Baron [d'Heaupet] spoke by no means kindly of her. She spoke of Chateaubriand as a very vain man—courting all parties to get a little praise. . . I shall call again soon. . . .

APRIL 6th . . . At home over books, etc., till late, when I went to J. P. Collier's to dinner; a very agreeable afternoon. There were Amyot, Sheridan Knowles, who was very flat and poorly—he said he was ill—until he was roused by brandy and water and then he became rather noisy (he has a sensible face, but he manifested no power of conversation: one would not have suspected in him the author of *The Hunchback*); Reynolds—he seemed today an agreeable man—I had not seen him for many years, since I conceived a dislike to him as the author of the parody on Wordsworth's *Peter Bell*; Dyce, the clergyman editor of Shirley's plays, an agreeable man, a professed admirer of Wordsworth. . . . The talk was literary and desultory; I incidentally heard that Thomas Holcroft was the author of a scandalous article entitled *Hazlitt's Last Hours*, in which Basil Montagu is attacked for refusing to Hazlitt just before £50 which Hazlitt wanted to give a worthless woman by whom Hazlitt was at the last fascinated. Reynolds is the author of the text of Miss Kelly's Recollections. I thought they had been by Lamb. . . .

APRIL 9th . . . I reached the Lambs at tea-time; I found them unusually well in health but not comfortable. They seem dissatisfied with their landlord and landlady and they have sold all their furniture, so that [they] seem obliged to remain lodgers. I spent the evening playing whist, and after Lamb and his sister went to bed I read in his album (Holcroft's *Travels*, pasted with extracts in manuscript and clippings out of newspapers, etc.). Lamb says that he can write acrostics and album verses, and such things at request with a facility that approaches that of the Italian *improvisatori*, but that he has great difficulty in composing a poem or prose writing that he himself wishes should be . . . excellent. The things that cost nothing are worth nothing. He says he should be happy had he some literary task. Hayward has sent him his *Faust*; he thinks it well done, but he thinks nothing of the original: 'How inferior to Marlowe's play; one scene of that is worth the whole! What has Margaret to do with Faust? Marlowe makes Faust after the original story possess Helen of Greece!'

APRIL 10th I read in bed all sorts of things. Looked into Tennyson's poems. They seem to have fancy but nothing else. We played three rubbers of whist after breakfast. I left them after one and walked home through the Green Lanes. . . .

MAY 9th . . . In the evening I went to the Antiquaries and afterwards to Lady Blessington. Strange I never leave her without increased kindness, and yet, having left her, I feel reluctant to go again. She told me this evening that she wrote her forthcoming novel, *The Repealer*, because she was urged to turn into a novel a pamphlet which she had written against O'Connell. She wanted £500 for a brother who is recently gone to India—her income not being large—and for that she wrote the book in five weeks. This is her story. Telling this to Masquerier, he said: 'She did not tell you what she gave to the person who assisted her. I know a poor man, who would be ruined were he named, who says that he writes for Lady Blessington, and is paid by her for his assistance!' . . .

MAY 22nd . . . I accompanied Naylor to the conversazione of Sass the drawing-master. . . . Old Godwin I spoke with. He began by saying he did not know me—said: 'It is ten years since I have seen you,' but chatted still and seemed irresolute whether he should be affronted with me or not. . . .

MAY 27th . . . Read in the *Spectator* of the week a regular puff of myself. It is said, speaking of Mrs. Austin's book, *Characteristics of Goethe*: 'We detect among the contributors the Englishman who is the most of a German among [the] English, who was acquainted with Goethe and Wieland, etc., who has written an admirable critical catalogue of all Goethe's works in the *Monthly Repository*. His recollections of Wieland are peculiarly graceful and instructive.' Such a compliment might have pleased me, but I suppose it to be written by Southern. Prandi says he has five guineas a week for doing the literary department of the *Spectator*. . . .

MAY 30th . . . I went out with Mrs. Aders to Pickersgill's to see his painting of Wordsworth. It is in every respect a fine picture, except that the artist has made the disease in Wordsworth's eyes too apparent. The picture wants an oculist. . . .

JUNE 5th . . . The next morning I set out on the longest of my summer excursions. I first saw the Martins at Birmingham and Liverpool. Then went to Wordsworth's, with whom I remained a considerable time, being partly at his house and partly at Ambleside and making an intermediate stay at Keswick.

Then Wordsworth accompanied me round the Isle of Man, and thence to Greenock, Oban, the visit to Staffa and Iona, and finally left me at Inveraray. . . .

[*Travel Journal.*] JUNE 14th [*Kendal.*] . . . I reached the Salutation Inn a quarter after five in capital spirits. Took tea in the common room and then strolled up to Rydal Mount, where I met with a cordial reception from my kind friends, but Miss Wordsworth I did not see—nor yet have seen. I was warmly pressed to take a bed, which I have hitherto resisted. I spent a few hours very delightfully, enjoyed the improved walk in Mr. Wordsworth's garden, from which the views are admirable, and had most agreeable conversation *de omni scibili*, with no other drawback from our pleasure than Miss Wordsworth's absence, and the state of her health. . . .

JUNE 15th . . . I had not yet seen Miss Wordsworth. I was at Rydal Mount by twelve, and I was admitted to her and had a comfortable chat with her before dinner. She looked surprisingly well to my apprehensive eyes, and I found her able to talk as usual, but she was not allowed to grow warm on politics, nor was I permitted to stay long, as even my talk was stimulating. I had time to relate a few of my travelling anecdotes. After dinner Wordsworth took me to a house building for Dr Arnold, master of [Rugby] School, where he had directions to give. Like every spot here, a beautiful site for a house . . .

JUNE 17th . . . Mrs. Wordsworth had also written to say that Wordsworth's son, etc., having postponed their visit I *must* take up my residence there. The weather continued very bad. I had therefore no other occupation than reading in Lord Byron the first canto of *Don Juan*, which amused me. . . .

N.B.—Wordsworth related to me this evening the origin of Lord Byron's animosity to him. Wordsworth wrote a letter to a lady warning her against hoping for public favour as a poetess on account of her sensibility and true poetic feeling, and remarked that the only two poets of the day who enjoyed popularity were men *one of whom had no feeling*, and the other had none but perverted feelings. This letter had been betrayed to Lord Byron, who assigned this to Rogers as the justification or, at least, excuse for his attack on Wordsworth. I would further add, with reference to Lord Byron's untrue anecdote, that he insinuates that he could authenticate it by poetic genealogy. If there were any origin in fact for the imputation, what poet so likely to spread a misapprehension or exaggerated rumour as Rogers?

JUNE 18th I rose early, packed up and sent off my luggage by the morning stage. . . . The rest of the day I remained with the family. I had an agreeable lounging day. I looked over the books. I had two short conversations with Miss Wordsworth, who is able only for a short time to bear the stimulus of conversation. . . . Wordsworth and I late, and in spite of the rain, called on Mr. and Mrs. Harrison, who have a handsome house at Ambleside. Mrs. Harrison is a cousin of Wordsworth. . . . I went to bed with a feeling of pride and satisfaction at being the guest of Wordsworth.

JUNE 19th A very wet day, so that I did not stir out of the house till evening, when I had a stroll with Mrs. Wordsworth on the terrace, and afterwards a walk with Mr. Wordsworth on the road to Ambleside with Mr. Hamilton. So all day was spent reading and talking. Wordsworth is become more diffuse in disputation, more like Coleridge. His topics are the alarming prospects of society from the prevalence of democracy, in which I share, though not to the same degree, and the *art* of poetry, in which I can only listen and receive instruction. I hear much that I cannot with propriety write down. My reading was Miss Wordsworth's journal, which I shall go through, of our Swiss tour. It is an agreeable refresher of my memory. . . .

JUNE 20th . . . I would have walked out after breakfast in spite of a clouded sky, but Wordsworth was interminable in his political tirades against the Ministry for their Church reforms, etc. . . .

JUNE 23rd . . . This idle sojourning must have an end. Tomorrow

Wordsworth junior, etc., will come, and I must remove to the inn. The weather is improving, and we might proceed on our tour, but Wordsworth has discovered that business will not allow him to set out for a fortnight. I must while away my time as I can at Keswick, etc. . . . I read in Miss Wordsworth's journal and I assisted in dragging her in her garden-chair in the garden. She enjoyed the varied scene. The improvement in her health is a sign of the more genial air which, in the absence of rain and winds, prevails. In the evening Wordsworth and I, accompanied by Mr. Hamilton, enjoyed a fine walk towards Grasmere.

JUNE 24th . . . Miss Wordsworth's journal occupied the greatest part of the day, except that I was not a little engaged by Wordsworth's very earnest political discussions. . . . At five we went to dine with Mr. Hamilton. . . . It was a very agreeable afternoon. We talked of English politics and German literature. I found Hamilton not at all favourable to the German language and opinions. He and Wordsworth agree on this subject as well as on another which will soon become a subject of national interest—the influence of America on our political institutions. They have a violent impression against the perilous and even mischievous course which the people and Government of North America are pursuing. They both think that the constitution gives the actual majority to the *mob*, and therefore the necessity of flattering the supreme rural power must lead to ruinous measures. John Wordsworth joined us in the evening. . . .

JUNE 25th . . . I drove Miss Wordsworth today in her chair in the garden. She is improving, and if the weather becomes warmer . . . she may become stronger. She is still very weak indeed. . . .

JUNE 26th . . . I left my very kind friends and had a very interesting walk [over the fells to Borrowdale]. . . . I put up at the Royal Oak, where I had a good bed. I had a 'crack' with Judith, the old woman who is in possession of Miss Barker's house. . . . Judith inquired with great kindness of *ould* Mr. Wordsworth and *ould* Miss Wordsworth, and, by the bye, my Langdale companion spoke of William Wordsworth [junior] as of one 'much talked of'. I believe he passes there for a greater man than his father. . . .

JUNE 27th . . . In the evening I went to Southey's, where I passed a very agreeable evening. . . . I had a cordial reception from the Laureate, and found the whole family very amiable. . . . With Southey I had a long and amicable chat on all kinds of subjects. On politics he was by no means so anxious and earnest as, but if anything rather more violent than, Wordsworth. That is, their turn of mind is different. He spoke with indignation of the old Tory branch of the administration, such as Lord Palmerston, etc., declared Stanley [Lord Derby] to be the most dangerous man among them, the most shuffling and shifting. Of the leaders, Lord Grey, Lord John Russell, Lord Althorp, he spoke rather in contempt than anger. On the whole, I could not often greatly differ from him, his greatest fault being that, like almost all, he is one-sided. . . .

JUNE 28th . . . After a poor dinner and a nap, etc., I went to Southey's . . . and I had a long and very agreeable desultory chat with the poet. He read me copious additions to the *Devil's Walk*, only too earnest. He says he shall leave behind him his memoirs. His articles in the *Quarterly Review* would make twelve such volumes as those two already published of moral and political essays. . . .

. . . I am now looking over Miss Wordsworth's Scotch journal. She travelled with her brother and Coleridge. Had she but filled her volume with their conversation rather than minute description! One saying of Coleridge is recorded. Seeing a steam engine at work, Miss Wordsworth remarked that it was impossible not to think it had feeling—a huge beam moved slowly up and down. Coleridge said 'it was like a giant with one idea.'

JUNE 30th . . . My evening I spent again with Southey—an agreeable evening. We read German and had the same sort of political and moral conversation which we had before. Southey is a most amiable man, and everything I see in him pleases me. . . .

JULY 3rd At length a change of weather—I hope so, at least. I had begun to despair of carrying my intended journey into effect. Now I have hopes. But I am apprehensive of Wordsworth's engagements and apprehensions. . . .

JULY 4th . . . It did not actually rain. I received a letter from Mrs. Wordsworth inviting me to return as Wordsworth cannot venture to set out for the Isle of Man *this* week. I know not what to do. . . . Took my tea as usual with Southey, and we had a pleasant chat. Southey read me a curious correspondence between himself and Brougham soon after he became Chancellor. Brougham . . . begged Southey to give him his opinion on the sort of patronage which usefully and safely might be given by the Government to literature. The letter of Brougham I thought wordy and full of commonplace. Southey's answer was a very good one—cutting, with all the forms of courtesy. Alluding to the new order which was at the time given to some distinguished men of science, Southey wrote: 'Should the Guelphic Order be made use of as an encouragement to men of letters, I for my part should choose to remain a Ghibelline.' This was repeated as a good joke by Sydney Smith to a friend of Southey's. . . .

JULY 9th . . . I had an agreeable chat with Miss Wordsworth though [she was] by no means well, and I dined with the Wordsworths. After tea I accompanied Mrs. Wordsworth to Grasmere—another delicious walk. . . . One charm of this district is its infinite variety, and one of the great excellencies of Wordsworth's poems and also his prose writing is the perfect discrimination between them all.

JULY 13th [*Whitehaven.*] . . . Before nine o'clock the Wordsworths [poet and John] came. . . . By half-past nine we were under way. . . . Nothing could exceed the beauty of the voyage. . . . On arriving at Douglas . . . we were surprised by the cheerful, pleasing appearance. . . .

AUG. 22nd [*Edinburgh.*] I received yesterday a favourable account of Miss Wordsworth's health.

SEPT. 13th . . . I reached Rydal Mount between five and six and received from my kind friends the same cordial welcome I had experienced three months before. I found Miss Wordsworth able to walk about the room without a crutch. . . . The evening was spent in relating to my friends the adventures of the last month.

SEPT. 15th . . . Had a discussion with Wordsworth on his favourite theme, the necessity of an establishment of the Church, and the reasonableness that the minority should contribute to support—a doctrine I accede to, while I assert the monstrous injustice of maintaining the English Church in Ireland against the will of the people. . . . I had also today agreeable chat with Miss Wordsworth. . . .

SEPT. 17th . . . Walked to Mrs. Fletcher's at Thorney Hough. A pleasant chat to me—perhaps not to Mrs. Fletcher, for I as energetically as I could exposed the dishonest course taken by her friend Jeffrey in the *Edinburgh Review* against Wordsworth's poetry. She on the other hand lauded the *Review* for its heroic support of liberal opinions when it was perilous to do so in Scotland, risking friends and fortune in the enterprise. . . .

SEPT. 18th . . . The greater part of the day spent with Wordsworth in most interesting conversation which, were it right, I would gladly insert here. Also heard Mrs. Wordsworth read the unprinted Scotch poems which at some future time will furnish a third series, not at all inferior to those of the two former journeys. Two sonnets I bring away with me, to be carefully made known. I had also very pleasant chat with Miss Wordsworth, I was glad of an excuse for staying, the more so as it is so very doubtful whether I shall ever see dear Miss Wordsworth again. . . .

NOV. 8th [*London.*] . . . I then walked to Edmonton. My first visit to Lamb in his new residence. Bating the circumstance that he is in the house where his sister has been, and, I fear I may add, is occasionally and regularly under restraint, it is a comfortable place. We had several hours of agreeable dummy whist—the greatest pleasure Miss Lamb can have. . . .

1834

JAN. 6th [*Brighton.*] Breakfast with Rogers and his sister by invitation. With them was Stewart Rose, a deaf and rheumatic man; he looks prematurely old. He talks low, so I should not have guessed him to be a man of note. Rogers was very civil to me, and there was an air of friendliness which is, I suspect, the mere surface of good manners. He is famous for being a good talker. I can record nothing perhaps that deserves notice, but still his conversation was pleasant to recollect. His most solid remark was on literary women: 'How strange it is that while we men are modestly content to amuse by our writings, women must be didactic. Miss Baillie writes plays to illustrate the passions, Miss Martineau teaches political economy by tales, and Mrs. Marcet sets up for a general teacher, not only in her dialogues,[1] but in fairy tales, and Miss Edgeworth is a schoolmistress in her tales.' We talked chiefly of literary and public men. Rogers praised Lord Liverpool for his liberality, which he learned late in life of Canning and Huskisson. When young he was the butt of his companions at college (at Christ's, Cambridge). There being a party at some gownsman's (I believe Canning), he broke in: 'I am come to take tea with you.' 'No, you are going to the pump.' They literally ducked him at the college pump. Yet the man who could submit to such indignity became Prime Minister. Canning, before he joined him, treated him very ill. Stewart Rose repeated some of the lampoons. Huskisson, Mackintosh declared, had done more to enlighten the nation by introducing to Parliament just notions on political economy. He had great difficulties to encounter. Of Lord Byron I spoke freely, and my freedom gave no offence. Rogers related the story Wordsworth told me of the reason why Lord Byron wrote against him. A private letter of Wordsworth's had been betrayed to him. But Wordsworth told the story better. . . . Rogers related that he brought Lord Byron and Wordsworth together to a *tête-à-tête* dinner. Wordsworth tried to talk his best and talked too much—he did not appear to advantage. Wordsworth was with Rogers when Lord Byron called to give an account of the assassination of Perceval. Rogers

[1] *Conversations for Children on Chemistry; on Natural Philosophy; on Vegetable Physiology; on Political Economy*, etc.

made inquiries about Wordsworth with obvious interest. He spoke of him with great liberality of praise, but remarked on his incapacity to tell a story, i.e. in verse. . . .

JAN. 8th . . . We dined with Horace Smith. A genteel dinner and a company I should presume far above the average of Brighton. . . . Our host is an excellent talker, and is full of anecdote. . . . Smith told us today, and with effect, the story of a Scotch merchant who, at the end of the year, being told by his cashier that the profits had been unusually large, called in his family to return thanks to the Lord for His mercies. But just as prayer was about to begin the clerk came in: 'Oh, sir, I made a sad blunder; I put down to the credit of the account the date of the year, 1808. It has not been at all a good year.' 'Oh, you may rise up then; we won't trouble the Lord just now.' Horace Smith acknowledged this evening that his *Gale Middleton* was written under the influence of the enthusiasm excited by the Reform Act. He regretted its party spirit. He is aware that it would have ruined him as an author were he young and had he a reputation to form. At his age and in his present circumstances it is of no consequence. . . .

JAN. 27th [*London.*] . . . Read this evening also Goethe's critical articles on Byron and other English literature. Nothing remarkable. His love of Byron annoys me. He significantly calls Scott the greatest of narrators. He describes his emotions on sitting down to read the *Life of Napoleon*, but writes no more. . . .

JAN. 30th . . . After a long delay I called on Lady Blessington. Sir Robert Wilson, as well as Count D'Orsay and a very genteel and I should guess able man, also came in. The Countess was so charming and all the others were so agreeable that I could not help resolving to be speedy in repeating my visit, and yet I suppose I shall again feel my own repugnance return. One thing, however, I shall not dare to do—ask Wordsworth for an original poem for her *Book of Beauty*. . . .

MARCH 14th . . . There were at Stephen's, Taylor, a clerk in the Foreign Office [*sic*], a man of some presumption if not talent, for he is coming out with two volumes of tragedies at once! Of his judgment and good sense I know but this in illustration, that when the alarm of the cholera took place two years ago he gravely proposed turning the Athenaeum into a cholera hospital. He is somewhat assuming in his tone of conversation and also somewhat of a dandy. . . .

MARCH 20th I had Barron Field and Shutt to breakfast with me, and also Lamb, who, I found, slept the night before in Southampton Buildings. It was but an uncomfortable visit. He would drink a large quantity of brandy and milk on his coming into the room at nine, saying that he had

had but one glass in the morning, and when he left me he would have more! He dines once a month at Cary's, and he is to breakfast with me when he is next in town. To have so excellent a creature, with all his infirmities, in one's rooms is delightful, but mixed with pain on account of the destruction he is rapidly bringing on himself. . . .

APRIL 1st . . . I went to the Countess of Blessington. Young Shee came in—a smart young man. Though Lady Blessington said nothing worth writing down this evening, yet she made herself so very agreeable and seemed so very desirous that I should soon call on her again, that I think I shall not again delay; and yet the old impression returns when I think of all that is said of her. She talked freely of Mrs. Landor—said she did not appreciate her husband. Mentioned the finding of Wallis at her house when she was ill and Landor was away, but I know not whether she meant anything. She spoke of Lord Byron's labour in writing as being greater than was generally supposed: and of Rogers she said that though she had known him do a vast number of munificent actions, yet his malignity in speech at least was such as to justify Lord Byron's satire—he spared nobody.

APRIL 21st . . . Went to Drury Lane and saw *Sardanapalus*. This is one of the most interesting of Lord Byron's works and it kept me in a state of reflection and thought at least, if not of feeling. Macready is most unfitted to represent the indolent voluptuary—he is a man of rigid earnestness of character in his features and air. Though he threw off a great deal of his nature, he could not qualify himself for the part by art; but the character itself is not in nature, it is a mere apology for certain habits and feelings which with egoistic speculation Lord Byron wished to present to the public. He has condescended to resort to clap-trap declamations against war which now and then had effect. Those against the priesthood were little noticed by the audience. In the dream Macready was very pathetic or rather terrible; Miss E[llen] Tree was tender but altogether cold, not at all the Grecian heroine whom Byron wished to portray. The scene with his wife seems a sort of personal apology for the author. Cooper as the virtuous hero gained his full portion of applause. On the whole a purely philosophical drama—it obtained more endurance than I expected—but it will not remain long on the stage. . . .

MAY 28th . . . I then called at Aders's. They were gone to dine with Coleridge. By the bye, Mrs. Clarkson related to me of the Coleridge family that lately the Colonel (the poet's brother and father of Coleridge's daughter's husband), has lately come into the possession of a large fortune. After a time he said to him: 'Oh, brother, you have not congratulated me on my good fortune.' 'Nor have you condoled with me on the loss of my annuity (£100 per annum as a member of the Royal Society of Literature, withdrawn by the present King). It was my all,' said Coleridge. And then the Colonel did *not* say: 'But, brother, I am now very rich, I was always in affluence—therefore I shall make it up to you,' or anything of the kind. Poor Coleridge, is I fear, beyond all hope of recovery or of any future exertion of his very great talents. . . .

MAY 30th . . . A very sad account of Coleridge; he can scarcely be seen by any one, and his condition is very fast breaking up. . . .

JUNE 15th . . . I went late to Lady Blessington. She was there with the Count [D'Orsay] and no one else. Perhaps for that reason I less enjoyed the hour's chat. She speaks very favourably of the young American poet Willis[1] and informs me that Landor has been writing a great deal. He wants £200 for a manuscript which [blank] is willing to print at his own entire risk and at the same time give Landor all the profit. But such a proposal would never be honestly carried into effect. It ought not to be expected, being unreasonable. . . .

JUNE 8th . . . A drive . . . to Highgate, where I called on Coleridge. Green, the surgeon, was with him. I stayed scarcely a minute with him. He was looking not quite so ill as six months ago, but he was in bed. No talk beyond a jocular compliment to me for my health. . . .

JUNE 10th . . . I concluded the evening as usual at the Athenaeum, where I read till one in the last *Quarterly Review*, which gives a very interesting account of Beckford's travels in Italy. He is excessively praised —and so have all his works been, even *Vathek*, to me one of the most odious books I ever laid eyes on. Like Lord Byron (an admirer of the book), Beckford seems to have had no other object of ambition than to exhibit power with an utter recklessness of moral purpose and not unwilling to excite horror and disgust. . . .

JUNE 19th . . . I had to breakfast with me Charles and Mary Lamb and Mr. Willis. Poor Mary Lamb was not strong—but Charles Lamb was quiet. Willis was pleased to have seen them. . . .

JUNE 26th . . . I rode down to Edmonton after an early dinner, where I took tea and had several hours of whist with Charles and Mary Lamb to their evident enjoyment.

JULY 4th . . . I dined with Talfourd in his new residence, Russell Square—a great start in his style of living, as he has made one in his practice. But he is unchanged in his manners, and being essentially a sound-thinking and right-hearted man, there is no present danger of his being corrupted by prosperity. We had a large party. The *star* was Miss Mitford. . . . She is not so entirely uncorrupted, and that by a prosperity

[1] Nathaniel Parker Willis, poet, traveller and gossip, author of *Pencillings by the Way*.

by no means so unequivocal. Her disagreeable, foolish father, the Doctor, was there, and wine made him a nuisance. . . .

JULY 17th I had an agreeable breakfast. Lamb was with me and quiet and pleasant. . . .

JULY 25th . . . Heard with sorrow of the death of a great man—Coleridge! He died with a strong expression of his sense of the unkindness with which he had been treated by his brothers, the Bishop[1] and the Colonel. . . .

[*Travel Journal: Germany.*] AUG. 11th [*Frankfurt.*] . . . Here, too, came Tieck . . . with whom I chatted agreeably. . . . He spoke of Coleridge with great admiration, and heard of his death with great apparent sorrow. . . . The most prominent individual, he who talked the most and the best, was Grimm, one of the *Gebruder* Grimm, the authors of the *Volksmärchen* and of the famous German Grammar. He is a lively talker with a very intellectual countenance—expressive rather of quickness than depth. . . .

AUG. 20th [*Heidelberg.*] . . . Mrs. Hoppner, with whom I had an agreeable conversation, chiefly about Lord Byron, who to the Hoppners always showed himself very amiable. She related some curious facts concerning Lord Byron which I never before heard so distinctly or on such good authority. His little child which died in Italy was by Miss Clairmont, who, Lord Byron declared, threw herself into his arms. He never felt the least regard for her. She had also a child by Shelley. On my remarking that I did not suppose that Lord Byron was intimate with Mrs. Shelley, Mrs. Hoppner assented to this, but said that had such an intimacy arisen, Shelley would have cared little about it. He thought such things natural. She said Shelley might, under other circumstances, have been an unexceptionable character; he had great qualities and genius. Lord Byron used to lament that he could not make such perfect verses as Shelley made. Lord Byron's vanity and excessive susceptibility to reproach and censure betrayed him continually into wrong actions. But he was capable of generous actions. . . .

NOV. 29th [*London.*] . . . I went to Covent Garden, where I saw Lord Byron's *Manfred* without any pleasure whatever except from the splendid scenery. There must be some merit in this poem since Goethe admired it, but as a drama nothing can be worse. . . .

DEC. 2nd I had a long gossip with Courtenay. I went about Wordsworth's Law Life shares which he wrote about, saying he should sell them by Courtenay's advice, they being at an unreasonable price. Courtenay mentioned to me that 22½ was the current price, but that a friend would take Wordsworth's shares at 23. On this, I said I would give

[1] A mistake. Two of his brothers were in Orders, but neither was a bishop.

Wordsworth 23½, which Courtenay at once accepted, and I have since paid Courtenay £117 10*s.* for the shares, which Pattisson will hereafter transfer to me. . . . Courtenay showed me his books and informed me that he had put a considerable quantity of money into Wordsworth's pocket by purchasing shares in the Rock Office. . . . Then I went to Lady Blessington; Willis was with her. I was alone with her, she made herself most agreeable. . . . We talked on public men. Lady Blessington talked with great frankness of her friends: of Lord Lyndhurst and Lady Sykes and young Disraeli[1] she related strange stories. But she declared her conviction that Lord Lyndhurst was privy to nothing dishonourable on the part of his wife, and cited him as an instance of the facility with which great men may be deceived by women. She spoke of a dinner the day before, at which Count D'Orsay was present with other political characters, at Lord Lyndhurst's, among whom was Mr. Barnes. This fact is stated in the *Chronicle* of today and will strengthen the injurious reports against *The Times* more than any other ascertained fact! Lady Blessington is impartial in her friendships. Among her intimates are Lord Lyndhurst and Lord Durham, Sir James Scarlett and Lord Grey. She is visited by Fonblanque, Disraeli, junior, and all sorts of ultras of every kind.

DEC. 30th This day I shall long recollect. I have not put on my shoes—I have been lounging over books but my mind has been wandering from them. I read in the morning papers[2] that *Charles Lamb died on Saturday*—one of the most amiable of men and an admirable genius. Yet he was outliving his faculties and his life was grown a burthen to him. His death must draw after it that of his admirable but wretched sister, who is now in a state of derangement and will probably recover only to hear of her irreparable loss and die. I wrote to Talfourd offering to attend the funeral and declaring that I wished to contribute to whatever might be required for her comfort.

[1] Benjamin Disraeli.

[2] *The Times* of December 29th 1834 had already carried an announcement of Lamb's death, followed by a short appreciation which may be attributed to its editor Thomas Barnes: 'DIED. On the 27th inst., at Edmonton, after a short illness, Charles Lamb, Esq., late of the East India-house, author of the *Essays of Elia*, and of other works, in the 61st year of his age. [Lamb was actually 59.] He was decidedly a man of genius; abounding with original thoughts, and not less remarkable for his power of moving the heart than of amusing the fancy. His amiable qualities converted even casual acquaintances into friends.'

1835

JAN. 1st I had a letter from Talfourd this morning. Lamb's death was after a short illness, an erysipelas, a breaking-up of the constitution. He died without pain. Miss Lamb is quite insane, yet conscious of her brother's death without feeling it, and able to point out the place for the grave. Talfourd left it entirely to myself whether I would go down or not to the funeral. There will be a sufficient number, he says—himself and Ryle (the executors), another from the India House, Moxon, Procter, Allsop, and Cary. Miss Lamb is not able to derive any comfort from the respect shown to her brother. After a long vacillation—the subject was on my mind all day—I resolved to stay here. I wrote accordingly to Talfourd. He writes me word that Lamb has left £1,100 three per cents, which I am greatly surprised at. . . .

JAN. 7th . . . I now regret that I did not attend Lamb's funeral. Neither Barry Cornwall nor Cary was there. Moxon consoles me by the assurance that there shall be published a complete edition of his works, like those of Lord Byron and Crabbe. I shall, by the bye, urge him to include *Mrs. Leicester's School.* He gives a very unfavourable account of the people with whom Miss Lamb is. She ought to remove to Miss James. . . .

JAN. 12th I resolved today to discharge a melancholy duty, and I went down by the Edmonton stage to poor Miss Lamb. It was a melancholy sight, but more to the reflection than to the sense. A stranger would have seen little remarkable about her. She was neither violent nor unhappy, nor was she entirely without sense. She was, however, out of *her* mind, as the ordinary expression is, but she could combine ideas however imperfectly. On my going into the room where she was sitting with Mr. Walden she exclaimed with great vivacity: 'Oh, here's Crabby.' She gave me her hand with great cordiality, and said: 'Now this is very kind; not merely good-natured, but very, very kind to come and see me in my affliction.' I began to stammer out something, I know not what, when she stopped [me]. 'Now don't you be chattering. I am glad to see you, but don't you be teasing me about Mrs. Anthony Robinson. She was a good woman, as good as ever breathed, but she behaved very ill to Mr. Creswell.' And so she ran on about the unhappy insane family of my old friend Anthony Robinson. It would be useless to attempt recollecting all she said, but it is to be remarked that her mind seemed turned to subjects connected with insanity as well as with her brother's death. She spoke of Charles repeatedly but not in a tone of the least sorrow. She evidently had an imperfect sense of her being in want. 'I can maintain myself. I will mend your stockings, and you shall pay me.' Said that when the lawyers had settled her affairs she would manage. 'You know that it is more difficult to settle property when there is a little than when there is a great deal: one wants a book and one a picture; it's very worrying.' She spoke of Talfourd's father and mother (who kept a madhouse) 'Mr. Talfourd was a much cleverer man than his son; he is only a man of industry like you, Mr. Walden; he saw everything and directed everything and was as quiet in the house as if he was not there.' Mr. Walden left us alone. I proposed as an amusement playing piquet with her; she played very well, but was tired at the end of a game, which she won, and she enjoyed winning. She inquired after the Colliers and made me give her Mrs. Proctor's, as well as Mrs. Joshua Collier's address. She spoke of the Wordsworths, said that Miss Wordsworth was ill-treated by her sister-in-law and the family—'all treat her ill; old maids are of no great use in the world, but it is a pity when they are cut off before their time.' She said Charles was shocked at the sight of Moxon's child. He loved the mother[1] and she him, but it would [not] do. The disproportion was too great in their age; but Moxon was not fit for her. 'She is such a nice, elegant creature, and he looks so dirty.' Except this last, every other judgment was, I hardly need repeat here, utterly wild and groundless. When alone she told me not to talk about her much, to say that she did not like to be talked about. She did not want to be visited, she was very comfortable, etc. I got her to talk about her age. She is nine years and nine months older than Charles, and will be soon seventy. She spoke of his birth, that he was a weakly but very pretty child, that he was long a-coming. She knew she had a little brother coming and was impatient to have him to nurse.

These are the recollections of the hour's visit. I have no doubt that if ever she be sensible of her brother's loss—this is knowledge without feeling—it will overset her again. I consider her as irrecoverable, and do not wish her to awake to a sense of her misery. I have no wish to see her again, an object of more compassion. She will live for ever in the memory of her friends as one of the most amiable and admirable of women. . . .

FEB. 16th . . . Saw Moxon today. He informs me that Mary Lamb is now quite recovered and bears her loss with unexpected composure. She expressed her wish to live in town, if she had the means, and Moxon informed her of what I had said and assured her she would not be suffered to want for anything. . . .

[1] Emma Isola, his adopted daughter.

FEB. 26th . . . Came home at eleven. Then began to skim Lady Blessington's *Conversations with Lord Byron.*

FEB. 27th I finished lounging over Lady Blessington's book. It has little worth reading and appears more insignificant compared with Hazlitt's *Conversations of Northcote.* One of the best conversations is that on the subject of the injustice with which the world treats some ladies with severity while others are overlooked altogether. The fair author gave the subject full attention and her reminiscences were sharpened to produce effect. After all, she knew Lord Byron only six weeks. She has not advanced her reputation either for candour or integrity. Nor does he appear as a great talker or thinker. His poetry, such as it is, is all he has to live on in the memory of mankind. . . .

MARCH 2nd . . . I may notice here what more properly belongs to tomorrow morning. Wordsworth is come to London at the suggestion of Lord Lonsdale, the Ministry having intimated a desire to give some place to William. At present, however, nothing has been found. Wordsworth had wished to transfer his place to his son, but that is inexpedient as there will be such an arrangement of the stamp and tax offices as may occasion the retirement of Wordsworth himself on a pension to which he as an old employé will be entitled and which his son could not claim. Among other matters Wordsworth consulted with me about his will. He has proposed my being executor with Mr. Courtenay, which I deem a great compliment to me.

MARCH 3rd. This was a busy and interesting day; I breakfasted with Mr. and Mrs. Wordsworth, Sir Robert Inglis called. Something highly respectable in his appearance; benevolence and simplicity are strongly expressed in his countenance. Mr. Rogers also called. He invited me to dine with the Wordsworths at his house today. I then walked with the Wordsworths to Pickersgill, who is painting Wordsworth in small for Dora Wordsworth, and we sat there a couple of hours—enlivening by chat to Wordsworth the dullness of sitting for a portrait. Called with Mrs. Wordsworth on Moxon. Miss Lamb is in very low spirits and is apprehensive about her circumstances. This she has been told is idle. She must come nearer London—arrangements shall be made for her comfortable and certain maintenance.

At six o'clock I returned to the west and dined at Rogers's with Mr. and Mrs. Wordsworth—Rogers himself did not dine—he was going out at eight. The visit was short. The very rooms would have made the visit interesting without the sight of any one. The pictures and marbles render them delightful—the most perfect taste imaginable. Wordsworth and Rogers disputed about the pictures and in a tone on Rogers's part sub-acid at least. Indeed, in general, Rogers betrayed, though faintly, that spirit which led to Byron's infamous verses. Wordsworth related an anecdote which, elsewhere and with cordial friends only, would have been kindly received, of a person calling on him and thanking him for procuring him an excellent wife. They were both lovers of his poems. He told also a second story of a German as calling on him with a like assurance, and mentioned Hills courting his present wife on a like occasion. Rogers on this related a parody-anecdote. Someone introduced to a lady a blue-stocking and *bel esprit* who burned with impatience to know the author of *The Pleasures of Memory*, but when the introduction took place she had never heard of the book. 'I never tell any other stories about myself.' This was followed by a significant pause: 'For I have none to tell.' I did not venture to look up. During the morning's talk Wordsworth was full of the Poor Law Amendment Bill, on which he will write a note in the appendix to his poems. At the Athenaeum early; a late call on Lady Blessington; she was alone. She told me tales of the Honourable Mrs. Norton, whom she declared to be the mistress of Lord Melbourne.

MARCH 4th. I saw Courtenay yesterday for a few minutes on Wordsworth's business (his will) . . . Called at Pickersgill's. Wordsworth there, but I did not stay. . . .

MARCH 10th . . . I then walked on to Mary Lamb. I found her not so violent in her grief as I feared she would be, but still afflictingly afflicted. She moaned sadly during my visit, complaining that she could not weep. She says she has made up her mind to stay where she is, against which I remonstrated. She confessed that one main reason is the fear of not having the means of living in London. This I declared to be an idle fear, and I urged her to consent to do what *all* her friends concurred in thinking right, without troubling herself with making any plans whatever. She played a single game of piquet, but without pleasure. . . .

MARCH 14th I called on Wordsworth by appointment at Pickersgill's. The small picture is much better than the large one. Wordsworth went with me to see the bust at Denman's; he thinks it a good likeness. I walked further with him and a nephew of his and afterwards called on Moxon. From him I heard the gratifying intelligence that the Trustees of the India House Clerks' Fund have resolved to allow Miss Lamb £120 per annum! This I have written to Talfourd. All anxiety is now at an end about her future subsistence. . . . An agreeable day. Should have mentioned that I called with Wordsworth on Copley Fielding. We had a very pleasant chat on painting, a subject on which Wordsworth talks well. He spoke severely of Martin (not even sparing Turner) and of all the analogous artists in poetry, etc.

MARCH 19th A call from Wordsworth and a consultation about his will. According to his account, his disposable property consists of more than two thousand pounds due to him out of his brother's estate, about two thousand in the Rock Office, including insurance for one thousand, and about four thousand which is invested in annuities. . . .

MARCH 21st . . . I went to Wordsworth. Served as his amanuensis to write from dictation a note to his new publication. . . .

MARCH 22nd Wordsworth came to me at nine and stayed with me till past three. Our whole time was spent in looking over and correcting his preface to the new volume of his poems. Especially a note on the Poor Laws—which will make enemies. . . .

MARCH 23rd After a little reading I went to Wordsworth at Pickersgill's. He returned with me to chambers and we spent several hours in reading his manuscript and I wrote from his dictation—rather a trying task. Wordsworth is accustomed to an amanuensis thoroughly patient and unpresuming to criticise—I could not be so patient and my interference was not always in vain. Wordsworth will aggravate antipathies by his polemical notes. His admirers will find additional cause to admire in his poems. . . .

MARCH 25th . . . Broken in upon by Wordsworth, with whom I made an appointment. In consequence I went at one to the Zoological Gardens, where I was joined by the Wordsworths. A very agreeable lounge in this very interesting spot. There a few animals of great interest. The rhinoceros to me a novelty. These grounds are now widely extended and with a tunnel extend on both sides the public drive. Here we met Julius Hare, with whom Wordsworth and I walked back. Having accompanied Wordsworth to his house, I dined at the Athenaeum. . . .

MARCH 30th . . . Returned to chambers to dress, and at half-past seven I went to Lady Blessington's, with whom I dined. There was a party of about twelve by which I was amused. The only person with whom I had much chat was Frederick Reynolds,[1] whom I helped to get into the Athenaeum, for which he expressed himself duly obliged. He talks with the ease and assurance of one who goes much into company, but I suspect him to be an ordinary person; he is quite so, in his judgment of Wordsworth. He spoke of knowing him. I believe, on recollection, that Wordsworth wrote for his Annual,[2] and was not pleased with the treatment he received from him. The amusing man of the party was a young Irishman, Lover, a miniature painter and an author; he sang and played

[1] Author of about a hundred plays, including *Eloisa*, a tragedy, and *The Dramatist*, a comedy.

[2] *The Keepsake.*

to himself and he told some Irish tales with admirable effect, one of King O'Toole and one of an Irish piper—in both, exquisite absurdities uttered in a quiet tone and dramatically constituted the charm. . . . [Others present included] Willis, the American, who spoke very little: by the bye, he is said to have a poem on the point of coming out. Chorley, the author of *Sketch of a Seaport Town* . . . Count D'Orsay of course did the honours. Lady Blessington quite well, but not very talkative. . . .

April 5th . . . At seven I dined with Rolfe; an interesting party, in all, twelve. The most remarkable man was (Lord) Jeffrey—alias Mr. Jeffrey, the Scotch judge, and so a lord by courtesy without being a nobleman. . . . It was an interesting afternoon. Jeffrey is a sharp and clever-looking man, and in spite of my dislike to his name, he did not, on the whole, displease me, though I introduced the subject of Wordsworth. He began by saying he was an admirer of Wordsworth, and yet he called him arrogant, impertinent, etc., chiefly with reference to his *Preface*. We did not more than skim the subject occasioned by his mentioning that Talfourd had written an article or two for the *Edinburgh Review*. Talfourd had seen him under the gallery of the Commons and Jeffrey meant to call on him. It seems, by the bye, that Talfourd's speech is considered generally as a failure, and yet Jeffrey said it was the speech of a clever man—he must, however, alter his style. It was a bold thing to quote Wordsworth twice. *The Times* has given one quotation; politics were talked, of course. . . .

April 18th . . . Rode down to Hampstead; dined at the Hoares' by invitation, the Wordsworths being there. It was but a dull evening. Henry Coleridge came after dinner and Miss Aikin, Mr. and Mrs. Le Breton, etc., came in the evening. All came to see the poet. Wordsworth was not in good humour during the dinner, but Coleridge brought a letter with bad news from Rydal. Wordsworth's daughter, Dorothy, is alarmingly ill—she eats nothing—so that the doctor advises change of air as the only means of preserving her. Wordsworth, therefore, means to go down to Rydal almost immediately; he will perhaps bring her with him. At all events he must return to have his teeth put in. He was in very low spirits, and I doubt whether Miss Aikin or the Le Bretons heard his voice during the evening. . . .

April 22nd . . . Then took the stage to Edmonton. I found Miss Lamb very much better indeed than could have been expected. She talked with me not indeed cheerfully, but with composure, and we have agreed that she shall remain for the present at Mr. Walden's. I am to send her French novels. I found her reading English Montaigne. After tea and a two hours' chat I walked back. . . .

MAY 10th . . . I began this morning Talfourd's tragedy *Ion*. The affectionate tone of the preface pleased me, and his explanation of the reasons why he printed his work is satisfactory. The poem will not disgust any one, and it will please all the lovers of literature. . . .

MAY 11th Read in bed the third act of *Ion*. This play of Talfourd's has originality of incident at least, and though too flashily written preserves the attention and, without any strongly marked character, gratifies by the general tone of the sentiments. . . .

MAY 13th . . . Finished this morning Talfourd's *Ion*. . . . On the whole this tragedy has raised Talfourd in my opinion. . . .

JUNE 1st . . . Then I went to the Athenaeum, where I read in Coleridge's *Table Talk* with very mixed feelings—pleasure greater than approbation, and very little concurrence in feeling. It was very fine, so I came home past nine to dress and then went to Lady Blessington's. I found her as usual very agreeable. We talked more freely than I had ever ventured before of our friend (Landor). I mentioned the idle report I had heard from Dr. Thomson that he was going to separate from his wife. 'That would not at all surprise me,' said Lady Blessington and Count D'Orsay, too. . . .

NOV. 12th [*Brighton.*] . . . We dined with Horace Smith, a small but very agreeable party, or rather Horace Smith is himself a party. His anecdotes he does, indeed, occasionally repeat, but he relates well, and that serves to excuse repetition. By the bye, Masquerier tells me that formerly Rogers, on Masquerier saying that I was with him, said in his sneering way: 'Can Mrs. Masquerier get in a word?' on which Smith said: 'I know few people who talk so much and so well at the same time.' On another occasion, Masquerier saying that I read walking and lost a book, Rogers said: 'If he were to drop a book out of his hand it should be Wordsworth, for as he worships him he would not object to going down on his knees to it!' Is there wit in this? I borrowed of Horace Smith some numbers of the *New Monthly Magazine*, and was amused by Campbell's *Letters from Algiers*. On the contrary, Coleridge's letters from Germany are not worth reading.

NOV. 22nd . . . I should have said yesterday that I received a most kind letter from Mrs. Wordsworth pressing me to pay them a visit in about a month—urging this as an act of charity. Such an invitation is irresistible and I sent an answer under Charles Buller's frank consenting to go down, provided a lodging can be procured where I can sleep and breakfast—dining with Wordsworth. . . . After nine I went to Serjeant Talfourd's, with whom I had a long and friendly chat about Mary Lamb, Charles Lamb's correspondence, etc. Talfourd says the letters are most delightful, but many are very exceptionable. The later letters, as well as writings, far superior to the earlier. A regard to living friends will render many suppressions necessary, as where writing to Manning, he says: 'Wordsworth says he could write like Shakespeare if he had a mind. So you see nothing is wanting but the mind.'

Nov. 23rd . . . I then went to the Athenaeum where I stayed the whole of the evening and read, *inter alia*, the third volume of Willis's *Pencillings by the Way*. He gives an account of his breakfasting with Charles Lamb at my chambers,[1] as in other cases putting for my name R. He speaks with great delight of Charles Lamb, and yet his account is calculated only to excite contempt. It might have been worse—he does not allude to some melancholy facts I mentioned to him. In his account of his interview with Wilson he makes Wilson say that he never in his life heard Wordsworth quote anybody's poetry but his own. This cannot be true, either Willis or Wilson has said the thing that is not. . . .

Nov. 29th I breakfasted with Mr. Rogers *tête-à-tête* and was with him from ten till one. A very agreeable morning and I left him with feelings of enhanced respect. He evinced a benevolence of disposition which I had not given him credit for. There was very little of that severity of remark for which he is reproached—candour and good sense marked all he said. We talked about Wordsworth, Lord Byron, and Goethe, and I have lent him Mrs. Austin's book. He seems sufficiently prepossessed in favour of Goethe. Of Lord Byron he spoke freely, no allusion of course, to the infamous verses against himself; but he expressed himself strongly of Lord Byron's malice and revenge. He said he would cherish resentment for a word and when the speaker had forgotten it, he would assail him by everything that could wound him. He mentioned his having through inadvertence repeated to him that he had [heard] Wordsworth say: 'I would not give five shillings for all Southey ever wrote.' 'I heard that Byron had printed this, but I went to Murray and declared that I would never see him or Lord Byron again if it were not expunged. It was expunged.' I told him that in fact it appeared in the new edition without his name but I guessed him at once; he was surprised at this. 'But,' said he, 'I have not the new edition and would not on any account possess it.' He spoke very highly of Wordsworth, but with qualifications which would not satisfy Wordsworth's admirers. He thinks he is likely, now, to be overlauded as before he was underrated. I was least prepared for his affirming that Wordsworth is a careless versifier—he thinks his blank verse better than his rhymes. On moral subjects and religion Rogers showed a seriousness I did not expect. He said it was most painful that he recollected so

[1] See *supra*, June 19th 1834.

distinctly his faults. 'But,' said he, 'every man has his kind moments and does occasionally kind actions, of course I as well as others, and it is distressing I cannot recollect them.' 'A Pharisee would,' I replied, 'and surely it is better not.' 'That I acknowledge, but still it is painful.' He produced a small volume which he praised greatly—*Clio on Taste*,[1] by J.U.—one Usher. . . .

DEC. 3rd . . . Went then to Moxon's. With him was Miss Lamb; she was very comfortable, not in high spirits, but calm, and she seemed to enjoy the sight of so many old friends. There were Cary, Allsop, Miss James. No direct talk about her brother. Wordsworth's epitaph she disapproves of; she does not like any allusion to his being a clerk or to family misfortunes. This is very natural; not even dear Mary can overcome the common feeling that would conceal lowness of station or a reference to ignoble sufferings. . . .

DEC. 20th . . . Then went to Serjeant Talfourd's, with whom and Moxon I dined. The evening till past twelve was spent in looking over Lamb's letters to Wordsworth and, when they were gone, Lamb's letters to Manning, which letters are the very best but they require a sedulous sifting. Wordsworth is very particular and has noticed as doubtful what appeared to us unexceptionable, and we were frequently embarrassed and finally I dare say Wordsworth will be dissatisfied as he will be very angry at several things in the correspondence published by Allsop which I have now finished. The worst passages are those in which a doubt is raised whether Wordsworth is a Christian, and Wordsworth's answer: 'When I am a good man then I am a Christian,' is equivocal, and will be taken in different senses. Fonblanque is enraged with the book, and all parties will abuse it alike.

DEC. 25th [*Rydal.*] Having breakfasted, I set out at eight and arrived at Rydal about half-past ten. I was set down at a small house opposite Mr. Wordsworth's lane—kept by a Mrs. Atkins—where I found a fire in the sitting-room intended for me. I was expected last night. Mrs. Wordsworth had left tea and sugar for me and I saw an omen of comfort in these lodgings in the agreeable countenance of my landlady. I, without waiting to dress, ran up to the Wordsworths, from whom I had a very kind reception. They approve of my plan of spending my mornings alone. I have yet had but a short chat with Mr. and Mrs. Wordsworth. The account of poor Miss Wordsworth by no means favourable, but Dora's case seems far more promising. . . .

We dined as they do usually here, very early. One is the dinner hour and the rest of the day was spent within except that we took a walk after

[1] *Clio; or, a Discourse on Taste: addressed by a young lady*, by James Usher.

dinner, that is, Wordsworth and myself, beyond Dr. Arnold's house with the Doctor himself to his house, and I came home at nine. Read till past twelve, when I retired, having at night begun Southey's *Life of Cowper*.

DEC. 26th . . . I have a bad memory and no skill in recording the finer parts of conversation such as may be repeated with honour. What I do recollect and could easily write down are what would expose me to the sort of imputation which Allsop has justly incurred. What it would be disreputable to print, it would be dishonourable to put in the power of others to print, and these idle memoranda *may* survive me. They *may not* if I live long and have ample warning. What I have to say of today will probably be an anticipation of my days during my stay here. I read in bed a couple of hours, for I awoke early. I sat within—not till dinner-time as it happened—for about twelve Mrs. Wordsworth passing in a gig proposed my taking Wordsworth out. I called on him and we had a fine dry walk up Grasmere lake, crossed it, and returned on the western side. I stayed with the Wordsworths, as I generally shall do, the rest of the day, and in the dark hour I walked with Wordsworth by Grasmere lake, also down to Ambleside—the excuse, to ask for a paper. We returned to our tea at six and at nine I came home, having ordered a fire in my bedroom at which I sat till twelve, when I read in bed till one. Such will probably be my life for the next few weeks. I am most comfortably situated. My kind and agreeable landlady makes me excellent toast and I have my own tea—a ham has been supplied by Mrs. Wordsworth. In the evening I take a morsel of bread and ham to keep off the foul fiend. Such is my home life. . . . A cottage-like apartment, very comfortable, a similar bedroom behind; for this I am to pay (Mrs. Wordsworth says) ten shillings a week and three and sixpence for fire—I dare say I shall be most honestly charged for the few things I consume. I must not, however, forget that I spent two hours this morning in looking over those of Lamb's letters which Wordsworth did not choose to send to Talfourd. There are several most delightful letters which one regrets not to be able to print immediately. There are also some which Wordsworth will allow me to copy in part and some from which notes may be taken, viz.: Lamb relates that having borrowed *Cœlebs*[1] of a careful, neat lady he wrote in it and returned it with this verse:

> If ever I marry a wife
> I'll marry a landlord's daughter,
> For then I may sit in the bar,
> And drink cold brandy and water.

[1] *Cœlebs in Search of a Wife*, by Hannah More.

DEC. 27th I read early Southey's *Cowper* till church time. I went to church: but a small congregation in this neat ornament to the village (a chapel-of-ease). Dr. Arnold officiated; he has the face and voice and manner of a man of talents, but his sermon was altogether cold—as bad as the morning itself: I sat shivering without my greatcoat. We dined at one; after dinner I walked with Wordsworth by Grasmere and to Ambleside though it rained a little; at nine I came home. Today full of conversation; it gave me great pleasure to perceive that both Mrs. and Dora Wordsworth are evidently gratified by my being here. They say I have already done Wordsworth a great service by taking him out of himself; both they and he are in better spirits than I could have expected, and Dora—a very sweet girl—is evidently in improving health; Wordsworth is somewhat less intolerant than he used to be and we have had very little sparring yet on politics. Of poor, dear Miss Wordsworth, I hear a melancholy account and I have not yet seen her—nor do I press it. . . .

DEC. 28th A day of uninterrupted quiet enjoyment. . . . I looked over an important document, Wordsworth's will, which required attention and thought, and I continued Lamb's letters till one. After dinner I chatted with Wordsworth *de omnibus rebus* and between three and four we set out notwithstanding the bad weather, for it had rained all the morning and threatened to rain again. We left a message at the door of Dr. Arnold. We strolled on to the shore of Windermere. The angry clouds left Langdale Pikes a grand object—more grand, perhaps, surrounded by black stormy clouds than illumined by the sun—and we made several calls. . . . At night I began reading . . . the *Life of Crabbe*.

DEC. 29th I awoke early and read in bed what I finished soon after breakfast. This *Life* has not much to interest me, because there is not much that interests me in Crabbe's poetry; I take no pleasure in his unpoetical representations of human life, and though no one can dispute that he had a powerful pen and could faithfully portray what he saw, yet he had an eye only for the sad realities of life. As Mrs. Barbauld said to me many years ago: 'I shall never be tired of Goldsmith's *Deserted Village* —I shall never look again into Crabbe's *Village*.' Indeed this impression is so strong that I have never read his later works—I know little about them. Of the *Life* the only parts that are attractive are the account of his extreme poverty and of his introduction to Burke, who at once raised him out of his desperately forlorn condition and made a parson of him. There are also several pleasing letters from the Quaker writer, Mrs. Leadbeater; also from Sir Walter Scott and some of Crabbe's own. I feel infinite respect for Crabbe and may read some two or three of his poems that I may have something like an idea of him.

I dined today with the Hardens at Field Head. John Harden fetched me in his gig—a pleasant drive—an agreeable dinner, and altogether a visit that I enjoyed. Our party consisted of a Mr. Rawlinson,—a barrister of no practice, but a gentleman, residing here, of considerable fortune, a very unpleasant man—his lady and Doctor and Mrs. Arnold. The Doctor is not very much to my taste.[1] He is a dry man and a clever rationalist; his opinions I like better than his principles—that is, he comes to conclusions which I cannot trace to his principles. . . . Wordsworth says and with truth that the Doctor ought not to be a minister of the Church of England. The Doctor is a Church reformer; he is a friend of Bunsen's, whom he, however, thinks to be a Liberal in politics! . . .

DEC. 30th At twelve I left my hospitable friends and had a delightful walk home. . . . Field Head is about five miles from Rydal. I found Wordsworth in low spirits; Miss Wordsworth's disease is taking a sad turn and he has lost all hopes. We dined late today, and before dinner I took a walk with Wordsworth. We met Hartley Coleridge coming to call on Wordsworth, an unlucky chance, for, as we dined late, Wordsworth could not but invite Hartley Coleridge to dinner. We had Mr. Carr to dinner and, therefore, the wine-bottles were not nearly empty. As soon as we sat down Coleridge drank wine with every one, and in consequence, though we were summoned very soon to coffee, poor Coleridge was already drunk—he was far advanced when he came. He went away as soon as the coffee was announced, and Wordsworth was so anxious about him that I followed him and led him to his lodging beyond Grasmere—he was quite unable to walk and fell four times. I had great trouble in getting him home. It broke into the evening sadly; I came home and read the *Life of Machiavelli*. . . .

DEC. 31st . . . Wordsworth broke in upon my reading by proposing a walk at half past eleven. We ascended Mr. Carter's plantations, and after dinner I walked there again in search of a lost handkerchief; with Wordsworth and Mr. Carr at Ambleside; a walk also with Mrs. Cookson, and at night I read over to the Wordsworths some of Lamb's reserved letters in order to pick out passages to be copied, and in this the evening was spent. At night I read in bed as before and looked over various pamphlets which Wordsworth had recommended to me, and these engaged me till late, of which hereafter.

[1] Dr. Thomas Arnold, who had been headmaster of Rugby since 1828. But see Crabb Robinson's entry for Jan. 8th 1836: 'I like him more the more I see him.'

1836

JAN. 1st . . . This morning I made some few extracts from Lamb's letters in order to forward them to Talfourd for his publication. The rest of the day was spent as usual, either in reading or chatting with Wordsworth. It was so bad a day that I took no walk beyond Wordsworth's house and at night I read to Wordsworth two chapters in De Tocqueville[1] with great pleasure. . . . Lately read *An Appeal to Dissenters by a Lay Dissenter*, a pamphlet of 1834 warmly praised by Wordsworth.

JAN. 2nd . . . In the evening I was permitted to see poor Miss Wordsworth. She was in her best state. She knew me but would talk very little with me. She went on repeating without intermission fragments of poetry —her brother's, Cowper's, Dr. Watts's—then repeating the Doxology, and the most melancholy act of all, carried away by the association of ideas, repeating the Amen in a loud tone and mocking a clerk accompanied by loud laughter. Otherwise she repeated the verses with great feeling and fine emphasis. These are her *best* moments—I believe that Wordsworth is now so convinced that her case is hopeless that he will be comforted by her death. Perhaps he, in that event occurring, might find means to go to Italy and I shall be happy to accompany him.

JAN. 5th . . . I have had much talk with Wordsworth on this sad question.[2] He says with the solemn earnestness of a Hebrew prophet that he would die a thousand deaths rather than consent to the appropriation clause in the Irish Tithe Bill! It is mournful to witness and alarming to anticipate the consequences of the opinions and prejudices of even good men on this most difficult of all subjects. I dined today with Wordsworth at Dr. Arnold's. An agreeable afternoon; though the main subject of conversation was one on which I have no pleasure in hearing Wordsworth talk—Goethe, whom he depreciates in utter ignorance. Dr. Arnold seems to be aware of the real objections to Goethe's moral character and is likely to overrate their importance. . . .

JAN. 7th . . . After an early luncheon I walked partly and partly drove with Wordsworth to Elleray, the residence of Lady Farquhar and Mr. Hamilton—the property of Professor Wilson. It stands above the lake of Windermere and enjoys a very wide view of the lake which I next morning saw, though disadvantageously; the mist obscured the lake. We had a very agreeable afternoon. Wordsworth exerted himself and Mr.

[1] *La Démocratie en Amérique.*

[2] The justice of forcing Irish Catholics to pay tithes to Anglican clergy.

Hamilton is a sensible man—a Whig, too—Lady Farquhar seems a very kind and interesting woman. On our walk Wordsworth was remarkably eloquent and felicitous in his praise of Milton. He spoke of the *Paradise Regained* as surpassing even the *Paradise Lost* in perfection of execution, though the theme is far below it and demanding less power. He spoke of the description of the storm[1] in it as the finest in all poetry, and he pointed out some of the artifices of versification by which Milton produced so great an effect as in passages like this:

> . . . pining atrophy,
> Marasmus, and wide-wasting pestilence,
> Dropsies and asthmas, and joint-racking rheums.[2]

in which the power of the final 'rheums' is heightened by the 'atrophy' and 'pestilence.' 'But,' said he, 'I would not print this and similar observations, for it would enable ordinary verse-makers to imitate the practice, and what genius discovered mere mechanics would copy.' 'Hence,' I said, 'I hold critical writings of very little use. They do rather harm.' Wordsworth also praised, but not equally, the *Samson Agonistes*. He concurred, he said, with Johnson in this, that this drama has no *middle*, but the beginning and end are equally sublime.

JAN. 8th The Lutwydges called on the Hamiltons this morning—an uncle of the Athenaeum Lutwydge and of the same class. An agreeable forenoon. Mrs. Wordsworth came at twelve and with her I drove home. The day tolerably fine. I dined with Dr. Arnold; I like him more the more I see him. The Hardens there, also Mr. and Mrs. Harrison.

JAN. 10th . . . I read at night and in the morning the notes to Shelley's *Queen Mab* as well as here and there bits of his poetry. His atheism is very repulsive, but the God he denies seems to be after all but the God of the superstitious. I suspect that he has been guilty of this fault of which I find I have all my life been guilty, though not to his extent,—inferring that there can be no truth behind the palpable falsehoods propounded to him. He draws in one of his notes a picture of Christianity, or rather he sums up the Christian doctrine, and in such a way that perhaps Wordsworth would say: 'This, I disbelieve as much as Shelley, but that is only the caricature and burlesque of Christianity.' And yet this is the Christianity most men believe. As poetry there is much very delightful in Shelley. Read till late in bed.

JAN. 11th Read in bed as usual. Before I had finished writing in this book I had a call from Wordsworth. He required me to look over his

[1] *Paradise Regained*, Book IV, ll. 409 sq.
[2] *Paradise Lost*, Book XI, ll. 486–8.

brother's will and advise in answering a letter from Lightfoot, the husband of his brother's widow. The consideration of this subject occupied us till dinner, after which I took a drive with the Wordsworths. We called on a fine old woman of eighty-three, a Mrs. Freeman—a pleasure to see such a person. Then at Mr. Carr's. . . . In the evening Wordsworth read to us several beautiful sonnets by Bowles and other moderns. I read at night till late.

JAN. 13th . . . It was a wet day and I spent the whole of it with the Wordsworths and in chatting, not reading. It may be worth mentioning that Wordsworth has himself intimated what so many other friends have done, that I ought to leave in writing, if not publish in my life, some account of my life. He is a severe and fastidious judge of writing of every sort and his recommendation is by far the most encouraging I ever received. It is very flattering, but I am by no means of opinion that I have talents of composition equal to the materials. From Wordsworth the recommendation has the more weight because he has very restraining opinions of the limits to be set to the repetition of anecdotes, the publication of letters; he has however, praised my anecdotes of Wieland and says I should do well to give an account of Goethe. He must think, though he does not say that, that I should also have much to say of himself.

By the bye his conversation has been very interesting lately, and had I not so bad a memory that a few hours suffice to obscure all I have heard, I might insert many a remarkable opinion, if not fact. He gave an account of *The Ancient Mariner* written in Devonshire when Coleridge and Wordsworth were together and intended to be published in the *Monthly Magazine* to pay the expense of their journey. It was to have been a joint work. But Wordsworth left the execution to Coleridge after suggesting much of the plan. The idea of the crime was suggested by a book of travels by [Shelvocke] in which the superstition of sailors towards that bird [the albatross] is mentioned. Wordsworth at the same time wrote many of his *Lyrical Ballads*—Coleridge wrote the first four lines of *We are Seven*. (Wordsworth says that Coleridge was in the habit of altogether denying miracles though he professed great attachment to Christianity. Wordsworth's own religion, by the bye, would not satisfy either a religionist or a sceptic.) Read at night De Tocqueville till late.

JAN. 14th A wet day, so that I was confined within doors and at Wordsworth's all day. . . . Reading no new book and chiefly engaged in newspaper reading and in political talk with Wordsworth, who is eloquent but tautological on some subjects—the Irish Church being the standing dish on all occasions.

JAN. 15th Having had no walk yesterday, Wordsworth was with me early this morning to walk to Ambleside in spite of snow, and I found a snow scene quite pleasant in this mountainous country. In consequence I returned to my room after our walk and read alone till near five in De Tocqueville, when I accompanied Wordsworth to Dr. Arnold's. I had sent the Doctor Mr. Malden's address of the Senate to the Council of the London University, which he warmly praised. Wordsworth had also spoken well of it. . . . Our afternoon was a very quiet one—less disputatious than usual—I was allowed to relate travellers' anecdotes, which were well received. . . .

JAN. 17th . . . By the bye I will here put down some scattered notes of talk with Wordsworth. What he appears to believe amounts to this and no more. 'The Atonement is a doctrine which has its foundation in that consciousness of unworthiness and guilt which arises from an upright self-examination—as all the orthodox doctrines are warranted by a humble spirit and all that is best in our moral nature. There is internal evidence for all these doctrines, which are a source of happiness. And the difficulty of comprehending the mysteries of the Gospel is no sufficient reason for rejection. It is not necessary to define with precision the doctrines thus received, and the Church of England has encumbered itself by needless and mischievous attempts at explanation. The Athanasian Creed is one of these unhappy excrescences. Nor does the idea of the personality of the Spirit come with such authority, or claim so imperiously our adoption, as the doctrine of the divinity of Jesus Christ. The thought that an infinitely pure being can receive satisfaction from the sufferings of Jesus Christ and accept them as a satisfaction for the sins of the guilty is declared by Coleridge to be an outrage on common sense. It is a hard saying, nor can I explain it to my satisfaction. I leave this as an awful mystery I am not called to solve. Coleridge used to declare that the belief in miracles is not a necessary part of a Christian's creed; but this is contrary to the express and uniform declaration of the Scriptures, and I have no difficulty in believing in miracles since I consider as superstition the imagined knowledge and certainty which men suppose they have as to the laws of nature.' This I believe is all that Wordsworth can be said to believe, and it is little. It is quite clear that he does not place any weight in the historical evidence, and when I said that I tried to believe, he said, 'That is pretty much my case.' . . .

JAN. 19th A day of reading like all the preceding. I read *Klosterheim* and De Tocqueville. It was also a very fine day and I was invited before dinner to walk out with Dr. Arnold, and a glorious stroll I had, skirting the west bank of Rydal Water up to the point of the Langdale Road where there is a view on Loughrigg Tarn, Elter Water, etc. The scene most beautiful; I enjoyed it four times today, for I returned rapidly to dine and after dinner renewed the walk with Wordsworth to meet the Doctor and his family on their return from an excursion to Dungeon Gill Force. On these walks I enjoyed chatting with the Doctor.

JAN. 23rd I finished this morning the first volume of *The Doctor*, which I shall be content with for the present. I have no doubt, whatever, that it is by Southey. Even its intolerance I fear does not exclude the idea. Towards the end he says of the Puritans: 'of whom it has long been the fashion to speak with respect instead of holding them up to contempt and infamy and abhorrence, which they have so richly merited'! This disgusts me so much that it has fixed me in the determination not to visit the Doctor [Southey] at Keswick this year. In this book there are beautiful serious chapters. The characters of the idiot and of the two Daniels are delightfully executed. The humour is coarse and the tone of the opinions harsh and sectarian with a sort of effort at good humour and kindness. Among the indications of its coming from Southey is the profusion of Spanish literature and old English odd citations. The only German book mentioned is one I gave him several years ago—all the *opinions religious and political are his*. . . .

JAN. 26th . . . By the bye, I wish I could here write down all Wordsworth has said about the sonnet lately—or record here the fine fourteen lines of Milton's *Paradise Lost* which he says are a perfect sonnet without rhyme. But I will hereafter find the passage. . . . Wordsworth does not approve of uniformly closing the sense with a full stop and of giving a turn to the thought in the [sestet]. This is the Italian mode. Milton lets the thought *run over*. He has used both forms indifferently; I prefer the Italian form. Wordsworth does not approve of closing the sonnet with a couplet, and he holds it to be absolutely a vice to have a sharp turning at the end with an epigrammatic point. He does not, therefore, quite approve of the termination of Cowper's sonnet to Romney:

> For in my looks what sorrow couldst thou see
> When I was Hayley's guest and sat to Thee?[1]

The lines in Milton are essentially a sonnet in unity of thought.

JAN. 27th . . . At five reached Mr. Parry's at Grasmere. A genteel dinner party. The Arnolds, Lutwydges, Captain Graves. . . . At night the Doctor [Arnold] accompanied me back. We walked over 'Old Corruption' for so the Doctor has christened in derision the original road between Rydal and Keswick. The first new road he has named 'Bit-by-bit Reform'

[1] Corrected from Crabb Robinson's misquotation.

(I proposed 'Juste Milieu') and the beautiful road by the lake, 'Radical Reform'. We found 'Old Corruption', here as elsewhere, perilous, and by night might have broken our necks. . . .

JAN. 29th . . . I am sorry to recollect that the next page, if ever filled by me, will probably record my departure from this delightful residence. By the bye, I overheard Wordsworth say last night to the Doctor that I had helped him through the winter and that he should gratefully recollect my kindness as long as he had any memory! . . .

JAN. 31st A very snowy day, so that my anxiety was excited. I am still apprehensive that I may be detained on the road. I am sensible of my imprudence in postponing my return till the very last day. I did not go to church this morning, being more usefully employed in drawing up a codicil to Mr. Wordsworth's will to provide against a contingency not likely to occur, but necessary to provide against, namely, the extending to children a bequest given to the sons in case of their death under peculiar circumstances. This occupied me both before and after dinner, being interrupted. I had a walk with Wordsworth and a call on Dr. Arnold. He is much pleased with Dr. Passavant's book. Wordsworth was today most earnest and painfully vehement on the eternal question—Irish Church Reform; but, in spite of my opposition on this vital matter, nothing could exceed his kindness. He expressed very warmly his thanks for my visit. After tea a long chat with him and the ladies on matters of business. It appears that this is the state of his affairs. He has about four hundred and fifty pounds a year from his place and a hundred from Sir George Beaumont for his life. This goes from him at his death. His property besides is small. There are about four thousand pounds in Mr. Courtenay's possession laid out in annuities which will probably produce a much larger sum, dependent on the lives of forty old men. Also he has Rock shares which produce enough to pay the insurance of his life for seven thousand pounds, and after his death they will produce another thousand. If he gets from his nephew the money lent to his late brother there will be two thousand more. Besides, he is now in receipt of something from his poems, perhaps two hundred a year. This may last several years. He may have a few odd hundreds besides some land worth a few hundred pounds, given to his daughter.

It occurs to me that I have not noticed as I ought Wordsworth's answer to the charge brought by Wilson against Wordsworth that he never quotes other poems than his own. In fact, I can testify to the falsehood of the statement; but Wordsworth in addition remarked: 'You know how I love and quote, not even Shakespeare and Milton, but Cowper, Burns, etc. As to the modern poets—Byron, Scott, etc.—I do not quote them because

I do not love them. Byron has great power and genius, but there is something so repugnant to my moral sense that I abhor them. Besides, even as works of mere taste, there is this material circumstance, they came too late, my taste was formed, for I was forty-five when they appeared, and we cannot after that age love new things. New impressions are difficult to make. Had I been young I should have enjoyed much of them, I have no doubt!' I forgot to mention that on Saturday I chatted with Miss Wordsworth. She was much more calm and reasonable than when I saw her before. She sang some of her brother's poems, which she seems to do as a relief from thinking. Her continual rubbing of her head showed the seat of pain. She evidently knew me, and was not irrational in anything she said.

FEB. 1st I left Rydal about eleven o'clock—I took leave of dear Miss Wordsworth. She was perfectly sensible, though her mind is greatly debilitated. From all my friends I took leave with feelings of great tenderness—my esteem for them all being greatly raised during this last most agreeable visit. For though the knowledge that Miss Wordsworth was suffering near us, and that Miss Dora was far from well, were painful to the healthful members of the family, yet these were become habitual to them, and the natural elasticity of the spirits happily enables even persons of strong sensibility like Wordsworth to resist the effect of such impressions and enjoy what was left of pleasurable emotions. So Wordsworth was capable of intellectual activity, and I had the satisfaction of knowing that I called it out. Therefore I call this visit agreeable. By the bye, before I quit Rydal I will add a note or two of Wordsworth's conversation. Talking of dear Charles Lamb's very strange habit of quizzing and of Coleridge's far more equivocal incorrectnesses in talk, Wordsworth said he thought much of this was owing to a *school habit*. Lamb's veracity was unquestionable in all matters of a serious kind. He never uttered an untruth either for profit or through vanity, and certainly never to injure others; yet he loved a quizzing lie—a fiction that amused him like a good joke or an exercise of wit. There was in Coleridge a sort of dreaminess which would not let him see things as they were. He would talk about his own feelings and recollections and intentions in a way that deceived others, but he was first deceived himself. 'I am sure,' said Wordsworth, 'that he never formed a plan or knew what was to be the end of *Christabel*, and that he merely deceived himself when he thought, as he says, that he had had the idea quite clear in his mind. But I believe that at the school the boys had a habit very unfavourable to the practice of truth. In my childhood I was very wayward and moody. My mother, who was a superior woman, used to say she had no anxieties about any of her children except William. She was sure he would turn out an extraordinary man, and she hoped a good man, but she was not so sure of that. He once tried to kill himself,' etc.

I was driven by Wordsworth's man James to Kendal—an honest fellow. . . .

FEB. 18th . . . I chatted at the Athenaeum with Rogers, who, I suspect, came there to look for me. He talked with great kindness of Wordsworth, who had written to him on business connected with his nephew's coming of age, but the letter he had not read. I was pleased with Rogers's expression of regard for Wordsworth, and therefore the more offended when at night Lady Blessington declared him to be a *bad man*—bad because, though he could do generous acts, he could mortally wound by his words. . . .

APRIL 19th . . . I had a letter from Wordsworth today—he solicits me to get money from my friends for a church at Cockermouth that wants building. I am annoyed by the application. . . .

APRIL 24th . . . A call from Talfourd. He has been written to by Wordsworth and Rogers also. It is a sort of fanaticism that Wordsworth thus expects from all his friends that for his sake they should subscribe to build a church! . . .

APRIL 26th . . . There died a few days ago another person who had a mighty influence on my early life—Godwin. I had lost all my personal respect for him. These are melancholy experiences in life. Godwin had no sense of *meum* and *tuum*. . . .

MAY 3rd I had a call from Landor just as I was going out. He was in excellent spirits and laughed as heartily as ever; yet I was sorry to learn that he does not mean to return to Italy. He says he will give four-fifths of his income to Mrs. Landor for herself and the three children and will live on the one-fifth himself. He says that for years Mrs. Landor has been making him ridiculous in the eyes of the servants and that he cannot possibly live with her. . . .

MAY 7th Landor came and breakfasted with me and I expected Kenyon. We had a very agreeable morning—I showed him my Goethe in the Gallery of Portraits which he said he liked but did not warmly praise and I suspect only tolerated, and we went together to the Exhibition. I pointed out to him the crack pieces. His judgment of these more like that of other men than of the old masters. He praised Landseer, but the picture he admired more than all others is Eastlake's 'Italian Peasants' First Sight of Rome at a Distance'. I thought the peasants too delicate and genteel, otherwise, great beauty in the varied expression. He spoke highly, too, of Etty's classical groups. . . .

MAY 13th My birthday, sixty-one complete! How near my grand climacteric! I had at breakfast Landor and Kenyon, and before twelve o'clock there came Wordsworth and his nephew and we had an agreeable chat till past two. Wordsworth and Landor agree on poetry better than on other matters, and where Wordsworth finds conformity in this he will be tolerant even of religious and political differences. I collected from the few hasty words that passed between us that he wants to make the very journey that I am desirous of making, so that I look forward to a very pleasant summer. . . .

MAY 14th . . . I set off on my walk which I found very pleasing—the most agreeable incident on my walk that I found dear Mary Lamb quite comfortable which I by no means expected. She was on a walk and was not at all flurried when she saw me. The best is that she now declares, but without any expression of ill-will, that she is tired of Edmonton and wishes to go to Miss James, who was with her lately and offers to take her. She only wants the approbation of Ryle, which she is sure of. I chatted but a short time with her, expecting soon to see her in town. . . .

MAY 15th I had to breakfast with me Wordsworth and his nephew and Landor. Before Landor came, Wordsworth beset me with his church-building solicitations, not in the shape of a personal application but of an account of what he has got—James Stephen has given him £50! A Mr. Twistleton called on him while we were at breakfast. I accompanied Landor to Talfourd's where we left our cards, and to Moxon's whom I told of Miss Lamb's inclination to come to London, at which he rejoices. . . . I then went to Lady Blessington's, where was a small party and several stragglers dropped in late between eleven and twelve. Not an agreeable chat; indeed, Lady Blessington does not improve. There came in Planché, a melodramatic writer, who praised a new piece by Dumas just come out in Paris in which angels, devils, the Virgin Mary, etc., all made their appearance. He praised the thing as sublime; even Landor praised. I alone was honest enough to call these things monstrosities, but the rest of the company seemed disposed to admire. . . .

MAY 16th . . . Then at a party at Miss Rogers's. Not many persons there; Milman, the poet, I was glad to know the person of. Lyell chatted very civilly with me, and Sydney Smith I got into a little talk with. His manner that of a person who knows that a joke is expected. He assumes a look of gaiety but he said nothing worth quoting. Speaking of a new review, the *British and Foreign*, he said: 'Hitherto it was thought that Lazarus, not Dives, should set up a review. The *Edinburgh* was written by *lazzaroni*.' He said the *Edinburgh Review* had done good. I said I hated it for its persecution of Wordsworth. By the bye, Sydney Smith said he never saw Wordsworth look so well, so *reverend*. 'But it surprised me—one always fancies a poet must be *young*.' He spoke to Wordsworth, as it seemed to me, in a tone of affected respect, or rather overdone. Several of the company looked askance on the poet as a sort of outlandish animal—and so is a poet among genteel folks. . . .

MAY 26th . . . The evening was interesting. I was at Covent Garden where Talfourd's *Ion* was brought out for Macready's benefit. It was most favourably received: Macready played well though he could not get over the want of youth; Ellen Tree played well but all the rest outrageously ill. The applause was immense and Macready and Ellen Tree were called out. After I had left the house it was demanded by the audience and given out for next week. I sat with Wordsworth, Landor, the Jaffrays, Ayrtons, and my brother. Wordsworth and Landor had dined with Talfourd. I had refused to dine and accompanied them to Talfourd's. He gave a supper on the occasion—a numerous party of legal and dramatic friends; I sat by Miss Tree and near Miss Mitford but left early to accompany Wordsworth who wanted someone to show him the way. I was a short time at the Athenaeum; I left Talfourd's after he had made a speech returning thanks for his health given by Macready, whose health he gave in return, but we could not wait for the speech of Macready's.

MAY 27th I breakfasted with Mr. Kenyon: Landor with him and a stranger. The day very fine and after calling on Miss Denman to see whether Landor could call on her, and by Kenyon's desire calling with Landor on his brother-in-law, Curteis, I strolled with Landor into the Zoological Garden where the four young camelopards would alone have repaid the trouble. They are the only creatures who ought to dance a minuet. These gardens are now greatly enlarged and improved, but the animals die fast and Landor says the clayey soil renders them insalubrious. I was walking with Landor till past three. . . .

JUNE 25th . . . On arriving at chambers I found an invitation to dine at Talfourd's to take *his* place as Wordsworth was come to spend a few days at his house and Talfourd was forced to dine out. I therefore went and we had an agreeable evening though I received the mortifying news that after all Wordsworth will not go abroad. He has worn out his spirits by being so long in London already. . . .

JUNE 27th . . . I concluded the evening by dressing at ten and going to Talfourd's. I found he had called on me and wanted me to dine with him—but I lost nothing by being away—chiefly Philistines: only Maule who was amusing; Wordsworth not in good spirits. I stayed late. There came in after me Ainsworth, author of *Rookwood*, an agreeable man, and Forster the *Examiner* critic. . . .

JUNE 30th . . . Wordsworth seems comfortable at the thoughts of going home, being exhausted. He has asked whether I would go on to Rome with him from Heidelberg in autumn; I answered yes, hastily, but I have written to Mrs. Wordsworth in an envelope that I should prefer next year. . . .

JULY 1st . . . I had a second note from Landor; he has been a week laid up at Lady Blessington's. I felt some awkwardness at not having been there before. I have since found that his note of last Saturday spoke of Gore House—I read it 'your house' by a blunder! He is going towards Italy immediately and would gladly be with me—but he is so excessively capricious that it would be difficult to manage with him. Quarrelling would be inevitable. . . .

[*Travel Journal: Wales, etc.*] JULY 26th [*Beddgellert.*] . . . I looked over the album of the house, in which Thomas Hood had written characteristically. I suppose it was his own writing. The name looked like an autograph:

> Here is a theme that never fails,
> To write or talk upon.
> The Undersigned has been in Wales,
> Jonah was but in One—
> THOS. HOOD.

AUG. 4th [*Dol y Melynllyn.*] . . . After our breakfast the yet unknown artist [Samuel Palmer], whose eye of deep feeling and very capacious forehead had inspired me with predilections for him, prepared to set out to one of the waterfalls I was come to see. I proposed to accompany him, and so an acquaintance was formed. He incidentally spoke of Blake as the greatest genius in art of modern times, though little known. This made me more interested in him. I spoke at length of Blake and my acquaintance with him and soon satisfied him that in calling Blake insane I was not repeating the commonplace declamation against him. He at length yielded to my statement, though he at first tried to maintain that in asserting the actuality of spirits he was but giving personality to ideas, as Plato had done before. On my mentioning my name, he said he had heard of me both from Blake and his wife. . . . I inquired whether Linnell is not a man of worldly wisdom. He understood the insinuation and said: 'Only *defensively*,' and he represented Linnell's conduct as having been very generous towards Blake. This is contrary to my impression concerning Linnell. . . .

AUG. 16th . . . I found an Annual luckily, and in it articles that afforded me unaffected pleasure, among others a successful imitation of

Coleridge by Praed, a satiric vision, *The Red Fisherman*[1]. . . . I read some pretty tales. . . . Altogether an amusing book. . . .

AUG. 28th [*Chepstow*.] . . . Reading Galt's *Annals of the Parish*. . . . It is well executed. . . . The sentiments are in excellent keeping and in one respect it has a character of importance. It shows incidentally the great change introduced in society during fifty years, for the worthy minister notices the introduction of tea and other domestic habits as well as the effect produced by the gradual change of a country village from being purely agricultural to manufacturing. The manners are something touching in the simplicity and there are some well-told family tales of the gradual rise and prosperity of Scotch families—all true to nature and fact. I have since been looking into another book, very inferior, by the same author, *The Steamboat*. . .

AUG. 29th [*Bristol*.] . . . Found myself at last at Mr. Cottle's—Joseph Cottle, author of king *Alfred*, and therefore in derision called by his own friends 'The Regicide'. He is a man of more than my age, with a club-foot and otherwise lame, so that he can walk with crutches only: he has a good . . . and has by no means a sanctimonious face . . . though there is a simplicity in his language which is not unpleasing. He was prepared for my call, and was very cordial in his reception of me. He lives in a comfortable house in a low neighbourhood and an air of neatness, not gentility, in all about him. My attention was drawn very soon to five miniatures—rather very small portraits of Southey, Coleridge, Lamb, and Wordsworth, besides one of a [blank in MS.]. Executed about A.D. 1798. Wordsworth's resembles more Edward Lytton Bulwer than himself now. All, Cottle assures me, excellent likenesses, Lamb's especially very beautiful, and therefore would be an excellent ornament to the forthcoming work. I thought I had already obtained the loan of it for Talfourd, but he retracted his consent to let me take it and said an excellent Bristol painter would make a capital copy of it for two guineas (Branwhite by name). I shall propose this to Talfourd. Cottle has also three larger portraits of Coleridge, Wordsworth, and Southey which I like less than the smaller. Cottle expressed a readiness to let Talfourd have any letter of Lamb's, but he had mislaid his papers and could not find any. I stayed several hours with Cottle, and our conversation was interesting. He showed me the preface he had written to his intended publication about Coleridge, but which I advised him not to publish. It consists of an account of his *démêlé* with the executors of Coleridge. He was applied to by Poole at the request of Gillman and Green for an account of Coleridge in his youth, as well as [for] some letters of Coleridge, all which he offered to

[1] *The Red Fisherman* was published in the 1827 issue of *Friendship's Offering*.

give them, provided they would publish them entire. This they refused to do. They chiefly objected to Cottle's relating how De Quincey gave Coleridge £300 in his youth—a fact which the relatives of Coleridge would have concealed, on which Cottle remarks: 'They, who pertinaciously refused to relieve his necessities, would have it concealed that others did what they ought to have done.' They also want to have suppressed a letter written by Coleridge to a Mr. Wade in which he gives an account of his sad habit of opium-taking; but Coleridge concludes this letter by solemnly requesting that this letter may be preserved and published after his death as a warning! On both points I think Cottle in the right, but I have recommended his taking [no] notice whatever of the executors. . . .

SEPT. 5th . . . I then went to Mr. Cottle's and had a very interesting conversation. He showed me an admirable theological letter from Coleridge on the future state, strongly inclining against the idea of an eternity of suffering, also a copy of a letter, far less creditable, to a lady, in which he affirms that his sonnet to Lord Stanhope was ironical—an exaggeration of French Jacobinism. Cottle himself remarked that his anxiety to stand well with the lady disturbed his memory! Poor Coleridge was not always correct in his facts. . . .

Cottle seems an uncertain man. I had made up my mind to have a copy of Lamb's picture by Branwhite for two guineas, when he said he thought he should use it himself.

N.B.—He read a letter from Coleridge praising in strong terms a tragedy by Wordsworth. He calls it 'absolutely wonderful.'

SEPT. 21st [*Margate.*] . . . I was reading today Henry Bulwer's *France*, which shows great acuteness and is full of sensible remarks.

SEPT. 22nd . . . I was engaged to breakfast with Rogers at Broadstairs. . . . I enjoyed the two hours with him. He is full of anecdote and generally has new ones. Today he has repeated four which I read only a day before . . . a sort of reproach to a professed story-teller. . . .

SEPT. 23rd . . . H. Bulwer has not the taste and imagination of Edward Bulwer [Lord Lytton] his brother, but I should think him a sounder thinker. Edward's manners are cold and forbidding. I have seen Henry but once at Lady Blessington's: there he was unpretending but chatty. What he would be at the Athenaeum, whether as silent and supercilious as his brother, I cannot say—I should think not. He is small and has no personal pretensions. His brother is somewhat of a coxcomb.

OCT. 27th [*London.*] . . . I went late to Lady Blessington's; Chorley was there. The usual chat; but it was not all agreeable chat. She did nothing but impress me unfavourably. She quoted absurd judgments given by Landor, whose critical decisions are ludicrously bad, as she herself and Chorley affirmed. She quoted him as affirming that James[1] is the greatest writer of the age and that Wordsworth can no longer write. Indeed, he is now satisfied that Wordsworth is nothing worth compared with Southey. Goethe is a great humbug and not equal to Madame Genlis, and these she repeated in derision. Yet Landor is her dear friend—I believe she really admires him! She was vehemently abusive of Rogers. . . .

DEC. 8th I finished and sent off letter to Landor on a subject worth noticing here. Landor sent me *A Satire on Satirists and Admonition to* [*Detractors*], a most unwarrantable publication which makes me quite indifferent now to the continuance of his acquaintance. The greater part is an attack on *Blackwood* and other satirists. But the detractor admonished is Wordsworth, and Landor here echoes the now stale reproaches on Wordsworth as an envious and selfish poet. . . .

1837

JAN. 6th . . . There were Mr. Thackeray and Dr. Outram. The Dr. Outram decidedly a weak, but I believe a very amiable, man; Thackeray a lively polemical spirit. The conversation spirited at the dinner-table. I could not go up to the ladies as I was engaged to Copley Fielding. A party chiefly of ladies, but it was agreeable. One interesting young man, a Trinity tutor, Blakesley, a friend of Worsley; rather an intolerant and assuming set, are these Cambridge scholars, admirers of Wordsworth, but they have both learning and talents. Blakesley had heard of Landor's pamphlet from Taylor but had not seen it, and he thinks it has been suppressed by Landor. He has received a very unfavourable impression of Landor, but adds, what I was not aware of, that Wordsworth slighted and shunned Landor when in town. . . .

JAN. 15th . . . I spent the rest of the evening at the Athenaeum, where I looked over a crazy review by Carlyle of Mirabeau's *Life*—occasional bursts of thought but for the most part mere idle whimsies and extravaganzas. He is a wrong-headed man—of genius perhaps, but the wrongheadedness is certain. The review was in the *London and Westminster Review*.

JAN. 16th . . . I also saw Southey. He immediately mentioned Landor's sad *Satire*, I told him that I had prevented the copy destined for him

[1] G. P. R. James, the historical novelist.

reaching him as Landor had caused it to be taken from Longmans'. He expressed his great regret at the publication, was sure it was founded on mistake, viz. the anecdote of what Wordsworth said of him; that Landor was always doing things he was sorry for afterwards; that people thought him crazy, or he would have been killed before now. We had a little talk about politics but not much. I advised him to reprint his *Wat Tyler* with a prose justification of the change in his opinions. . . .

JAN. 25th I had Southey and Serjeant Talfourd at breakfast. They were unacquainted with each other before and have too great diversity of taste and opinion to become intimate, but they had an agreeable though short conversation; their common friend, Charles Lamb, the bond between them and the intended publication of Charles Lamb's Letters the business they met on. They concurred in thinking it on the whole to be wished that the publication could be postponed till Miss Lamb's death; but that can hardly be, as the engagement to Moxon, or at least the understanding between them, is that an early publication should take place. Talfourd left soon. I walked out with Southey to a bookseller's and to Singleton's the portrait painter who is making a very Jew of him. . . .

FEB. 3rd . . . I wrote to Wordsworth. In my letter I gave him a short account of things concerning my own family and I promised to be ready; I gave, I fear, unwelcome advice, not to include in the new edition the note on Poor Laws, but rather print a pamphlet on the subject. I also advise rather delay than the hastening our journey. I took this to Moxon; I found him troubled by an intimation made him by Rogers that Talfourd thought him inattentive to Miss Lamb, and but for my dissuasion he would have remonstrated with Talfourd. These remonstrances do seldom any good. However, I am to see Talfourd about the publication of the Letters. Just as I wrote the above—about ten p.m.—Talfourd called on me, with whom I had an interesting and agreeable chat. He is sorry that he has inadvertently said anything to Rogers that could be considered strong enough to allow of a repetition and left with me a few lines that will be some relief to Moxon. He says that his opinion has changed recently. I trust my interference in this matter will be of use. . . .

FEB. 5th . . . Called on Moxon and, by a judicious use of a note Talfourd gave me, I have stopped what might have become a serious quarrel. Moxon was appeased and has written a conciliatory answer. . . . Reached Lady Blessington's after ten; with her D'Orsay, Dr. Lardner, Trelawny, Edward Bulwer, a stranger whose conversation interested and even pleased me till I knew he was young Disraeli. He talked with spirit on German literature. Landor's *Satire* was spoken of as it deserved by everyone. Disraeli declared it was impossible to give publicity to it: its fault, that it had no satire in it; so, feeble and unmeaning. It was an amusing chat. Bulwer much more of a dandy than Disraeli; he was supercilious in his manner.

FEB. 23rd . . . I breakfasted with Samuel Rogers. He was so very friendly and kind that I should have thought him a flatterer if I had been rich or powerful or had not been *tête-à-tête* with him. We had a long and interesting chat *de diversis rebus*—Landor, Wordsworth, Southey. He is a good teller of anecdotes: some I have put in my book.[1] He spoke with great affection of Mrs. Barbauld, but thought Miss Aikin had not treated her aunt well; Mrs. Barbauld complained that Lucy had never shown her the manuscript of her *King Charles* or *King James*. Of Southey he spoke with respect as to his genius and moral virtues, 'but he is essentially a narrow man and an enemy to the improvement of the common people. He is anti-popular.' Of Wordsworth he spoke with less cordiality than I could have wished, but he said nothing that was not true, viz. as to his too secular spirit [?].[2] We talked of slander and the truth blended with it; Adam Smith said to Rogers: 'Wilkes said to me: Give me a grain of truth and I will mix it with a great mass of falsehood so that no chemist shall ever be able to separate them.' Talking of composition he showed me a short note in his *Italy* which he says took him a fortnight to write. It consists of a very few lines: Wordsworth has amplified it in his poem on the picture of Miss Quillinan by Stone. Rogers says, and I think truly, that the prose is better than the poem. The thought meant to be powerfully expressed is that the *picture* is the substance and the beholders are the shadows. This led me perhaps injudiciously, to show Rogers my note[3] to the *Elegiac Stanzas* as the only lines that will survive me. He seemed to be pleased with me and wrote my name against the passage in his copy. I related many anecdotes of Goethe, etc., and he expressed a hope to see me again soon. . . .

MARCH 6th A letter from Wordsworth announcing his intention to be here on Friday and to leave London as soon as possible. I must therefore now in earnest set about getting ready for the journey. . . .

MARCH 11th . . . Moxon and Wordsworth came and we had an interesting chat. Wordsworth will stay till Saturday—a great relief to me: I hope now I shall have time for every[thing]. Wordsworth brought an invitation for me to breakfast with him at Mr. Taylor's; Brockedon and Kenyon also invited. . . .

[1] Robinson made a small collection of anecdotes, which is extant.

[2] The last four words cannot be deciphered with any conviction.

[3] Crabb Robinson supplied the introductory note to Wordsworth's *Elegiac Stanzas* on Goddard, the young American who was drowned in the Lake of Zurich in 1820.

MARCH 15th . . . To St. Thomas's Hospital, where I saw Mr. Green and lent him five books (German philosophy) with notes by Coleridge. . . . At Moxon's I fell in with Wordsworth and he took me to Courtenay's. After we had together got our passports, Courtenay advised us strongly to buy a carriage and post it and gave us an account according to which we should spend only £250 each, though we might remain out six months. For both the account being 180 days at £1 1*s*. per day £200; 2,500 miles at 1*s*. per mile £125. Loss on a carriage £35. Extras 10*s*. per day £90. Unforeseen contingencies £50: equals £500. Wordsworth declared that he had his £250 ready, and I consented readily and I rejoice at the determination; only I told Wordsworth I knew not how to make a purchase. . . .

MARCH 16th . . . I had a letter from Walter Savage Landor, giving me an account of his daughter having formed an unhappy connection with a cousin, of whom Landor gives a bad account. Landor says his children will see me with pleasure, and he is sure from my friendship that I shall suggest just sentiments to them. He says nothing about his wife. I had written to him to ask whether I should call on them or not. . . .

MARCH 17th . . . I went early to Wordsworth and walked with him, Henry Taylor, etc., to look at Mr. Hallett's carriage at Turner's, Long Acre, of which I had heard the day before, and that pleased us so much that Wordsworth and I at once agreed to give £70 for it, and having consulted Mr. Courtenay about it I went to Mr. Marmaduke Robinson and paid him the money for it; I gave him a cheque of Moxon's for £200 and he paid me the balance. This business occupied me nearly all the forenoon. That I should ever buy a carriage for my own use seems quite incredible. I am now satisfied I have done well, and I should be unwilling to travel any other way. . . .

Our tour lasted from Sunday, 19th of March, to Monday, the 7th of August, and I have preserved short memoirs of it. It included a journey through France along the Corniche road to Pisa, by Volterra to Siena; thence to Rome. After a month there, we returned by the three Tuscan monasteries to Florence; thence through Parma to Milan and then turning eastward by the lakes of Como, Iseo, and Garda to Venice. We crossed the Alps by the new road along the valley of [the] Piave and that of the Drave through Werfen, Hallein, etc., to Salzburg. After an excursion to the Austrian Salzkammergut proceeded to Munich, Stuttgart, and to Heidelberg and then through Brussels to Calais.

[*Travel Journal: Italy, etc.*] [*Paris.*] . . . I am now the associate and shall soon be the sole companion of no less a man than Wordsworth, and with him the intention of us both is to visit all Italy. . . . I shall . . . content myself with inserting very brief notes of the country we pass through. . . . I doubt much whether I shall ever do more, for I am a bad journalist. . . . I feel unable to record even the interesting remarks which Wordsworth is continually making—and it is his society that will distinguish this from all other journeys and it is to accommodate him that I have altered my usual mode of travelling. He cannot bear night travelling, and in his sixty-ninth[1] year needs rest. I therefore at once yielded to his suggestion to buy a carriage for the journey. . . . It is a barouche . . . Moxon offered to be our companion, and we have found him very friendly and agreeable on our journey. He is, however, to return from Paris to England when we leave for Italy.

MARCH 22nd . . . With Wordsworth I did not fail to have occasional bursts of conversation on Landor and on poetry. It may not be unworthy of mention that Wordsworth heard only of Landor's *Satire* from Quillinan in Portugal. He said he regretted Quillinan's indiscretion, and he felt much obliged to all his London friends for their never mentioning the circumstance to him. He never saw nor means to see the *Satire*, so that it will fall ineffectual if it were intended to wound. He had heard that the pamphlet imputed to him a depreciation of Southey's genius, but as he felt a warm affection for Southey and an admiration for his genius he never could have said that he would not give five shillings for all Southey had ever written. He had in consequence written a few lines to Southey. Notwithstanding his sense of the extreme injustice of Landor towards him, he willingly acknowledged his sense of Landor's genius. As to the image of the sea-shell, he acknowledged no obligation to Landor's *Gebir* for it. From his childhood the shell was familiar to him, and the children of his native place always spoke of the humming sound as indicating the sea and its greater or less loudness had a reference to the state of the sea at the time. The circumstance, however, gave him little annoyance. The malignancy of one person was balanced by the kindness shown by so many friends in their silence. . . .

MARCH 27th . . . We set out soon after six and proceeded to Nemours to breakfast. The rock scenery of the forest greatly delighted my friend, so susceptible to the beauties of nature, and I anticipate a sonnet at least. . . . It is now near midnight . . . and Wordsworth is sleeping in an alcove, and has in his sleep been declaiming some unintelligible verse. He has been chatty today and talked about the poets. He said Langhorne is one of the poets who had not had justice done him. His *Country Justice* has true feeling and poetry. He praised Béranger, and said he is eminently popular. All classes love him. He was not aware till I informed him of the fact,

[1] Sixty-seventh is correct.

that Béranger owes a great portion of his popularity to having flattered the vices and bad passions of his countrymen.

MARCH 28th . . . The views of the Loire which we afterwards enjoyed were of great interest to Wordsworth. Goldsmith's lines in *The Traveller* made an impression on him in his youth.

APRIL 2nd [*Avignon.*] . . . Set off in a cabriolet to Vaucluse. . . . Wordsworth was strongly excited, predetermined to find the charm of interest, and he did. There is no verdure, but perhaps on looking more closely Petrarch may not have praised his retreat either for shady groves or meadows—and the stream of the Sorgues is eminently beautiful. The rocks are almost sublime, at least very romantic. Having taken a luncheon at the mouth of the cavern we ascended the heights above, and Wordsworth made a longer ramble among the rocks behind the fountain. . . .

APRIL 3rd [*Nîmes.*] I took Wordsworth to see the exterior of both the Maison Carrée and the Arena. He acknowledged their beauty, but expressed no great pleasure. He says: 'I am unable from ignorance to enjoy these sights. I receive an impression, but that is all. I have no science and can refer nothing to principle.' He was, on the other hand, delighted by two beautiful little girls near the Arena [and said]: 'I wish I could take them to Rydal Mount. . . .'

APRIL 4th . . . I took Wordsworth to the gardens, which pleased him much more than the antiquities. The interior of the Arena did not seem strongly to affect him. Indeed, he confessed that he anticipates no great pleasure from this class of object in his tour. . . . Wordsworth has already frequently expatiated on the superiority of English climate. Within a few hours we have suffered from both heat and cold.

APRIL 5th . . . To relieve the ennui of a very dull drive I read this afternoon Beckford's *Vathek*, with renewed disgust. It is not to be denied that it is a wonderful production if it were really written before the age of twenty[1] [?] and in a foreign language. The latter fact must be qualified and it will still be an extraordinary work. But the laborious accumulation of crimes and horrors, with whatever imaginative power, excites only an uncomfortable feeling of the waste of powers neither harmoniously combined nor of the highest quality.

APRIL 10th [*Antibes.*] . . . This place pleases Wordsworth more than he expected.

APRIL 12th [*San Remo.*] This was a delightful day, which Wordsworth heartily enjoyed—a compensation for the labours and discomfort of the journey through France. . . . During the greater part of it we enjoyed admirable scenery under the most favourable circumstances, except that

[1] *Vathek* was written in 1782, when its author was twenty-two.

the spring verdure was still wanting. . . . [Through Monaco to] Mentone. I would gladly have stayed here, but Wordsworth was rather anxious to get on. This is a delicious spot. . . .

April 14th [*Savona.*] . . . Wordsworth and I set out early on a walk in this quiet and agreeable town. There is a port, and before it a greensward just at this season, which delighted Wordsworth more than objects more extraordinary and generally attractive. . . . We ascended to a couple of monasteries, the one of Capuchins with an extensive view of the sea, and then to a former Franciscan monastery, now desecrated. Wordsworth took a great fancy to this place, and thought it a fit residence for such a poet as Chiabrera, who lived here and whose epitaphs refer to Savona. We sauntered here a long time. . . .

April 15th [*Genoa.*] Wordsworth left me early to take a short walk, but as usual, following the humour of the moment, he did not return till eleven. . . .

April 19th [*Massa.*] . . . After dinner we ascended a knoll of land between the town and the disagreeable flat that borders the shore, and there enjoyed a scene that Wordsworth seemed to admire more than any we had met on our journey. . . .

April 20th . . . Early in the morning we set out on a walk which Wordsworth guessed must be interesting, being in a glen through which a stream flowed, and I soon found that it was, in fact, the glen in which runs the river [Frigido], and in which I had enjoyed myself on my former stay at Massa. We went on and were so much delighted with the romantic beauties of this glen terminating in mountains covered with snow that, in spite of violent rain, we went on. . . . Wordsworth esteems it one of the most remarkable spots he has seen on his journey, and he did not see the very finest point. At that point the mountains were very precipitous and near and awfully grand, and a path led to the recesses in which the stream had its origin called the Sorgente.

April 25th [*Acquapendente*] . . . Wordsworth has little pleasure in antiquities, but every form of natural beauty attracts him. . .

April 26th [*Rome*] . . . I called on Miss Mackenzie. . . . She is very desirous to give Wordsworth the use of her carriage and she has friends at Albano (the Sismondis) who are very desirous to see him. . . . Wordsworth seems disposed to enjoy Rome and felt quite as much as I expected at the sight of St. Peter's and at the view from the Pincian. . . .

April 27th This has been a very interesting day. To Wordsworth it must have been unparalleled in the number and importance of new impressions. . . . About seven o'clock in the morning, being fine, I took Wordsworth pretty nearly the same walk which I by accident took on my arrival here near seven years ago, in the course of which we entered the Campo Vaccino, noticing all the well-known objects in that sublimest of Cow Fields, and having walked round the Coliseum, by which Wordsworth seemed sufficiently impressed, to the Temples of Janus, Vesta, Fortuna Virilis, the porch of the Portian Gate, and also the Pantheon, which Wordsworth seemed to think unworthy of notice compared with St. Peter's. . . . We then called on Mrs. Theed, who took us to 45 in the Piazza di Spagna, where we engaged lodgings at the rate of ten scudi a month apiece. . . . We rode with her [Miss Mackenzie] to St. Peter's, by which Wordsworth was more impressed than I expected he would be. . . . Wordsworth is no hunter after sentimental relics. He professes to be regardless of places that have merely a connection with a great man, unless they had also an influence on his works. Hence he cares nothing for the burying-place of Tasso, but he has a deep interest in Vaucluse. The distinction is founded on just views and real, not affected sympathy. . . .

April 28th . . . We chatted with Collins, the landscape-painter, who is a great favourite of Wordsworth's. . . . We concluded the evening by taking tea with Miss Mackenzie, who has been most kind indeed. She and Wordsworth got into literary chat. He evidently showed himself to be desirous to be agreeable in her eyes, and therefore no doubt will be so.

May 2nd I was glad to be relieved by some variety of society. . . . I introduced Wordsworth to the Colliers, and from them he will receive attention and Mr. Collier will accompany him on his walks. I have therefore made arrangements for our spending this afternoon separately. Wordsworth, I trust, will be able to find sufficient interest in Rome notwithstanding his faint interest in antiquities. . . .

May 4th . . . Introduced Wordsworth to Bunsen. He talked his best to Wordsworth and with great facility and felicity of expression pointed out to us monuments from the history of Rome from his own windows. I never heard a more instructive, delightful lecture in ten times the words. . . .

May 5th . . . At breakfast Wordsworth was made happy by letters from Mrs. Wordsworth. . . . We took tea with Miss Mackenzie. There came Dr. Meyer, the German, and with the Rev. Mr. Hutchinson, a Mr. Muir, who came on purpose to see Wordsworth, and most amusingly dogmatised about poetry. It was even ludicrous to hear him declaim against the form of the sonnet as utterly worthless in the presence of the greatest master of the sonnet. Wordsworth himself was amused by the incident. . . .

May 6th . . . After breakfast we made calls on Severn, who had a subject to talk on with Wordsworth besides art—poor Keats, his friend. He informs us that the foolish inscription on his tomb is to be superseded by one more worthy of him. He denies that Keats's death was hastened by the article in the *Quarterly*. It appears that Keats was by no means poor, but was fleeced by Haydon and Leigh Hunt. Brown[1] is to write a life of him. . . . Wordsworth confesses it a duty rather than a pleasure to make the circuit of palaces as well as churches. . . .

MAY 10th We rose early and had a delightful walk before breakfast. We ascended the Coliseum. The view of the building from above enhances greatly the effect and Wordsworth then seemed fully impressed by the grandeur of the structure, though he seemed still more to enjoy the fine view of the country beyond. He now wishes to make the ascent by moonlight. . . .

MAY 13th . . . We then drove to Hadrian's Villa, which delighted Wordsworth for its scenery and amused me by its ruins, and after an hour and half there went on to the Sibilla. . . . We inspected the old rocks among which the cascade fell, and the new fall which has been made by a tunnel. The change was necessary, but it has not improved the scene. The new fall is made formal by the masonry above. . . . The old fall had the disadvantage of being hidden by projecting rocks, so that we could only see it by means of paths cut, and then but imperfectly. This alone would have been a great disappointment to Wordsworth, but he was amply compensated by the enjoyment the Cascadelles afforded him from the opposite side of the valley, from which you see two masses of what are called the little falls, and at the same time the heavy mass formed by the body of the river. . . . Altogether Tivoli has left an agreeable impression. . . . By the bye, Wordsworth called the Cascadelles 'nature's waterworks.' . . .

MAY 15th . . . I . . . had a most agreeable chat with Dr. [John] Carlyle, who read me some excellent memoirs of a conversation with Schelling. . . . I took tea with Wordsworth at Bunsen's. The Bunsens were unaffectedly surprised at our intended departure so soon, and were very friendly indeed. Wordsworth was in good spirits and talked well about poetry. He made the Bunsens feel—and I can see they are sensible of his worth: perhaps they only suspect it. I copied for Bunsen the Antiquarian sonnet. On language and Church matters, not the same harmony between them. On politics Wordsworth is less tolerant. . . .

MAY 16th Wordsworth went early to Severn to breakfast, and have his portrait taken. . . . I now called on Mr. Harvey, our landlord as agent for a Mr. Moore. Wordsworth had before paid him what he owed. Harvey

[1] Charles Armitage Brown.

asked if he was the poet, and said: 'He seems quite an economist and man of business'—but this not offensively, and he very pressingly invited us to dine with him on our return....

MAY 17th ... I looked into Thorwaldsen's studio. He has a very fine statue of Gutenberg—fine, for its significance. That of Lord Byron has no value in my eyes, either on account of the man or of the work itself. It is pretty rather than elegant. I am told it has been denied admittance in Westminster Abbey. It is too late to be particular on such an occasion. Surely a memorial to even so anti-religious a poet as Byron may be admitted where the inscription to [J. Gay] stands:

> Life is a jest, and all things show it.
> I thought so once, [but] now I know it.

Wordsworth says that Bunsen has informed him that from the particular friends of Byron he has learned that Lord Byron had an impression that he was the offspring of a demon. In a moment of disease he may have suffered such a thought to seize his imagination....

MAY 19th [*Albano.*] This day was nearly lost to us as travellers, for the weather was wet, and we were kept within all the forenoon.... I am glad that Wordsworth has had a day's rest, as he is too apt to complain of fatigue and to imagine himself weak. I hope I shall not be as old as he is five years hence....

MAY 22nd This was a busy day, for I had to prepare for our final departure, make calls, etc.... I dined with Miss Mackenzie.... Nothing can exceed her kindness to Wordsworth and me. She seems to feel for Wordsworth the affection of a daughter, and he is much pleased with her. She was affected when we took leave, and, I believe, sincerely grieves at our departure. ... She has ... had great pleasure in showing us the attentions, which have afforded Wordsworth and me our chief gratification. But for her house Wordsworth's evenings would have been deplorably dull. Wordsworth wants the cheering society of women, and Miss Mackenzie's house was open to him every evening. He has invited her to visit him at Rydal, and I have no doubt she will accept the invitation....

MAY 23rd ... The scenery of [Civita Castellana] and from thence onward to Narni delighted Wordsworth much. But at Narni he was put out of sorts by not seeing the famous broken bridge. He went on while the horses were putting to, but I neglected to give him directions what to do....

MAY 24th [*Terni.*] ... I had seen the famous cascade before but never to so great advantage. Then I thought it the very finest waterfall I had ever seen; and Wordsworth declared it to be also the most sublime he ever beheld. The upper fall is sublime as seen from above, from the mass of water, and the great extent of the fall, which is said to amount to three hundred feet. The rebound of the water is such as to resemble a cloud, so that the well-known proverb applied to a wood may be literally parodied. You cannot see the cascade for the water. . . .

MAY 27th We left Arezzo about eight. . . . We left the high road to Florence soon and were driven [on] good cross-country roads into the very heart of the Apennines and especially into the Val d'Arno, *superiore* as I suppose. At least we soon came in sight of the Arno, and we had it long afterwards to the great joy of Wordsworth. It is not unqualifiedly true that the rose would smell as sweet by any other name—at least, not the doctrine that that famous expression is used to assert. We do feel the pleasure enhanced when we find ourselves in a beautiful spot and find that that spot has been the theme of praise by men of taste in many generations. . . .

MAY 29th Today Wordsworth and I had a little quarrel; he was rude because I was forced to resist his too large demands on my good nature and this had some influence in making me decline going with him today.

JUNE 1st [*Florence.*] . . . Niccolini called and I introduced the poets to each other, but they could have little pleasure in conversation for want of a common language. . . . We then took a walk round, went out at the Croce gate, crossed the Arno over a suspension bridge, and then had a delightful walk up to the San Miniato.

JUNE 4th [*Visit to Landor's.*] . . . The only bad points in the affair are these. Mrs. Landor is certainly a very weak woman, but I think respectable in her conduct. My suspicions on this head are removed, and I have no doubt her provocations have been very great indeed. She complains of personal violence, even beating, and I can believe such things. She allowed me to say she would be happy to receive Landor on principle and no reference to the past. Julia is a very fine and indeed interesting girl. I do not think her attachment to her cousin is of such a kind as to endanger her health, but she feels very much her father's conduct. She cried several times when I talked about him; she has given me a note to him from which I expect more than from anything else. I had written thus far when it occurred to me that I should do better by forwarding Julia's note to her father than . . . writing to my brother. Accordingly I wrote a short letter to Landor giving an account of his family. . . .

Mrs. Landor complained of Landor, and accused him of beating her and of making himself an object of terror to the children. She said he had a good heart but a very bad temper. She seems to be quite dependent on him. He allows her for the maintenance of the family forty crowns a week, which certainly is no bad allowance. He told me that he took for himself one-fifth of his income and left four-fifths. That may be true. She says that he every year pays off debts. She related to me that he ran away from her when she was in Jersey, a short time after their marriage. And unless I am strangely mistaken she said that they had lived together as brother and sister ever since she was thirty-six years old! All these are strange and incredible things were Landor not a very strange man. Many particulars I omit. Notwithstanding all this, she allowed me to say that she should be happy to see him. So I said no more than I was warranted in saying. She showed me a letter from Landor's sister offering her an asylum; from his brother praising very highly Edward Landor, a nephew, who has confessed his attachment to Miss Landor, and she is more than a little attached to him.

JUNE 7th [*Bologna.*] . . . The rest of the day was spent by me more pleasantly than by Wordsworth. He has been all day very uncomfortable —annoyed by the length of the streets. He is never thoroughly happy, but in the country. . . . We went to the gallery, where Wordsworth found very little to interest him. . . . But Guido is surely a delightful painter. . . . Domenichino, too, has great ability . . . and there are some fine heads by Giotto. . . .

JUNE 9th [*Milan.*] . . . I have been pleased to hear again the German language, and though in a small and not well-furnished room for sleeping, yet I am comfortable and only afraid that Wordsworth will be impatient and want to hurry me away. . . .

JUNE 11th . . . We drove to the very celebrated Certosa, four or five miles on this side Pavia. . . . It so surpassed our expectations that even Wordsworth did not regret the journey. It is the richest church I ever saw, not in its architecture, but in its sculpture. . . . Wordsworth was annoyed by the large parties who were seeing the church, and to avoid them, left it, and we went up the tower together. We saw everything quietly. . . .

JUNE 12th To make up for the insignificance of the day before, this was one of the most agreeable of the whole journey, enjoyed by Wordsworth more than any other, yet we had to encounter fatigue. . . . Just before we reached Como the scenery became very grand. . . . At Como . . . all other feelings were for the time overpowered by the fortunate occurrence of meeting with the Ticknors, a great and unexpected pleasure. They, too, were going up the lake by the steamboat, and thus we united to the pleasures of the scene the gratification of chat with a clever family. . . . The view of this most beautiful of lakes was in itself to me an unmixed pleasure. Wordsworth blended with it painfully pleasing recollections of his old friend Jones, with whom he made the same journey in the year 1790, and who died a few months ago. He also had a still more tender recollection of his journey here in 1820 with his wife and sister twice, during the first of which only Monkhouse and I were with him. . . . A hot and disagreeable drive [from Como back to Milan], but I read as long as the light lasted in the *Life of Scott*, by Lockhart, which Ticknor had lent us. We arrived after eleven. . . .

JUNE 13th . . . I accompanied Wordsworth up the cathedral. A small sum . . . is required of each person, and no one accompanies the traveller —an excellent arrangement, and, as Wordsworth truly observed, the cheapest of all sights for which anything is paid. For it is a most interesting sight. The view of the surrounding country is not to be despised, but that is the least part of the sight. Its singularity consists in the effect produced by the numerous pinnacles on the roof of the church—three rows on each side, each surmounted by a figure and all of marble. . . .

JUNE 14th [*Bergamo.*] . . . This day was, perhaps, the very best of our journey to Wordsworth. At least, it partook most of that character which expresses his personal taste. It was a day of adventure amid beautiful scenery. . . . We . . . rambled up to the old town of Bergamo, for our inn was only in the suburb below. I was much pleased with the walk. I have seldom seen a more pleasantly situated provincial town in Italy, or indeed in any country . . . Bergamo being built, as it were, on the first step of the series of hills which end in the Alps. I strolled alone into the city . . . only hurried too much and found Wordsworth not returned when I reached our inn. . . . We left our inn between ten and eleven. . . . We went . . . to Pallaguola [Palazzolo?] . . . a pleasing little town. Here the post-road terminates. . . . We had a pleasant drive through cross, but very good, roads to this little town situated at the foot of the lake of Iseo. We put up at a humble inn . . . kept within doors till the evening set in. Then a lad of the house guided us through long lanes of stone walls to the side of the lake. The view . . . very grand. Several ridges of lofty mountains; the latter streaked with snow. The day was intensely hot. Finding a conveniently retired spot I had the luxury of a bathe. I enjoyed it greatly. Wordsworth and I had separated. He returned after dark, having enjoyed his solitary ramble. . . . In bed late, having read both evening and during the day Lockhart's *Life of Walter Scott*—a made-up book, the writer, like his subject, carrying on literature as a trade, and being desirous above all things to make a large book for the sake of the large pay. The best parts of what I have yet read are those traceable to Scott himself—extracts from his letters and anecdotes of his own telling. . . .

JUNE 15th I rose early and wrote part of the above. Then I took a delightful walk . . . and had a fine view of the lake. . . . The *Life of Scott* was my companion. . . . Called away by the departure of the boat at eleven. It was the humblest vehicle in which gentlemen ever made a party of pleasure—a four-oared broad boat with a sail. The company about four sheep, one horse, one ass, one cow, about ten steerage passengers, cabin passengers about four or five besides Wordsworth and myself. We had the shelter of an awning near the helm, but so ill-contrived as to allow of no comfort in a posture between lying and sitting. The day was hot and at one time we were becalmed. No attempt to use the oars. It was hot to suffocation. I managed to read in the *Life of Scott*, for the motion was so slow that the scenery, fine as it was, did not fully occupy my mind. We went near twenty miles in four and a half hours. Towards the end of the lake, as we drew near Lovere, it improved in beauty, and on arriving the country was so inviting that we resolved to explore the neighbourhood till it became dark. We walked up the road to Bergamo, from whence the views of the lake are exquisitely beautiful. . . . We rambled several hours, indeed, till it was dark. We then found a respectable inn . . . where a comfortable dinner was supplied . . . and after this we had the use of a large room. Wordsworth slept and I read Walter Scott's *Life*. . . . At twelve we re-embarked on our boat [with] other animals, both biped and quadruped. . . . It was about 3 a.m. when we arrived [at Iseo].

JUNE 16th We rose between six and seven and . . . were driven fifteen miles to Brescia . . . [where] we were glad to lie by for a few hours in the middle of the day. . . . We stayed here till half-past four, and were then driven . . . to Desenzano . . . [which] we reached . . . at dusk. We were put in good rooms fronting the lake [Garda]. . . . A long slip of land . . . runs into the water dividing the lake into halves and ending in . . . the promontory of Sirmione, where Catullus had a villa. Wordsworth had a strong desire to visit this point, but the sight of it hence will probably be sufficient to satisfy him. A fine view towards the head of the lake determined us at once to make use of a small steamboat which . . . [on] Saturday goes to Riva. . . .

JUNE 17th . . . At seven in the morning . . . we embarked on a small but pleasant steamboat which took us in six hours to the head of the lake to Riva. . . . After dining Wordsworth took a boat and went to . . . Torbole. I walked a couple of miles to this Torbole and from thence ascended the mountains above. . . . I met Wordsworth on his return, he having taken a boat half the way. . . .

JUNE 18th [*Riva.*] . . . We walked out before breakfast and took the road to Arco, above the lake. Wordsworth soon left me, as he was annoyed by the stone walls on the road, and I sauntered on to a little town, walled. . . . After refreshing myself . . . I strolled back . . . and then read in my room Lady Mary Wortley Montagu's [*Letters*], which formed my resource today. I sat in my room till past one, when I became very uncomfortable. Wordsworth said he should return and take his breakfast. His non-return made me fear an accident had occurred, and, this idea having seized me, I could not rest, but walked out in search of him, being aware that in case of accident, I being dressed so much like him, should be informed of it. It was oppressively hot, but I went on and guessed that he would be attracted by the appearance of a village and castles on the mountains. I went in that direction. The sound of a waterfall caught my ear. I knew it must catch his. I pursued it, came to a mill, found he had been there and had breakfasted there. He was gone higher up. I went higher and found a man who had seen him near Riva. This relieved my apprehensions. I returned. He was there and we dined at three. . . . In bed at eleven o'clock after a very agreeable though, during some portion of it, anxious day.

JUNE 19th [*Verona.*] . . . We hastened from the inn to the amphitheatre. . . . Wordsworth did not seem to enjoy the amphitheatre. The restoration of the steps seems to have taken away all the poetry and effect in his eyes. When I saw it first I was more impressed, but then I had not seen Rome. . . .

JUNE 22nd . . . Wordsworth was gratified by our entrance into Venice. The view of the picturesque palaces on the Canale Grande was very interesting, if not beautiful. . . . We enjoyed ourselves much in the short walk we took on the Piazza. . . .

JUNE 23rd . . . We called on the Ticknors . . . and . . . Wordsworth accompanied them to hear Tasso chanted by gondoliers, for which I had no curiosity. . . .

JUNE 26th *Titian's House*. . . . Two pictures delighted me most, perhaps because they were not new to me: 'The Four Ages of Man,' a favourite of dear Lamb's; he valued an engraving of it, and a 'Deposition from the Cross.' . . .

JUNE 27th . . . We thus found four days in fact enough for Venice, Wordsworth being so indifferent to mere sights. Venice on the whole I have enjoyed more than before, because I have seen it more at my ease. . . .

JUNE 28th . . . Met Wordsworth and Mr. White [an American], an amiable young man who won on Wordsworth by being very attentive to him personally, but his qualities apparently are negative. . . . Our first day's journey [homewards]. . . .

JUNE 30th . . . Wordsworth overslept himself this morning, having for the first time on his journey, I believe, attempted composition, and in the forenoon I wrote some twenty lines by dictation on *The Cuckoo* [*at*] *Laverna*. We therefore did not leave our nice comfortable inn [at Sillian] till seven o'clock.

JULY 1st . . . Wordsworth himself [who had desired to take the 'new' route they were following], I believe, regrets now that we did not turn to the left as we quitted the mountains at Toblach and take the high road to Innsbruck. But I hope to make a comparison hereafter of what I have seen and what I missed. For though I feel no desire to visit Italy again, I should not hesitate another journey among the Alps, so much greater and more unmixed is the pleasure which mountains give than what cities afford us. . . .

JULY 2nd . . . Golling. Salzburg . . . one of the very prettiest *small* waterfalls I ever saw (I mean small as to the volume of water), but the height of the fall is considerable. . . . A short post brought us to Hallein, where I was fourteen years ago in company with two young men. . . . We then came to see the famous salt works, which Wordsworth has no curiosity about, and we then went on to see what I hope to see again today, the grand lake, the Königsee. Hallein lies finely, as every place does in this country. I took a walk alone, Wordsworth being engaged in composition—rewriting his verses on *The Cuckoo at Laverna*—and I read a chapter in Walter Scott's *Life*, being satiated with beholding fine scenery.

JULY 3rd . . . We . . . had a very delightful day's excursion to the Königsee. The drive to Berchtesgaden is most delicious, and more perfectly beautiful country than this of Salzburg can't be imagined. . . . Wordsworth enjoyed the whole day and declared it most charming, though the lake itself did not, I believe, answer the expectations he had formed of it. . . .

JULY 4th This day also has been very agreeably spent. . . . We . . . pursued our course to Salzburg . . . and Wordsworth was enchanted with a scene which combines the most pleasing features of English scenery . . . with grand masses and forms. Especially before Salzburg the avenues and the fine grass quite won my companion's heart. . . . In the evening Wordsworth and I met on the heights near the castle, where I found him greatly delighted with the scenery as uniting every variety of beauty and greatness. . . .

JULY 5th . . . I had accounts to make out, etc., after breakfast, and Wordsworth went out and left me alone. I met with a packet of the *Allgemeine Zeitung*, which interested me more than the fine scenery of Salzburg. I had before read of the death of William IV. I was anxious to know what immediately followed. I learned from these papers that the new Queen Victoria has already appointed Whig ladies her maids-of-honour, which shows that for the present her tastes and predilections are on the liberal side. Wordsworth not coming home early, I dined alone, and after dinner walked . . . I found Wordsworth on my return. . . .

JULY 6th . . . We left Salzburg . . . and . . . the Salzkammergut has not failed to afford us all the pleasure that could be reasonably expected.

JULY 7th [*Ischl.*] . . . We made an agreement with a *Pferdephilister* to have a horse to Weissbach for ten *Zwanziger*, but when the horse came, and we were ready to start, he insisted on fifteen. This disgusted my companion, for whom alone the horse was wanted, so much, that he rejected it, and we set out on foot and we were well pleased with the result. . . . We walked down the valley of the Traun by the side of the rapid river in a narrow glen for near a league, and then turned into a vast pine-wood valley along which for perhaps two leagues we sauntered. We walked slowly, Wordsworth resting frequently, and I took one or two naps . . . and early in the afternoon we came to the lake of Alter and the little hamlet of Weissbach. . . . We sauntered in the evening by the lake. . . .

JULY 10th . . . I did not reach Ischl till past one, having been on foot since eight. Wordsworth had been there since eleven, having been taken up by an empty carriage. . . . I found Wordsworth bent on departing. Ischl is not at all to his taste, being a bathing-place . . . with something of an attempt at gentility and a sort of smart people. . . . We set off—it was past four—and drove to Aussee. . . .

JULY 12th [*Hallstadt.*] . . . After breakfast Wordsworth set out on a boat-excursion for which I had no taste. I preferred sauntering along near the lake. . . . Wordsworth returned at two.

JULY 15th . . . The new King of Hanover has abolished (*aufgehoben*) the Hanoverian constitution! Of so violent a man as the ex-Duke of Cumberland anything may be expected. . . . Wordsworth has related to me an anecdote that on an occasion on which the Duke of Cumberland intimated to the Duke of Wellington that he would do a certain act, the Duke replied: 'If so, I will impeach your Royal Highness.' . . . We left our inn a little after six without taking any breakfast and went two stages to breakfast, i.e. to Weisham [? Westerham] and Rosenheim. . . . We were a little annoyed by being rudely treated by a German gentleman . . . who, contrary to the post regulations, though he arrived last at Weisham [?] contrived to get the first horses. He had had some words with Wordsworth in my absence, whom he called *Der Brummbär*. He was most insolent and very un-German in his manners. . . .

JULY 16th . . . We set off about 7 a.m. and had a charming drive . . . to

Tegern See. . . . Wordsworth drew my attention to the fine figure of the female peasants—stout forms, short necks, and faces masculine and yet comely. . . . We found at the foot of the lake a palace, the summer residence of the Dowager Queen of Bavaria. . . . Beyond I found a building called the *Parapluie*, from its form, though Wordsworth said parasol would have been a better name. Here I stayed a considerable time. Read with delight extracts from *The Excursion*. . . . I read the whole of the admirable tale of Margaret from *The Excursion*. After two I found Wordsworth at the inn. He had seen all I saw and a great deal more. . . . We took a short walk after dinner, for the rain had abated. . . . It is apparently fine now. But Wordsworth says the air is full of water and we must expect continued bad weather.

JULY 17th [*Munich*.] . . . I was accosted by Clemens Brentano . . . in his wild and gay tone of conversation not much altered. He was accompanied by two of his nieces. . . . On returning to the inn I introduced Wordsworth to the whole party, who dined at the table d'hôte. . . . Brentano was in *his* way courteous in French, though he rattled about religion in a way that could but half amuse and half disgust Wordsworth. Brentano took us to the house of Professor Phillips, who speaks English, that he might give Wordsworth information about St. Francis, but he was not at home. Brentano also gave me a note to the conductor of Cotta's business here that he might show me some German translations from Wordsworth, whom I at once recognized as an old acquaintance, Mr. Oldenburg. . . . He speaks English, is very desirous to serve, and will be of great use to Wordsworth. . . . I looked over the translations from Wordsworth in the *Ausland* by Freiligrath. They seem in general done with feeling and talent. By the bye, Freiligrath has translated *The Ancient Mariner*. Wordsworth's translations are anonymous. . . .

JULY 18th . . . Early in the morning we met with the courier of the Ticknors, who arrived here yesterday. We accordingly called on them and had a very pleasant chat. . . . I was rejoiced on Wordsworth's account, who very much wanted a companion.

JULY 22nd [*Ulm*.] . . . I was pleased with some respectable young men in the dining-room. . . . One of them found a striking resemblance between Wordsworth and Jung, alias Heinrich Stilling, and I told them who Wordsworth is. . . .

JULY 23rd [*Wurttemberg*.] . . . Wordsworth got into political chat with an English lady and talked very illiberally against the Dissenters. . . .

JULY 24th After breakfast Kölle[1] accompanied us to the Royal Park. . . . We talked on German politics and the conduct of the new King of

[1] An old friend of Crabb Robinson who chanced to be in their hotel.

Hanover. Wordsworth was very rude because Kölle unluckily made use of the word 'Tory.' Kölle kept his temper, but was greatly disgusted by his tone and conversation, and will make a very unfavourable report of him. We afterwards all went to the museum.

JULY 25th . . . While on the road Wordsworth expressed a readiness to go with me to Frankfurt if I wished it, but a desire to avoid the rich city, and I at once made up my mind to accede to his wishes as I have always done. . . .

JULY 26th [*Heidelberg.*] . . . After five accompanied Wordsworth to the Schlossers, where we took tea and had a very pleasant evening. Schlosser and Wordsworth seemed to take pleasure in each other. . . . Schlosser showed us his house and books, etc., and he told me interesting particulars of the death of Fräulein Gunderode, which Bettina in her *Briefwechsel eines Kindes* has sadly misrepresented. Schlosser says he believes the letters which appear to have furnished the matter of some of Goethe's sonnets were written by Bettina after the sonnets. This I do not believe. But in other respects I agree with Schlosser in thinking the book betrays a great want of real delicacy and moral feeling. . . .

JULY 27th . . . I called on Geheimrat Schlosser and had an interesting chat with him on his *History of the Eighteenth Century*, from which he read me some extracts, and showed me a quotation from a letter of mine to Benecke which he made in the original language and names me with a compliment. From a writer of so great distinction this is an honour, but at the same time a liberty which few English writers of eminence would have allowed themselves to take. I do not yet understand in what connection he has made the quotation. It consisted in a not ill-expressed characteristic of Mandeville. . . .

AUG. 2nd [*Louvain.*] I found opportunity today . . . to read some *Galignanis*. They contained an account of the borough elections, and, on the whole, I have been pleased with what I this day and have since heard. It gives me great pleasure that Roebuck has lost his seat at Bath, though it gives me no pleasure that two Tories have got in for Bath, my old acquaintance General Palmer being thrown out. . . . Wordsworth at dinner today said neatly: 'Mr. Roebuck is the best friend the ministers have, for his blackness makes their darkness show like light.' . . .

AUG. 3rd . . . We hurried off from our inn and with difficulty reached the railroad office at half-past six. We reached Antwerp in an hour and a quarter—a journey that used to take five hours. Wordsworth and I were in a very genteel carriage called a 'Diligence,' for which we paid each three francs. A still higher place is the 'Berline,' but which differs only from the 'Diligence' in having arm-chairs for all the travellers. We had no one with us. Judging by my feelings only, I should have thought the velocity much below that of the road between Manchester and Liverpool.[1] . . .

Aug. 5th . . . We came . . . as far as Cassel. . . . Wordsworth was greatly delighted with the view from the heights of the small town, and would prefer this place as a residence to any one he has [seen] for a long time. The plain is so enriched by fine wood as to afford delightful drives. . . .

Aug. 7th . . . There was too much wind to allow of sleep when we were out of the harbour. . . . A single discharge relieved me and going then on deck I was in comparative comfort. Wordsworth had had a much worse night and more severe sickness. . . . We had a very agreeable passage after we were in the Thames, and reached the Custom House about three o'clock. I instantly ran to Paynter's chambers, leaving Wordsworth with the carriage. Brittain . . . sent for horses and between five and six we had our things packed. The officers behaved very liberally and we were charged nothing for our few books and prints [?]. I told them who my companion was, and that probably in some measure influenced their conduct. My luggage was dropped at the Temple gate, where I alighted, and after dining at the Athenaeum and taking tea at Jaffray's I called on Wordsworth at Moxon's. I found him in good spirits and certainly in as good health as when he set out—I think even better.

And so ends this interesting tour. It will probably be not altogether unproductive, though Wordsworth has for the present composed part only of a poem on *The Cuckoo at Laverna*.

Aug. 9th . . . I have received the *Letters of Charles Lamb*. There are two to me and a civil mention of me by Talfourd. . . .

Aug. 12th . . . Strolled with Lamb's *Letters* which I had been enjoying a great part of the day. . . . As I advance in perusal of Lamb's *Letters* they delight me more. It is a pity that those at the beginning of the volume are poor. Many readers will stop at the beginning. Talfourd has showed great judgment in the veil he has thrown over what ought not to be too palpable and intelligible.

Aug. 14th I breakfasted with Mr. Samuel Rogers and had an agreeable two hours' chat with him. S. Rogers was very courteous, on reflection rather more than I can hope to be a permanent feeling, assuming it to be perfectly sincere at the time. He chatted confidentially with me about Wordsworth, but I had no pleasure in being complimented at his expense; nor dare I believe to the full extent of Rogers's statement that Wordsworth speaks of me with admiration for my taking him on a journey [?]. Still it is agreeable to believe that there is some foundation for

[1] See *supra*, p. xiv.

such a report and Wordsworth must have spoken not unkindly to permit Rogers saying so much. Of Talfourd, Lamb, Wordsworth, etc., Rogers spoke kindly and without satire. I have a pleasure in testifying this. The rest of the day I spent lounging. . . . I saw Wordsworth late at Moxon's and late in the evening I read[1] the third volume of Lockhart's *Life of Scott*. The book is intolerable and must injure both the subject and the writer. It is a memoir of the trade of book-making and exhibits the poet in the very lowest point of view imaginable.

AUG. 15th . . . I went on with the *Life of Scott*—worse and worse as it goes on. I am glad to find the opinion of the world at large agrees with mine. . . .

AUG. 16th . . . A dinner at Rogers's: the party, Miss Rogers, Mrs. Courtenay, and Mrs. Bellenden Ker—a very pleasing young woman—nothing blue-stocking about her or flighty in her manner; I never was more mistaken in my preconceptions of a person. Courtenay and his son there, out of their place, at least the father out of his; Wordsworth and Empson, so that with our host, Wordsworth, and myself we were within the prescribed number. The day passed off well. I escaped my sleepy fit. The conversation not polemical; the parties too equally divided for controversy. Rogers rather annoyed me. Empson repeating that I had boasted that I had never lost my temper or my spirits, I said: 'That is, I am afraid, not true now.' Rogers said: 'That is a reflection on Wordsworth,' and he remarked we sat as far from each other as possible. Wordsworth looked grave; I treated this as a joke, but Rogers should not have said this. Has Wordsworth said anything? He is, however, very friendly towards me. . . .

AUG. 17th I breakfasted with Rogers again this morning; Empson went with me. Wordsworth had removed thither on account of Moxon's house being under paint. A very interesting chat with Wordsworth about his poetry. He repeated emphatically what he had said before to me, that he did not expect or desire from posterity any other fame than that which would be given him for the way in which his poems exhibit man in his essentially human character and relations—as child, parent, husband, the qualities which are common to all men as opposed to those which distinguish one man from another. His sonnets are not therefore the works that he esteems the most. Empson and I had both spoken of the sonnets as our favourites. He said: 'You are both wrong.' . . .

AUG. 23rd . . . Went down to Edmonton. I found dear Mary Lamb in very good health, and she has been so long well that one may now hope for a continuance; I took a walk with her. She led me to Charles Lamb's

[1] This word is uncertain, it may be 'recid', i.e. 'received'.

grave (which she showed me without emotion). As usual I amused her by playing piquet, and she seems by no means so wretchedly situated as I before thought—yet I desire removal. . . .

AUG. 27th . . . Panizzi has obtained the Chief Librarianship of the British Museum over the head of Cary, whom I thought the best-entitled. But it seems that on account of his infirmities (he has been insane) even the Archbishop of Canterbury thought him disqualified. . . .

SEPT. 2nd . . . I had engaged to call on Wordsworth at Moxon's, and was there by eleven. He approves of my going with them to Hereford, and I am to order places for Friday. . . .

[*Travel Journal: Hereford, etc.*] I felt dissatisfied with the journey because I returned so early in the season, and therefore I resolved on making a short excursion by way of supplement to the Italian tour, and as Wordsworth was going to Hereford to visit his brother-in-law near the city, I proposed to him to go to Hereford, and accompany him on the Wye, etc., his daughter being of the party. Accordingly

SEPT. 8th We set out in the *Mazeppa* Hereford coach. . . . The journey was one of the very dullest I ever took, and Wordsworth said the same. [It lasted from 6 a.m. till half-past ten.] . . .

SEPT. 9th Young Mr. Hutchinson came for the Wordsworths to take them to Brinsop, and, between eleven and twelve, Mr. Monkhouse also came. He had heard of my being here and came for no other purpose than to fetch me . . . to the Stow, Mr. Monkhouse's farm in Whitney parish, sixteen miles from Hereford.

SEPT. 11th . . . A visit to the Hutchinsons. . . . Wordsworth had inflamed eyes and has in consequence found it impossible to compose. . . .

SEPT. 13th . . . I met Wordsworth driving to make a call on Sir Robert Price. I therefore joined him, and, entering the park when he alighted to make his call, I rambled about the park. . . .

SEPT. 14th [*Hereford.*] I ascertained this morning that there is no passage boat now between Ross and Chepstow. This took away all hope and desire to make an excursion down the Wye. I walked in the castle grounds, and found the wind so sharp as to satisfy me that this season does not suit Dora Wordsworth, and that a journey ought not to be made by her. . . . I therefore made up my mind to go to Liverpool, [to meet his brother.] I hesitated whether I should not go this morning and perhaps I should if I had not been deeply interested in *Waverley* [lent him by Mrs. Hutchinson], which I have only just finished. . . .

SEPT. 15th . . . It was alarmingly fine, for I feared Wordsworth might come and be inclined to pursue the journey originally intended, and now

I should have disliked that, my plan being otherwise fixed. He never came, nor was there any one from Brinsop. . . .

SEPT. 16th I rose early and placed myself on the box of the Liverpool stage. . . . The day was wet: relieved from all apprehension that Wordsworth might think me capricious in not making the excursion with him to Chepstow. . . .

OCT. 21st [*London.*] . . . I went to Covent Garden where I saw Lord Byron's *Werner*. I had not even read it. The fine acting of Macready gave me great pleasure: otherwise the play gave me no great pleasure. It is dissatisfying. . . .

OCT. 22nd . . . The day was made amusing by Miss Martineau who pleased me better than before. She told me a number of curious anecdotes of Willis, whom she represents to be little better than a swindler. Her account of American persons was very interesting and not at all offensive by any assumption on her part, though she speaks like one who is conscious of having a right to speak and form a judgment. . . . Miss Martineau gave an amusing account of Mrs. Trollope, who, she says, was admitted to no decent society in Cincinnati. . . .

OCT. 27th . . . Miss Martineau . . . pleased me by speaking with perfect frankness of her former poverty: she had not five shillings. Her books had put her in possession of an income. . . . Mr. Robertson, editor of the *Westminster and London Review* [*sic*] . . . assured me from personal knowledge that the *Edinburgh Review* does not now pay its expenses nor does it regularly pay its contributors. The *Quarterly Review* is the only trimestrial review that does. . . .

NOV. 21st . . . Miss Martineau gave me good news about the progress of a copyright bill in America for the benefit of English authors which will rejoice Wordsworth. . . .

NOV. 25th . . . I had then to go to dine with Mr. Crawford, 27 Wilton Crescent—a family party and relations and also Carlyle. I found Carlyle so very outrageous in his opinions that I have no wish to see him again, and I avoided saying anything that looked like a desire to renew my acquaintance with him. He spoke of Dr. Channing[1] with contempt as an unreadable commonplace writer, and I was sorry that Crawford concurred in this opinion. He quite disgusted me by his avowed approbation of the annexation of Texas and of the holding the negroes in slavery. It is a natural aristocracy, that of *colour*, and quite right that the stronger and better race should have dominion! He said, however, some striking things in which if not absolutely true there was notwithstanding some truth: as that [no] man ever did any great good to society under the influence of

[1] William Ellery Channing.

benevolent motives. Men were impelled by instinct and impulses of passion to do great actions. This, he said, after the expression of great contempt of Dr. Channing's *Essay on Buonaparte.* He was, however, personally civil to me, and though I shunned particular conversation with him I said nothing discourteously that I am aware of.

NOV. 29th . . . I then called on Miss Harriet Martineau; she was evidently gratified by my warm praise of her brother's *Rationale*[1] and I dare say forgives me for not admiring as she does the style and wild opinions of Carlyle. . . .

NOV. 30th . . . I went to the Athenaeum, where I read a portion of *Oliver Twist*; a very able and quite original work of fiction—exhibiting very pathetically, but repulsively sometimes, the sufferings of the very poor. It is the history of a parish apprentice—the tendency bad but the work one of pure genius. . . .

DEC. 1st . . . I read another chapter of *Oliver Twist*, a book that almost exceeds the allowable measure of human suffering and the temporary success of villainy, but I suppose all is to be made right at last, as we hope a future state is to redress the seeming wrongs of the good in this world.[2]

DEC. 6th . . . I also wrote to Landor acknowledging his *Pentameron*; I was glad of the opportunity of praising with sincerity this delightful book. I praised what I have copied, his fine remarks on the atheism of Lucretius and the orthodoxy of Dante; I noticed a conceit in Charles Lamb's way on the birds and clouds not being damned. I jokingly noticed some passages which look like a covert attack still on Wordsworth, and I very briefly hinted at his family matters and gave a rapid account of our journey—I believe the letter will please him. . . .

DEC. 11th . . . I had this morning a letter from Landor, so absurd, in answer to mine, worse than absurd. He does not trouble himself to notice mine, or thank me for my civility or show pleasure at my commendations, but sends me loose verses! I will break with him. . . .

DEC. 19th [Bear Wood.] The only incident of the day . . . was that I . . . called at Miss Mitford's. She was unwell. Her old father we chatted with. In the morning he is conversable. He has the air of a gentleman of the

[1] *Rationale of Religious Inquiry*, by James Martineau.

[2] In his later reminiscences, compiled between 1845 and 1853, Crabb Robinson added: 'My first notice of the writings of Dickens, as far as I can perceive. . . . Dickens is a fine writer and excellent man. It is to be lamented that he is ambitious of living genteely and giving dinners to the rich. With an income of three or four thousand a year, and sometimes much more, he may at length, it is to be feared, leave his children to be maintained by the public. He is delicate in his appearance and some slight tendency to be a fop. He is liberal in his opinions, charitable, and a good chairman at public dinners.'

old school, an aristocratic air with which he masks his poverty. Living in a miserable hovel, he has been maintained by his daughter, who now writes popular books for their support after he had spent £20,000 she gained in the lottery. . . .

1838

JAN. 8th . . . One person in particular whose conversation interested me more than any I have met with for a long time, his name, Milne,[1] a young man, member for Pontefract . . . a Conservative, but one who thinks that the Catholic Church ought to be established in Ireland! This shows him to be a thinker. He is besides a man of varied reading and of most catholic taste. He is a great lover of Wordsworth and of Goethe too: besides, he is an acquaintance of De Lammenais, of whom he relates that the apostate *abbé* has of late become very intimate with George Sand! Yet he seems to think that De Lammenais is a sincere Christian after all. Milnes, however, is fond of paradoxes. He spoke in approbation of persecution, if it could be efficient—the old Catholic apology. . . . He . . . praised the writing of one Maurice, who wrote *Subscription no Bondage* and other writings of High Church theology, but on such philosophic principles as to be an object of suspicion to the commonplace orthodox. By the bye, of the commonplace people, the Baldwins, to whom I lent Lamb's *Letters*, did not read much of his letters because of his having praised Dr. Priestley. They thought him unsound. Poor, dear Lamb! Talfourd put in these letters as the only few he could find in which Charles Lamb showed the least sense of any kind of religion whatever; but I could not say this to the Baldwins.

JAN. 17th . . . Began *Pickwick* a few days ago. I like the book much more than I expected.

JAN. 20th . . . Reading in *Pickwick*, whom I am acquiring a real taste for. . . .

JAN. 26th . . . Read *Pickwick*. . . . A call from Milnes. He talked pleasantly about German literature. I showed him my translation [of *Egmont*] and lent him books. We shall become acquainted. . . .

JAN. 29th . . . A call on Harriet Martineau; my respect for her judgment diminishes daily, but not my esteem for her character. She is an excellent person. I called to lend her Voltaire, etc. . . .

[1] So written in the MS. But it is clear that Crabb Robinson is writing of R. Monckton Milnes.

FEB. 7th I read for an hour in *Pickwick*, who does not improve as he advances, but in whom I am more interested. . . .

FEB. 16th I finished *Pickwick* this morning. A book that had very much more amused me than I expected, though I cannot on reflection rank it high as a work of art. Neither Pickwick himself nor the greater number of the persons are, after all, characters at all. Only Sam Weller the faithful servant, and his father the old coachman, are characters. The rest are dull, commonplace people. Such characterless persons are good to relieve the marked and too emphatic actors, but when they are the staple of the author's persons they are very tiresome, and mere vulgarity is a bad foundation for humour and too much of *Pickwick* is mere slang. Still, Dickens has genius and will do much. . . . Dined with Edwin Field; Miss Rogers and M. Sharpe and Dr. Hutton there, and later came Joanna Baillie. It was Joanna Baillie that I went principally to see. Nothing could be more agreeable than her person and manners as an old lady, nearer eighty than seventy, I am told, nothing more unimportant and insignificant than her conversation—yet nothing in the slightest degree *against* her reputation, for there was no occasion for display. She inquired about Wordsworth and recognised me as having called on her formerly with him. The conversation not in any way literary or controversial, yet no *ennui*. I recollect nothing that was said by any one, and only that I passed an agreeable evening. Of Joanna Baillie I should add that she has a broad Scotch accent, though she has left Scotland more than sixty years, and that she has the appearance of a woman of strong practical good sense. . . .

FEB. 18th . . . I dined by invitation with Rogers—a mere family party. That is, Miss Rogers and all the Sharpes, no one else. I remarked again and more strongly than before a decided unfriendliness towards Wordsworth, which is so predominant a feeling as I think to go far towards justifying Lord Byron's attack:

> Hunts your weak point out, then shows it
> Where it injures to disclose it.

Though the last line may seem inapplicable, since I am not likely to be affected by such things. I cannot help thinking also that the inference is justly drawn:

> 'Tis but envy when all's done.

MARCH 14th I finished this morning Milnes's *Memorials of a Tour in Greece*, which I had great pleasure from. It is the book of a young writer

—the verses careless, the style loose, but wise thoughts and feelings, to be expected from an admirer of Wordsworth. He will become, I expect, an excellent writer. . . .

MARCH 16th . . . I left my card at Milnes's with a civil note about his poems. . . .

MARCH 21st This morning was spent in finishing the sixth volume of Walter Scott's *Life*, which has raised him greatly in my estimation. His conduct after the calamity had arisen was exemplary. . . .

APRIL 27th . . . I called on Lady Blessington—more than a year since I called. She would have been cold if she had not been indifferent. She was unusually agreeable—no flattery to me, no abuse of others. D'Orsay looked haggard as if he had been unlucky at Crockford's. James Smith besides there. I stayed very late. I am glad I renewed my visits: it would have been prudery not, yet I like Milnes the better for not sending her his poems.

MAY 7th . . . I finished the first volume of Gillman's *Life of Coleridge*. A deal too much that is old and very little new, and unworthy omissions both of Coleridge's letter on his opium-eating, and of De Quincey's early generosity to Coleridge; a palpable preference of the hero to truth. Too uniformly eulogistic and too anxious a desire to make a good Church of England Trinitarian of him. . . .

MAY 20th My breakfast party went off very well indeed as far as talk was concerned; I had with me Landor, Milnes, and Serjeant Talfourd. A great deal of rattling on the part of Landor. He maintained Blake to be the greatest of poets, that Milnes is the greatest poet now living in England, and that Scott's *Marmion* is superior to all Wordsworth and Byron, and the description of the battles better than anything in Homer! but Blake furnished chief matter for talk. I had but little talk about Landor's family when we were left alone. . . . He made no inquiry about his wife or other children. He is most uncomfortable and unhappy and it is painful to be *tête-à-tête* with him. . . .

MAY 22nd A delightful breakfast with Milnes, Rogers, Carlyle, who made himself very pleasant indeed, Moore, Landor—a party of eight. Rogers angry with being forced into Landor's company. Moore very civil to me, whom he on other occasions has cut. Talk very good, equally divided. Talleyrand's recent death and the poet Blake were the subjects. Tom Moore had never heard of Blake—at least not of his poems. Even he acknowledged their beauty. I left at one. . . .

MAY 24th . . . Southey has intimated a readiness to travel with Kenyon and me in July in Normandy and Brittany. So this will probably take place. . . .

JULY 6th . . . I went late to Lady Blessington's. It was a relief to hear that Landor had left London and, as I can justify apparent neglect, I am not anxious to do it. He was at the Coronation, and rampant, it is said. . . .

JULY 16th . . . I looked again into Lofft's curious volume [*Self-Formation*], and also into Milnes, whose last work, *Memorials of Foreign Travel*, will certainly fix his reputation as a poet. A pity that he has contrived to get a character for foppery and arrogance. . . . But he will get over this.

AUG. 17th . . . Began at the Athenaeum tonight that marvellous but to me interesting book *Sartor Resartus*, by Carlyle.

On the 28th I went to Dover, and on the following day I met at Boulogne Southey and his son, a Mr. Senhouse, Southey's friend, my friend Kenyon, and his friend Captain Jones. They had hired two carriages, and with them I set out next day on a short tour through Normandy into Brittany and by the Touraine to Paris. . . .

The Southeys left soon. I remained with Kenyon and Jones till the 31st of October.

During the tour not an unpleasant occurrence with any one of my companions, and greatly improved my intimacy with Kenyon.

[*Travel Journal: France.*] AUG. 28th . . . I hope tomorrow to meet at Boulogne with our party—the Laureate and his son Cuthbert Southey, a Mr. Senhouse, his friend, an elderly gentleman of great promise, my friend, John Kenyon and his friend Captain Jones—a party of six which will, I expect, be found too numerous to be able to travel together long. . . .

AUG. 29th . . . The Southeys and Senhouse I found well and all seeming in good spirits and humour. . . . I read to Southey the passage in my *Supplement*[1] about himself and Wordsworth, with which he seemed contented. . . .

AUG. 31st [*Abbeville.*] . . . The party were in very good humour all day and Southey especially in excellent spirits—an unassuming and agreeable companion. I began to read the history and introduction to Southey's *Lives of the Admirals*, which Captain Jones had brought with him and which I found a pleasing book. . . .

SEPT. 4th . . . My friends had the happy disposition to find everything agreeable and therefore the really beautiful valley in which Rouen stands could not but be pleasant. . . .

SEPT. 26th . . . It was the suggestion of Southey that he should like to see Chinon on account of its connection with Joan of Arc. . . . It was here

[1] To Thomas Clarkson's *Strictures on a Life of Wilberforce* (1838). Crabb Robinson was a passionate believer in the abolition of the slave-trade, and a close friend of Thomas Clarkson (1760–1846), the campaigner against slavery. The *Strictures* was, in fact, largely written by Robinson in defence of Clarkson, who had been unfairly criticized.

that [she] recognised, according to the legend, Charles VII, and on this account Southey wished to see the castle. . . .

Oct. 6th [*Paris.*] . . . I called on the Southeys in the evening. . . . Southey has, I believe, not been in the Louvre and cares for nothing at Paris but the old book-shops. This is a singular feature in his character. But with this indifference to the living things around him is closely connected his faculty, the poetic faculty, of beholding the absent as if present and creating a world for himself. . . . Southey read to me part of a pleasant letter to his daughter in which he said: 'I would rather live in Paris than be hanged, and could find quiet spots to reside in, in the country round. The people look comfortable, and might be clean if they would, but they have a hydrophobia in all things but one. They use water for no other purpose than to mix with their wine—for which God forgive them.' In this letter he said that the tour had been made without a single unpleasant occurrence, and that six men could not be found who better agreed. This seems complimentary. He might have added: Three of them devoted themselves entirely to the service of the other three, performing every labour, and consulting their wishes and giving them the best of everything. Southey himself is sensible of this. I doubt whether the others are. At least no expression of being aware of it. . . .

Oct. 9th . . . The Southeys . . . went off at a quarter past four. . . . This was but a broken day, being the last attentions shown to the Southeys. Southey left us with a friendly farewell to the 'faithful fellow-travellers.' . . .[1]

Oct. 23rd . . . I lounged in the Tuileries with *Sartor Resartus*, which even for its style delights me—perhaps but few besides, for one must be German to relish it. Yet there are wise and admirable things scattered about with great profusion. And all a treatise on clothes. A supposed treatise by a supposed professor in the University of Weissnichtwo, who bears the horrid name of 'Devil's dung', *Teufelsdröckh*. This disgusted me and prevented, I believe, my looking into the book for a long time. . . .

Oct. 29th . . . I shall finish this book at the Athenaeum. When not read too frequently it is delightful, but the style is best when it can be considered as humour. When it is purely pathetic, it is constrained. Carlyle's thoughts are better than his descriptions. All the love tale of Professor Teufelsdröckh is dull enough. . . .

Oct. 30th . . . I called with a p.p.c. card on Samuel Rogers. I found him at home. He accompanied me to the Louvre, and pointed out to me a

[1] In his subsequent reminiscences Crabb Robinson wrote: 'None of us on setting out were aware to how great a degree the mind of the Laureate was departed. . . . He had lost all power of conversation, and seldom spoke. Yet he was always amiable.'

number of the best pictures, most of which were favourites of mine. . . .

Nov. 11th [*London.*] I went to the Athenaeum, where I went on reading *Oliver Twist*, which is now published in the form of a novel. . . .

Nov. 19th . . . Finished *Oliver Twist*—an excellent but not faultless book. Its merit lies in the truth of the picture of the condition and sufferings of the poor; its greatest fault that Oliver Twist has no character; he is but the poor parish boy, victim of the state of the law—or rather, would be if by most romantic incidents, by no means well made out, he did not recover property. The unfortunate girl, Nancy, and her murderer Sikes are most admirably wrought—so is Bumble the Beadle; but Monks, the half-brother of Oliver Twist, is a failure. The Jew is also powerfully conceived, and the conclusion is wrought up with admirable power. Read an article on Carlyle in the *Dublin Review*. The Catholic party would gladly get Carlyle on their side, but the attempt fails.

Dec. 7th . . . I went to bed to read *Nickleby*, which I read both then and early in the morning. *Nickleby* is certainly not equal to *Oliver Twist*. One is tired of the succession of troubles arising from poverty in conflict with meanness. I leave Nickleby with actors. The exhibition of the Portsmouth company is amusing though a caricature, but it ought not to last long. The author always passes over which [*sic*] should be the main incident; as he in *Oliver Twist* omits the trial of the Jew, so here he omits the acting of Nickleby. He is but a sketcher of scenes; he cannot construct a story. Could not that [be done] by somebody else? He is a master of comic character drawing.

Dec. 28th On the Whitehaven coach at eight, and set down at Rydal after ten. Mrs. Wordsworth had taken rooms for me next to Agnes's—in a genteel house where I shall be very comfortable. My rooms are excellent, Mrs. Fleming a respectable person. I had a most kind reception from every one of the Wordsworths, and the rest of the day was agreeably spent with them. William was there from Kendal; I found all well except Miss Wordsworth, and she better than when here before. She came down after dinner and stopped with us a short time. She repeated some of her own poems very affectingly. Interesting conversation with Wordsworth: he was very civil about the *Strictures*, which he praised cordially. All here rejoice in Clarkson's triumph. On religion Wordsworth talked with his usual sagacity. He apologised for making salvation depend on opinion, by the suggestion that only depravity of will could prevent that examination of evidence which must lead to the conviction of truth; but he would not affirm that such a principle applied to the Athanasian Creed, which he pretended not to justify, but wishes to remove. Wordsworth's health is good. I dined and took tea with my friends. . . .

DEC. 29th [written on Jan. 1st] I have little to say of the three days just spent here, not having memory to record the wise sayings that occasionally fall from my friend here. The incidents were simply these: That in the forenoon I called, with Wordsworth, on Dr. Arnold, of whom I shall have frequent occasion to speak, and with them I walked to Ambleside, where I left a small parcel with Mrs. Cookson and called also on the Harrisons. I dined, of course, and took tea with the Wordsworths, and after a rubber of whist—a new practice of the Wordsworths—I came home at half-past nine and found a good fire in my bedroom. I began Dr. Arnold's *Rome*.

DEC. 30th As in duty bound, I went to church; a thin audience. A most dull business, the reading bad, the preaching worse. Even the Wordsworths can say nothing for their parson. A wet day. We dined at one, and in the afternoon I had a short walk with Wordsworth in the garden. Then to Ambleside; a call on Miss Fenwick, Wordsworth's friend, the patroness of Henry Taylor, a rich maiden lady—a sensible and agreeable woman. She enjoys good books and courts clever people. She admires both Carlyle and his writings. I am now reading her Carlyle's *History of the French Revolution*. It is a fascinating book to those who are once caught by it, but the Wordsworths and nine out of ten readers cannot endure it. I have a difficulty in letting it out of my hand, and when they say, 'It is not English,' I can only answer: 'It is as good.' I wish I could have altered a very few ultra-Germanisms. I read it every morning in bed, when my head may be supposed clearest; at night I read Arnold's *Rome*.

DEC. 31st I accompanied Wordsworth to Mrs. Luff. She was most friendly; declared: 'I quite love you for your defence of Clarkson.' She is a great friend of the Clarksons. . . .

1839

JAN 1st I kept within till Wordsworth called with Dr. Arnold. I talked with the Doctor about his book in a tone that could not but be agreeable. It is, indeed, to me a good book. The morning very wet. I had no walk but for half an hour in Wordsworth's garden. Miss Fenwick at dinner; she was detained till near eleven by the non-arrival of carriage. Though we had a long evening I had no ennui and was hardly drowsy. I found more sympathy than I anticipated with Miss Fenwick. But she too is for Clarkson. It is true I have lost way by confessing that I now and then see Lady Blessington. But I lost none in declaring Kehama to be John Calvin's God. We had all sorts of literary gossip. Wordsworth talks well with her and she understands good talk and seems quite liberal as well as intelligent. She is really a very agreeable person. Home late, and read only in *The Doctor* tonight.

JAN. 2nd Had a difficulty in shutting Carlyle after breakfast to write these memoirs, so much taken by it. I continued reading with great pleasure Dr. Arnold's *Rome*, and having now finished the first volume—the whole yet—I will just say . . . I now feel a strong interest in Roman history, which I never did before. I had a call from Mr. Ball the Quaker with Wordsworth, and with Wordsworth I made a call on Miss Fenwick. I dined with Dr. Arnold alone, Wordsworth being afraid of the cold. Sir Thomas Pasley there; very pleasant visit. The Doctor very friendly, though he is aware I wrote against him as Fellow of the London University. He said: 'I am no longer a Fellow, therefore we are no longer enemies,'—but no other allusion. . . . We talked easily about the religious controversies,—took all I said in good part. He is evidently bitter against the Oxford Tract men. Wordsworth is rather friendly towards them.

JAN. 3rd I remained, as is my practice, till Wordsworth called, in my room. Between one and two he came and we called at Dr. Arnold's—he was from home. We went on to Miss Fenwick. Wordsworth talks his best with her. He spoke of poetry—on occasion of Miss Barrett; he said: 'Her poems are too ideal for me. I want flesh and blood; even coarse nature and truth, where there is a want of refinement and beauty, is better than the other extreme. At the head of this natural and sensual school is Chaucer, the greatest poet of his class. Next comes Burns; Crabbe, too, has great truth, but he is too far removed from beauty and refinement.' I told him that in this he unconsciously sympathises with Goethe. Dined as usual; a short rubber. William Wordsworth [junior] very poorly; so Dora. At night read as usual.

JAN. 6th . . . In the evening I read part of Gladstone's new book on the connection between Church and State. The tone is mild and gentlemanly and it is more liberally written than I expected; but I do not see much talent or good writing in it. . . .

JAN. 7th . . . I read after dinner to Wordsworth some things in Carlyle; Wordsworth cannot enjoy Carlyle. He has a habit of opposing to everything that is said—a something not the same—and therefore what is not his own he does not like—as if there were not an infinity of relations as well as of modes of viewing things and as if all in their place and way might not be true. This is the greatest defect in Wordsworth's great mind; that it begins to ossify: he is beset by fixed ideas, he does not retain the facility of shifting his position and seeing things on all sides. We had an agreeable evening, divided between whist, Carlyle, and Gladstone. But the more I read the more ordinary I think his [Gladstone's] understanding. He has taken so little trouble to inform himself that he actually asserts that nearly all the old Dissenters of Charles II are become Unitarians!

JAN. 8th . . . I went to Wordsworth this forenoon. He was in bed of a cold. Read to him Gladstone's book, which I like only in parts, chiefly those parts that show the evil of Catholicism. . . .

JAN. 15th . . . Today the Wordsworths went all to Miss Fenwick's for a few days' visit. She pressed me to take a bed there, which I declined, but accepted of her invitation to dine with her as long as the Wordsworths were with her. Southey, too, was invited for a few days, and he came this afternoon. We had but a dull dinner, partly occasioned by Southey's silence. He seemed in low spirits—perhaps occasioned by the state of his daughter (Kate's) health. Wordsworth was rather chatty and I seconded him; still, though the afternoon passed off with nothing unpleasant, it was not what, in such society, might have been expected. . . .

JAN. 18th . . . I walked out with Wordsworth. We met with Dr. Arnold, and with him I walked alone. We talked of Southey; Wordsworth spoke of him with great feeling and affection. He said: 'It is painful to see how completely dead Southey is become to all but *books*; when he comes here he seems restless, as if from a sense of duty, and out of his element. He is obliging and amiable, but indifferent to everything; I, therefore, hardly see him for years together.' Now all this I had observed on the journey. Rogers noticed it as a subject of reproach, Wordsworth only of sorrow. Dr. Arnold said afterwards: 'What you said of Mr. Southey alarmed me. I could not help saying to myself: "I am in danger of becoming like him; shall I ever lose my interest in things and retain an interest only in books?" ' 'If I must,' said Wordsworth, 'lose my interest in one of them I would rather give up books than men. Indeed, I am compelled in great measure by my eyes to give up reading. Yet with all this Southey was an affectionate husband and is a fond father.' . . .

JAN. 22nd . . . A party at dinner—the Pasleys and Hardens, and the afternoon went off very agreeably. I amused myself with Miss Arnold, while Wordsworth declaimed with Dr. Arnold and Sir Thomas Pasley. Wordsworth seems to have adopted something of Coleridge's tone, but he is more concentrated in the objects of his interest. I am glad to find that neither he can accompany Gladstone in his Anglo-Papistical pretensions, nor Dr. Arnold neither—indeed, the Doctor is less of a churchman of the two. . . .

JAN. 26th . . . I read with deep interest the third volume of Carlyle, of whom Wordsworth pronounces a harsh judgment. It is not only his style that he condemns, but his *inhumanity*. He says there is a want of due sympathy with mankind. Scorn and irony are the feeling and tone throughout. There is too much truth in this, and it is too strongly confirmed by the opinion so strongly expressed by Carlyle at table at Crawford's, in favour of the continuance of negro slavery by the Americans, which he, one might hope in a spirit of paradox only, was led to profess, even at war with his innermost feelings. . . .

JAN. 28th I went early to Wordsworth to talk about the Copyright Bill which Talfourd is to bring forward and a petition which Wordsworth and others are individually to send in. Wordsworth has drawn up one in which he is too desirous to express his own impressions and cares, too little about the impressions it will excite in others. . . .

JAN. 29th Looked over last night and this morning the new edition of Southey's works for the sake of the new matter—in prefaces. I found nothing in it to excite a desire to read again the poems I formerly read, or those I am unacquainted with—I have always thought more highly of Southey's prose works than his poems; but, believing him as a thinker to be either quite wrong or only partially right on all the great points of religion and politics, I cannot possibly rank him very highly. Still, he is a most excellent man and of great general ability and a beautiful stylist in prose.

Wordsworth read to me some twelve or more new Sonnets—for the greater part excellent. His faculties as a poet are certainly not on the decline; I was the whole of the afternoon and evening with him.

This morning I amused myself by re-writing a petition Wordsworth had drawn up in favour of the new Copyright Bill of Talfourd. Wordsworth adopted a few of my suggestions in himself writing it over again.

JAN. 31st . . . I also finished Carlyle's *History*, the bad taste of which I concede to Wordsworth, but not that it is written in a spirit of derision towards the aristocratic and ecclesiastical sufferers under the Revolution. I wrote to Talfourd today expressing my regret that he had been unable to remove Miss Lamb during her late illness. . . .

FEB. 1st Reading as well last night as this morning the second pamphlet written by Wordsworth against Brougham in 1818. They were on the General Election and are a very spirited and able vindication of the voting for the two Lowthers against the Radical parvenu, and have in them very little that I now dissent from. They show Wordsworth in a new point of view. He would have been a masterly political pamphleteer. There is nothing cloudy about the style; it is full of phrases such as these:

'Whether designedly for the attainment of popularity or in the self-applauding sincerity of a heated mind.' 'Independence is the explosive energy of conceit making blind havoc with expediency.' . . .

FEB. 7th [*London.*] . . . Then I called on John Wordsworth and afterwards on Quillinan. It was useful, my call. I found [J.] Wordsworth had given offence to Quillinan and therefore did not wish to meet him, but on going to Quillinan he also told me the ground of offence. I found it not difficult to remove an unfriendly impression; I told Quillinan that John Wordsworth was not unfriendly towards his pretensions (with Dora), and the end was that, calling twice on John Wordsworth and twice on Quillinan for the purpose, they agreed to shake hands in my chambers on *this* day, but Quillinan was forced to leave town. He wrote me a note thanking me for my interposition, quoting the text blessing the peacemakers, etc. They had shaken hands, etc. . . .

MARCH 4th . . . I made my first call at Francis Hare's: only Mrs. Hare's sister at home—at least she was the only one I saw. Mrs. Shelley I was rather surprised to see there; her son there, a loutish-looking boy, quite unworthy his intellectual ancestors in appearance. If talent descended, what ought not to be the issue of Mrs. Wollstonecraft, Godwin, Shelley, and Mrs. Shelley! . . .

MAY 1st . . . I heard Carlyle's first lecture on Revolutions. It was very interesting, though all the ideas were familiar to me, and too diffuse. A great number of interesting persons. . . .

MAY 4th . . . The Wordsworths called. Wordsworth proposes that I should join him in giving our carriage to Mr. Hutchinson on his paying all the expenses, to which I readily assent. I have offered Wordsworth two of my pictures bought at the sale [of Aders's pictures]. Not yet fixed on by him. . . . I hurried . . . to Carlyle's lecture. The second pleased me less than the first. A violent declamation against the Pope would please the Protestants, but generally I think there was more originality in the style than in the thoughts. The subject was Luther. He got applause once only—that was in apology for intolerance when opposed to that tolerance which is only another word for indifference. . . .

MAY 7th . . . Lord John Russell and Lord Melbourne announced their resignation. To Wordsworth a grievous occurrence—it will postpone the Copyright Bill and prevent the arrangement about his office. . . .

MAY 16th . . . Calls at Marshall's, where I found the Wordsworths, and on Miss Fenwick; a confidential chat. She tells me that Dora Wordsworth is at last to marry Quillinan with Wordsworth's forced permission, not approval. There is no other objection to the union than want of fortune. A serious talk with Miss Fenwick. . . .

May 18th . . . I heard Carlyle's last lecture today. It pleased more than others, yet I could not assent to his depreciation of the Brissotins nor be pleased with his merely saying of Robespierre that he was *unlovable*. Of the Terrorist leaders, Danton, Marat, and Robespierre, he is the apologist on the ground that they had a deep and sincere feeling for the *wrongs* sustained by the masses against the privileged orders; while the Brissotins he condemns as logicians and men guilty of the *crime* of being revolutionists through vanity. . . .

May 24th . . . I spent the rest of the forenoon with Landor. He talked of his two new tragedies on Joan of Naples[1] with amusing frankness. One of them is better than anything that has appeared since Shakespeare; both written in a few days. They are praised by James the novelist very highly, even beyond Landor's own opinion. They are soon to appear. I accompanied Landor to the diorama, a very declining work of art. . . . Then I accompanied Landor to the Exhibition, where I ended the forenoon. The heroes of the Exhibition are Landseer and Maclise; yet Maclise is introducing a sort of diabolical style, very high fierce colouring, but he has invention and power. Etty has a most voluptuous, even gross, 'Rape of Proserpine.' There is a little picture by Uwins that I prefer to all these—a long panel picture—a scene in Italy—a delicious thing. Turner, hotter and more uncomfortable than ever. I dined at the Athenaeum and called by invitation of Wordsworth late at the Marshalls'.

May 26th I had at breakfast Wordsworth and Dr. Thompson and Mayer,[2] also Layard, whom I had asked before. Mrs. Wordsworth was to have come, but she had just heard of the death of her elder brother. The breakfast went off well enough, though Wordsworth would discuss the Church question—a tiresome one. . . .

May 28th. I had another breakfast that gave me more trouble than pleasure—Landor, Mayer, Thompson, Kenyon. . . . Landor praises excessively my Francia; Perugino, and the Albrecht Dürer I have been forced to give up. In other respects an amusing visit. Landor entertains by his wild talk at all events. . . . A call from Mrs. Aders. She took away the picture of an old woman by Albrecht Dürer which I bought for £3 and which Miss Lawrence begged for, and I have most unwillingly parted with. My account of pictures bought at the sale stands thus: I bought a 'Sandbank', Ruysdael, £2; Wordsworth takes this. 'St. John in the Wilderness', Agnani, [?] £2 2*s*.; I wish I had it not. 'Virgin and Child,' Van der Weyden; Wordsworth takes this. 'Descent from Cross', Hemling

[1] *Andrea of Hungary* and *Giovanna of Naples*.

[2] Enrico Mayer, an Italian politican, was a friend made by Crabb Robinson on his first visit to Italy.

[i.e. Memling], £14 3*s.* 6*d.*; Masquerier says he would not give it house-room; Aders thinks it thrown away. I am not sorry I have it, for it has great expression. 'Portrait of Old Man,' Hans Schäuffelein, £5 18*s.* 6*d.*; I like it much. 'Holy Family', Pietro Perugino, £31 10*s.*; Landor says Raphael did not paint finer, but he says it is by Lorenzo di Credi. I love it much; it is the crown of my purchases. 'Annunciation,' Carlo Dolci, £13 13*s.*; Landor says twice as much as it is worth. 'St. Catherine,' a Francia, £6 6*s.*; the piece I love most after the Perugino. Total £79 10*s.*

N.B.—The pictures taken by Wordsworth are presents—he made a selection from the six smallest. The loss of the Albrecht Dürer has vexed me not a little. . . .

MAY 31st . . . Returned to chambers and read *Nickleby* till I dressed for a party. This book goes on improving as a novel without being more pleasant as a picture of manners. . . .

JUNE 11th . . . In the evening I was at a most interesting party at Kenyon's. The Websters: Mrs. Webster the most interesting American lady I have ever seen. Also at Kenyon's, . . . Dickens, with an interesting face, but rather a disagreeable expression. . . .

JUNE 22nd . . . Called first on Quillinan, who wants my advice or assistance. He has the offer of the secretaryship of a new joint stock bank, if he could bring some good men into the concern. This I cannot do, for I know none of that class of persons. If he can get this place he may be able to marry—and dear Dora would then be able to marry. . . .

JULY 24th . . . I read another volume of *Vivian Grey*, which I felt no inclination to finish. The same occurred with *Sense and Sensibility*—a rare occurrence in novel-reading. Nor shall I think of reading anything else by the younger Disraeli. . . .

JULY 25th . . . I spent this forenoon reading Ainsworth's *Rookwood*—a genuine romance which interested me during the day I was reading it, but I felt ashamed of the lost time. Only the ballads and flash songs have left an impression of merit and talent in the writer. . . .

AUG. 29th . . . I had an early dinner and then I walked to Edmonton, where I stayed more than two hours with some difficulty to fill up the time. Poor dear Mary Lamb was ten months ill lately and these severe attacks have produced the inevitable result. Her mind is gone, at least it is become inert. She has still her excellent heart—is kind and considerate and her judgment is sound—nothing but good feeling and good sense in all she says; but still no one would discover what she once was. She hears ill and is slow in conception. She says she bears solitude better than she did. She is afraid to come to town, lest she should suffer under a renewal of her periodical alienation of mind. She did not press me to stay till the last coach, and so after a few games of piquet I took the seven o'clock stage. . . .

SEPT. 22nd . . . I was reading yesterday and today *Sense and Sensibility*, which I resumed at the second volume. The last volume greatly improves on the first, but I still think it one of the poorest of Miss Austen's novels —that is, inferior to *Mansfield Park* and *Pride and Prejudice*, which is all I have read.

SEPT. 27th . . . I read yesterday and today a novel by Theodore Hook— the first and probably the last. I have seldom read a novel so uninteresting. Gilbert Gurney is an ordinary character, and the tale is of ordinary events —merely to exhibit comic characters and situations. . . .

OCT. 31st [*Brighton.*] . . . I finished the first volume of Boz's *Sketches*. These are clever pictures of manners, with a sprinkling of romantic incident. His best articles are his representations of low-life. Yet such reading tires soon and one feels that one does not want to know more of such worthless realities than one is forced to come in contact with. It is only the great masters of Dutch painting that can render enjoyable their still and low-life.

NOV. 11th . . . We had a party with us—more interesting than usual . . . and a very interesting old man, [George] Thomson, the friend of Burns and publisher of his songs. His correspondence with Burns is well and honourably known. He is about eighty years old, and he fiddled and sang Scotch songs all the evening—his vitality is marvellous. His daughter was there, an agreeable woman. . . .

NOV. 24th [*London.*] . . . I dined with Rogers. . . . However, the old gentleman, in spite of his determination against it, is becoming manifestly old. . . .

DEC. 15th . . . Moxon's in the evening. By the bye, a letter lately from Wordsworth: Southey continues very weak—no hopes of his recovery, as it seems.

1840

JAN. 2nd . . . Read within these few days further articles in Carlyle's *Miscellanies*. His article on Jean Paul is deeply interesting, though I cannot always fathom him. His article on Schiller flattering from the general concurrence in opinion.

JAN. 11th . . . I also read a fine article of Carlyle's on the state of German Literature. His other article on the German Playwrights I liked less; it is somewhat flippant. That on Heyne, though in a tolerant spirit, is inferior. By the bye, he has sent a civil message to me and he is now willing at least to be on friendly and respectful terms with me. More I cannot expect or even desire—he being what he is and I what I am. . . .

JAN. 24th . . . I finished at the Athenaeum this morning Macaulay's beautiful article on Lord Clive in the *Edinburgh Review*. A wise article, distinguishing happily between the praise due to a man for a preponderance of good over evil in his public conduct and that unqualified eulogy due only to the perfect moralist. Macaulay rises every day in my esteem. I believe he will be a powerful aid to the Ministry. . . .

JAN. 29th . . . I walked on to Chelsea; Carlyle and his brother the Doctor were not at home. I chatted with Mrs. Carlyle—a sensible woman—a short time. Carlyle had before called on me, and there[fore] I was not unwilling to overlook his former manifest desire not to keep up his acquaintance. . . .

FEB. 5th . . . To my great pleasure. . . . Madame D'Arblay has left Miss Burney £200 per annum for her life. . . .

FEB. 21st Quillinan breakfasted with me—very friendly. It seems that the reason why the intended marriage was not carried into execution was the discovery that certain property of his is encumbered. Dora is in town and everything remains in the same unsettled state in which it has so long been. . . .

FEB. 22nd . . . I dined with H. N. Coleridge; no one there but Dora Wordsworth and Quillinan except a silent young Irishman, possibly a pupil. I presume that Dora and Quillinan being thus invited together is a sort of public annunciation of the connection intended to be consummated between them. Quillinan, it seems, insists that Wordsworth shall give his daughter away. This, I think, is going too far. Wordsworth, I suppose, does not actively oppose the marriage, but submits to what he cannot successfully oppose. . . .

FEB. 29th . . . Called on Miss Fenwick. . . . We talked about poor Southey. His death is now desired by his best friends. . . . Dined with Miss Rogers. . . . It is more and more manifest that Rogers's activity of mind is declining, yet he says strong and sarcastic things still. . . .

MARCH 27th [*Bath*.] I breakfasted self-invited with Landor and I afterwards took him out with me. He had called with me yesterday on Miss Burney and she had proposed our calling on Manning, the Chinese traveller and friend of Charles Lamb. We found Manning quite the invalid—he had suffered from paralysis and this had occasioned his wearing his beard, which was iron-grey, long and bushy. His conversation was cheerful and he seemed glad to engage Landor to renew his call.

Landor was struck by the beauty of his face. They are likely to relish each other's conversation. Landor was as usual wild in his talk; when alone, he inquired with feeling about his children. By the bye, Milnes speaks of Arnold as being a wicked boy. Landor will also call on Miss Burney, for I perceive that he, after all, wants occupations and objects of interest. . . .

MAY 5th . . . Heard Carlyle's lecture on Heroes, the first lecture. I own there was but little in it and that little not *effectively* delivered. The Jaffrays there; chatted with old Sterling. No applause—I fear the lectures will injure future attempts. . . .

MAY 8th . . . Attended Carlyle's second lecture on the prophetic character of great men illustrated by Mahomet. It gave general satisfaction, for it had uncommon thoughts and was delivered with unusual animation. He declared his conviction that Mahomet was no mere sensualist nor vulgar impostor, but a real reformer. His system better than that of the Christianity current in his day in Syria. Milne[s] there; Mrs. Gaskell, with whom I chatted pleasantly; with the Jaffrays on return. Everybody pleased. Yet I doubt whether the lecture was really sound and true. My ticket, however, is numbered 248; it was one of the last. . . .

MAY 12th . . . I went to Carlyle's lecture—on the Hero as Poet. His illustration taken from Dante and Shakespeare. I brought nothing away worth the walk—nor indeed any thought that I wished at the time to retain. No allusion to the fierce spirit or the judicial character of the poem. He once only got a clap, by asking whether we would give up Shakespeare for our Indian Empire, and he took advantage of this to make his escape. He had a very good-natured audience, and I took care to say only to the friends what I say here. . . .

MAY 15th . . . I went on to a lecture of Carlyle's. A better than the last by far, but still I have not recovered my liking to such unformed and unarranged pouring-forth. This fourth lecture was on the Hero-Reformer; his illustrations Luther and Knox. He was at home on this subject and felt zeal on behalf of the old Puritans. . . .

MAY 19th . . . I heard another of Carlyle's lectures, on the literary hero, illustrating the character by Burns, who was no literator or book-maker, and Rousseau, who was scarcely so. Johnson was a professional author but hardly merited his distinction. Much cant in this lecture against scepticism. . . .

MAY 22nd This day was rendered interesting by a visit from one of the most remarkable of our scholars and men of science, Professor Whewell.[1]

[1] William Whewell (1794–1866), soon to be elected Master of Trinity College, Cambridge. For his physique, see *infra*, 26th January, 1845.

He breakfasted with me and my nephew; the occasion of his visit was to look over his translation of *Herman and Dorothea* with the original and particularly some corrections I had made in his translation. He acknowledged nearly all my corrections. Whewell is a poly-historian and on account of the multifariousness of his pursuits is sneered at by those who have only one pursuit. Someone said Whewell's *forte* is *science*. 'Yes,' said Sydney Smith, 'and his *foible* is *omni-science*.' The geologists affect to despise him. Wordsworth would not tolerate his English hexameters; even Milman does not. I gave him my lines in answer to his, but he did not read them and of course will not like them either for form or matter. I spent the morning out.—At Carlyle's last lecture, on Cromwell and Buonaparte; much better on the English than the French usurper; but on the whole these lectures have lowered, not raised, Carlyle in my opinion. . . .

[Crabb Robinson was busily engaged this summer in writing his *Exposure of Misrepresentations contained in the Preface to the Correspondence of William Wilberforce*. His book was published by Moxon on July 31st.]

AUG. 9th [*Bear Wood*.] . . . In the evening Miss Mitford came and took tea with us. She talked with great warmth of Kenyon, with kindness of Talfourd, with kind feeling of everybody. She is really an amiable person, most generous, Kenyon says. She seems disposed to be kind to everyone.

DEC. 11th . . . I received today Landor's *Fra Rupert*, a drama of great beauty of style, but in which I could not take any great pleasure.

DEC. 18th . . . I went out early to breakfast with Rogers. . . . I enjoyed my chat with this excellent man. He grows more kind every day. . . . He spoke very freely of Wordsworth in a way I could not hear without regret but could not object to. . . . I wrote to Landor today on his *Fra Rupert*, anxious to say all I could with truth that would give him pleasure and therefore honestly congratulating him on the full possession of his powers, contrasting his state with poor Southey's. . . .

DEC. 21st I finished this morning Coleridge's posthumous *Confessions of an Inquiring Spirit*, of which the most remarkable feature is that it contains an eloquently-expressed denial of the doctrine of plenary inspiration, which makes the supposed inspired writer the mere organ-pipe of a foreign spirit. The writings lose all individuality and characteristic worth—because dead and inoperative, and I expressed my pleasure in the book in a letter to H. N. Coleridge. Indeed, in publishing this liberal book he has redeemed his fault in giving publicity to some illiberal sentiments of the poet in his *Table Talk*. . . .

DEC. 22nd I went out early to breakfast with Rogers, calling by the way on Moxon to inquire for messages to Rydal. A most agreeable chat with Rogers; he was very cordial, communicative, and lively; gave us copies of the cheap editions of his *Italy* and poems, though he had before given us the better editions, and he pointed out to us his beautiful works of art and curious books. I could not help asking what is to become of them. 'The auctioneer,' he said, 'will find out the fittest possessor hereafter—he who gives money for things values them. Put in a museum nobody sees them.' I allowed this of gold and silver, but not of books such as his Chaucer, with the notes Tooke wrote in it when in the Tower, with minutes of the occurrences that then took place; so Tooke's copy of the *Trial of Hardy*, etc., with his notes. 'Such books you should distinguish with a mark and say in your will: All my books with the marks set out—to so-and-so.' I fear he will not pay attention to this . . . .

DEC. 24th [*Rydal.*] . . . I found at the Wordsworths', William and Miss Fenwick, and all of them seeming well, except poor Miss Wordsworth, and she is better. She came down, but could not stay many minutes. I was in high spirits, and a great deal of pleasant talk, *de omnibus*. . . .

DEC. 25th . . . On coming out of church Dr. Arnold stepped in for a moment with Wordsworth. I went to an early dinner, after which I took a walk with Wordsworth. We called on Mrs. Luff and accompanied her to Ambleside. . . .

DEC. 26th At one I called on Dr. Arnold and walked with the family to Ambleside; Miss Arnold, indeed all the family, as amiable as ever. . . .

DEC. 30th . . . I have been delighted with Shelley's *Letters*[1] from Italy in the second volume of his Prose Writings. His taste is most delicate and altogether there is a captivating moral sentiment throughout. His contempt for Christianity is strongly expressed and is a stain on the book, but even that I believe was a very honest mistake; I am glad however to find that he was fully sensible of the deformities of Lord Byron's mind and character. One does not, however, see why he should, with his own habits and life, express himself with such abhorrence of *Childe Harold*. His politics violently Radical; *anno* 1819 he seriously advised his friends to sell out of the English Funds; he looked forward to a revolution as inevitable and believed the strangest fables, the news of the day, such as the Inquisition in Spain murdering seven thousand people before they succeeded in effecting a revolution; marvellous ignorance occasionally, thinking Godwin's answer to Malthus triumphant.

DEC. 31st . . . I chatted with the ladies on the Mount. By the bye, I have not yet mentioned that Miss Wordsworth is amazingly improved. She can talk for a time rationally enough, but she has no command of

[1] *Essays, Letters from Abroad, Translations and Fragments*, 1840.

herself and has the habit of blowing with her lips very loudly and disagreeably and sometimes of uttering a strange scream, something between the noise of a turkey and a partridge but more shrill than [either]. She can be withdrawn from this only by being made to repeat verses, which she does with great feeling, quite pathetically. We played whist after tea. . . .

1841

JAN. 1st . . . After dinner I called with Wordsworth on the Arnolds. Charmed with the account Mrs. Arnold gave of their family habits. On the first day of the year the father and mother dine with the children in the schoolroom as their guests, the children sitting at the head of the table, etc. She also told me of the *Fox How Miscellany* which appears this day, all the family contributing an article to the magazine. One would not have expected this in a schoolmaster's house. . . . Began at night to look over Coleridge's *Remains*, in which I found very great delight.

JAN. 5th . . . There was a dinner party at the Mount. The Arnolds, the Robinsons, etc., in all twelve, and the afternoon was singularly agreeable. The ball of lively discussion was kept up with ease, and yet I can recall as little of this as of the *tête-à-tête* chat with Spedding. Spedding, I ought to say, is a clerk in the Colonial Office, a liberal thinker, in politics rather more than a Whig, for he advocates the ballot. He is not a brilliant and learned man, but clear-headed and judicious and associates with the best of his age, between thirty and forty only. He is seemingly free in his religious opinions, but religious in his tastes and feelings—he does not oppress by superiority but encourages by sympathy. . . . I also finished today an *Essay on Cicero* by young Hallam. Spedding says that Hallam's *Remains*[1] give no adequate idea of the promise his precocious talents presented to the world.

JAN. 21st After breakfasting and packing up I went to the Wordsworths after ten. Wordsworth read me a beautiful manuscript poem, *The Norman Boy*, which will be popular. A peasant lad builds a hut and plants a cross on it. At twelve I left my friends with renewed and enhanced regard and with warm expressions of kindness on their part and invitations for another year. . . .

FEB. 14th . . . I finished this morning *The Old Curiosity Shop*. The

[1] Arthur Hallam, Tennyson's friend, son of the historian, who published the *Remains* privately in 1833, the year of the young man's death.

pathetic parts are among the best things Dickens has written. The character of Nell is quite ideal and that of Kit the servant boy also in a way ideal, but true to nature. Quilp, the attorney, who is drowned at last, is a very monster of baseness, and not natural—he has no human quality. I shall read no more of Dickens's things in numbers. . . .

MARCH 15th . . . I was taken into the Reform Club and there fell in with the Right Honourable [Thomas] Babington Macaulay. A short but gratifying conversation with him. He began on the subject of my Wilberforce controversy: 'I have never thanked you for the book you gave me long ago; I wish you to know that I altogether disapprove of the conduct of the Messrs. Wilberforce and did so from the beginning.' Not in the order in which he said so, but this was the substance: 'I have a sort of hereditary respect for them, but I know very little about them; I believe them to be pious and sincere men; quite in earnest; but they are incapable of anything generous or liberal or kind. This they take from their mother (or mother's family) I cannot say which.' I said that I had out of respect for his feelings not sent him the second book. He smiled and said he had read it; he looked as if he meant I should think that he thought it indiscreet to say how much he approved of it. All he said was: 'I do not quite agree with you on all points as to Mr. Clarkson's egotism; but that is a trifle, and it was most ungenerous to treat so eminent a person of his years and after such a life, in such a way.' I began to refer to the estrangement between Clarkson and his father, when he said: 'I was not aware there was anything that amounted to estrangement; I know my father thought that not enough was said about Stephen.' I said: 'That is admitted in the *Strictures*. I hope you were satisfied with Clarkson's apology and with what he said about your father.' He said with great warmth: 'Oh quite, quite!' On Wednesday I wrote to Mrs. Clarkson giving her an account of this conversation and at the same time pressed on her my wish that Mr. Clarkson should write to me an acknowledgment of my services, lest the Wilberforces should represent him as disclaiming my aid. . . .

MARCH 22nd . . . Read in bed Hurwitz's *Hebrew Tales*. I called on Moxon and paid for the *London Encyclopaedia*, of which I have sent a copy as a present to Wordsworth and Dora with a playful letter assigning as a reason for including Dora that I feared Wordsworth would otherwise burn it as an offering to the *manes* of the Copyright Act—the book being published by Tegg. . . .

MARCH 29th I went out after writing the above to breakfast with Milnes, and an agreeable meeting it was. There were poets, host included, viz.: Kenyon, Barry Cornwall, Browning, author of unreadable books, and Alfred Tennyson, who looks a bandit of genius—also Harness, Mrs.

Procter, Hayward and myself and some others I do not now recollect. We stayed late, the talk lively and no one prominent—but Kenyon quite silent. . . .

April 3rd I had a genteel and plentiful breakfast which was not honoured as it deserved. Mr. and Mrs. H. N. Coleridge did not come; I had Dora Wordsworth and Mr. Quillinan (about whom I heard news with pleasure which I ought to have heard before, but better late than never. They are shortly to marry). . . .

April 19th [*Bath.*] . . . Having dined, I went in search of the Wordsworths—I found them at number 12 North Parade, and had a very kind reception. A general invitation from Miss Fenwick. Wordsworth wrote to me, he said, yesterday, to thank me for my magnificent present, and from what they all say I have no doubt they really find it a very acceptable gift. By the bye, I have already in private asked Miss Fenwick to advise me about a present for Dora on the forthcoming marriage. Miss Fenwick: 'Why think of anything more? Dora is grateful for your *Encyclopaedia*.' But I told her that that was not so meant, and she promises to think of it. . . . During the evening I heard of the new poems written as well as of old poems to be published, nearly a volume already collected, and I heard with, I hope, a pardonable gratification of my vanity, that the Italian series is to be dedicated to me. . . .

April 21st . . . Then strolled in meadows with *Sartor Resartus*, which gives me very great pleasure on a second perusal. His humour I can relish, and his philosophy (essentially that of Coleridge) not unintelligible. . . . Read again in Carlyle till seven, when I went to Wordsworth. Took a stroll of an hour with him. Then had tea and a cordial gossip with them. Miss Fenwick has decided my present for me, a teapot and cream jug, so this will be done with ease and is business settled. . . .

April 25th I read Carlyle in bed as I did yesterday and with great pleasure. *Sartor* is full of genius though of unhappy taste. . . . I made calls on Miss Burney, looking over her will, and on Landor; he was in high spirits, declared himself to be the happiest of men; he praised Dickens as being with Shakespeare the greatest of English writers, though indeed his women are superior to Shakespeare's. No one of our poets comes near him. I dined with Miss Fenwick and drank tea with her after going with the Wordsworths to hear a Mr. Tottenham, a very popular preacher. He pleased Wordsworth and Dora, and not at all Mrs. Wordsworth. She thought him a ranter. Wordsworth says Mrs. Wordsworth would have a man preach out of a mummy-case. . . .

April 26th . . . Went to the Wordsworths. Took a short walk with Mrs. Wordsworth and played whist with the ladies. Finished *Sartor*

Resartus, a book I had enjoyed without requiring others to enjoy it too. It is only an acquired taste the relishing it. . . .

April 27th . . . I went to breakfast with Landor and spent nearly four hours with him. He took me a beautiful walk to Weston and pointed out sweet scenes to me with great interest. His sense of beauty of all kinds is his most enviable quality. Were his moral as well as his aesthetical judgment equal to the strength of his feelings he would be an estimable man. . . .

April 28th . . . I dined with my nephew and I left him at five that I might call on Joseph Cottle—he lives now on Knowle Hill with his sister Mrs. Hare, and her I found living in a charming place on a height. I was induced to stay and take tea there and postpone returning till half-past eight, and I really enjoyed my visit and it has led to Wordsworth's acceptance of an invitation. He means to take his ladies there tomorrow. Mrs. Hare seems a sensible woman: he, in spite of writing bad poetry, is a very worthy man. . . .

May 11th [*London.*] I then went . . . to Emanuel's, where I got a teapot and cream jug, a bridal present for Dora Wordsworth, who I trust was married today to Quillinan. This was a business glad to have got over. . . .

June 6th . . . I walked out with the intention of calling on Mrs. Wordsworth at the Marshalls', but forgot my gloves and could not go in. I then walked on to the Athenaeum, where I wrote a letter to Mrs. Wordsworth. . . .

June 13th . . . I breakfasted with Kenyon; only Landor there and Milnes and Forster; an amusing morning, but nothing to remark on. Landor did not bring Walter with him, his second boy, an interesting youth. . . . The afternoon passed over very well; Wordsworth in very remarkable good health and looking quite handsome. . . .

June 15th . . . I left my bridal present for the Quillinans at Mr. Moxon's. . . .

July 5th . . . At four at Mrs. Hoare's. There the Wordsworths, Quillinans, and also the Doctor [C. Wordsworth], Master of Trinity. He was very lively—decided in politics. The poet quiet; I took the poet and Quillinan to see Miss Sharpe's garden. A very agreeable afternoon. . . .

July 10th . . . Wordsworth called on me. I walked out with him. . . . Wordsworth has seen Peel about the Copyright Bill, whom he is labouring to secure—not yet determined who is to succeed Talfourd in that business.

I had a dinner party of eight today given in consequence of Wordsworth's coming to me. It consisted of Wordsworth, Copley Fielding, and Dr. Carlyle, Booth at the bottom, Cookson, Harness, and Dr. Wood. It did not go off so well in consequence of the too great length of the table. We were not near enough and groups were formed, but I believe my company pleased each other. Harness and Dr. Wood got very comfortable together; Kenyon and Fellows came in after dinner. Kenyon made himself, as always, agreeable; Cookson pleased with my friends. Fielding was particularly pleased with being invited and so I believe was Booth. Wordsworth talked chiefly *tête-à-tête*, but he seemed to be in a good mood. On the whole he is improved as a companion since his last being in London. He is not triumphant at Tory success.[1]

JULY 14th . . . Went out after breakfast and called on Mrs. Quillinan to engage her to come to me; I then went to see Mary Lamb, at length happily removed to 41 Alpha Road, Regent's Park, to a sister of Miss James. This happy event has been effected by the interference of Barry Cornwall, *alias* Procter, who is a Lunatic Commissioner, and she rejoices at having escaped from a place far removed from all her friends and where she was not even kindly treated. She had offered to come and see me and perhaps I shall ask her to accompany the Quillinans and Coleridges. . . .

JULY 19th . . . Then I made calls on Mrs. Quillinan, on Mary Lamb to secure Mary Lamb's coming to me tomorrow. . . .

JULY 20th . . . My second dinner went off quite as well as the first. It consisted of Mr. and Mrs. Quillinan, Mr. and Mrs. H. N. Coleridge, and Mary Lamb. Mary Lamb took but little part in the conversation, but enjoyed herself quietly. The other ladies very agreeable. H. N. Coleridge talked very well: in short, everyone as he should be.

JULY 22nd . . . In the forenoon I called on Mrs. Quillinan and dear Mary Lamb. Pleased her by looking over her old books. She was quite comfortable. . . .

AUG. 2nd [*Hastings*.] . . . My day was spent in reading *Ivanhoe*, which I heartily enjoyed, caring nothing for criticism. I was sufficiently interested in the story to care for nothing else. . . .

AUG. 15th [*London*.] . . . Mary Lamb not at all well, I fear she will soon be ill again. She moaned sadly, but even if ill she will be better off than at Edmonton. . . .

AUG. 19th . . . I then went to the Athenaeum, where I amused myself by copying some marginalia of Coleridge in *Letters concerning Mind*, by Petvin, a book I found at Miss Lamb's on Wednesday and brought away. This occupied me the forenoon. . . .

AUG. 20th . . . I went to Mary Lamb, carrying her a cake and some fruit received from Bury. I chatted a little with her. . . .

[1] In the recent general election.

On Wednesday the 25th I set out on a five weeks' journey into Devonshire. . . .

[*Travel Journal.*] AUG. 29th . . . I began today *Barnaby Rudge*, which promises to be one of the most delightful of Dickens's works. He improves in general style. . . .

AUG. 30th . . . Reading *Barnaby Rudge* . . . and have only this *now* to say—that the character of the selfish Chester seems the most original of the author's invention. It is the combination of quiet imperturbable ease and good humour with utter heartlessness which constitutes the originality. . . .

SEPT. 1st I arose very early, but I had so worked myself into the tale of *Barnaby*, the idiot (who thus far is not important), that I would not walk out till I had finished a part before breakfast. Then I took a short walk with *Barnaby Rudge* and the book occupied me all day. . . . Dickens will lose popularity with the saints, for he too faithfully exposes cant. . . .

SEPT. 4th . . . The picture of the riots of Lord George Gordon's mob is excellent and has poetical truth whether it be historical or not. . . .

SEPT. 5th . . . Finished all of *Barnaby Rudge* yet published. . . . I will read no more till the story is finished. . . . I will not expose myself to further anxieties. . . .

OCT. 7th . . . Calling on Mary Lamb I found her again ill, but Mrs. Parsons says she is not unhappy and I am sure she will be kindly treated. . . .

OCT. 13th . . . I had accepted conditionally an invitation to dine with Booth today, that is if Mrs. Marsh,[1] the author of the *Two Old Men's Tales*, should be there. She did go and I had a very agreeable evening. The party consisted of the Hutton family and the Marshs. Mr. Marsh is a gentleman and nothing more and Mrs. Marsh is a fine woman, middle-aged, no assumption and yet her look and manner show she has a consciousness of being somebody—a thorough Liberal and humane to the utmost, being against the Government on the sugar question. The Marshs were in pecuniary difficulties when Mrs. Marsh became a writer, but they are in affluence now. . . .

NOV. 5th . . . I continued skimming as I did yesterday a disagreeable novel meant to be philosophical and an attack on the modern Liberal school of philosophy—the younger Sterling's[2] *Arthur Coningsby*. The incidents and character of the French philosophy very coarsely treated. . . .

NOV. 17th . . . [At] Mrs. Montagu Bourgoynes . . . I met [at Brighton]

[1] Mrs. Anne Marsh-Caldwell (1791–1874).

[2] John Sterling (1806–1844), son of Edward Sterling of *The Times* and the subject of Carlyle's biography (1851).

with Mrs. Ogle, the lady at whose suggestion Wordsworth has written a poem, *The Peasant of Normandy*. She is a pretty young woman, a warm admirer of Wordsworth and would be very agreeable if she were quite free from affectation. She wrote to Wordsworth and he was pleased with her letter. She discriminates in her admiration. Mrs. Montagu Bourgoyne, when a young lady, saw Dr. Johnson at Mrs. Thrale's. He was out of humour with Mrs. Thrale and the company; said 'the green peas were good for the pigs,' took himself into the garden and fed the swans and was kind to her and went away without going into the drawing-room when they returned from their stroll in the garden after dinner. . . .

Nov. 28th . . . I dined with Rogers, a *partie carrée*, Rogers, Captain Jones, and Turner, R.A. Jones (it was his first visit) did his *most* to make himself agreeable: oh, the mass of commonplace which was expectorated by him that day! yet not at all unpleasant, I dare say, to entire strangers. He makes himself agreeable. Turner is a man of real genuine talent—I may say genius. But in society he is rough (not coarse),[1] sarcastic, and looks at least as if he could be cynical. . . .

Dec. 12th . . . I dined with Talfourd. . . . There was a jovial looking man, Rev.—Barrow[2]—or what was it?—the author of the *Ingoldsby Legends*, a humorist whom I cannot fancy in the pulpit. . . .

Dec. 15th . . . I next called on Moxon. We talked about Wordsworth and his *not* now publishing his poems. Moxon complained of the bad state of the bookselling business. The returns are not a sixth of what they were a year ago. . . .

Dec. 24th . . . [At] Kendal we [the Quillinans and Crabb Robinson] could not find place in the only mail and came to Rydal in a covered car, which brought us for £1 to Mr. Wordsworth's door before the Whitehaven mail. We overtook Wordsworth. . . . I found everybody well at the Mount (William Wordsworth [junior] also there). . . . Wordsworth was exceedingly kind, and informed me of his intention to dedicate some hundreds of lines to me—a most flattering and honouring distinction. We played a little whist and I came home—that is, to my old lodgings at the bottom of the hill—after nine o'clock.

Dec. 25th My first day was without incident. It being a festival not kept by Dissenters, I was under no obligation to go to church and I, therefore, stayed at home all the forenoon. I wrote the above memoirs and was otherwise occupied. I saw no one but the Arnolds, whom I chatted with from my window. We dined at one and after dinner I

[1] In his later reminiscences, Crabb Robinson lengthened 'not coarse' into 'not to say coarse'.

[2] Richard Harris Barham.

accompanied Wordsworth a short walk. We called on our way on Mrs. Arnold. She was as charming as ever. . . .

DEC. 26th . . . After dinner I took a walk with Wordsworth to his old servant Mary—an annual Christmas call. He was very cordial and communicative. He informed me that he had when last in town altered entirely the arrangements of his will; he had substituted for executors his son William, Mr. Cookson, and his bailiff[1] Mr. Carter instead of Courtenay and myself on account of my age; he thought it would relieve me from a burthen. I told him I entirely approved of this, as I most sincerely do. . . . An evening of chat and without any reading.

N.B.—Greatly pleased with the warm cordiality both of Wordsworth and everyone, including Miss Fenwick, towards myself—a just reason for congratulation undoubtedly. . . .

DEC. 27th I read this morning early Dr. Arnold's very interesting inaugural lecture as Professor of Modern History. Distinguishing history as the record of the acts collectively of men . . . opposed to biography, those of the individual man. Liked the whole except the too confident annunciation of this being the last age of the progress of mankind; as if there could not be a third. This I intimated to the Doctor himself when he called afterwards, and I stated to him Lessing's views. . . . I was interrupted . . . by Wordsworth, who called for a walk to Ambleside. . . .

We had a dinner party: Mr. and Mrs. Robinson, Mr. and Mrs. Harrison, and Mr. Faber.[2] This ultra-Puseyite High Churchman, whom I had taken a dislike to, pleased me today very much. He has been a long journey with Mr. Harrison's son to Constantinople and has written a book about the state of religion in the countries he passed through. He is a lively narrator and very spirited talker. His prejudices are strong, or should I rather say his opinions are *one-sided* and *violent*? He speaks with abhorrence of the French Protestants and says the Huguenots were always a factious and worthless set. Their representative Henri IV. Like him ready to change their religion (manifestly false, why did not they?). He speaks with equal contempt of religion in Prussia and of the Prussian Government. The King wishes to establish a Church without rights and entirely dependent on the State. Faber is one of those who would make the Church independent. In nothing do I so much dissent from him as in his admission that he thinks the true Church ought to be supported by pains and penalties. He is not friendly to Romanism; says Lingard's *History* is one consistent *lie* throughout. He says Wiseman is not an honest

[1] The shorthand appears to stand for 'bailive', but the term 'bailiff' is inappropriate. Carter was at first a clerk, who later became a general factotum to the Wordsworths.

[2] F. W. Faber, who became a Roman Catholic and established the London Oratory.

man and has been convicted of false quotations. Yet with my utter dissent from much that Faber said, his manner pleased me and I should like to see him again. Came home as usual and sat up late reading a *Times* newspaper.

DEC. 28th I . . . went early to Wordsworth and challenged him to a walk. Faber walked with us, an interesting talk. . . . I would not take leave of him without letting him know how much I disliked some of his Church notions. . . . We called at Dr. Arnold's for the *Examiner*, and he accompanied us on a walk before dinner. . . .

DEC. 31st . . . I read at home till one, when we dined to accommodate the servants, who had a treat. After dinner I walked out with Mrs. Quillinan to Mr. Roughsedge's and then I went on to Grasmere, joining Wordsworth at Mary Fisher's. We took early tea and in the evening we played whist as usual, called on Miss Wordsworth, etc. There came this evening the new *Quarterly Review*, a very interesting number. Wordsworth gave Henry Taylor a set of sonnets on capital punishment, which he has wrought into a long article on Wordsworth's Sonnets; an article much too preaching and prosy to be suited to the delightful extracts on which he comments. The new Sonnets are admirable, but not all equally lucid. . . .

1842

JAN. 2nd I read in the morning, early, the third and fourth lectures of Harwood and afterwards a sermon by Dr. Arnold—I can enjoy opposites. These occupied me till church time. A couple of hours of ennui there were followed by a short walk with Wordsworth before dinner and after dinner a delightful walk with him by the Rydal Head, towards the cove that shuts up this little valley as all the valleys of the Pyrenees are shut up. A fit scene this for chat about Italy. Wordsworth talks of the past journey there with pleasure and builds castles of a second journey with Miss Fenwick, Mrs. Wordsworth, and myself. . . .

JAN 3rd . . . Wordsworth at Dr. Arnold's mentioned his having dedicated a poem[1] to me and his attempt in vain to bring in my name. It is too mean for verse! I fear, too, there will not be an allusion to it, so the dedication may be lost in a subsequent edition.

JAN. 5th The first thing I did this morning in bed and after breakfast was to read Faber's Education Sermon, which I read here last year. I

[1] *To Henry Crabb Robinson*. Prefatory lines to *Memorials of a Tour in Italy, 1837*.

dislike it less than I did before; I see more distinctly that Faber is as a Churchman quite consistent, but it is a consistency that is likely to drive men out of it both ways, up or back to Romanism or down and forward to Dissent. . . .

JAN. 6th . . . I have neglected making memoranda of Wordsworth's conversation while here. It has been remarkably agreeable. Today he talked of poetry. I can now remember that he held Pope to be the greatest poet, but Dryden to have the most talent—the strongest understanding. Genius and ability he opposed—as others do. He said his preface on poetical language had been misunderstood. Whatever is addressed to the imagination is essentially poetical, but very pleasing verses deserving all praise, but not so addressed, are not poetry. . . .

JAN. 12th . . . Dr. Arnold had promised to walk out with me today, and did not come till past one. We then had an interesting walk, and as today (Thursday) there is a fall of snow, it was probably the last day of the season when such a walk could be taken. We went up the Rydal Beck towards the Rydal Head, crossed the mountain, and returned by the Scandalebeck. I could not have made the walk alone, nor scaled the walls, but with the Doctor's aid it went off well; I enjoyed the walk, though at last we were forced to hurry, in order not to be too late for dinner. . .

JAN. 16th . . . I went up the Mount at one and did not leave till nine as usual. I read the paper, etc. My letter to Sir Robert Inglis approved. I read at night Dix's *Life of Chatterton*—a poor composition. It contains some newly discovered poems. I never could enjoy Chatterton—*tant pis pour moi*, I have no doubt—but so it is. This morning I have finished the little volume; I do feel the beauty of the Mynstrelle's song in *Ælla*—and some of his modern poems are sweetly written. I defer to the highest authority, Wordsworth, that Chatterton would have probably proved one of the very greatest poets in our language. I must, therefore think he was not a monster of wickedness, but he had no other virtue than the domestic affections very strongly. He was ready to write for both political parties at once. I think Horace Walpole has been too harshly judged. Chatterton was not the starving genius he afterwards became when Walpole coldly turned his back on him. But certainly Horace Walpole wanted generosity. . . .

JAN 17th . . . The evening spent as usual. We had our rubber of whist and a kind, cosy chat at last. Wordsworth read the intended dedication to me. 'Cheerful companion and experienced guide and long-tried friendship,' are words of kindness I feel to be honouring; but he is dissatisfied with the word 'cheerful' and '*tried* friendship' as too strong, 'experienced' would be better. . . .

I asked Wordsworth this evening wherein Chatterton's excellence lay. He said his genius was universal; he excelled in every species of composition, so remarkable an instance of precocious talent being quite unexampled. His prose was excellent, and his powers of picturesque description and satire great. . . .

JAN. 18th . . . I went up the Mount, took leave of all my kind friends, and at ten o'clock Mrs. Quillinan and I were packed up in a car and drawn in three hours to Kendal. . . .

JAN. 27th . . . I dined with Talfourd—only the Moxons and Mary Lamb there. Poor dear Mary Lamb was very flighty in her talk, so that I fear she will soon be very ill again. She has had too much going out lately. . . .

JAN. 31st . . . Began Madame D'Arblay's journal. It is not without interest as a picture of manners in those days of formality. . . .

FEB. 8th . . . I rose late and breakfasted by self-invitation with Rogers. He was alone and very amiable. Talked with great kindness of Wordsworth and everybody else. . . .

FEB. 10th . . . Finished Madame D'Arblay's first volume, which has a deal of tiresome twaddle, but has some capital Johnsoniana, and it offers a lively picture of what was then considered the best society. . . .

FEB. 17th . . . I forgot yesterday to put down an incident of some interest. Calling on Moxon he showed me a proof of the forthcoming volume of Wordsworth's *Poems*. It contains the following inscription on the title page of *Memorials of a Tour in Italy*, 1837:

To H.C.R.

Companion! by whose buoyant Spirit cheered,
In[1] whose experience trusting, day by day
Treasures I gained with zeal[2] that neither feared
The toils nor felt the crosses of the way,
These records take, and happy should I be
Were but the Gift a meet Return to thee
For kindnesses that never ceased to flow,
And prompt self-sacrifice to which I owe
Far more than any heart but mine can know.

I am perfectly satisfied with these lines. They are neither poetical nor encomiastic—so much the better. They come from the heart, and the highest praise, after all, that I can receive is that I am an object of regard to such a man.

MARCH 2nd I finished this morning *Barnaby Rudge*, a novel full of

[1] Crabb Robinson writes 'To'.
[2] Crabb Robinson writes 'joy'. Probably the first version was as he transcribed it.

talent and wisdom—as a story full of faults, there being many characters left mere shadows, such as the younger Chester and his love, Miss Haredale. The charm of the tale lies in the comic characters. . . .

MARCH 7th . . . Called on Moxon, with whom I left the eighteen spoons I bought at Emanuel's . . . and I wrote a short letter to Mrs. Wordsworth . . . referring to my present, and I wrote also to Mrs. Quillinan expressing my satisfaction with the *Dedication*. . . .

MARCH 14th . . . I called afterwards on Moxon, proposing a double volume to Wordsworth's poems, one to be volume the seventh. I then went to the Athenaeum, where I read a long report in *The Times* of last Friday containing an account of a sad case of the Brydges family in which Quillinan defends in *forma pauperis* and is charged with participating in fraud. There can be no doubt that he acted most incautiously and weakly in signing deeds, and being an assenting party to transactions which were of a most iniquitous character; but still I am perfectly convinced of his honour and integrity, and I wrote a letter to that effect to Mrs. Quillinan, which I hope will be a comfort to her, but it is, after all a melancholy mode of escaping from an imputation on one's honour by allowing that the fault must be transferred to the head. . . .

APRIL 19th . . . Today I was glad to read in *The Times* a declaration from the Vice-Chancellor that he believed Mr. Quillinan was free from all intention to commit any fraud, but he is made liable with some four or five others to make up the difference between £22,000 and £7,000, besides costs, which will be a sad dead weight lying on him, and prevent his doing anything for his wife.

APRIL 25th . . . At Moxon's I learned that Wordsworth would not let a single copy be sent to the papers. This is injudicious. His pride is wounded. I know not what to do. I am afraid to order it to be done at my own cost; he might be offended. . . .

APRIL 29th . . . I wrote to Mrs. Wordsworth chiefly to suggest the danger to the sale of Wordsworth's new volume from his not allowing any copies to be sent to the papers; in consequence it has been noticed by no one. . . . To Samuel Rogers, to whom I had invited myself to breakfast. I stayed till twelve with him. He was as amiable as ever, and he spoke with great warmth of the new volume of Wordsworth's. 'It is all gold—the least precious is still gold.' He said this accompanying a remark on one little epitaph which he said would have been better in prose. He quoted someone who said of Burns: 'He is great in verse, greater in prose, and greatest in conversation.' So it is of all great men; Wordsworth is greatest in conversation. This is not the first time of his preferring prose to verse. . . .

MAY 4th . . . I finished Wordsworth's poems. On the whole better pleased with the new than the old poems, and I like the least the Salisbury Plain incidents.[1] The *Epistle to Sir George Beaumont* is beautiful—indeed, all is beautiful, but the question occurs: Why was not this published before? or, Why is it published now? . . . Then I went in search of Wordsworth, who came before nine. While Mr. and Mrs. Wordsworth drove to Spring Street, I walked with William, and I sat an hour with them. The Wordsworths are come on business, and most heartily do I wish them success to get if possible something for their son William. But I have only faint hopes of success. But little talk today.

MAY 9th I had my breakfast party, which enabled me to give pleasure to several friends. It consisted of Mr. and Mrs. and William Wordsworth, the Cargills, the Westons, Miss Bayley, and Trotter—all rejoicing in the sight.

MAY 11th . . . At eleven I went to the Quillinans. Mrs. Quillinan is looking very poorly, and her father is anxious about her. Quillinan was going to call on Miss Rogers, where there had been a breakfast party—*inter alia*, Miss Stanley, the lady I was introduced to at Bunsen's (Miss Rogers joked at my familiarity), and Washington Irving. His person not at all attractive, rather coarse, but he is really a man of genius. Wordsworth called with me on Mary Lamb. She received us with composure. And then Wordsworth and I followed Rogers and Washington Irving and Mr. Leslie to the painter's house, where we saw a very pleasing picture of the christening that lately took place—making for the Queen. . . .

MAY 12th . . . I . . . called on the Wordsworths. We had an interesting chat about the new poems. Wordsworth said that the poems: *Our walk was far among the ancient trees*, ii, 297; then, *She was a phantom of delight*; next, *Let other bards of angels sing*, i, 158; and finally, the two sonnets *To a Painter* in the new volume—but of which the first is only of value as leading to the second—should be read in succession as exhibiting the different phases of his affection for his wife. . . . I went to meet Mr. Plumer Ward. I found him a very lively and pleasant man in spite of his deafness. He related that soon after his *Tremaine* appeared he was in a party when the author (unknown) was inquired about. Someone said: 'I'm told it is very dull.' On which Ward said: 'Indeed, why, I have heard it ascribed to Mr. Sydney Smith.' 'Oh, dear, dear no! That could not be; I never wrote anything dull in my life.' . . .

MAY 20th . . . After this I went to the Athenaeum, etc. My dinner party had been a subject of solicitude, and therefore I had to go into the city before I went to the Athenaeum. . . . I went to Alsager, and with difficulty found him. It was a lucky choice, for, besides gratifying Alsager very

[1] *Guilt and Sorrow, or Incidents upon Salisbury Plain.*

much, Wordsworth too was particularly pleased to see him. Sat next him and was in excellent spirits, but talked with almost every one. . . .

MAY 26th . . . Went to Quillinan's, where I spent several hours; Wordsworth, etc., came home late from the Lords, where the Copyright Bill had been discussed, and may be considered as substantially passed, though not formally. William Wordsworth walked back with me. He was not in spirits. He is about to succeed his father as Distributor of the Stamps. This is an arrangement which Wordsworth has been anxious to make, that in case of his death William should not be unprovided. But William is honourably minded and cannot take anything from his father's limited income, so for the present he rather loses than gains. The emoluments of the office have been greatly reduced by the Whig economical reforms. However, there are hopes that Wordsworth will have a pension given him, but he will not accept less than has been given to any one that has three hundred pounds.

JUNE 1st . . . I dined with Mrs. Hoare. All the Wordsworth party were there, including the Doctor, who made himself agreeable; but nothing occurred worthy of note during the day. Wordsworth talked about his own affairs with feeling; if he got a pension he expected he would be able to go abroad and live a year in Italy. In that case I would join him. Except this, nothing to remember of the day. . . .

JUNE 8th . . . She [Mrs. Basil Montagu] accused Wordsworth of great selfishness and even ingratitude for past kindnesses and expressed herself with passionate ill-will, which annoyed me. I am afraid there may be some little foundation for this. . . .

JUNE 10th . . . I went early to Moxon's, Wordsworth being there. A large party of authors. Milnes, whom I am to breakfast with on Wednesday, Campbell, Sir John Hanmer, etc. It was not till past one that I could get Wordsworth away, to take him to Mrs. Aders. He sat full two hours to her. I fear the likeness will not be a good one. . . .

JUNE 13th . . . Milnes informed me of the death of Dr. Arnold. A really afflicting event. . . .

JUNE 14th After breakfast I called at the Wordsworths. They were all in affliction at the death of the Doctor. He is said to be only fifty-two.[1] What a happy house at once broken up! Bunsen's remark was: 'The *History of Rome* is never to be finished.' . . .

JUNE 15th . . . She [Mrs. Aders] has nearly finished Wordsworth. It will not be good. A fierce expression and no character. . . .

JUNE 20th I went after breakfasting with my brother, self-invited, to Forster's to hear him read to Kenyon, etc., some of Dickens's letters from

[1] He was younger than that. Arnold was born in 1795.

America—better letters I never heard read. The descriptions most animated, satire and sublime painting admirably intermixed. I was gratified by finding that he had not been deceived by the gross flattery of the people; he sees through them. He confirms my dislike of the people. Their want of honesty is not so flagrant as their grossness of manners, but it is as certain. . . . These letters must form the nucleus of a work on America which might be one of the most efficient ever written. . . .

JUNE 21st . . . Mrs. Aders had done two copies of Wordsworth, which I made into a parcel and carried to Mrs. Quillinan. She was struck, as I was, with a want of truth in the eye, which does not suit a profile; otherwise not unlike. . . .

[*Travel Journal: Tyneside, etc.*] JULY 6th . . . I was surprised at her [H. Martineau's] appearance. She looked well, and then and ever since talked not at all like an invalid. In fact, under the salutary influence of laudanum she has long periods of mental repose and she is during these times able to enter into conversation with all her former spirit . . . and she talks well. . . .

JULY 9th . . . A very interesting chat with Miss Martineau about her own affairs. She showed me her correspondence with Mr. Hutton and also with Charles Buller, which showed that she refused a pension offered by Lord Grey and also by Lord Melbourne. *Four times* did she refuse, and she stated her reason to Buller at length. She could not take what was the produce of taxation and what others were better entitled to than herself. £150 was offered. . . . She receives many attentions from all classes of persons.

JULY 10th . . . The more I hear Harriet Martineau talk about herself, the more I am interested in her character. Mrs. Reid remarked today that her character is most egregiously mistaken in general—that she is perfectly feminine in her feelings and tastes and would have preferred being wife and mother to literary celebrity. She became an author merely for bread, having first from impulse written and acquired a habit of composition when she wrote merely for pleasure. Her judgment seems sound on all points unconnected with America. She read to us this evening an admirable letter from Emerson about her brother who died, which will make me interpret more favourably his *Essays*, which I have brought with me. Miss Martineau thinks him a more original character than Carlyle and morally a superior man, whatever may be thought of his literary powers. I began in bed and finished in the morning one of Miss Martineau's tales in the *Playfellow* called *The Crofton Boys*. . . . It is a wise and highly moral tale which would improve any schoolboy—remarkable for the perfect truth of the narrative. Not an occurrence or a word in conversation that reads like a fiction. The feelings and tone in conversation of school, with no attempt at idealisation.

JULY 12th . . . My reading at home today was another of Miss Martineau's *Playfellow* [stories] and the most picturesque and agreeable by far. The picture of Norwegian life and manners is quite charming: *Feats on the Fjord* . . . It is wonderful how much wisdom Miss Martineau has thrown into a very pretty story.

JULY 20th [*Ambleside.*] . . . I instantly went back to Rydal where I had a cordial reception from my friends, with reproaches for not taking up my residence with them. . . . The poet was looking thin but not unwell. I dined with them and after dinner walked with them to Fox How. Mrs. Arnold I was consoled by finding not only able but ready to talk of the Doctor. . . .

JULY 21st . . . I remained with her [Mrs. Arnold] till it was time to dine with Wordsworth. . . . We had a most delightful walk which lasted till half-past seven o'clock, and which was one of the most enjoyed that I recollect at any time in this country. We went up Loughrigg, not the straight path but circuitously. We had first a fine view of the Windermere scene and afterwards of the Loughrigg Tarn, which Wordsworth especially admires. Then we went round till we had a delicious point overlooking Grasmere, and here Wordsworth pointed out to us the Point Rash Judgment and the vicinity of the Wishing Gate—altogether a delightful succession of beautiful scenes. . . .

JULY 26th . . . I lay by the way [Bowness to Kendal] reading Emerson's *Essays*. . . . After dinner wrote a letter to Harriet Martineau in which I gave a free opinion of Emerson, having before read his essay on *Spiritual Laws*. . . . I was reading Emerson great part of today, but could get no relish for him. As in his earlier essays, truisms and paradoxes are strangely blended. More originality in the words than the thoughts.

JULY 28th . . . [Yorkshire manufacturing villages.] The brown houses, though of the soil, are frightfully offensive, and so far offend Wordsworth's theory that houses should be of the colour of the soil. . . .

AUG. 20th . . . I finished the fourth volume of *Madame D'Arblay*. I am far from agreeing in the most contemptuous review in the *Quarterly*, which declares it to be the worst book of the kind ever written, and that Madame D'Arblay was insincere and altogether an ordinary and very offensive person. . . .

AUG. 23rd . . . Called on Mary Lamb. She has not been long visible. I found her quite in possession of her faculties and recollecting everything nearly. She was going to call on Thomas Hood . . . and I walked with her. . . .

SEPT. 11th . . . Engaged reading, chiefly Sydney Smith. I have now finished the first volume of his works, consisting of articles published in the *Edinburgh Review*. On the whole they have somewhat lessened my impression of his merit as a writer. His humour is easy and pleasant, but rather shallow and commonplace. It lies in a great measure in ridiculous and commonplace epithets. The two subjects treated of in this volume in which he is most successful are *the Methodists*, and on *University and general education*. He cannot be said to have taught anything, but he has recommended and given circulation to useful practical truths. All his articles are in favour of humane reform, viz.: emancipation of Roman Catholics, the chimney-sweeping children, the poor from the game laws, lunatics from cruel treatment, our convicts under transportation, and the people at large from religious fanaticism. But, after all, he does not appear in these first articles, which come down to 1819, so great a comic writer as I expected. . . .

SEPT. 20th . . . I walked to the library and read in the new *Quarterly Review* an eloquent and philosophical article on *Tennyson's Poems*. One long extract brought tears into my eyes. The reviewer has done justice to Wordsworth's profoundly reflective and philosophic poetry at the same time that he eulogises *Don Juan* in a way that I cannot at all sympathise with . . . and in the evening I went on with what I have since finished—*Peter Plymley*. Sydney Smith has maintained his characteristic humour in these letters very successfully, but his pamphlet on *The Ballot* is the most masterly union of wit and logic, irresistible argument and irresistible pleasantry, that I ever met with in combination.

SEPT. 22nd . . . I spent the evening as usual, having begun Miss Austen's *Persuasion*.

SEPT. 23rd Another day of quiet reading. I went on with *Persuasion*, finished it, began *Northanger Abbey*, which I have now finished. These two novels have sadly reduced my estimation of Miss Austen. They are little more than galleries of disagreeables and the would-be heroes and heroines are scarcely out of the class of insignificants. Yet I ought to be suspicious perhaps of my own declining judgment. . . .

OCT. 18th I had a very gratifying letter from Wordsworth today. Sir Robert Peel has offered Wordsworth out of the Civil List a pension of £300. This was quite unexpected. It is the death of the Marquis of Wellesley which has set this sum at liberty. Wordsworth writes with great pleasure of it. I went at night to Mrs. Quillinan to rejoice with her about it; she is quite delighted. Now probably Wordsworth will go in the spring to Naples, or rather in the autumn. . . .

OCT. 20th . . . Occupied . . . partly looking into Dickens's *America*, a book which will do good; it will be very popular and influential. His opinions on slavery will have great weight and they are what they ought to be. . . .

OCT. 29th . . . In the evening at the Quillinans'. Mrs. Quillinan looked very poorly. They go to Rydal on Monday, their lodgings being under repair. The pension of Wordsworth is now in all the papers, and I rejoice to find that not a single paper, as far as I can hear, or a single person even, sneers or snarls at it. . . .

NOV. 1st . . . I then went on to Mary Lamb and had a short chat with her. Quite well in health, but she is growing very old and her deafness makes it difficult to keep up a conversation with her. . . .

NOV. 2nd I breakfasted this morning with Samuel Rogers *tête-à-tête*. . . . Very little said about Wordsworth's pension, which, however, Rogers says he rejoiced in. . . .

NOV. 14th . . . Then I went on to Mrs. Barrett. At her request I had the fifth volume of *Madame D'Arblay's Memoirs*. I had no other suggestion to make to her than that she should correct minute faults of style, the book being full of the most outrageous faults of language—obsolete words and affectations, quite ridiculous. For these she was more than judiciously thankful, and means to correct some of the more flagrant. I was better pleased with Miss Burney's amour with D'Arblay than with any part of her life besides. Her prudery towards Madame de Staël was very childish whose letters, on the contrary, are the gems of the work. . . .

DEC. 3rd . . . I began to read with interest an *Imaginary Conversation* in the new *Blackwood*, by Landor. It is between Porson and Southey on the poetry of Wordsworth and betrays all the malignity of the author. He alludes to the slanders of his poem and he repeats all the old trite ridicule on the most exceptionable of Wordsworth's early writings. I do not so much object to Porson's vituperation against Wordsworth—it is in character—it is spirited and fair in the way of abuse, but it ought not to have been met in so mawkish and drivelling a way as Southey does, at least in the first quarter, for I have read no further yet.

DEC. 19th I called on Kenyon after breakfast, and was glad to find that he felt as I did towards Landor for his scandalous critique on Wordsworth. Like me he has no wish to see him again, there is so much malignity mixed up with his best compositions. . . .

DEC. 24th [*Rydal.*] . . . Mrs. Wordsworth . . . was looking but thin, while Wordsworth was looking remarkably well. . . . An agreeable evening diversified by a rubber at whist. . . .

DEC. 25th . . . The Wordsworths dined at one and I had a very agreeable chat at and after dinner. Every one in good humour. In the afternoon I walked with Wordsworth. . . .

1843

JAN. 1st . . . After an early dinner I had, however, a delightful walk with the poet to the church lately erected on the road leading to Langdale, a picturesque object in a splendid situation, but, within, a naked and barnlike building. A very interesting conversation which I regret my inability to record. It was on Goethe and his poetry, on his own poetry, and, sad bathos, even on myself. The latter subject I will advert to because of its relative importance though absolute insignificance. He again pressed on me the drawing up reminiscences of the great men I have seen in Germany, and by the earnestness of his recommendation has made me more seriously resolve to execute my long-formed purpose. He approved of the title *Retrospect of an Idle Life*, to which I object only because it seems to embrace my whole life, and I think it is only abroad that I can find fit materials for a publication; but he thinks otherwise. Of Goethe Wordsworth spoke with his usual bitterness, and I cannot deny that his objection is well-founded—that is an extreme defect of religious sentiment, perhaps I should say, moral sense—and this suffices, says Wordsworth, to prove that he could be only a second-rate man. Wordsworth, however, does not deny that he is a great artist—but he adds this, in which I do not agree: In Shakespeare and Homer we are astonished at the universality of their penetration. They seem to embrace the whole world. Every form and variety of humanity they represent with equal truth. In Goethe you see that he attempts the same, but he fails. In Milton and Spenser there is not the attempt. You have admirable representations, and what the authors mean to do they actually do. Goethe's *Tasso* and his *Iphigenia* Wordsworth declares to be flat and insipid; but then he knows them only in translations. He has formerly said the same of *Herman and Dorothea*: he expressed disgust at the *Bride of Corinth*, which Herder called *scheusslich*. I have no time to write more now—only adding that Wordsworth repeated today his sonnet on *Wansfell*, which he declares to be one of his most perfect as a work of art.

JAN. 5th . . . I was sorry to be taken from them[1] to accompany Wordsworth and Faber on a walk. Their conversation I was not competent altogether to follow, but certainly Wordsworth's tone was that of deference towards his younger and more consistent friend. . . . Wordsworth denied Transubstantiation on grounds on which, says Faber, 'I should deny the Trinity.' Faber objected to the sonnet on [Pope] Alexander III putting

[1] Law's *Letters to Bishop Hoadly*.

his foot on the neck of the Emperor,[1] and says it is founded on a flagrant falsehood . . . Wordsworth declared in strong terms his disbelief of eternal punishment, which Faber did not attempt to defend. . . .

JAN. 16th . . . Having breakfasted, I went up the Mount and spent more than an hour with my friends. Their attachment to me is warm and affectionate, and Miss Fenwick seems to have caught the feeling. Nothing could be more cordial than her shake of the hand when I took leave. . . .

MARCH 19th . . . I then went on to dear Mary Lamb's. But how altered she is! Deafness has succeeded to her other infirmities. She is a mere wreck of herself. I took a single cup of tea with her to while away the time, but I found it difficult to keep up any conversation beyond the mere talking about our common acquaintance, and that is a discourse about the dead. . . .

MARCH 26th I breakfasted with Rogers. . . . It was an unusually pleasant morning. There were, besides Kenyon, only Twopenny and also Thomas Moore, who came in uninvited. The conversation was very pleasant. Rogers and T. Moore both related anecdotes which I regret I cannot now recollect. . . . Moore was very unassuming and very agreeable; Rogers unusually animated. Rogers said: 'The three works of fiction that I would exhibit to foreigners as specimens of English genius are the *Robinson Crusoe*, *Lilliput*, and *Brobdingnag*.' . . .

APRIL 1st . . . I went to the Athenaeum, where I stayed till one reading with great interest Quillinan's *Imaginary Conversation* in *Blackwood*, between Landor and the editor. It is admirably conceived. . . .

APRIL 2nd . . . I had an interesting chat with Moore about Goethe. On inquiry he assured me he never received the letter I sent him from Weimar in 1829 containing an account of my conversation with Goethe about Lord Byron, and he wishes me to collect from my papers the substance of what I recollected. He says he shall probably have an opportunity of making use of it as there is an intention to collect his prose writings. . . .

APRIL 5th I had a letter from Wordsworth this morning informing me that he had declined the laureateship, and on going out I found that it was announced in the papers that he had done so, alleging . . . advanced age (he becomes seventy-three on the 7th instant). This I approved of and rejoiced in; but I have now heard (the 6th) that he has yielded on a second application, which I am sorry for, as I am sure his motives will be misconstrued. . . .

APRIL 6th I have already mentioned having had a letter from Quillinan.

[1] *Ecclesiastical Sonnets*, XXXVIII. *Scene in Venice.*

He writes in good spirits about his attack on Landor as well as on Wordsworth's acceptance of the laureateship. . . .

APRIL 8th . . . Called first on Mr. E. Darwin[1] and gave him £25 for the testimonial for Miss Martineau, which he received as a good omen. . . . He told me that Miss Martineau has not more than £150 per annum. . . .

APRIL 9th I finished this morning in bed reading Newman's *Sermons*—at all events a book of great power. . . .

MAY 5th [*Bury*.] . . . So I went to the library. There I took up Trelawny's *Younger Son*, and was so much excited by it that I carried it home and read what formed in the original edition the first volume. But I will not go on with it. It is a very uncomfortable book. It is the history of an ill-educated man. . . . I met the author in Italy and afterwards at Lady Blessington's—a weather-beaten elderly man. I said to Landor: 'You know Trelawny?' 'Oh, yes, he is my friend.' 'I've heard he was either pirate or smuggler, I forget which.' 'For the matter of that I dare say both.' But this was said with a laugh and not to be taken seriously. In all that I have read of the novel and the rest which I looked over, I found all the numerous mottoes taken without exception from Byron, Shelley, and Keats. . . .

MAY 30th . . . Having breakfasted, I wrote a letter to Quillinan giving an account of myself, adding a joke of Landor's which Kenyon told me. 'I am told a Mr. Quillinan has been attacking me. His writings, I hear, are *Quill-inanities*. . . .'

JUNE 4th I breakfasted by appointment with Rogers, and Thomas Moore was there. The elder poet was the greater talker, but Moore made himself very agreeable. He expressed himself as seriously apprehensive of the result of the Repeal agitation. Rogers showed him some manuscript verses, rather sentimental, but good of the kind, by Mrs. Butler. Moore began, but could not get on; he laid down the manuscript and said he had a great dislike to the reading of poetry. 'You mean new poetry,' Rogers said. 'No, I mean *old*. I have read very little of any kind of poetry.' Rogers spoke very depreciatingly of the present writers. Moore did not agree. He assented to a warm praise of Tom Hood by me, and declared him as a punster equal to Swift. But the article (good poetry) is become of less value because of its being so common. There is too much of it . . .

AUG. 2nd [*Bury*.] . . . I . . . heard Mr. Cobden address the farmers . . . against the Corn Laws. I was very much pleased with his manner and style and even with the matter. . . .

AUG. 8th . . . I forgot to mention yesterday that I had had a letter from

[1] Erasmus, brother of Charles Darwin, the naturalist.

John Wordsworth of Keswick enclosing a Russian letter which he wants me to translate, addressed to an impostor calling himself Count Osolinski. I took it to the Athenaeum, where Hall undertook to show it to Kohl, the Russian traveller. . . . This matter occupied my attention, though it was hardly right in Wordsworth to advise his nephew to send it to me; but this comes of having the character of a good-natured man. . . .

AUG. 14th . . . I enclosed for Mr. Taylor a copy of Southey's letter to me declining to come to London for any emolument however great. I was authorised by Walter to offer him £2,000 if he had been inclined to come, but my letter was only general.[1]

[*Travel Journal: Brinsop.*] SEPT. 27th . . . I found the Wordsworths quite well . . . I spent the rest of the day very pleasantly with my friends.

SEPT. 28th The Wordsworths and Mrs. Hutchinson were engaged to take an early dinner with two maiden ladies of a certain age, the Miss Whalleys, and I accompanied them to Hereford, being driven by Mrs. Wordsworth, in a taxed cart. We found them two very benevolent old maids, quite delighted to receive at their house the great poet, though I suspect they know very little about his works. But they seemed most respectable old ladies notwithstanding. . . .

SEPT. 29th I was driven over to Mr. Monkhouse's by Mr. Wordsworth. . . . I forgot to mention that the news arrived yesterday of the death of Miss Joanna Hutchinson, the youngest sister of Mrs. Wordsworth and Mr. G. Hutchinson. This much affected Mrs. Wordsworth and saddened our yesterday evening at Brinsop. . . .

SEPT. 30th . . . Drive home. As we went Monkhouse was evidently gratified by the visit of the poet, and Wordsworth also enjoyed his visit, for he has a great regard for Mr. Monkhouse both on his own account and that of Thomas Monkhouse, our companion in Switzerland in 1820. This has been, he said, a visit both of duty and inclination, and therefore particularly agreeable. . . .

OCT. 31st I had an offer from Mrs. Talfourd to take me to see Mary Lamb, who lately put out her shoulder bone. We found her better than we feared. The bone is not set, which she is not aware of. Mary Lamb is eighty on the 3rd December next. She was in spirits, inquired after my brother, but talked rather ramblingly. This accident has brought her to herself sooner than would have been. . . .

NOV. 4th . . . I had an interesting chat with Fonblanque. . . . Sydney Smith joined us as we were talking. He received our compliments for his letter about the Americans. He was vastly pleasant. . . .

NOV. 12th . . . We fell in with Horace Smith, with whom we chatted

[1] See *supra*, March 10th, 1817.

pleasantly. His health is not good just now. I never thought his conversation equal to his reputation. Smith has made a fair epigram, which I have entitled:

BRIGHTON ATTRACTIONS

Sea without ships and, without trees, land
Three miles of glare and a beach without sand.

DEC. 6th I received early Harriet Martineau's *Life in* [*the*] *Sick Room*, a deeply interesting volume, anonymous. . . .

DEC. 12th . . . I had received from Quillinan a letter recording the very warm praise of the Wordsworths of Harriet Martineau's *Life in* [*the*] *Sick Room*, even more than I expected, for I thought the want of positive religion would prevent the enjoyment I could otherwise have so confidently anticipated, and I could not do better than copy the letter and send it to Harriet Martineau, at the same time apologising for a seeming breach of confidence towards Mrs. Reid. I also wrote to Quillinan vindicating Harriet Martineau for what he calls her 'falling short,' and justifying her conscientious abstinence from religious professions. I wrote also to Quillinan on the doubt I entertain whether I shall be able to go to Rydal this Christmas. From Moxon I learn that Harriet Martineau is quite satisfied with the reception the book has received already, but my letter will give her greater pleasure for Wordsworth's praise. . . .

. . . Having finished the book, I cannot but consider it as one of the very best, indeed the best she ever wrote. It is to be applauded for its perfect honesty and freedom from cant. I took care to praise her to Quillinan for her exuberant natural piety, which not even Unitarianism could extinguish. The book is full of acute and original remarks. It is full of bursts of eloquence. . . .

[*Travel Journal: Rydal.*] DEC. 24th . . . I went to the church and heard a sermon and the service performed in a manner that impressed me unfavourably. . . . Wordsworth even praised the sermon! After a few words of chat with Mrs. Arnold . . . I went up to the Mount, where I dined and after dinner I accompanied Wordsworth to Ambleside, where I took tea with the Quillinans . . . and walked home with Wordsworth.

DEC. 25th . . . James . . . gave notice[1] to Mr. and Mrs. Wordsworth. They followed soon and I had from them every consolation that friendship and kindness can administer. . . . I had a call from Quillinan in the evening as well as from Wordsworth several times. . . .

DEC. 26th . . . I was put into Miss Wordsworth's carriage and drawn

[1] On Christmas Eve Crabb Robinson fell downstairs at his lodgings, and had to spend several days in bed, James Dixon, the Wordsworths' servant, acting as his nurse.

to the Mount. I was put into a room adjoining James's sleeping place. He is an excellent nurse. . . .

DEC. 27th . . . I have found it very difficult to talk and Mr. and Mrs. Wordsworth have therefore been short in their visits. . . .

DEC. 28th . . . The Wordsworths went to dine with the Quillinans. . . .

DEC. 30th . . . In the evening, finding Mrs. Arnold was below, I got James to dress me and surprised them at their tea. I was cordially greeted and I was in excellent spirits and chatted freely enough. . . .

DEC. 31st . . . I had a pleasant two hours' chat below. . . .

1844

JAN. 4th . . . We went early and took tea with Mrs. Arnold. Mrs. Ward and her son . . . who has been travelling in Germany, alone there. He is a sensible and *liberal* man—at least he took the liberal side in argument against the poet on the subject of the despotism of the King of Hanover and the intolerance of the late King of Prussia. An evening taken up with disputation. . . .

JAN. 5th . . . A very interesting letter from Harriet Martineau . . . partly consisting of a well-expressed statement of the effect she promises herself from her vindication of her ideas of the dignity of human nature in opposition to the common notion of human depravity. Even Miss Fenwick could on this only remark that she believed there was a great deal of mistake and that persons might mean the same, using different words. This letter is excellent and was, I have no doubt, meant for my friends.

JAN. 6th . . . We went to Mrs. Fletcher, with whom we dined and stayed till nine. . . . The conversation rather heavy, but not amounting to dull. Mrs. Fletcher spoke with moderation of her Scotch friends, especially of Jeffrey. She saw Southey at Edinburgh on the appearance of the *Edinburgh* review of *Madoc*. Southey felt it much as a matter of interest. He saw at once that it would be decisive of the immediate fate of the work. And so it proved. His profits at the end of a year were £3 15*s*. Mrs. Fletcher expressed her disapprobation of the note on Wordsworth by Lord Jeffrey. She thinks that he ought to have explicitly acknowledged two things,—first that public opinion had greatly changed concerning Wordsworth, and he ought also to have pointed out some half-dozen poems and acknowledged their worth. Wordsworth was very chatty today. . . .

JAN. 7th . . . An agreeable chat with the Wordsworths. Wordsworth not in good spirits. He has been with Mrs. Quillinan, who is in a poor state of health, I fear. . . .

JAN. 12th . . . Mrs. Quillinan came today. She is very much of an invalid and fills both Mr. and Mrs. Hutchinson [? Wordsworth] with very great anxiety, and not without too much cause, I fear. . . .

JAN. 22nd . . . A very agreeable chat with Miss Fenwick about a present I want to make to Wordsworth. She says I must not give so large a present as I wish, not more than £5. On being satisfied, she proposes I go and do this.

JAN. 24th My last morning I spent most agreeably with my friends. I never left them with a warmer feeling of gratitude for kindnesses towards all of them. I gave great pleasure to James by presenting him with a second-hand silver watch. . . . Miss Fenwick is very cordial indeed. Her feeling amounts to friendship, which from such a pious woman is a good sign. . . .

JAN. 30th [*London.*] . . . I went about buying a set of tea and breakfast things for Wordsworth at Daniell's. I did not attend to Miss Fenwick's injunctions, and bought a set of china with gilt rims for £6 18*s*. A full set except that I had only six breakfast cups and saucers, and consisting of eighty pieces. They are, however, neat rather than gaudy and I have no doubt will please. . . .

FEB. 21st . . . In the course of the evening and the next morning I amused myself by reading Hood's *Whimsicalities*. Hood is not one of my favourites, but I cannot deny his power. I like best his simply good-humoured pictures of humble character [in] low life—his Mrs. Gardner, for instance, a good Cockney who has but one passion, flowers, of which she never speaks, but in the first person singular—a source of very obvious and rather too easy jokes. Ease is both the merit and the temptation. He writes so easily that he gives himself no trouble. There is a class of his works which I do not like because the *kind* is offensive, and that is the horrible; but sometimes he happily blends the serious with the comic, even when the comic comes as a damper or disappointment: for instance, in *The Defaulter*, you have a picture so drawn that you are sure the hero has embezzled, from his suspicious conduct. It turns out that he is only the happy father of a babe after fifteen years' waiting. So a ghost appears, only to give notice to the heir: 'There's tippence due for salt at No. —— and not booked.' Of the purely horrid is the poem *The Forge*, very vigorous, but offensive. But he is declining in his puns.

FEB. 22nd I continued reading Hood. I have now finished the second volume and am glad there is not a third to read—such things soon tire. . . .

MARCH 13th . . . The only really interesting circumstance was that I saw Miss Edgeworth! I noticed, without knowing who she was, a little old woman, with a very fair complexion, dressed in white handsomely—a face strongly marked with an expression shrewd, if not shrewish. She reminded me of Mrs. Barbauld, so that [when] W. Lloyd told me she was in the room I knew it must be the lady I had seen: I could not get near enough to her to hear her voice. . . .

MARCH 18th . . . I stole away to go to an evening party at Guillemard's, which I was lucky in being able to do, for there was Miss Edgeworth. I got myself introduced to her. . . . She has not seen the Aikins. She was dressed in white, but not so grandly as at Murchison's—or did the novelty of her appearance give dignity to the impression? Miss Edgeworth does not impress me with the notion that she is particularly amiable or kind. There is a sharpness in her physiognomy not at all agreeable. . . .

MARCH 30th . . . I breakfasted with Kenyon. With him . . . Browning, the crazy poet, but a sensible man in prose conversation. . . .

APRIL 9th . . . I had matter for agreeable thought before I went, in a letter from Mrs. Wordsworth informing me that my tea equipage was handselled on Mr. Wordsworth's [birthday]. A note from Miss Fenwick confirmed her intimation that my present had been very acceptable. . . .

MAY 25th . . . Reading *Coningsby*. It is full of cleverness, and the exposure of Croker under the name of Rigby is most excellent. There is also a very clever but extravagant and hardly serious eulogy of the Jews, as if they were the great race of men.

MAY 26th . . . I went on with *Coningsby* and finished the second volume. The book is full of stimulating and at the same time of offensive matter. The worst I have mentioned. Theodore Hook is as bad under the name of Gay as Rigby is good representing Croker. Theodore Hook says nothing that any ordinary [man] might not have said. The election scene is spirited and not extravagant, but very true. . . .

MAY 30th . . . I continued at the Athenaeum all day to finish *Coningsby*, which has given me great pleasure, more than I could have expected from such a man as Disraeli. I came home late.

JUNE 16th . . . Cookson . . . told me that Wordsworth is violent against the Bill,[1] as his brother tells him, but is quite uninformed on the subject. . . . I went to Miss Fenwick's, with whom I dined at luncheon hour and had a very agreeable chat. I found her as amiable as ever and found her very quiet and even admitting the justice of the Bill. My brief reply she

[1] The Dissenters' Chapels Bill, untiringly supported by H.C.R., which was passed by the House of Lords on July 15th 1844.

seems to have found unanswerable and though not for, at least, not against the Bill. Wordsworth must be instructed. Mr. and Miss Rogers called while I was with her, and Miss Fenwick was, I believe, pleased with the unexpected compliment. We talked *de omnibus*, less about Church matters than usual. Miss Fenwick is much pleased with Dr. Arnold's *Life and Correspondence*, in spite of her imperfect sympathy with the Doctor. . . .

JUNE 17th . . . The subscription for Southey's monument is going on. Kenyon and most of the committee give £10 10*s*. I shall give £5. This is to be in Westminster Abbey. . . .

JUNE 24th . . . I ventured to remark on the single defect of Wordsworth's character. He has lost his love of liberty; not his humanity, but his confidence in mankind. . . .

JULY 3rd . . . A letter to Mrs. Wordsworth chiefly on the Bill and on Wordsworth's opposition. Wordsworth being of opinion that Dissent should not be endowed, I urged that he ought rather to be for than against us. . . .

JULY 25th . . . I amused myself by reading the first two numbers of *Martin Chuzzlewit*, which I fear will have matter very clever, but at the same time disagreeable. Dickens's great fault is his predilection for very mean and despicable characters, out of proportion in number; and, besides, he makes goodness contemptible. . . .

AUG. 13th . . . Called on Bernard Barton, the Quaker poet. Just the simple man I expected to see from Charles Lamb's account of him—a mixture of shrewdness withal. I dare say a very good man. . . .

AUG. 20th . . . On the journey I read Nos. 10–12 of *Martin Chuzzlewit*. The book has become interesting, but on reflection it is unpleasant. Dickens's picture of the Americans is gross caricature, and it has no air of truth about it. The settlement in Eden might have been made by Englishmen. The great fault of the book is the profusion of low characters. . . .

AUG. 24th . . . I finished *Chuzzlewit* at night; a book that I do not wish to look into a second time, so generally disgusting are the characters and incidents of the tale.

OCT. 14th . . . I then went to the Athenaeum, where I spent the rest of the day, reading nearly the whole of a most amusing book of travels in the East, *Eöthen*, meaning 'From the East,' there being a wilful neglect of all useful and instructive matter, and the mere humanity of the scenes and country being dwelt on. This occupied me till late.

NOV. 28th . . . Sam Naylor brought me a handsome copy of the *Reynard the Fox*, which is dedicated to me—the first book that ever honoured my name by putting it in front. . . .

NOV. 30th . . . I breakfasted with Samuel Rogers by self-invitation. . . . Rogers was in his usual quiet calm spirits.[1] He said he should be ashamed of himself if he could not bear such a blow at his age. It would amuse him to try on how little he could live, but he should not be put to the trial. 'There is, if all be lost, enough to pay everyone and to spare. We are not ruined.' This was said without any affectation or emphasis. . . .

DEC. 21st . . . I went westward and first bought a handsome shawl in Regent Street, which I carried to Mary Lamb. She received it with manifest pleasure, and I had a nice chat with her. She is removed to a more comfortable house. . . .

[*Travel Journal: Rydal.*] DEC. 26th I heard Wordsworth last night read prayers from Thornton's collection. He read with remarkable effect and beauty. He told me this anecdote. The Duke of Wellington being on a visit was told by his host that he had family prayers in the morning. Would he attend? 'With great pleasure,' said the Duke. The gentleman read out of this book. 'What! You use fancy prayers?' He never came down again. He expected the Church prayers, which Wordsworth uses in the morning. . . . I am glad to find . . . that neither Carr nor Wordsworth is altogether a partisan of the Puseyites whatever their tendencies may be. . . .

DEC. 27th . . . To Mrs. Fletcher's, with whom I dined . . . and Hartley Coleridge. . . . Hartley Coleridge behaved very well, and did not drink much. He read some verses I could not comprehend, as he read them very unpleasantly, on Dr. Arnold, and he sang a comic song which kept me very grave. He left us quite early, Wordsworth says to get beer at other houses. . . . A very pleasant chat with the Wordsworths and Mrs. Quillinan at night. I read to Wordsworth [the] Wilberforces' letter.[2] To the ladies I had read Mrs. Clarkson's letters before. They all consider the Wilberforce apology to be no apology at all. . . .

1845

JAN. 4th . . . Mrs. Quillinan was come to the Mount, and she spent the evening with us and was able to play whist with us, and so contributed to the amusement of the evening, though she was and is in a very feeble state. . . .

[1] Rogers's bank had been broken into and 'plundered of more than £40,000 in bank notes, besides several thousands of gold and also securities abstracted. . . . Samuel Rogers bears the loss heroically.' [*Crabb Robinson.*]

[2] An apology for their statements about Clarkson in the *Life* of their father.

JAN. 6th . . . I wrote from dictation of the poet some corrections of his *Letter on Railroads*, a disagreeable task. . . .

JAN. 10th . . . I read Tennyson's poems today. There is one on *Locksley Hall* of incongruous contents. One expects an antiquarian romance, and meets with complaints of a jilted lover, who becomes a declaimer about social institutions, and a comparison of the savage and civilised state. Another poem, *The Vision of Sin*, is a crazy rhapsody—perhaps a riddle I have not sense to solve. I copy three grotesque stanzas: 'A gap-toothed man' lights at a ruined inn and says:

'Slip-shod waiter . . . Empty scarecrows, I and you.'

All this is unintelligible. I extract part of the same address I fear [?] from which a meaning may be extracted.

'Friendship! to be two in one . . . Frantic love and frantic hate'

Tennyson is beyond all doubt a poet, but I suspect his poetry is worth little or nothing.

JAN. 11th . . . *The Two Voices* very ambitious, but if I go on about Tennyson my volume would soon be filled.

JAN. 14th . . . It being very fine, Wordsworth challenged me to a walk. I went with him to Ambleside. . . . I then called with Wordsworth on Dr. Davy. . . . This morning Wordsworth came down late to breakfast, being detained late making a sonnet which he gives to me to do what I like with, but I am not to name him as the author. It belongs to a class of which he has written very few.

YOUNG ENGLAND[1]

A SONNET

Young England! What is then become of Old
Of dear Old England? Is our Mother dead—
Dead to the very name, that once could shed
Such glory round us? Nay, it keeps its hold
In the true filial bosom's inmost fold
And will for ever. Alfred at the head
Of all who for her rights watched, toiled and bled
Knows that this prophecy is not too bold—
What! How! Shall she be ruled in thought and deed
By beardless boys, an imitative race,
The servile cattle of a Gallic breed?
Dear Mother, if thou *must* thy steps retrace,
Go, where at least meek innocency dwells.
Let babes and sucklings be thy Oracles.

JAN. 16th . . . The Davys . . . gave a handsome dinner. The party consisted of the Gregs and Miss Martineau, the Fletchers and Mr. Graves.

[1] This draft differs in lines 2, 3, 4, 6, 9, 11 from the final version.

But by tacit consent the conversation was on purely indifferent matters. This was better than controversy. Mr. Greg being himself a mesmeriser,[1] and as well Wordsworth as Dr. Davy and Mrs. Fletcher being decided disbelievers, an attempt at discussion would have endangered the good will of the parties to one another. Wordsworth was very chatty, dividing his talk between his neighbours, Miss Martineau and Mrs. Davy. She also shared hers between the poet and Mr. Graves. Mrs. Fletcher was between Mr. Greg and me, and I had for my other companion, Mrs. Greg. I was placed between two very interesting women, and tried to be as pretty-behaved as the poet. I was much pleased with Mrs. Greg, a very sweet woman indeed. Mr. Greg is a clear-headed man. I thought I remarked a shyness between the poet and him. They spoke little or nothing to each other. I intimated to Mrs. Greg that it was distance only, and the fear to make new acquaintance, that prevented Mrs. Wordsworth calling on her. I have arranged that Miss Martineau is to call today here. . . .

JAN. 22nd . . . Miss Martineau is so much pleased with the country that she thinks of residing there for six months. I doubt whether she would become cordial with the Wordsworths. . . . Wordsworth was very poorly.

JAN. 26th [*London.*] . . . A call from Moxon, who brought an invitation to dine with Rogers. . . . Lushington, Mrs. Norton, Spedding, Alfred Tennyson, Moxon, Robinson, Kenny. Rogers told us that a lady [Mrs. Caroline Norton] was coming who was very desirous of seeing Tennyson, but he did not name her, and she did not come till dinner was half over and went away very early. She was not named nor did I guess who she was, so little did she resemble the lady I had seen in full dress at Bunsen's formerly. Her tone of conversation was very easy, like one who is accustomed to good company, but she said nothing remarkable. She named herself incidentally. The only subject on which I talked was Bettina, of whom she spoke admiringly. There was nothing to be remembered. Tennyson did not hesitate to say that he shuddered sitting by her side, a strange remark from a young man. Tennyson himself was a much more interesting person. I had a long chat with him, *tête-à-tête* at table and in the drawing-room, chiefly about Goethe, of whom he has a high opinion, with the common notion that he wanted heart. He acknowledged the inferiority of Schiller. I related anecdotes of him. He was searching in his questions. I felt unequal to reply to some. Alfred Tennyson is intimate with Carlyle. I asked him to call and look at my Wieland. I suspect he will not come. It is probable he has taken or will take an impression

[1] He claimed to have relieved many sick persons. Harriet Martineau had recently been cured by mesmerism of her long, and supposed incurable, illness.

from Carlyle. I spoke to him freely about his poetry, and complained of his obscurities. He said he was pleased that I preferred his *Vision of Sin*, which few would like. He himself particularly liked *The Gardener's Daughter*. The tale of the woman who pined away when she found her poor lover a lord, he said, was founded on fact. Alfred Tennyson is a fine fellow in his physique, almost as powerful and rough as Whewell. Lushington is a young barrister, and like Spedding, a friend of Alfred Tennyson, refined in his manners. All three talk with consciousness: *Nur die Lumpen sind bescheiden*. . . . Rogers in good spirits. No inquiries about the Wordsworths—a want of memory, I dare say. I did not venture to read *Young England*; it does not take here, I find. . . .

JAN. 27th . . . I took tea with Miss Sturch. No one with her, but Mrs. Jameson and Mrs. Bayne and Kenyon and Fellows. It was a very agreeable evening. Mrs. Jameson and I agreed unusually well. She talked her best. She has lately risen much in the estimation of society, and is now received in the highest literary circles, and this has not made her offensively confident. She spoke of Sydney Smith as incurably ill. He will not survive long, it is thought; but he will retain, it is expected, his humour to the last. A few days ago he declared that he had dreamed he was in a madhouse, and that there was shut up with him Harriet Martineau and the Bishop of Exeter. . . .

Feb. 24th . . . Today's papers announce the death of one of our very ablest writers, Sydney Smith. . . .

APRIL 24th . . . I found Mrs. Quillinan less of an invalid than I feared to find her. They breakfasted with me, and I then walked out with Quillinan and I called at Moxon's, where I found Wordsworth looking very well and about to make arrangements for going to the Queen's ball this day (Friday). He is to stay at Moxon's for a few days and then go to Mrs. Hoare's. . . .

MAY 3rd . . . I dined with Mrs. Hoare—rather a flat dinner, chiefly owing to Wordsworth being very silent. He seemed unwell, and is suffering in his eyes. Perhaps, too, he is suffering more than all from the journey of his daughter to Portugal, which it is intended shall take place in a few days. Mrs. Quillinan's health is so bad as to justify any apprehension on his part, but she was looking better today. . . .

MAY 7th . . . To Moxon's, where I found Wordsworth: he was cheerful. I found Mrs. Quillinan had left London on Tuesday. . . . Rogers came in. Wordsworth gave an account of his being at the levee—an idle act his going, for he exchanged not a word with the Queen. . . .

MAY 16th . . . And then I went to the Athenaeum, where I was seduced by the opportunity to begin Disraeli's *Sybil*, a new volume that will be the object of general curiosity for six weeks. I have not finished the first volume; will therefore only say that its palpable object is to exhibit in coarse contrast the two nations—rich and poor. . . .

MAY 17th . . . And then went to the Athenaeum, where I stayed the rest of the day, having obtained the second volume of *Sybil.* An unsatisfactory and not very stimulating book. . . .

JUNE 3rd . . . I went to see Mary Lamb and I played a few games of piquet with her. A clearer proof of the decline of her faculties cannot well be than that she was unable to play. She could distinguish the cards, but was unable to play with even the ordinary skill. . . .

JUNE 19th . . . On our arrival we found waiting for us the American poet, Bryant.[1] . . . I had been reading in the morning some half-dozen of Bryant's poems. They are agreeable enough, and he may be the greatest American poet, but still I met with nothing that will tax my memory to [retain].[2] There are no striking thoughts or even expressions which will give life to the poems. They are chiefly descriptive and sentimental, all quite moral and pure and very little nationality. We kept it up till late. Lively chat.

JUNE 20th . . . Bryant is rather reserved than modest, but I liked him sufficiently to give him my card and desire him to call on Wordsworth. . . .

DEC. 10th . . . Called on Mary Lamb—a painful call—her articulation is become so bad as to be unintelligible. I had a great difficulty in understanding her. Glad to find she had a good-natured boy who came to play cards with her. Gave him half a crown. . . .

DEC. 17th I went on my annual visit to Wordsworth. . . .

DEC. 19th [*Rydal.*] . . . Mr. Wordsworth was at the lane with James, and I had from him and Mrs. Wordsworth the cordial reception I have always had. They only in the house, which I never saw before so empty. Poor Miss Wordsworth no better than she used to be and no society. We had a great deal of talk, both of persons and things. The only interesting circumstance is this: on my reminding him he had not executed his purpose of introducing in the new edition a note expressing his regret that he had ever uttered a word favourable to Puseyism, he said his only reason was that he was at last quite tired—a very insufficient reason. And I fear he will never do it. Nevertheless, he expressed himself strongly against Faber. . . .

I took a walk with the Wordsworths to Ambleside. We looked into the shell of Harriet Martineau's new house, whom we met on the road. Called on Miss Fenwick in Mrs. Quillinan's old lodging. . . .

[1] William Cullen Bryant, who edited the *New York Evening Post* for fifty years.
[2] MS. 'remain'.

DEC. 20th . . . Then I proceeded to Harriet Martineau, whom I found blooming in health. She is industriously working on her Forest and Game Law Tales, and, though her first volume does not appear to be popular, the modern tales will probably be more attractive. While with her, she received a cheque from Moxon for £50 on account of her *Life in the Sick Room*. Moxon had given her £75 before for her first edition. . . . She is full of family affection as well as of general kindness. . . .

DEC. 22nd . . . One thing [about Harriet Martineau] is delightful, nay, two things—her good health and the cordial terms on which she is with everyone here, notwithstanding so many are unbelievers [in mesmerism] and even scornful unbelievers.

DEC. 23rd It is curious to observe how no one seems to be either very glad or very sorry at the late political changes,[1] as if every one felt that the post of Prime Minister is not an enviable one. No one knows what to expect or what to wish. . . . The indifference of Wordsworth to the results of the present political party arrangements is remarkable. He seems to expect no good from the success of any one. It is also remarkable that Harriet Martineau is also rejoicing in the return of Sir Robert Peel to power, and in the exclusion of Lord John Russell from office. . . .

DEC. 24th . . . The family here have been grievously afflicted by news from Rome. They have lost their youngest grandchild, a wise and most interesting child of four years of age. Wordsworth has been composing verses which will be much talked of hereafter, but must be kept strictly secret for the present. Therefore, I merely record that I have had the credit of making an improvement in a line and been thanked for it. There had been written:

> That from my thoughts may steal into thy mind.[2]

This I strongly objected to. I proposed instead:

> That hence may fitly pass into thy mind,

which has been thankfully accepted.

1846

JAN. 7th . . . Wordsworth this evening related a pretty anecdote of his cook-maid. A stranger who was shown about the grounds, asked to see

[1] Lord John Russell had just resigned and Peel been summoned to form a ministry.

[2] The line now reads:

> 'That issuing hence may steal into thy mind.'
>
> *Lines Inscribed in a Copy of his Poems sent to the Queen*, l.22.

his study. The servant took him to the library and said: 'This is master's library, but he studies in the fields.' . . .

JAN. 10th I left my excellent friends at half-past two, Wordsworth accompanying me to the end of the lane. . . .

FEB. 4th [*London.*] . . . A letter from Wordsworth in low spirits received on Tuesday. This morning I heard of Dr. Wordsworth's death. The poet will feel this, for he is a man of strong family feeling and his brother was an amiable man.

FEB. 21st . . . Called on poor Mary Lamb—a melancholy spectacle—she is unintelligible in her speech. I will never call again but to make her some little present. . . .

MARCH 9th . . . Kenyon had but a small party, and I promised to go after dinner. Browning and others with him. Browning, whom I could not for a long time sympathise with, has at last made himself quite agreeable. Home late. Read at night Hood's serious poems. I had no notion of the earnest strength of his serious verses. I was aware only of his comic merit and chiefly as a punster.

MARCH 27th . . . We then went to Weekes's studio and saw his bust of Southey for Westminster Abbey—a spirited likeness, but it approaches caricature, as Southey's own countenance does. . . .

MAY 21st . . . A long-looked-for letter from Wordsworth. I am sorry to remark that his hand is becoming illegible. . . .

JUNE 29th . . . An omnibus to Hampstead and dined there with the Hoares to meet the Quillinans on their way from Portugal to Rydal. Mrs. Quillinan looking very well. Quillinan himself, thin but not ill. I enjoyed the afternoon hearing their report of their journey. Mrs. Quillinan seems to have had high enjoyment, especially from the south of Spain, a country I more than ever wish to see. . . .

JULY 11th . . . [Called] on Mary Lamb. Her speech inarticulate. No wonder she is infirm. She was born Dec. 1764. A visit to her is now painful. . . .

1847

JAN. 12th My annual visit was unusually curtailed this year. I went late, and instead of four weeks, stayed little more than two. The only occurrence of note was that William Wordsworth brought his bride to his father's on the 30th of January. . . .

JAN. 13th . . . Found the Wordsworths all quite well and John on a visit. . . . I saw the Quillinans also, and in the evening we played whist. . . .

JAN. 18th . . . Wordsworth was himself this evening. Till today he has been quite silent as if the vigour of his mind were gone; but he has been quite himself. . . .

JAN. 19th . . . We dined with the Quillinans . . . and after dinner we all came home to tea, there being a party of fifty, with the servants. Whist as usual.

N.B.—This was the day fixed for the marriage of William Wordsworth and Miss Graham at Brighton. . . .

JAN. 20th . . . A dinner party at Mrs. Davy's, which went off well. . . . Mr. Wordsworth there. He has recovered his spirits, and has been chatty enough during the last two days. . . .

JAN. 30th . . . William Wordsworth was to bring home his wife today, and to lessen the embarrassment of her situation, I went early to Charles Arnold, and we together mounted Loughrigg, ascending and descending by Fox How, a delightful walk, both for the scenery and our conversation, which was most interesting. . . .

This morning I had more talk with Wordsworth than on any day since I came. He had his usual flow of conversation. We spoke of literature. He delivered an opinion very unfavourable to Hallam's judgment on all matters of taste and literature in his great *History*. . . .

FEB. 14th [*London.*] I breakfasted with Rogers this morning, and an agreeable morning we had. There were three Sharpes, and Empson [and] Prandi, and a new man to me, Kinglake, whose person, manners, and tone of conversation all pleased me. A good deal of public anecdote was given by Rogers, who is fond especially of relating his conversations with Wellington, whose wisdom and patriotism he warmly [praises], and he always justifies his praise. . . .

I had been invited by Miss Fenwick to spend a few days with the Wordsworths at her house, and I went accordingly on the 9th March.

MARCH 9th [*Bath.*] . . . I was set down by an omnibus at 8 Queen Square, where Miss Fenwick now resides. Besides a niece, Mr. and Mrs. Wordsworth were there. I had a most friendly reception from all, but as well the poet as our friend the hostess look poorly—not absolutely ill, but old and feeble. Mrs. Wordsworth is the best of the party. In truth, we are all growing old, and they, perhaps, say of me what I have written of them. I was the liveliest of the party. We had nevertheless grave talk, except that after tea we had a rubber. . . .

MARCH 12th I succeeded in persuading Mr. Wordsworth to take a walk with me. We went over the new bridge direct to Witcombe, and passed by the graveyard in which my mother's body has lain for more than half a century. We had rather a fatiguing walk over the heights and I was afraid it would be too much for my companion. But he was not so fatigued as I was on our return. . . .

MARCH 13th . . . My first call was on Walter Savage Landor. He received me very cordially and rattled away about pictures and persons most delightfully. We both abstained from all allusions to his attack on Wordsworth which occasioned our subsequent estrangement. He did not ask me where I was nor make any inquiry about myself. . . . He tells me that the new edition of his works differs much from the old.

MARCH 16th This was a fine day and the morning was well occupied in part in a call made by me and Mr. Wordsworth on the Miss Sollys,[1] who yesterday wrote a very odd note requesting Mr. Wordsworth to fix a time for their calling on him. Mrs. Wordsworth was angry at this pushing themselves, but Wordsworth was kindly disposed, and at my suggestion consented to call on them with me, which we did. And their conversation was better than from their absurd letter, accompanied by an execrable sonnet, might have been expected. The whole incident was ridiculous. . . .

MARCH 18th [*Devizes.*] . . . It was about ten when I called . . . and introduced myself to the Doctor [Brabant, on whom he had left a letter of introduction], with whom I have become acquainted in the course of four hours more intimately than I recollect with any man. He is about sixty-six years of age, is a small man with a scholar-like, gentlemanly appearance and talks well. . . . It was through Coleridge that he was induced to study German theology, Coleridge having told him that Paulus entertained the same opinions which he professed. He seems to have known Coleridge well, of whom he related this, that he has repeatedly heard him say: 'I have known many men who were religious because they were good, but never one that was good because he was religious.' He also repeated a pun of Coleridge's against poor Amos Cottle. 'He wrote a poem that bore a lie on the title page, for he called it *Alfred*, and it was never *halfread* by any human being.' He [Brabant] spoke highly of Coleridge. He has several very interesting letters from Coleridge which, at my suggestion, he will give to Mrs. Coleridge. . . .

APRIL 12th [*London.*] . . . I took an omnibus to Hampstead, where I dined with the Wordsworths at Mrs. Hoare's. He is looking much better and was cheerful and chatty. Mrs. Wordsworth also cheerful. Good

[1] 'Two ladies of a certain age . . . whom I had seen before. They called on pretence of inquiring whether I had received their card, but evidently in the hope to see Wordsworth . . . who was gone upstairs. . . . Altogether their behaviour was strange. They are said to be flighty, one especially, but very respectable morally.' [March 12th, 1847.]

accounts from Mrs. Quillinan. Moxon was there, and we walked back together. . . .

April 14th . . . [Call] on Mrs. Coleridge with whom I had a chat about her father's poetry, his philosophy, etc.; a long talk. . . . I also read through the recent Oration by Green—Hunterian Oration, which has been so much admired for its eloquence, and which is a more luminous exposure of some of Coleridge's principles than has been yet given to the world. I have been writing to him today, congratulating him on the work and on the progress of public opinion in favour of the Master's notions. . . .

April 16th . . . I began Coleridge's *Remorse*, which I was so pleased with that I could not but finish it in the morning. Never felt more strongly the great difference between the poetical and the dramatical. How beautiful in the one, how worthless in the other, point of view.

April 26th I went early to Wordsworth at his nephew's in the Westminster Cloisters, and sat with him while young Wyon took a model of his head for a bas-relief medallion, and I hope also he will cast a die and have a medal of him. . . . Mrs. Wordsworth was very low about Mrs. Quillinan, and while I was there a letter came, and Wordsworth was called out of the room. I did not see him again. The account was not favourable. It is uncertain whether I shall see him again during his stay, as Mrs. Quillinan's state may make him leave immediately. . . .

April 29th . . . I went to Dr. Wordsworth's to inquire about the Wordsworths, and learned they went away on Monday evening. The news continued to be alarming. . . .

May 1st . . . Quillinan has announced that his wife's life is drawing to a close. This will be the death of Mrs. Wordsworth, I fear. Quillinan wrote with composure. His condition will be deplorable, for he lives on his wife. . . .

May 19th . . . Mrs. Quillinan is as she was. The Wordsworths are resigned. . . . I have been engaged lately reading Mrs. Coleridge's preface to the new edition of the *Biographia Literaria* of her father. She has very ably, and not with gross partiality, apologised for his infirmities—of intellect, not moral defects.

May 20th . . . I wrote letters today to Mrs. Quillinan, a taking of leave, having received a very kind and also a cheerful letter from Quillinan speaking of her as happy and resigned—a remarkable letter under such circumstances. . . .

May 23rd Anxious to run over a book I ought never to have undertaken to read—Thackeray's *alias* Titmarsh's *Journey from Cornhill to Cairo*—I occupied myself this morning with the book. Occasionally amused, but, on the whole, it is a book I could not relish—the levity of the tone is offensive. The only description which I could attempt to realise is that of Cairo, aided merely or chiefly by the panorama I saw on Saturday. . . .

MAY 24th . . . I was gratified by a short note from Quillinan. A letter I wrote to Mrs. Quillinan on her death-bed, as we all suppose, has been received, as I hoped, by all the family, and even gratefully acknowledged. In Quillinan's letter he mentioned the death of Mary Lamb, of which I had not heard. . . .

MAY 28th . . . I attended dear Mary Lamb's funeral. A coach fetched me, in which were Talfourd and Forster. We were driven to St. John's Wood, where we found Moxon, Ryle, and Martin Burney, and after taking some refreshment drove to the Edmonton churchyard. . . . [Later] we went to Lamb's old house, where a cold luncheon was provided for us. We chatted about our dear old friends. . . .

JUNE 6th . . . I had reserved the evening to myself that I might hear a lecture from Cooper, the Chartist, who was imprisoned for sedition, has been eulogised by Talfourd, who wrote a bepraised poem, *The Purgatory of Suicides*, and from whom I expected to hear coarse and passionate eloquence. I have seldom been more disappointed. The subject, 'The Life and Genius of Byron.' I sat out an hour of desultory rambling which had not one redeeming virtue. His manner rather finical and precise, like that of the Fordhams, no energy or power, and the substance commonplace appeals to vulgar feelings such as might be supposed would please the second- and third-rate audience of the National Hall. But he has not much attraction for them, it seems. There were not above two hundred or two hundred and fifty people there, the hall not half-full. The topics were abuse of lords, praise of the working-man, not much about Byron—of course, the greatest poet after Shakespeare. Speaking of his domestic quarrels, he said that it had been said that poets were not suited to domestic life. 'I heard Mr. Wordsworth express himself strongly on this. "It is a libel on all poets, on me, too, for," the old man said, "I am a poet as well as Lord Byron." ' When he began to read an extract from *Childe Harold*, after foolish praise, I flitted, for he read very ill and inaudibly. . . .

JUNE 19th . . . Mrs. Twining[1] gave a sad account of the Wordsworths. The poet is said to be quite disconsolate. He said to Mrs. Arnold: 'My daughter is dying, Mrs. Wordsworth will quickly follow, and then I shall go.' . . .

JULY 6th . . . Read in the *Quarterly Review* a flattering review of Mrs. Quillinan's Portugal Journey.[2] It comes too late to give pleasure.

[1] *Née* Mary Arnold. [2] *Journal of a Portuguese Tour.*

JULY 10th This morning I received a short note from Quillinan, dated yesterday: 'At 1 a.m. my precious Dora, your true friend, breathed her last.' Hardly a word more. . . .

. . . I read a very favourable review of Mrs. Quillinan's book in the *Edinburgh Review*. Such is the effect of a name! The *Edinburgh* makes up for injustice to the father by over-praise of the daughter.

OCT. 14th . . . I had a most interesting call on Talfourd. He read to me some letters by Charles Lamb on the tragical event which threw a cloud over both his sister and himself. I have given a decided opinion that these letters ought to be made public, both for his and her sakes, though they reveal the fact that even he was once in confinement. The additional volume of letters will be of great interest, beyond even the preceding. They will supply an apology for all one wishes away in his delightful works. . . .

OCT. 30th I saw Mr. Rooper this day and talked about Charles Lamb, whom he recollects playing with as a little child, and Lamb's grandmother was housekeeper in the house of old Plumer, the member of Parliament for Hertfordshire. . . .

[*Travel Journal: Rydal.*] DEC. 18th I set out on a visit to this place under circumstances unusually melancholy. I was to visit my friends after they had sustained the heaviest affliction in the death of their only daughter, Mrs. Quillinan, and the ordinary enjoyment of this Christmas visit I could not expect. Mrs. Wordsworth wrote early to say I was still to come, and probably the hope is that I may serve to amuse the poet, and that my animal spirits may provoke some cheerfulness. I shall rejoice if it prove well-founded. . . .

It was near ten when we [Crabb Robinson, Jane Wordsworth, and her cousin] reached Rydal Mount. Of course, a kind reception, but still a mournful one in both my friends.

DEC. 19th I felt very heavy [the result of a fall at Birthwaite station]. Mrs. Wordsworth proposed my sitting still all day, and I therefore did not pull off my slippers. Mr. Wordsworth, too, stayed at home, but I sat alone in the dining-room, while he was alone in the further sitting-room. Mr. Quillinan called and dined with us. . . . We had several calls. . . . and I was not at all out of sorts. . . . I read with great interest the notes added by Cuthbert Southey to the third edition of Southey's *Life of John Wesley*—chiefly consisting of the marginalia of Coleridge in his own copy. They exhibit the vast superiority of Coleridge to Southey in intellect, though I concur in Southey's strong antipathy to Calvinism rather than in Coleridge's mystical half acquiescence. . . .

DEC. 20th . . . The evening was very dull. We dined at five and after dinner . . . I proposed playing whist, but Mrs. Wordsworth only shook her head, and Wordsworth did not speak the whole evening and retired early. . . .

DEC. 22nd This has been but a bad day. I set about the small volume of Henry Taylor's poems, just published, which I read with great pleasure. They are full of thought, and the style is very elegant. . . . Before dinner came Hartley Coleridge, and he stayed the rest of the day. He was very chatty, and his talk was that of a thinking man, but it is an effort to follow him, and I felt it a relief at night when he went away. Yet could he abstain from liquor he might be anything in society with a little trouble.

I am sorry to find that a very bad feeling has arisen between Wordsworth and his son-in-law. Wordsworth has never been to Quillinan's house, and this so offends Quillinan, that he says he has lost all respect for him. I have tried to soften him, but in vain. Quillinan is a proud man, prone to take offence. . . .

DEC. 24th This day has been like the preceding—somewhat more sad. At breakfast I proposed to Wordsworth that we should call together on Mrs. Cookson. I had touched a wound. He burst into tears, and he has hardly spoken a word the whole day since. . . .

I read out *The Ugly Duckling* from Andersen's tales; but it did not draw out a word from Wordsworth, beautiful as it is.

DEC. 25th *Christmas Day* This would have been a very mournful festival but for the attention of Mrs. Davy, who kindly invited me to dine there. . . . I reached Rydal after four, when I had a call from Mr. Greg. Wordsworth was able to chat cheerfully, though at church he sobbed all the time. I knew this would be a most painful anniversary. . . .

DEC. 26th This has been a more cheerful day. Wordsworth was in a composed state at church in the forenoon, and has been so during the time that I have seen him, but that has not been much. . . .

DEC. 28th . . . I walked out with Wordsworth, and called on Mr. Robinson. . . . The day was fine and the walk, I hope, was of use. . . .

DEC. 29th . . . Returned to walk with Mr. Wordsworth, whom I was glad to have persuaded to a walk, but he was silent. . . . I after this called on Quillinan who is as melancholy as Wordsworth.

1848

JAN. 4th . . . Mrs. Wordsworth this evening put into my hands a number of letters from Charles Lamb, which I am to take with me to

London and offer such to Talfourd as I may think fit to print. But perhaps he has had them already? . . .

JAN. 5th . . . I looked over Browne's *Vulgar Errors* with Coleridge's notes. . . . It has fortunately happened that, as through Wordsworth's sorrow that admits of no consolation and dear Mrs. Wordsworth's also, this visit has allowed me little comfort within doors, so I have had an unusual degree of pleasure out of the house, especially at the Davys'.

JAN. 7th . . . I spent the evening at home, but Wordsworth was as moody and silent as on the other evenings, so that the evening has been but a painful one. I had newspapers to read, which filled up the time.

JAN. 8th I rose early and packed up my things, when I took a nap before James brought me the hot water. Talked with him about the excessive grief of Mr. Wordsworth. James said: 'It's very sad, sir. He was moaning about her, and said: "Oh, but she was such a bright creature," and I said, "But do you not think, sir, that she is brighter now than she ever was?" And then Master burst out into a flood of tears.' Was a better word ever said on such an occasion? . . . I left my friends at ten. Mr. Wordsworth burst into tears as I left him. He was unable to take leave of me. . . .

JAN. 20th This day I did make a beginning in examining Lamb's letters lent me by Mrs. Wordsworth. I first read those to Wordsworth contained in the printed volumes, and I have already found a few well worth copying. Others, on the contrary, certainly not fit for publication. . . .

FEB. 2nd . . . A very satisfactory letter from Quillinan. It is evident that the relation between him and Wordsworth is very much improved.

FEB. 6th . . . I then called on Talfourd and gave him all those letters of Lamb to Wordsworth which I thought might, without giving offence, be printed. I found Talfourd at work on Lamb's papers, and I believe he will complete his publication of Lamb's *Letters* with the love with which he began it. . . .

FEB. 24th . . . Read with some pleasure the first number of Thackeray's *Vanity Fair*, said to be the best of his works. The picture drawn of a cunning and selfish girl, a governess, trying to catch a rich officer from India is capital and promises a great deal.

MARCH 5th . . . I also read No. 2 of *Vanity Fair*—very spirited and truthful portrait painting by Thackeray. I shall probably read the whole. . . .

MARCH 17th . . . At Moxon's—paid for books. He gives a better account of Wordsworth. A good sign that he is preparing an edition of his prose works. This I heartily rejoice at. . . .

MARCH 26th . . . I breakfasted with Rogers and met there by my introduction Layard, and also Moxon and Carrick, who has been making the most striking likeness I have yet seen of Wordsworth—a miniature full length. But it is too sad a likeness: it has an expression of fixed and irremovable grief. Rogers was not in a good-tempered mood. . . .

APRIL 7th . . . I dined with Tagart—an unusually agreeable dinner. The party small and quite select. There were the Dickenses. Dickens himself had the post of honour. He did not affect the *bel esprit*, but talked like a man of judgment on the news of the day. . . .

APRIL 16th . . . I dined with Field and found there a very agreeable party: Emerson, who, however, did not talk much or say anything worth noticing; Wilkinson, a very remarkable person, a mystic, a follower of Swedenborg and a great admirer of Blake. We talked only about Blake. He will call on me to see what I have by Blake, and I expect Emerson also. . . .

APRIL 26th I finished in bed this morning a very bad book, over which I hurried and lost all the time I spent over it—the *Gipsies [of] Spain*, by Borrow. . . .

APRIL 27th . . . I had a chat with . . . Talfourd about Moxon, who has really sold Lamb's books to some American. Talfourd is displeased with this, and reasonably. [Moxon] tells him that these were worth nothing, and that he got only £10 by them. This cannot be true, and if true so much the worse. Moxon told me at first that he would give the books to the University College; but afterwards said they were not worth their accepting. Talfourd has made use of all the letters of Lamb to the Wordsworths which I sent him.

MAY 2nd . . . Last night I had seen a card left by Emerson in the day, and this suggested the idea of inviting him to dine with me at the Antiquaries' dinner, and Hunter approving of this, I did so and it answered admirably well. . . . I took Emerson with me and found he was known by name, and I introduced him to Sir Robert Inglis, afterwards to Lord Mahon. He would have been taken to the chairman's right hand, but I prevented that lest there should be a mistake in asking for money from him; but he was noticed by a number. He was placed between Collier and me, but I gave up my place to Hunter, and the evening passed off with great cordiality. . . . Emerson retired early, after responding to his health briefly and well. . . .

MAY 10th I read early a number of *Vanity Fair*—a book of humour I have been unluckily drawn in to read—and it is so clever that I must go on with it, though I ought not. Thackeray aspires not to the spasmodic energy of Dickens, but there is a quiet exhibition of natural qualities and humorous contrast in ordinary life that is very refreshing. Miss Sharp, the cunning and intriguing governess, is a capital piece of painting. . . .

MAY 22nd . . . I went to the Athenaeum late and stayed till near one reading a number of *Vanity Fair*. The numbers five, six, and seven are become dull. The Osbornes are too insignificant and the Crawleys too low. Rebecca, the governess, when she gets a husband becomes an ordinary creature. Miss Crawley, the rich aunt, and Mrs. Bute Crawley, the legacy-hunting kinswoman, are well described, but one cannot care for them. The characters want strength and significance.

MAY 27th . . . I finished . . . a number of *Vanity Fair*, which I am going on with with no great pleasure. . . .

MAY 28th . . . Read a chapter in *Vanity Fair*. The pathos of the widow of Captain Osborne is excellent . . . and the truth and keeping of the Crawleys are worthy of all praise. . . .

MAY 30th . . . I read today two chapters of *Vanity Fair*. This book I like only in parts. No. 12, containing an account of the death of old Sir Pitt Crawley, is very humiliating by exposing infirmities that in a less degree will be found in many. The truthfulness of the odious Rebecca, Mrs. Crawley, almost makes her endurable. The artistic merit of the picture tends to reconcile oneself to the original, or rather the moral disgust that it excites is qualified by the critical approbation of the copy. . . .

JUNE 1st . . . I read today in *Vanity Fair*, No. 14. Deeply pathetic is the contrast between the grief of the mother giving up her child to his grandfather and the boy's heartlessness. . . .

JUNE 6th . . . I heard Emerson's first lecture on the Laws of Thought. I could not keep awake, as I never can over sermons. The lecture was full of sparkling thoughts and *naïvetés*, but I brought away with me only this one thought: that the laws of thought were the same as the laws of the natural world, there being a system of analogues, as I should say, *in rerum natura*. A good audience there and a number of acquaintance. . . .

JUNE 10th . . . I went to Emerson's third lecture, which pleased me far better than the first; yet my memory is so bad that I can report nothing of what I heard. The most remarkable point he urged was the high dignity of Instinct. His manner was very impressive occasionally, but in general feeble. . . .

JUNE 13th . . . I heard Emerson's fourth lecture, which was full of brilliant thoughts; but I was unable to connect them. He praised Owen and called Fourier a great man; yet he seemed to speak of all their efforts as hitherto unsuccessful. Wilkinson whispered to me: 'All lies,' but my attention was at the moment flagging. . . .

JUNE 15th . . . Heard Emerson lecture on Eloquence. Less original, but more intelligible. . . .

JUNE 16th . . . I came home early and read in my bedroom Longfellow's *Evangeline*.

JUNE 17th which I finished this morning. An uncomfortable work. The lovers, forced from each other on their wedding day by the tyranny of the English in Nova Scotia, meet only when Evangeline as a Sister of Mercy closes his eyes, dying of the plague. The poem opens in Acadie, the old name of Nova Scotia. They meet in New England. The conclusion is pathetic and the lines worth quoting. Emerson says that Wordsworth spoke highly of Longfellow and regretted his name. . . . Heard Emerson's last lecture, which everyone seemed [*sic*]. It was on Aristocracy and contained nothing to offend the highborn. He expatiated on the influence of the *individual*. Perhaps many think his lectures uninstructive, but everyone likes the man. . . .

JUNE 18th I had a breakfast party which went off very well. Emerson, whom my friends came to see. . . . Emerson very pleasant in talk. I was in spirits. . . .

JULY 12th . . . I learned from Talfourd that the second publication of Lamb's *Letters* is coming out, and he gives a promising account. Among the notabilia Alaric Watts was there [at a ball given by Talfourd], who reminded me of our having met twenty-five years ago. In a wordy style, but still with feeling, he related a generous act of Talfourd's towards himself in returning fees in a hard lost case merely on the ground of his being a literary man. Talfourd replied to the compliment in good taste. . . .

JULY 15th . . . at the Athenaeum, where I was diverted from reading *Konversations Lexikon der Gegenwart*, as a help to my reminiscences, by my anxiety to finish *Vanity Fair*, which is well wound up by the marriage of the faithful Dobbin to the fond wife and the final prosperity of Rebecca, the cunning governess. . . .

JULY 25th [*Lincoln.*] . . . I had a letter from Quillinan in the forenoon. He gives a good account of Wordsworth and of all friends. . . .

JULY 26th . . . Received a kind letter from Mrs. Wordsworth.

JULY 30th . . . Found the latter part of Lamb's letters written in his best style. He had acquired his peculiar humour. The early letters are of an ordinary character, and I thought them, as I first read them, likely to disappoint the general reader, though the matter is deeply affecting.

AUG. 2nd I strolled about . . . reading Talfourd's delightful volumes of *Final Memorials of Charles Lamb*. . . .

AUG. 3rd . . . Emerson . . . left England, I find, quite satisfied with his reception here and with reason. . . .

Aug. 5th I then went westward. Called on Moxon. Chatted about the *Final Memorials*. He agrees with me that the account of Wainewright is a blotch and stain on the book. By the bye, there is in the *Athenaeum* a severe article as respects Talfourd's style, but everywhere justice is done to Lamb. The *Inquirer* gives as specimens his two letters to me. The article is poor: I hope it will not be thought to proceed from me.

Oct. 18th . . . Then I had a call to make which interested me, on Mrs. Coleridge but I did not discharge the commissions I had in making the call. We spoke about Scott and more about her father. She is justly incensed against Cottle for his second publication, which I have never seen, and is sorely put to it when she has to meet the reproaches cast on his [her father's] memory. But she is even more impartial than one could have expected. She incidentally betrayed a degree of soreness at the freedom and depreciatory tone with which Wordsworth is accustomed to speak of others, she said; but I dare say she meant her father. We agreed in our disgust at Cottle's printing a very offensive letter by Southey against Coleridge. But she contended that Cottle ought not to have printed Coleridge's letter about his taking opium, but left that to his children—from which I altogether dissent. . . .

Oct. 21st I read in bed last night and also this morning in *Dombey and Son*, which begins to interest me much. I had tears in my eyes when I left off this morning, No. 6, at the leave-taking of Walter by Florence. Her character is well conceived—thus far at least. . . .

Nov. 3rd I finished *Dombey and Son*. . . . I found Mrs. William Wordsworth looking better than I expected. She is a sweet woman. She gave but a poor account of her father- and mother-in-law, but says Mrs. Wordsworth seems now to be in health the worst. He is very uncertain, and can occasionally abstract himself from his daughter. But he cannot go to Quillinan's house, which Quillinan is convinced is out of his power. . . .

Dec. 15th . . . Went in omnibus with Le Breton to Field's. A dinner-party to see Mr. Clough,[1] with whom I was much pleased in spite of his youth. He has a most prepossessing countenance and manner. I was gratified by his courteous address towards me, saying we had several common friends, and he spoke very highly of the Arnolds. It was an agreeable afternoon. . . . Clough will breakfast with me on Thursday. I stayed at Field's till past ten. . . .

Dec. 19th . . . Then I dressed for a grand party at Serjeant Talfourd's. He is offended at Wordsworth's having taken no notice of the Dedication to him of the *Final Memorials of Lamb*, and I think with reason. . . .

Dec. 21st I had a breakfast party to meet Clough. Agreeable enough,

[1] Arthur Hugh Clough (1819–1861), the poet.

without advancing our object.[1] Clough pleases, but does not show much [*sic*]. . . . Had a meeting of the University Hall Council. A committee was appointed to confer with Clough and ascertain his religious views, for Mrs. Arnold will not guarantee them. . . .

On the 26th I made my annual visit to Rydal Mount. . . . As it was the shortest, so it was the most uneventful of any of my late journeys. It was distinguished by one single incident, the death of Hartley Coleridge, which took place on Saturday the 6th of January. The interment took place on Thursday the 11th. During the performance of the ceremony I sat with Mrs. Wordsworth. . . . I dined out but three times. . . . But the time at home was greatly improved by the far better state of Wordsworth's spirits, who was calm and collected. . . .

[*Travel Journal: Rydal.*] DEC. 26th I had postponed my usual Christmas visit to Rydal Mount because I wished to avoid being present on a day which could not be of festivity, as the loss of Mrs. Quillinan is still too deeply lamented and too easily brought to recollection. I therefore . . . this morning . . . set out on my journey by leaving London in the express train at 9 a.m. . . . *The Times* . . . and the *Life of Collins* the painter occupied me all day. The book, an ordinary work, which to one unacquainted with the art could give no pleasure. I saw a little of Collins in Italy when travelling with Mr. Wordsworth in 1837, when I liked him well enough. He was civil to me on account of my companion. But I declined his further acquaintance in London, Mr. Daniell having told me that Collins had said to him: 'I would not shake hands with a Unitarian knowingly.' I would not defraud him of so small a gift as a token of good will surreptitiously. I valued him as an artist only for his fresh and *healthy* landscapes. . . .

DEC. 27th . . . I was set down at the bottom of the hill at Rydal a quarter before ten, and that good creature James was in waiting for me. I found my friends vastly improved in appearance, and I have had this single day more talk with him than during my whole last year's visit. The two grandchildren were there, which enlivens the house. But it was somewhat saddened by the severe illness of Hartley Coleridge, whose death is expected almost daily. After a cordial breakfast and the customary inquiries were gone through, Mr. Wordsworth and I walked out to call on the Cooksons and inquire about Hartley Coleridge at his cottage. . . .

DEC. 28th . . . Soon after breakfast the news was brought that a great change had taken place in Hartley Coleridge, so that it was thought he would recover. The diarrhoea had been stopped. His lungs were better,

[1] The appointment of Clough as first Principal of University Hall, then in course of foundation.

and he had an appetite. And at this time came his brother, Derwent Coleridge, whom I had never seen. He is, compared with Hartley, a handsome man, and with his father compared, a stout healthy man. He is a laborious scholar, at the head of a normal school at Chelsea,[1] a churchman who professes orthodox, and he has a character to lose. Probably inferior far even to his brother, he will probably go through the world with credit. He has been backward and forward all day, and he talks with ease and no prudery. He has been a resource. . . . Wordsworth . . . has been very cheerful all day. . . .

DEC. 29th . . . After dinner, some literary talk with Derwent Coleridge. Without any pretence to his father's genius, he has his tone occasionally and he can make use of what he has, which is what the great man could not do. . . . I accompanied him to tea at Mrs. Arnold's. Harriet Martineau there. . . .

DEC. 31st This has been, as usual, a very dull day, being Sunday. For decorum I went to the chapel. . . . Miss Martineau stepped in, with whom I walked back after she had chatted a short time with the Wordsworths. She is now full of a prospect of forming here building-societies for the benefit of the poor in imitation of the Birmingham societies. She, in the meanwhile, lectures to the poor people on sanitary measures, and even the Wordsworths and Carr acknowledge that she is doing some good by them. . . . Harriet Martineau has actually taken to the management of land, and has a man-servant. She sells butter and milk, keeping a cow, and is elated with the prospect of setting a salutary example to the young women. . . .

1849

JAN. 1st . . . I also called on Mrs. Arnold . . . I learned from Matthew Arnold that Clough writes him word that he is in disgrace with the Unitarians because he declines reading prayers at the University Hall. But, he says, quitting Oxford because he will not conform, it would be absurd to become a Unitarian conformist. . . . I dined with Mrs. Fletcher. . . . Derwent Coleridge was to have been with me, but he found it necessary to sit up with his brother Hartley, who is again worse, and his recovery is again despaired of. . . .

JAN. 2nd . . . I first called at Mrs. Arnold's with Wordsworth. She was

[1] i.e. St. Mark's College. Derwent Coleridge was a great friend of Praed and edited his collected poems. See *infra*, Sept. 17th, 1864.

not visible, but I had a pleasant chat with the sons, etc. . . . It was a dull evening; cards not being yet introduced, and Wordsworth being silent and somewhat moody, we were dull. . . .

JAN. 3rd . . . I sat up till one reading *Jane Eyre* . . . having borrowed it from Mrs. Fletcher. This novel, of which I will say nothing yet, has given me very great pleasure indeed. It is an extraordinary work, and in the first volume, at all events, I have found nothing to justify the character of a wicked book which Lady Richardson gives to it.

JAN. 4th . . . I made a call . . . with Mrs. Wordsworth on Harriet Martineau. Whatever she be as an authoress, there can be no doubt that she is an excellent house-manager. . . . She keeps a cow, poultry, and pigs, and is planting a large kitchen-garden. She is becoming a farmer, and while she does this, she writes every month a number of Knight's *Pictorial History*, for which she receives £40. Her activity and indefatigable industry deserve all praise. I made no other call today, my whole time being spent, as well evening as morning, in the perusal of a very excellent novel, *Jane Eyre*, of which I read today, volume two.

JAN. 5th . . . In the evening I read to Mr. and Mrs. Wordsworth my reminiscences of my Holstein journey. I thought it read poorly as to style. Mrs. Wordsworth said it was very interesting. Wordsworth said little, but he was attentive, and Mrs. Wordsworth [said] he was more attentive than to anything that had been read to him for a year.

I finished today *Jane Eyre*, from which I had received very great pleasure. . . .

JAN. 6th . . . I finished Clough's poem in hexameters,[1] a playful composition narrating the adventures of a set of Oxford students in the Highlands. . . . It is full of university and college jokes—some unintelligible even to the Arnolds. There is a very friendly review in *Fraser's Magazine* by Kingsley, author of *The Saint's Tragedy*. There is gaiety in this *jeu d'esprit* and the opposite of Puritanism. . . . It was after finishing this that I heard . . . that Hartley Coleridge was just dead. This was between two and three o'clock. He was in his fifty-second year. He was pitied and beloved by everybody in the valley, and many a man will echo the words: 'I could have better spared a better man.'

JAN. 7th This day was devoted to *Mary Barton*. . . . It is a book I would rather recommend others to read than read myself. It is a very good and edifying book and honourable to Mrs. Gaskell who wrote it. . . .

JAN. 8th . . . Mr. Wordsworth and Mr. Coleridge having to fix a site in the burying-ground for poor Hartley's body, I walked with them to Grasmere . . . and walked home with Wordsworth. He was chatty today,

[1] *The Bothie of Tober-na-Vuolich.*

and talked on critical subjects—a proof of the recovery of a more healthy state of mind, otherwise the mournful visit to the graveyard where Mrs. Quillinan's body lies would have overpowered him. Coleridge dined with us and was also quite cheerful. He purposes printing unpublished poems of Hartley, which, with the old volume, would make two of verse, and there may be one of prose. He [has] seemingly an excessive admiration of his brother. This is a family weakness—the family over-estimation. . . .

JAN. 9th I read early in bed a sensible essay on *Poetic Life* from Henry Taylor's *Notes on Life*. . . .

Mrs. Wordsworth has given me up all my letters, which I have been indexing and putting in order. They are numerous; a few only worth preserving.

JAN. 10th . . . I had a long chat with the poet after breakfast. He talked cheerfully on literature. Indeed, his spirits have been unexpectedly well during the preparation for Hartley's funeral. . . . I have now finished sorting the letters I have written to the Wordsworths, which I must take with me. I wish they had not been given me. . . .

JAN. 11th . . . I had only to go to the Nab, where [Hartley] Coleridge's body lay. . . . At twelve the body left the cottage. In one carriage the medical men were. In the other, Derwent Coleridge, Mr. Wordsworth, Quillinan, and Angus Fletcher. I sat with Mrs. Wordsworth while the funeral took place; and when at half-past three I entered the mail at the bottom of the hill, Wordsworth got out of the coach. . . .

JAN. 13th [*London*.] . . . I went late to the Athenaeum, where I read *inter alia* a canting article in the *Quarterly Review* in which Jane Eyre is declared to be an unregenerate character and no Christian therefore. This religious part said to be the addition of Miss Rigby. The novel is collated with *Vanity Fair*, and Becky and [Jane] both are made use of as pegs to introduce benevolent remarks on governesses.

JAN. 15th . . . I was attracted by the sight of Macaulay's *History*, of which I will read at least the Introduction. Though it did not prevent my dozing, it interested me much.

JAN. 16th . . . A call on Sara Coleridge. She manifested a feeling for her brother Hartley I cannot comprehend. A woman's tears must be very much on the surface to fall for a brother she had not seen for twenty years. . . . I was occupied reading Macaulay's *History*. The first introductory chapter, being a sort of review of English history, is a very eloquent history, but a work rather of rhetoric than of philosophy.

JAN. 18th . . . An important meeting at the University Hall at which a vote in favour of Clough succeeded, moved by Busk and seconded by me. . . . Some difference of opinion about the expression of a resolution in favour of a chaplain, as Clough will not read prayers. . . .

JAN. 24th . . . I finished the first volume of Macaulay. The disgust he excites towards James and the Tory principles must have a salutary effect on the public mind. It will shame the High Church and Tory party. . . . Kenyon took me to and from Tagart's, with whom I dined. The party was not large, and more agreeable than dinner parties usually are. The chief persons were Dickens, whose conversation was perfectly natural and yet earnest, speaking benevolently on the topics of the day—nothing of the wit or literator, but altogether the sensible and respectable man. The American minister and his lady were there. . . .

JAN. 25th . . . Though I had other things to do, yet I could not resist the temptation of reading the second volume of Macaulay's *History*, which is quite as interesting as a novel. . . . His book will be a sad blow on the High Church and Tory party. It will effectually destroy the remains of the old prestige in favour of the Stuarts. . . .

JAN. 30th My principal call this morning was after reading my old letters and journals of 1811–12, when I heard Coleridge's lectures, to call about them to Mrs. Henry Coleridge. I showed her my notes, unfavourable as they were. . . . I received today from Murray the third edition of Henry Taylor's *Notes on Life*. He has inserted an anecdote I told him of Schiller's saying to me that on principle he would not read much in foreign languages because it injured his own delicate perception of his own. Taylor has taken occasion to introduce an extravagant compliment to me, forgetting that *celui qui exagère diminue*. He speaks of me as 'the friend of Schiller and of most of the other great men of letters of his times in England and Germany—indeed I may add, the friend of all men great and small who stand in need of his friendship.' I must write and remonstrate with him, but how to do it I do not know well—to avoid the imputation of affectation or ingratitude. . . .

FEB. 7th . . . Finished Macaulay's delightful volumes today.

FEB. 11th I had at breakfast Roscoe and Oastler, and they brought with them their friend Bagehot,[1] one of the University Hall, a young man of talent. An agreeable two hours. . . .

MARCH 4th An interesting morning. I had asked T. Stansfeld and his son to breakfast with me, and they came, but I left them early to breakfast with Monckton Milnes, with whom I remained till half past two. There was a company of ten at table, including the host, and of these about half were men known to the world. . . . Thomas Carlyle, always a remarkable man in company, though his talk generally is, as it was

[1] Walter Bagehot (1826–1877), the economist.

today, mere spasmodic growls—abusing the present age, the Government, and men of letters, etc. He broke in every now and then with his declamations without much effect. . . .

MARCH 20th I have this morning been reading Layard's *Nineveh* in bed. It has gained great popularity owing to favourable criticisms. I wonder where he got his learning. He has shown an industry for which no one gave him credit, though I told his mother he would turn out well when he had sown his wild oats. . . .

APRIL 22nd I rose very early and breakfasted with Chapman. Several Americans there and Mrs. Gaskell (authoress of *Mary Barton*). She is a woman of agreeable manners, with a hale, florid complexion, with nothing literary about her appearance. She pleased me. . . .

APRIL 25th . . . Received at night a parcel from Mrs. Coleridge consisting of a copy of her recent publication, a sort of second edition of the first two volumes of Coleridge's Lectures on Shakespeare, which I have been looking over. She has printed extracts from my two letters to Mrs. Clarkson giving an account of Coleridge's lectures, 1808, and they do not read amiss, and I am not so ashamed of them as I was when I read them in my own handwriting. She speaks in a note civilly of me, without, however, any compliment which could be thought flattery. This pleases me. . . .

APRIL 27th . . . Lady Blessington . . . is going to France. Her debts are only £5,000 and her house will supply £10,000. She earns £800 per ann. by literature and has £2,000 p.a. . . .

APRIL 28th . . . Mrs. Gaskell . . . I like the more the more I see her. . . .

JUNE 18th . . . After dinner I went to a small party . . . several of the young men of University College. Bagehot, who has all the external marks of genius; it is a promising set, these young friends of the University College. . . .

JUNE 20th . . . But it was Froude himself the seeing of whom was an object of interest. He is quite a young man with a pleasing countenance and manners, those of a young Oxonian, quite gentlemanly. He thanked me for my kindness to him,[1] which he said was no ordinary kindness, and said this with apparent earnestness. I disclaimed any merit beyond a wish to serve him. He told me he was going to Manchester, where was one Ballentine[2] or Valentine, editor of a paper, once a workman, whom he spoke of as the first man there. Bunsen, he said, had been very kind to him. Bunsen holds English orthodoxy in abhorrence. He thinks Carlyle a greater man than Coleridge, and his *History of the French Revolution* to be ranked next to Thucydides and Tacitus. As a thinker, above all Germans except Goethe. The strength of his convictions places him above

[1] A favourable review.

[2] Thomas Ballantyne.

all others. This I am far from assenting to. I am glad I have seen Froude, but I hardly wish for his further acquaintance. . . .

JUNE 21st–26th On the 21st I took a trip to Malvern with Moxon. . . . Our object in the journey was to see a beautiful country and see the Wordsworths, who were with the youngest of the Hutchinsons, Mrs. Wordsworth's nephew. Miss Fenwick, too, was there. . . .

[*Travel Journal: Malvern.*] JUNE 21st . . . We had not been there [Westminster Hotel] long before we saw on the road before the house Miss Fenwick, driven by the Rydal James, and Mr. Wordsworth accompanying her. A hearty greeting. We accompanied Miss Fenwick to her house door, very near the hotel, and I walked then to the parsonage, where was Mrs. Wordsworth and the Hutchinson family. . . . We returned soon to tea. . . .

JUNE 22nd This was a day of great fatigue, but also of considerable enjoyment. A picnic party had been formed by several ladies to take tea on the top of the hill about five miles from Great Malvern, called the Camp, and *we* were, of course, invited to be of the party. . . . Between two and three [Moxon and I] were joined by Wordsworth and Mr. George Hutchinson, when we set out on our walk. Mr. Wordsworth was soon forced to mount one of the three small carriages which formed the mass of the procession. . . . There were three middle-aged ladies, seven or eight young ladies, and one other gentleman, a Mr. Preedy. . . . And at the top of a height beyond the camp we were all refreshed by tea made by the company. . . . After tea we ascended another knoll, round the top of which is an evident entrenchment. . . . I . . . did not reach home till . . . nine.

JUNE 23rd . . . Mrs. Hutchinson and Mrs. Wordsworth were going to make a call on Colonel Raper at a distance of two miles. They rode and Mr. Wordsworth was to walk and I accompanied him. . . . The walk . . . had nothing remarkable in it. Mr. Wordsworth and I returned about half-past two. . . .

JUNE 24th . . . I called at Miss Fenwick's, where were the poet and his publisher, and where Mrs. Wordsworth and Mrs. Hutchinson joined us. . . .

JUNE 25th . . . Between ten and eleven I accompanied the Wordsworth party on a visit to Mrs. Fearon . . . about seven miles. . . . Mrs. Fearon . . . had with them . . . Mr. and Mrs. Taylor, the father and mother of Henry Taylor. Mr. Taylor is an old man of seventy-seven, but in vigorous health, a man full of life and a man of intelligence. He took Mr. Wordsworth and me a walk and showed us a rich rural scene. . . . No want for conversation. . . . After tea I called on Miss Fenwick and the party at Mrs. Hutchinson's and took a cordial leave of all. The only time this visit when Wordsworth talked freely and in his old style was with Mr. Taylor. I was particularly pleased with Miss Fenwick on this visit. . . .

JULY 19th [*London.*] . . . I read early Wordsworth's *Waggoner* in bed with great pleasure. Donne[1] had praised it highly. It did not use to be a favourite with me; but I discerned in it today a benignity and a gentle humour, with a view of human life and a felicity of diction which rendered the dedication of it to Charles Lamb peculiarly appropriate. . . .

JULY 26th . . . News arriving that [Talfourd] had been appointed judge, an appointment that seems to give general satisfaction. . . . The repose of judicial life harmonizes better than the wranglings of the Bar with the temperament of the poet. Talfourd is a generous and kind man and merits his good fortune.

OCT. 4th . . . I walked to Gibson's, Westbourne Terrace, and dined with him there—only his father and mother. Newman and Clough were there and I enjoyed the afternoon much. Newman made himself very agreeable, and Clough also, with whom I walked back. He is modest and amiable as well as full of talent, and I have no doubt that we have made a very good choice in him of a Principal for the University Hall. I explained to him as well as I could our position, and I hope he will form now no unreasonable expectations. [Francis] Newman told us that Maurice refused to join the Ladies' College in Bedford Square if he (Newman) were a professor, and though Newman offered to withdraw he still would not join. Maurice is certainly a very anomalous and strange character and perhaps overrated for ability. Clough does not announce his opinions on religion, and is wise.

OCT. 29th [*Sheffield.*] . . . By Broom Hill to the Mount—a row of houses in which lives James Montgomery the poet. We [Mr. Philipps and the diarist] called on him, and though we had but a few minutes to spare they were very agreeably spent. I recollected spending one evening with him at Charles Aikin's,[2] when Jane Porter was present. This evening rested on my memory, and to my surprise I found Montgomery recollected it too and me also. He reminded me of an argument on Wordsworth's poetry, and on a criticism in the *Eclectic Review* with which I was very angry, written by Montgomery himself, but unknown to me. He said: 'Our controversy amused others, Miss Wesley, for instance, who knew I was the writer. I recollect your saying: "The worst of all is that the fellow has a sense of Wordsworth's beauties, after all." ' He spoke with great esteem of Mr. Wordsworth and showed me with pride the first volume

[1] William Bodham Donne (1807–1882), afterwards Librarian of the London Library and Examiner of Plays in the Lord Chamberlain's office.

[2] May 13th, 1812.

of his poems, a copy of which Wordsworth sent in exchange. 'My brass for his gold,' said Montgomery. Wordsworth had written a very kind note expressing admiration of the pious use to which Montgomery had applied his genius. I should say that the former interview with Montgomery must have been above thirty years ago. Montgomery is now seventy-seven years old, has a pale face and delicate countenance. He has of late years attached himself to the Church—that is, the Evangelical. . . . I enjoyed this short chat with him much.

OCT. 31st . . . I wrote a long letter to Quillinan giving an account of my journey and accepting an invitation for Christmas, though Mrs. Fletcher will not be there and Wordsworth is, I fear, lost to society. . . .

NOV. 27th I was able to reach Rogers's [from Brighton] by half-past ten and there I found the usual Tuesday's breakfast party, viz. Samuel Sharpe, Dr. Henderson, Mitford, and Dyce, and we had a lively chat, which Sharpe and I broke up at half-past twelve. Rogers was, as he always is, prompt to repeat his favourite anecdotes and quote his favourite passages; but the old man is growing fast on him. Every visit may be the last, therefore I do not like to omit any, yet the anticipation of an early cessation of these is painful. . . .

NOV. 30th . . . I went late . . . to the Athenaeum, where I unluckily have entangled myself into reading *Shirley*, which I do not much like. . . . A few days since I had a very kind letter from Wordsworth himself, expressing the wish to see me at Christmas. . . .

DEC. 3rd . . . I wrote two long letters—one to Mrs. Wordsworth chiefly on the uncertainty of my going to Rydal at the Christmas as usual, and the other to Mrs. Coleridge, who sent me a letter from Miss Fenwick. They both want me to write to Wordsworth to induce him to make a settlement on a niece of Southey who is in poverty. I wrote at length showing that I ought not to do so as I do not know Miss Southey myself and could only write being set on by others, and this indirect and circuitous mode of making the application would be justly offensive. I also went on with the novel of *Shirley*. . . .

DEC. 4th . . . I had a very pleasant chat with Clough before I went out. I shall be able to make parties with him for breakfast. . . .

DEC. 5th I was gratified by a letter from Mrs. Coleridge declaring that she had been instructed by my letter and that she concurred in what I wrote and would not apply to Mr. Wordsworth for Miss Southey. . . .

DEC. 15th . . . I was engaged yesterday and today writing to Quillinan announcing my not going to Rydal at Christmas [owing to a carbuncle], and Dr. Boott has written to the same effect to Mrs. Davy, so I shall not be suspected of caprice. . . .

DEC. 31st I was accidentally led to read *The Winter's Tale*, and that led me to Coleridge's *Notes on Shakespeare* and especially to the *Selections from his Correspondence* in the second volume published by Mrs. Coleridge. His humorous style in some articles which Blackwood published, seems on the whole lumbering and clumsy, though it is rich in the serious thought at the bottom. But I do not wonder that he never became really popular. A religious set strove to make use of his name as an authority, but it is after all hard work. Quite as much against orthodoxy as for it may be found in his works. . . .

1850

JAN. 3rd . . . I had a letter from Quillinan informing me that Richmond[1] had been at Rydal, where he amused them all. How can Wordsworth tolerate a man who asserts that the six great English poets are Chaucer, Shakespeare, Spenser, Milton, Wordsworth, and Martin Tupper! . . .

JAN. 29th . . . I read today Emerson's *Swedenborg*. A great deal that I do not at all understand, but coupled with so much that I do, that I am deeply interested in this new book of *Representative Men*. It is very suggestive. It makes me humble.

FEB. 4th . . . I read today Carlyle's first *Latter Day Pamphlet*, *The Present Time*. His contempt towards the Americans powerfully expressed, and I could not but enjoy it; and yet on the whole the tone of this writing, like that in *Fraser* on *Slavery*, is very disgusting. He is a man I have no wish to see again, and I perceive that he has now disgusted readers in general. These extravagancies are to be ascribed to excessive vanity. He prides himself on exciting wonder, and does not care for exciting disgust. He likes it. . . .

MARCH 10th . . . Clough is a great deal too silent. There is a danger lest the faculty which never appears should be denied. . . .

MARCH 19th . . . [Carlyle's] *Latter Day Pamphlet* on *Model Prisons*. It is a pity there is so much truth in what he says, as there is nothing but scorn and contempt of what is most amiable among men. His derision of the Philanthropists is not altogether unfounded, but in spirit very offensive. . . .

MARCH 25th I took Mr. Clough to see Mr. Rogers. No one else with him. Clough, I believe, gave pleasure, for he received a second invitation.

[1] The Rev. J. C. Richmond, an Anglophile American, a friend of Robinson and Wordsworth (and of Tupper).

Rogers was very full of anecdote, and Clough, on a hint from me, more communicative. . . .

APRIL 5th I continued reading the clever but worthless and even tiresome *Trois Mousquetaires*, which I ought never to have begun. . . .

APRIL 20th . . . Carlyle—of whom I read a *Pamphlet*, *New Downing Street*. The only sentence of practical sense and meaning is a declaration in favour of Sir Robert Peel as one who may be a redeemer. . . .

APRIL 23rd . . . But the day will have a black mark in the annals of the age, for on this day died the greatest man I had ever the honour to call friend—Wordsworth.

APRIL 24th . . . On my arrival I found a letter from Quillinan announcing the death of my great friend the poet only an hour before. His sons were with him, and Mrs. Wordsworth had the comfort of her nearest relations. Every consolation which death admits of was here, of which the chief was the full sense that the departure was after a long life spent in the acquisition of an immortal fame, 'the perfect judgment of all-seeing Jove,' the reward of a life devoted to the service of mankind, the spread of truth married to immortal verse. . . .

APRIL 28th I spent great part of the forenoon in writing a paper for the *Bury Post* on Wordsworth, with which I am by no means pleased. It is an account of the Wordsworth controversy with the *Edinburgh Review*. The article on Wordsworth in today's *Inquirer* is very good, and I have ordered a copy to be sent to Quillinan. The *Examiner* also is good, but not equal to the *Inquirer*. The best by far of the newspaper articles is that of *The Times*, which is admirable. . . .

APRIL 29th . . . I talked with Monckton Milnes. He thinks Wordsworth should have had a public funeral. He even approves of Carlyle's *Pamphlets* —an opinion I found it difficult to tolerate. . . .

APRIL 30th . . . Then at the Athenaeum, where I wrote a letter, for a letter had come from Quillinan informing me of the funeral. Mrs. Wordsworth herself had attended, and I was expected. I regret much I did not go, for in general it seems that it was thought I was there. Everyone speaks as he ought of Wordsworth, and so all the papers. . . .

MAY 3rd . . . I went to Mr. Cookson, who is one of the executors of Mr. Wordsworth's will, and with whom I had an interesting conversation about Wordsworth's arrangements for the publication of his poems. He has commissioned Dr. Christopher Wordsworth to write his *Life*, a brief memoir merely illustrative of his poems, and in a paper given to the doctor he wrote that his sons, son-in-law, his dear friend Miss Fenwick, Mr. Carter, and Mr. Robinson, who had travelled with him, would gladly contribute their aid by communicating any facts within their knowledge. But the property in these works remains with his family. . . .

May 10th . . . At Moxon's also, from whom I was sorry to hear that Talfourd did not scruple to talk in company unkindly of Wordsworth. . . . Archdeacon Hare . . . wished for my concurrence in a committee meeting to concert a plan for a monument for Wordsworth, perhaps on Monday at the Bishop of London's. Talked after with Arthur Stanley and Dr. Whewell on the same subject. Wrote a second note to Quillinan on this subject. . . .

May 13th . . . At quarter-past four I attended a meeting at Mr. John Coleridge's to consider of a monument for Wordsworth. I made the thirteenth. Present: Bishops of London and St. David's, Archdeacon Hare and Milman, Mr. John Coleridge, Rogers, Scott (Professor) and Boxall,[1] and four whose names I did not learn. There was little or nothing said worth remembering. The archdeacon had drawn up a resolution, which was objected to for its phraseology and referred to a sub-committee. It was agreed that there should be a bust in Westminster Abbey and a suitable memorial in Grasmere church, and if there should be a surplus of subscriptions (not likely) it is to be considered what is to be done with that. The Bishop of Llandaff suggested a scholarship at St. John's College for a native of the Lakes. John Coleridge objected to scholarships. The Bishop of London wished for something connected with literature—almshouses seemed to want an object. Rogers was uncomfortably deaf and understood little of what was going on. I left before the close of the business and hastened to an omnibus. . . .

May 14th . . . At the Athenaeum I wrote a long letter to Quillinan. Archdeacon Hare there; he gave me the corrected resolutions to copy, which I sent to Quillinan. A larger body of the Committee named, viz. Bishop of Oxford. How will he relish his companions? The Bishop of London alone has subscribed and given £25. I wish to subscribe all I can with propriety. . . .

May 16th I also wrote to Quillinan in answer to letter from him on the Wordsworth monument. At the Athenaeum I chatted again with Hare about the monument. John Coleridge, son of the J[ustice], is secretary. I am on a sub-committee. I suffered myself to be put down for £20 subscription at the persuasion of Hare, but I think I have done wrong; it will look like assumption. But Hare said: 'If you don't, there is a danger lest no one go beyond £10; at present only the Bishop of London has given more, viz. £25.' . . .

[1] Later Sir William Boxall: a portrait-painter, who became Director of the National Gallery.

MAY 19th I had an unusually agreeable party at breakfast. Matthew Arnold and Clough, Boxall, and Cookson. The two latter I introduced and they had much to communicate about the monument, Boxall being one of the sub-committee with me and Cookson being to be on the committee. I talked with Arnold on German matters, particularly Goethe. . . .

MAY 20th . . . I had a letter from Quillinan calling my subscription munificent—others will call it ostentatious and presumptuous. . . . Kenyon has written to me against the having an institution. He will give £5 for a monument only, he would give £25 for a suitable monument, but he will give nothing for a school or a church. He has written me a sensible, but to some an offensive letter. . . .

MAY 25th . . . I breakfasted early with John Coleridge at Boxall's. Our business was to add to the committee for raising the monument. I succeeded in getting the secretaries to insert the names of Madge as already appointed, and of Donne, Donaldson, and Hunter, to be written to for their consent to be appointed; I also communicated the purport of a letter from Quillinan with enclosures from Lough, etc. Among the incidents is that of Sir Robert Peel declining to be on the committee because he does not 'see his way' through the business. The announced subscriptions amount to £200, but I do not expect a large increase. . . .

MAY 30th I spent a great part of the forenoon in writing on Wordsworth. My paper is not at all to my taste. I hope I shall never be called on to print anything again. . . .

MAY 31st . . . I called on Boxall, paid him my subscription of £20 for the monument, and then called on Moxon and Dr. Wordsworth. I saw only Mrs. Wordsworth and I gave the first volume of Coleridge's early writings. I was fully engaged on this business. I wrote on the subject to Quillinan and I also wrote to Donne and Donaldson to have their names on the subscription. Boxall says the subscription goes on well. The Queen and Prince Albert will subscribe. This is the best fact I have to mention. I distrust the business talent of those who will manage this business. . . .

JUNE 21st . . . Read the first half of volume one of Leigh Hunt's *Autobiography*. I could not but feel interested, because I knew so much of those he wrote about.

JUNE 22nd . . . Boxall told me last night . . . that it was resolved that there should not be any institution—merely a full-length figure of Wordsworth in Westminster Abbey. Any surplus may be given to the Grasmere memorial. This I gladly communicated to Kenyon, as I have no doubt he will now give the £25 originally proposed. . . . I made a call of enquiry at Rogers's. He has broken the cap of his hip-bone. He may recover, but he will never walk again without crutches; he has seen no one yet but his own family. . . .

JUNE 23rd . . . I had written to him [Kenyon] informing him of the change of plan as to the monument and that it is to be merely a monument in Westminster Abbey. He will, therefore, give £25 with pleasure. My only apprehension now is that a sufficient sum will not be raised for a statue. Monckton Milnes complains that there is not the feeling for Wordsworth which there was in his day at college. . . .

JUNE 26th . . . Finished Leigh Hunt's *Autobiography*. The book leaves an impression more favourable to his moral than his mental qualities, as if he were a well-disposed man with no worse vice than vanity. . . . My chief call was on Samuel Rogers, who is lying on his bed, and his appearance was ghastly. He will never be able to walk, and it is to be feared that the want of exercise will destroy his health. He is not sensible of the extent of the injury, for he says he will never go out again without an attendant!

JULY 4th . . . I had this morning a letter from Quillinan. Mrs. Wordsworth very much dislikes the full-length of Wordsworth. . . . Dr. Wordsworth leads one to fear that the expense of the licence for the monument will be very great. . . .

JULY 26th . . . I began today and read two books of *The Prelude*, the autobiographic poem of Wordsworth, with which I am delighted; but it will give great offence—of which hereafter. . . .

JULY 28th Read *The Prelude* in bed. I was reading with great enjoyment *The Prelude* all the forenoon. . . .

JULY 30th . . . I finished the first hasty perusal of *The Prelude*, which I think very beautiful; but I find myself so dull that I shall with difficulty execute my purpose of writing a short paper on it for the *Reformer*. . . .

AUG. 6th Donne called on me this morning and with him James Spedding, one of those men of solid talent of whom I stand in awe. We had a half-hour's agreeable chat. He says that he believes Bacon did not write the *Paradoxes*. Spedding has devoted his life to the study of Bacon, whose life he means to write. . . .

AUG. 14th . . . On Thursday 15th August I set out on a visit to Rydal, where I remained a week. I went to see Mrs. Wordsworth, whom I found admirably calm and composed. No complaint or lamentation from her. I went also to talk with Dr. Wordsworth about the *Memoir* he is writing and with Miss Fenwick. . . .

AUG. 16th [*Travel Journal: Rydal.*] Wordsworth [John] and I were met by a stranger—Pearson—who accosted me by my name. . . . He knew I was here and wished to talk with me about Charles Lamb. We chatted a few minutes, but he was an admirer of Carlyle, so we did not harmonise. . . . By the bye, Miss Wordsworth is, I think, much improved in health. Mem.: This day Mrs. Wordsworth attained her eightieth year, and on the same day, 1804, Mrs. Quillinan was born.

AUG. 17th . . . I had three interesting conversations, first with Mrs. Wordsworth, then with Miss Fenwick, and then with the Doctor [Christopher Wordsworth] as to the expediency of mentioning a delicate subject in the forthcoming Memoir, and I have the satisfaction of believing that I shall have contributed to a determination in which all parties will be agreed, and the having done this will have rendered this my short visit a very valuable one.

AUG. 25th [*Bolton Abbey.*] . . . I found Miss Martineau as happy and full of zeal as ever. She is full of work and full of confidence both in the utility of what she does and of her capacity to do it. She is writing for Knight's *History of England*, and by way of change, writes Sanitary Tales for Dickens's *Household Words*. . . .

AUG. 30th [*London.*] . . . I called on Samuel Rogers. I found him greatly improved in appearance, reading by his bedroom window. He has been out of the house twice and is going to reside at Brighton with his sister. He made kind inquiries after Mrs. Wordsworth and spoke very favourably of Tennyson's *In Memoriam* as full of deep feeling, though Tennyson is often very obscure.

SEPT. 12th . . . I had an agreeable evening reading . . . passages from the *In Memoriam*, which I am more and more pleased with, and from Shelley. . . . His small poems [I] recognised as very beautiful, especially the *Skylark*; but I could not relish the *Adonais* as I do the *In Memoriam*. By the bye, the *Prospective Review* does ample justice to Tennyson, but with an admixture of blame.

SEPT. 28th . . . Also at the Athenaeum I began to read the *Autobiography of Alton Locke, Tailor and Poet*, by Kingsley. So pleased with the beginning that I must go on with it.

OCT. 3rd . . . Reading and finishing *Alton Locke*, the Chartist novel, embracing most of the stirring topics of the present day. A tale of considerable ability, but leaving the sentiments of the reverend author in considerable doubt. I suspect him to be a liberal striving to be orthodox. . . .

OCT. 4th . . . I finished *Alton Locke*, which is a powerful novel, though unsatisfactory at the close, the result being that Chartism has no legitimate root but in the death of Christ for all men. The conversion of Alton is rather rapid at the close, and being converted there was nothing left for the author to do but to kill him. It would have been beyond his strength to make him live in conformity with his new life. . . .

NOV. 2nd . . . I forgot to mention a call from Moxon on Friday. Dr. Wordsworth is going to put the *Life* of Wordsworth into Murray's hands. This is unjust to Moxon and will be against the interest of the family, for Moxon will give more than Murray for the work, and Murray refused the poems. . . .

NOV. 26th . . . I went round by Moxon. He told me that Mrs. Wordsworth and the family had written very strongly to the Doctor in favour of *his* being the publisher of the *Life*. Perhaps he may, as Murray's offer is not a good one, viz. to publish the book on commission and give a bill for the profits at nine months. Moxon says he will give a sum and pay beforehand. The Doctor, Moxon thinks, is looking only to the profit—he halves it with the family. . . .

DEC. 7th . . . I wrote [to Aspland] about dear Charles Lamb's inquiry whether he had not a right of action against Capel Lofft for writing stupid letters under the signature 'C.L.', by which he (Charles Lamb) was injured in reputation. . . . At the University College Clough was elected professor[1] in the room of Scott. . . .

DEC. 11th . . . Monkhouse . . . is glad as I am that Moxon is to publish the *Life*. . . .

1851

JAN. 18th . . . I met at Mr. John Coleridge's the sub-committee for the Wordsworth monument, a very genteel dinner. The business of the monument was gone into but not much done. Only £1,100 subscribed and about half paid; yet this is enough, they say, and the secretaries are to address to artists a circular request for design. The party was not large. The most interesting person was Ruskin, who talks well and looks better. I have told him of the Flaxman Hall, of which he had not heard, and he will see it with me and call to see my Wieland, etc. I have also interested him about Blake. He has a very delicate and most gentlemanly countenance and manners. . . . I found that I kept my place at table and was respectfully treated. . . .

FEB. 1st . . . Was employed in reading Tennyson's *Princess*. The playful grace and unpretending good humour of this *Medley* are quite captivating. Tennyson succeeds evidently in the genteel comedy or pedestrian blank verse in which Cowper excelled. The theme not unlike Shakespeare's *Love's Labour's Lost*, but treated very differently. . . .

[1] Of English Literature.

FEB. 3rd . . . I finished *The Princess* today. It is an elegant trifle, and with graceful irony the true relation of the sexes is pointed out; but it has numerous faults of construction and is very carelessly written, the versification very unequal.

FEB. 8th . . . I called at Chapman's and there saw Miss Mary Ann Evans (George Eliot), translator of Strauss—no recommendation to me, certainly, but the contrary, and yet there was something about her which pleased me much both in look and voice. She spoke of Harriet Martineau's and Atkinson's letters as studiously offensive.[1] It seems as if this book is absolutely atheistic! . . .

FEB. 12th . . . I breakfasted with Rogers. . . . Afterwards Ruskin stepped in. He seemed to have forgotten me, but was obliging in his manner when I referred to our dinner; but I did not renew my wish that he should come to see the Flaxman Gallery. . . .

FEB. 13th . . . I came home luckily, for I had a letter this morning from Dr. Davy about the Grasmere monument to Wordsworth. He requested me to let a young artist—Woolner—have the Chantrey bust in order to make a medallion for the monument, and while writing to desire he would call tomorrow. He did call, and I gave him the bust and I wrote to Quillinan telling him what I had done. . . .

FEB. 18th [*Brighton.*] We [Masquerier and Crabb Robinson] had calls soon after breakfast. The one to be mentioned was that of Faraday, one of the most remarkable men of the day. The very greatest of our discoverers in chemistry, a perfect lecturer in the unaffected simplicity and intelligent clearness of his statement, so that the learned were instructed and the ignorant charmed. His personal character admirable. Masquerier was kind to him when he was young and poor and altogether unknown, and now that he is a great man he does not forget his old friend. . . .

MARCH 4th . . . I devoted all the day to the reading of Atkinson's and Miss Martineau's letters on the Formation of Man, and went over half the volume with no pleasure and yet with less disgust than I expected. I have not fallen in with any atheistical sentiments, but the arrogant tone is offensive. . . . Altogether a disagreeable book. I am not sorry that my intimacy with Miss Martineau has of late so much declined: I shall make no *sacrifice* if I break with her entirely.

MARCH 7th . . . In the forenoon I took a cab to Stanhope Street, Mornington Crescent, . . . and there looked at the medallion of Wordsworth just modelled by [Woolner], who has made it for the Grasmere monument. It is a form I especially like, though the putting it up now

[1] *Letters on the Laws of Man's Social Nature and Development*, by H. G. Atkinson and H. Martineau, 1851.

by the Ambleside people in their impatience, while the chief monument is undetermined, is to be regretted.

MARCH 9th . . . I finished the book of Atkinson and Harriet Martineau. Charles Knight, it seems, has advertised that he is not going on with a work she was to have written: her name, however, does not appear. This will open her eyes if anything will. . . .

MARCH 18th . . . Wordsworth showed me the proof sheets of the *Life*, in which I am sorry to see a canting commonplace remark on the perils to which Wordsworth was exposed in his youth at Paris, which might make one utterly ignorant of Wordsworth's personal character imagine he had been guilty of some immorality! I wrote a short letter on this to Quillinan.

MARCH 21st . . . Then I called on Moxon about the *Life*. In the first proof, which I supposed to be the revise, John Wordsworth showed a passage of which I have spoken in the last page. Quillinan sent my letter to the Doctor, he and Miss Fenwick and Mrs. Wordsworth all agreeing with me; but Moxon is sure that the objectionable passage has been expunged, and at all events it will be if Mrs. Wordsworth requires it; and I wrote a letter to Quillinan to say as much. On my way I called at Boxall's and he told me that Dr. Davy and seven others refuse to pay their subscriptions to the Wordsworth monument; something so outrageous that it is hardly conceivable that any gentlemen could act so. . . .

MARCH 25th . . . From Moxon I learned what provoked me—that the injudicious paragraph about Wordsworth's residence in France is retained, which I thought had been omitted, and I wrote to Quillinan in consequence. . . .

MARCH 27th . . . A call from John Wordsworth just after a letter from Quillinan. Quillinan would submit to the Doctor's insertion of the offensive paragraph, but I advise him and his mother to prohibit it absolutely. Moxon will do what they wish. . . .

APRIL 2nd . . . I had a call from Quillinan quite unexpected. I am sorry to find that Dr. Wordsworth has not yielded to remonstrances. . . .

APRIL 11th I received last night a copy of the *Life of Wordsworth*, of which I have yet seen no part but that which respects my journey with him in 1837. So much I perceive that the Doctor has treated me kindly and with respect. I wrote a note of acknowledgment to him. . . .

APRIL 27th . . . I stayed at home . . . reading Wordsworth's *Memoir*, in which I continue to take a deep interest. I do not find anything seriously to [incomplete in MS.]. If not the whole man is given, portions are faithfully, though inevitably in magnitude disproportioned to the other portions of his character. . . .

MAY 14th . . . I had interesting talk with Ruskin, who said he was

Henry Crabb Robinson in old age

From a photograph by Maull and Company, at Dr. Williams's Library, London

ashamed at not having been impressed by Wordsworth's landscape sonnet[1] which I repeated, and I left a better impression than he had before received of Goethe. He has hitherto not been to see the Flaxman Gallery because he had not time to see it as he ought. . . .

JULY 10th . . . My first call was on Moxon. There I heard of the death of Quillinan, which Mrs. Wordsworth's note had made me apprehend. It is some consolation that his death will not leave his daughters in a worse condition, but be rather a relief. He was an amiable man, and the kindly feelings of the Ambleside people will be now generally excited. It is a great drawback on the hoped-for pleasure of a visit there. . . .

AUG. 28th . . . I heard from Cookson that the Wordsworth monument is going on and that the artist will take the money subscribed, whatever it may be. . . .

SEPT. 7th . . . I was not at Kenyon's house till near twelve. With him I found Walter Savage Landor, who was in a somewhat subdued mood all day. In his judgments not at all extravagant—his laugh only as joyous and sincere as ever. . . . Our party was increased by Browning, whom I found more agreeable as well as more healthy than ever. The talk was critical and anecdotic, and the latter easier to set down than the former. . . . Browning . . . is so far from being timid that he and Mrs. Browning are going to Florence, notwithstanding her *Casa Guidi*. Procter accompanied Browning. . . .

SEPT. 18th [*Rydal.*] After a long delay and several procrastinations, I have renewed my visits to this hospitable house. Last Christmas I was prepared to come if Mrs. Wordsworth had wished me to come, but she herself through Quillinan proposed my deferring my visit . . . which I gladly assented to. . . . On arriving at the Mount . . . I had a cordial reception. . . . I was glad to find that Mrs. Wordsworth was, as I have since found her, cheerful, in spite of the repeated bereavements she has recently undergone. . . .

SEPT. 27th I left my excellent friend Mrs. Wordsworth before eight o'clock with an apprehension that this may be the last of my visits to her, not that I fear her death, but I fear that Rydal and Ambleside may cease to be visitable places. They are changing. Even James is become incapable from infirmity of managing a horse and it is laid down [*sic*]. . . .

SEPT. 29th . . . I read with great admiration rather than pleasure Beddoes's tragedy—the first three acts of *The Fool's Tragedy*.[2] . . .

[1] 'Praised be the Art whose subtle power could stay.'

[2] The verse drama *Death's Jest Book, or The Fool's Tragedy* was published anonymously in 1850, after the suicide of its author, T. L. Beddoes, in January 1849. The composition had occupied him at intervals since 1825.

SEPT. 30th I have since read the rest of this beautiful tragedy. It has marvellous power, and as the work of a young man, raises deep regret at his early death. It is replete with horror, with a grotesque combination with comedy, and also delicious songs. It deals in the supernatural and is exuberant with imagery and excessive passion. In the same volume is the tragedy of a minor, *The Bride's Tragedy*. . . . It is full of beauties and will please more than the other. The author was nephew of Miss Edgeworth.

OCT. 3rd [*Bath.*] . . . I first called on Landor. He was very friendly, but he is so uncertain a man that I should fear being intimate with him. The Miss Hughes have told me an anecdote of him, corroborated by his own original letter; so that there can be no doubt. A lady, a great admirer of Landor, meeting him at the Miss Hughes' began in extravagant terms praising his articles in the *Examiner*. He must have misunderstood her to suppose that he was a writer for pay; that offended him to such a degree that he called her *impudent*, and insulted her in the grossest terms. Leaving the house, he sent a letter to the Miss Hughes, which I read; it was to this effect—that he had never in his life seen so impudent a woman as the one he saw at their house. 'It must be because I have not acquaintance with the worst of your sex. However, if you take an interest in her, *I will return good for evil and procure her a ticket for the penitentiary*.' Truly he must be mad—but where does madness begin and responsibility end? . . .

OCT. 4th . . . I went to Landor's and chatted till past ten with him. He was as friendly as ever. I understand he talks very cordially about me. *Tant mieux*.

OCT. 30th [*London.*] . . . I attended the Council of University Hall. We resolved to give notice to our Principal that his connection with us is to cease at the end of the present session, for we find that our pupils are fewer this year than they were last, so that we cannot possibly go on as we are. It seemed to be the general opinion that Clough, though a most amiable man, is by no means the man to preside over an establishment like ours. He wants authority and also activity. A letter was read from him declaring very coolly that he could suggest nothing by which our numbers could be increased. This was unsatisfactory to even his most zealous friend Edwin Field, and he concurred in the vote. . . .

NOV. 7th . . . I read an *Athenaeum* and I began Carlyle's *Sterling*, which he will make interesting in spite of his faults. At all events it begins well. . . .

NOV. 8th . . . I was detained and attracted by Carlyle's *Sterling*, of which I read this evening enough to make me anxious to go on with it. Indeed, next day, Sunday, I read a little more. The character of Coleridge is admirable, the best thing in it, and yet a brilliant passage exposing the vanity of his imagined religion is precisely what may be with equal truth said of his own. The style is somewhat less extravagant than usual, but it is not free from his peculiarities. It is the subject, after all, which chiefly attracts me. Sterling is a man I feel an interest in. There is no extravagant admiration of him by his biographer, which is a great merit.

Nov. 12th . . . I took luncheon at the Athenaeum, meaning to go further, but I found Carlyle's *Sterling* so attractive that I could not leave. . . .

Nov. 14th . . . I read in Carlyle's *Sterling*. This takes up time, but it reconciles me greatly to Carlyle. The book has much that is excellent. . . .

Nov. 15th I was within all the forenoon after a call on Mrs. Fletcher, which was a very agreeable one. I obtained from her the £5 she had given to the Wordsworth monument—she declaring the Doctor [Davy], her son-in-law, though a most honourable man, to be no man of business. I left a note at Boxall's informing him of this and congratulating him on his being made an A.R.A. . . . Of the party[1] were Kinglake, author of *Eöthen*, . . . a gentlemanly and agreeable man, with a cast of expression very Jewish; but nothing remarkable in his conversation. . . .

Nov. 17th . . . Also finished the *Life of Sterling*, by Carlyle—a book which has given me the greatest pleasure and all but made me forgive his brutal paper on *Slavery* in *Fraser* last year. . . .

1852

Jan. 28th . . . Then I drove . . . to Thackeray's lecture at the Marylebone Institute. It was the last of the series and well delivered, having been read before. The subjects Sterne and Goldsmith. Sterne in rather a canting style abused for his impurity, and Goldsmith [praised] for his goodness. At the close the public were absolved from the imputation of neglecting men of letters. On the whole the matter not sterling, but the form graceful. I asked him why he did not incidentally mention Charles Lamb. He said he could not venture on him. He admired Charles Lamb greatly. . . .

Jan. 29th . . . I read an *Athenaeum* and I lounged over Miss Mitford's *Literary Life*. Most pleased with Praed's capital *vers de société*. He was quite a master in that style. . . .

Feb. 4th . . . Left home early, having promised to call at Angus Fletcher's studio in order to look at a bust he is making of Wordsworth. He has, I think, succeeded in making a strong likeness, but, as I honestly

[1] A dinner at Sir Francis Goldsmid's.

wrote, I am conscious of not having that delicate perception that constitutes taste. . . .

MARCH 4th . . . Pickering [H. W. Pickersgill?] has a full-length of Wordsworth, his own property, which he looks forward to as of great value to his family in the next generation. It is a well-conceived painting. . . .

MARCH 19th . . . I began and read the first number of *Bleak House.* It opens with exaggerated and verbose description. London fog is disagreeable even in description, and on the whole the first number does not promise much, except an exposure of the abuses of Chancery practice. The best thing is the picture of a desolate condition of a natural child, but she is removed out of it before sympathy is much called out. . . .

APRIL 8th . . . Read No. 2 *Bleak House.* Dickens retains his admirable talent at scene-painting. . . . Two delicious characters: that of a benevolent man who won't be thanked—an impersonation of goodness, the good genius of *Bleak House*, and a childlike thoughtless creature who allows young women to pay his debts and thinks he does them a kindness by making them feel they take care of him 'who for himself can take no care at all.'

MAY 4th . . . Accompanied Donne to Chapman's, where was a meeting of authors, etc., to announce an opinion against the Booksellers' Association—to put down the cheap vendors. Dickens in the chair. The best speakers by far were Tom Taylor, who was playful and convincing. . . . Professor Owen spoke feelingly and produced a serious impression. Carlyle, John Mill, and others wrote letters. Several booksellers spoke on the other side, but were not listened to. . . .

MAY 13th . . . William Wordsworth and I went to see his father's intended statue, and calling on Kenyon in our way he accompanied us to the sculptor's, Thrupp, 30 Gloucester Place. We found Thrupp's statue a sitting figure. Wordsworth is bent over—not a book as originally designed, but—it is not yet clear what—something in his hand. I had not a sufficiently clear impression to venture on criticism, except that I wished the muscles of the right hand to be relaxed, not compressed. Both William Wordsworth and Kenyon thought the statue would prove good. . . .

JUNE 18th . . . I read at Bear Wood Nos. 3 and 4 of *Bleak House.* It has an excellent picture of Walter Savage Landor as Mr. Boythorn. His fierce tones, tenderness of heart, and exaggeration in all his judgments described with great truth and force. . . .

JUNE 27th . . . I finished the anti-slavery novel,[1] which I was pleased with notwithstanding its very Evangelical tone. All the classes in America

[1] *Uncle Tom's Cabin*, by Mrs. Harriet Beecher Stowe.

are fairly represented and the manners of the Southerners painted with honour and spirit. Written by a woman. Ophelia, the New England Abolitionist, and the heartless wife at New Orleans are well contrasted. Quite as candid and fair as such a book can be. It is reprinted cheap in England from the tenth American edition. It is said to have made many converts to Abolitionism. The hero, Uncle Tom, is a pious negro who submits to every cruel infliction as an apostle would, and his persecutor is perhaps too unmingled a monster. . . .

[*Travel Journal: Edinburgh.*] SEPT. 1st . . . The only novelty of importance is the Scott monument—full of crockets and petty ornaments not unsuited to the character of his poetry. . . .

SEPT. 2nd . . . We went to the little theatre, not the Royal, and saw *Rob Roy* with no great pleasure . . . and I was rather unpleasantly affected by hearing portions of Wordsworth's *Rob Roy* sung. His verse does not admit of being vulgarised. I felt that thoughtful verse does not gain by being set to music. It is degraded. One does not sing axioms of wisdom.

SEPT. 9th [*Rydal.*] . . . I called . . . on Mrs. Davy, with whom I had an interesting chat chiefly about Harriet Martineau. It seems that she is at Belfast, that she is engaged to write there a series of articles describing the state of Ireland—to be published either in the *Daily News* or *Household Words*, according to the subject. She is a chief contributor to *Household Words*, and also makes £200 by what she writes in the *Daily News*, the paper of largest circulation after *The Times*. . . . Harriet Martineau lets her house whenever she leaves Ambleside, so that I should think she must be saving money. This I am glad of, as with all her faults there is more of good than bad in her. Her talents are great, and her intentions benevolent. Mrs. Arnold remarks that her spoken judgments on persons and things of the day are very unsound, yet that her written judgments in her *History* are unexpectedly correct. . . .

SEPT. 15th . . . I could not leave dear Mrs. Wordsworth without a painful feeling that it is not unlikely to be the last time of my visiting her. While we both live I should be sorry to omit coming once a year, and she would regret not seeing me. Yet we are of necessity declining every day and possessing fewer of those qualities which interest others. . . .

SEPT. 22nd . . . Clough is about to try the experiment of America, where he may be able to establish himself in some college as a professor. I fear he wants the faculty of getting on.

OCT. 3rd . . . Moxon . . . joined me at Kenyon's, with whom was Browning. A *partie carée.* The afternoon was a pleasant one. Browning talked agreeably, but there was nothing remarkable in anything he said. I am afraid I talked the most. . . .

Oct. 6th . . . With Kenyon I found an interesting person I had never seen—Mrs. Browning, late Miss Barrett. Not the invalid I expected. She is a handsome oval face, a fine eye, and altogether a pleasing person. She had no opportunity of display and apparently no desire. She has not the very amiable appearance of her husband. There is a singular sweetness about him. . . .

N.B.—I have never read Mrs. Browning's poems. She addressed me as if she had known me before. I had lent her books though I had never seen her. I hear that she advocates the cause of Louis Napoleon, which, unless in a very qualified way, would be an evidence of wrong-headedness. Yet it is said she considers him as really the people's choice. This would prove great credulity.

Oct. 14th . . . Then I came to the University College, where Clough, who had already resigned his professorship of English Literature, yet delivered his lecture prepared on the History of English Literature. But admirable as the substance was, so ill delivered was this lecture that it gave little pleasure. . . .

Nov. 16th . . . I spent the whole of the day afterwards at the Athenaeum, for I found Thackeray's *Esmond*, vol. i, at liberty, and took advantage of the circumstance and was reading it between five and twelve with great pleasure. It is one of the most agreeable novels long read. The two noble ladies, the Catholic dowager and her successor, as far as the first volume goes, very finely painted. The latter ought not to be called, as some critic does, an aristocratic Becky. The first appearance of Sir Richard Steele is felicitous.

Nov. 18th [Day of the Duke of Wellington's funeral.] . . . Reaching the Athenaeum a little after 8, I found Thackeray's *Esmond* at my service, and I was engaged nearly all the day—that is from half past eight a.m. till half past seven p.m.—reading it. . . .

Nov. 20th . . . Then I went to the Athenaeum, where I was able to finish *Esmond*, and with great pleasure. This is a capital novel, and in this respect it is quite artistic: that the romantic catastrophe harmonises admirably with the historical elements. . . . Among the best parts of the tale are the exposure of Marlborough's selfishness and treachery and of other public men. Sir Richard Steele is introduced with effect; Swift unworthily; Addison not ill. . . .

Nov. 23rd . . . I have renewed *Bleak House*—read No. 5—also without any pleasure. But from Dickens one may expect something good to follow what is insignificant.

Nov. 26th . . . I continued *Bleak House*. Having begun this poor work I am constrained to go on, little as I like it. . . .

Nov. 28th I finished this morning Beattie's *Life of Campbell.* I could never relish Campbell's poetry, and wonder at the honour showed him in a burial in Westminster Abbey. He wrote *down* to the mediocrity of the age. . . .

Nov. 29th . . . At seven I went to Robertson's[1] and had two hours of interesting talk with him,—on his position here [Brighton] in the pulpit; also about Lady Byron. He speaks of her as the noblest woman he ever knew. It seems Lady Lovelace is dead and that Lord L. and Lady L. have both acted very ill. . . .

Dec. 11th . . . I read . . . Hood's capital *Ode to Rae Wilson*, full of satire and liberal thought, very offensive to the godly Scotch Sabbatarians. . . .

Dec. 12th . . . All my reading today was confined to the *Inquirer* and the poems of Thomas Hood. . . . Hood is really a poet and excellent both in the humorous and the grave. *The Bridge of Sighs* is one of the best I ever saw. . . .

1853

Jan. 9th . . . I read . . . in Moore's poems. His political squibs are his very best. I find now, looking over the complete edition of his works, that he has written very many things that one can well spare. . . . I finished the second volume of Moore's Life.[2] It raises my opinion of the man infinitely and makes me better acquainted with his works. But his political poems are far too many. . . .

Feb. 9th . . . Read at night an amusing paper in *Household Words*, exposing the impudent imposture of the evoked spirits [spirit-rapping]. Precisely the same account which Dr. Ashburner gave me the other day, except that the Doctor narrated as a dupe what Dickens exposes *en esprit fort.*

March 8th . . . I was seduced by laziness and the attraction of Miss Brontë's *Villette* to stay at the Athenaeum till late. Villette is the name of a French [*sic*] town; the supposed authoress, a Miss Snowe, is a young woman who has to live by her wits. Two-thirds of volume one bring her to the establishment of Madame Beck at Villette. She is a model of selfishness and shrewdness—a character. I suspect the book is a collection of character sketches, in which the authoress excels. Carlyle is become

[1] The Rev. Frederick William Robertson. See *infra*, Aug. 16th, and Sept. 13th, 1853.

[2] *Memoirs, Journals and Correspondence*, ed. by Lord John Russell.

a member of the Athenaeum. He was unexpectedly friendly towards me.

MARCH 11th . . . I went to the Athenaeum where I stayed all the rest of the day till six. My object was to finish *Villette*. It disappoints at the end. . . . It is a novel of thought—too much preaching, in fact, and disquisition on points of education and physiology—and written in a strange style of bombast, so that the impression is disagreeable at the close. . . .

APRIL 17th . . . I had just time to finish the third volume of Thomas Moore's Life. It filled up three years of his life and shows him as a very ordinary tuft-hunter—a feeder on the great. It has lowered him in my opinion. His ill-will towards Wordsworth is discreditable to him. . . .

APRIL 18th . . . I went to the Athenaeum where I began the fourth volume of Moore's Life. In his diary mention of me not written in a friendly spirit, yet not uncivil. . . .

APRIL 27th . . . I finished the fourth volume of the worthless Life of Moore. . . .

APRIL 29th . . . I was diverted from my intended evening calls by the Haymarket playbill and saw Browning's play, *Colombe's Birthday*—very obscure in style. Heard little and understood less, nor did Ellen Tree satisfy me. . . .

MAY 24th . . . At Mrs. Reid's between three and four. There were assembled some twenty or thirty of Mrs. Reid's acquaintance to be introduced to the object of general curiosity. [Mrs. Beecher Stowe] herself looks young, agreeable, and quite unpretending—her voice only disagreeable, being Yankee-ish. . . . A far more interesting person was Lady Byron, to whom Mrs. Jameson introduced me. . . .

JUNE 3rd John Mallett . . . accompanied me to see the sitting figure of Wordsworth by Thrupp—very striking. In consequence, I have written to Samuel Rogers to induce him to see it, which he can from his carriage. . . .

JUNE 7th . . . I forgot to go to Moxon to meet Derwent Coleridge about having a picture of the poet by Allston engraved. I am put on the committee! to have it done. I have since seen the picture. It has great beauty, more expressive of the poet's tenderness than power. But it deserves to be engraved, and I willingly take part in the work and shall subscribe for several copies.

JUNE 9th . . . I amused myself by writing a paper for the *Athenaeum* on Moore's account of the dinner at Monkhouse's thirty years ago, which Boott recommends me to send to the *Athenaeum* and I mean to do. . . .

JUNE 19th . . . I read Thackeray's Pope lecture. Thackeray does not rise in my estimation, and it is the subject, not the treatment, which makes me relish the book. Any fresh biography of Addison, Swift, or Pope could not fail to delight me—at least, to interest me. . . .

JUNE 25th . . . I called . . . at the Athenaeum office and had the pleasure of reading 'H.C.R.' in the morning's number.[1] The paper itself is better than I feared it would be. . . .

JUNE 26th I was alone at breakfast, which gave me time I did not profit by as I ought. I lost time in musing over my letter on Lamb and Moore in the *Athenaeum*, which I liked at first, and the kind words about it of Kenyon . . . etc. made me think it really good. But I have been reading it again, and found numerous improprieties of expression and points feebly put. . . .

JULY 5th . . . A dinner at T. Talfourd's . . . Moxon . . . The Justice made himself agreeable. Probably not pleased with my paper on Lamb, as he did not allude to it; but Moxon likes it. . . .

JULY 6th . . . Having had a letter from Boxall, I wrote yesterday at the Athenaeum a long letter to Harrison declining to let Dr. Davy transfer my intended subscription, five pounds, to the Wordsworth monument to the Ambleside window, which is no proper memorial of Wordsworth, and I justified my not joining in church building, which I approved of churchmen doing, on the ground that, with very limited means each individual must be guided by personal considerations. . . . Let me supply an omission. At Talfourd's was Charles Kemble, who, but for his deafness, which is severe, would be very agreeable. With the aid of a tube he can maintain a *tête-à-tête* conversation. He expressed great pleasure at my relating anecdotes of the old time—my love of Mrs. Siddons; but Charles Kemble spoke of his brother as a greater artist than his sister. Charles Kemble said incidentally that all his children were lost to him. He knew nothing about them—in an angry tone, too. . . .

AUG. 16th . . . And in the afternoon Dr. King wrote to me informing me of the death of Robertson of Brighton. Take him all in all, the best preacher I ever saw in a pulpit—that is uniting the greatest number of excellencies, originality, piety, freedom of thought and warmth of love. His style colloquial and very scriptural. . . . He combined *light* of the intellect with *heat* of the affections in a pre-eminent degree. . . .

SEPT. 4th . . . I breakfasted with Samuel Rogers. For the first time alone, or at most the second time since I have known him. Dr. Beattie preferred going to church. No wonder! Poor Rogers's conversation is becoming painfully indicative of a failing memory. After twelve I left him, he having pressed me to dine with him. . . . I returned to dine with Rogers, of which dinner I have nothing further to say except that he pressed me much to breakfast with him again this morning. He was, as usual, acrimonious and affectionate at the same time towards the same

[1] See *supra*, June 9th.

person, both morning and evening referring to Wordsworth's refusal to consent to his daughter's marriage with Quillinan. . . .

SEPT. 11th . . . I called today—the only time—on Moses Ricardo.[1] He, too, seems grown old: he looks a different man. He is one of those whom I find it difficult to tolerate who will prefer Sortain[2] to Robertson. And yet, unless Sortain be grossly calumniated, he is morally as inferior to Robertson as he is most certainly intellectually. I knew that Ricardo thought meanly [of him] on the score of integrity and veracity. . . .

SEPT. 13th Aspland jumped at my offer to prepare an obituary paper on Robertson, and this, therefore, became my occupation for this and the following day. It is now in the printer's hands. I fear a middle thing, containing more than a mere paper giving an account of the man required, and yet nothing as a paper of thought. I am glad I attempted no more, for I should have written what I should have been ashamed of, compared with a short, excellent paper in the last number of the *Inquirer*. . . . In the evening called by desire on Lady Noel Byron, a call which I enjoyed and which may have consequences. She looks even an old woman; and, recollecting her history and as the widow of the most *famous* poet England had in our day, not the greatest, I felt an interest in her as I went, and that was greatly heightened when I left her. From all I have heard of her I consider [her] as one of the best women of the day. Her means and her goodwill both great. She lives to do good, says Dr. King, and I believe him. . . . She wanted my opinion as to the mode of doing justice to Robertson's memory. She spoke of him as having the best head on matters of business of any one she ever knew. 'I have consulted lawyers on matters of difficulty. Robertson understood these better than the lawyers. He unravelled everything, and explained everything at once as no one else did.' She spoke of the Life to be composed, and suggested that one might be composed like that of Margaret Fuller. This was done afterwards in a letter to me I received next morning, in which she said an inducement was to have my aid in writing it—a flattering opinion. Unhappily I know that I make an impression at first by my manner which I am unable to keep up. . . .

SEPT. 18th . . . I had finished the first volume of Haydon's very interesting Life.[3] Better by far than I could have expected. . . .

SEPT. 23rd . . . I read in bed this morning a chapter in Haydon's Life. It grows in painful interest. But I must not forget that I never saw a picture by him which gave me pleasure. Could he have been made to feel

[1] Brother of David Ricardo, the economist.

[2] Joseph Sortain.

[3] *Autobiography and Journals of B. R. Haydon.*

the truth of Mrs. Barbauld's *Essay on Inconsistency*, he might have cured himself of the folly of expecting the vulgar to have the refinement of the few. . . .

SEPT. 25th . . . Street[1] the architect, though High Church, pleased me unexpectedly. He is a man of sense, and agreeable in his person and conversation. . . .

OCT. 9th . . . Calls from Clough. He is returned from America, and has a place in the Education Board. He was only at Boston. The Yankees were friendly to him, and he likes them. He is, however, glad to come back. He looks well and is fatter. . . .

NOV. 4th . . . I slept for the first time on a spring mattress, and I have found the effect very agreeable. Formerly in Germany I slept on a sofa with a spring seat. I never slept better than last night, and I am now lying on it while writing and find it very pleasant. . . .

NOV. 15th . . . A call on Mrs. Wordsworth in Dean's Yard, and sat with the ladies, but I declined staying to lunch and seeing the Doctor. Dear Mrs. Wordsworth wants me to hear him preach; I fear she thinks he might convert me. . . .

NOV. 28th . . . I took an omnibus into the city, having before, by the bye, as soon as I had breakfast gone to the Euston Road railway station, and there in her carriage taken leave of dear Mrs. Wordsworth in her way to the north. . . . Took an omnibus to the Athenaeum. There I . . . stayed till past nine, being diverted from my intended [plans] by Reade's novel *Peg Woffington*, a delightful picture of the manners of the dramatic and gay life of the time of Colley Cibber and Mrs. Clive, when Garrick was commencing his career; the merit lying more in the description than in the thing described, being profligate. But there is a mixture of pathos and gaiety very attractive. . . .

DEC. 11th . . . A call from Clough; he was as pleasant as man can be. Did not absolutely talk about his intended marriage, but looked it all, and invited himself next Sunday. . . .

DEC. 18th . . . The Americans have made Clough even loquacious compared with what he was. I like him. . . .

1854

FEB. 11th . . . We dined with Rogers. . . . Rogers was also silent. . . . The impression he has made on me is that long life is a very doubtful

[1] George Edmund Street (1824–1881), architect of the London Law Courts.

blessing. But then he is twelve years older than I am, and he was weakly in youth. . . .

FEB. 12th . . . Until this visit to Brighton the only matter of a serious kind on which Lady Byron spoke with me was the publication of Robertson's Life and Remains. But that subject was soon dismissed, and she soon introduced matters of a more delicate kind, and by her confidence I felt honoured. Yet during these communications given for the sake of advice asked for, there was very little indeed that I could not put down here with perfect propriety. The least important alone of these subjects were introduced by me, viz., the relation between Lord Byron and Wordsworth, etc. She spoke highly of Wordsworth and his poetry, and I, relating the incident at Lamb's chambers of Wordsworth's expressing his disgust at the unhandsome treatment of the *minor* Lord poet by the *Edinburgh Review*, she mentioned the warm admiration Lord Byron expressed of Wordsworth's dignified manners, and as to his Satires, she considered these as unserious wantonness. I informed her of the loss of my letter which contained a full account of all Goethe said of Lord Byron. She made no particular remark on this, nor in general on Moore's conduct, but she has authorised the insertion in some future *Edinburgh Review* [of] a contradiction of the statement in the sixth volume of the *Life*, that she had declared her approbation of Moore's *Life of Lord Byron*, which she never would do. In all she said to me about Lord Byron there was a manifest wish to spare him. He could not subdue his passions. She denied that he was malignant, but he was reckless. She produced to me a copy of Medwin's *Conversations*, with marginal notes by her. She desired me to read a few on the spot, and then say whether it should be preserved. I was of opinion that she should take care to leave a written reply to all calumny. It is only since her daughter's death, etc., that she has felt it of importance that the second son[1] of Lord Lovelace should entertain just notions concerning her. He ought to entertain just notions of her. She hopes to have a good influence over him. I like his appearance much. She speaks of him as full of talent and strong affections, but has a tendency to waywardness. How can it be otherwise? Having read some of these marginalia I remarked to her that she must be careful not to assert a *negative pregnant*. She was not acquainted with the word. She is too upright to commit the fault wilfully, and will guard against inadvertently committing it. I also recommended her not to notice *light* imputations, which, at the worst, would only affix on her the minor charge of vanity. It would betray a want of feeling to care for such matters

[1] Ralph Gordon Noel Milbanke, later Lord Wentworth, second son of Lord Lovelace, whom he succeeded, and grandson of Lady Byron.

in the presence of serious matters. She took this very kindly. She praised warmly her governess as an admirable person. Lord Byron was worked on by others. No allusion to the cause of their separation—that is, its nature, except that it was necessary. I now find that here in London it is supposed to have been *incest*. I had thought it was still worse. I have found today that Mrs. Boott is inclined to think that Lady Byron ought not to have abandoned her husband. This is a woman's judgment. I am not supplied with any special means of judging except what my increased respect for her supplies. The next, and practically the most important matter on which she asks for my assistance, is a governor for this grandson—the second. He must be a man of dignity, to enforce authority; of gentleness, to secure love; a sufficient scholar, etc. I know no one. . . .

FEB. 21st . . . At Mrs. Swanwick's I chatted very agreeably with James Martineau, and also with Newman; but Newman is losing ground with the public from his anti-Christian zeal, as many people will consider his anxiety to make his *un*belief known. . . .

FEB. 22nd Read in bed Talfourd's *Rambles*. He is too much of a Smelfungus. His criticisms on Rome are very unequal. I have since finished the volume. It has amused me. . . .

MARCH 13th . . . My attention was diverted from books to the really sad catastrophe which was announced in the evening papers. Talfourd, soon after delivering the charge to the grand jury at Stafford, was seized with apoplexy and died in half an hour! My acquaintance with Talfourd had long been on the wane, and was just beginning to revive, at least with Lady Talfourd . . . and now it is suddenly ended. This is a terrible blow to his family. . . .

APRIL 27th . . . Moxon . . . is about to publish Talfourd's last works. Lady Talfourd would publish his Life, but that is not desirable, otherwise than as a short memoir. I read today Dickens's few but deeply feeling lines—sentences on Talfourd in *Household Words*. A little overdoing is to be expected, but it is not excessive here. . . .

APRIL 30th . . . Boxall . . . introduced to us seniors the strange topic about to amuse and scandalise the public—a suit in the Ecclesiastical Court by Mrs. Ruskin against husband *impotentiae causa*, the real ground being extreme neglect in matters in which he wanted not the power but the will to do his duty. . . .

MAY 1st . . . Another matter was on my mind this morning: an application from Phillips through Papworth for permission to have a mould made from my bust of Wordsworth. Papworth did not know that this was by Chantrey. I doubt the propriety of this. I, however, called on Scharf, and I mean to speak with Thrupp and possibly with Lady

Chantrey as to the means of getting a suitable memorial of Wordsworth in the Crystal Palace. Of this more hereafter....

MAY 2nd ... I was taken by Mrs. Byles in her carriage... to Thrupp's where we looked at Wordsworth's bust. It is a fine figure of an *old* man, and yet the poet should not droop so. The bard is lost sight of. Thrupp tells me that his bust was offered the Crystal Palace for five pounds, and that the mould does not cost more than two pounds, so that I am not so much obliged to them as I thought....

MAY 6th ... My first business was to call on Lady Chantrey and inquire whether she would approve of my letting the Crystal Palace have my cast of Wordsworth to make a mould from. She satisfied me that this ought not to be done. Sir Francis wished all the moulds to be destroyed, that casts might not be multiplied. And she destroyed all. Moulds from casts are not so good as from the marble. ... I wrote accordingly to Papworth. My next call was on Benson Harrison, from whom I heard that Mrs. Wordsworth has recovered the use of her cross-eye, and is become blind in the eye formerly straight and now become cross, the eyes having thus changed their position! Dr. Gibson tells me that this fact is not unknown to him, and he mentioned a case which he printed....

MAY 26th ... I dined at [Erasmus] Darwin's. A party—himself not [there], for he caught cold. His brother Charles (a fine fellow in person as in character)....

JUNE 2nd Finished the last *Prospective Review* by reading on Leopardi [whom Crabb Robinson had met in 1831] ... a sickly poet of high reputation. ... His person not unlike De Quincey's in the impression left of it, like mother of pearl....

I read the *Hard Times* with increasing pleasure....

JULY 19th ... A letter from Mrs. Wordsworth pressing me to go soon. Miss Wordsworth has become happy and still. A blessed change, writes Mrs. Wordsworth, preparatory to the last change. She, I perceive, thinks Miss Wordsworth cannot long survive, and therefore would have me go....

AUG. 5th ... I had the pleasure of a walk with Grote[1] to Regent Street. I found him very liberal and intelligent. It was the best part of the day....

AUG. 9th ... Called at Rogers's. From Moxon I had heard of Rogers having had a fit, and his life was not expected; yet he had again rallied and Dr. Watson says he may get over it—still!...

AUG. 10th–22nd [*Visit to Rydal.*] ... At Birthwaite I was recognised by William Arnold, author of *Oakfield*. ... William Arnold is an invalid,

[1] George Grote (1794–1871), the historian.

but really a fine fellow. I was glad to hear Lady Byron had engaged him for a year as a tutor for her grandson, and I wrote to her saying how much pleasure this gave me. In return she wrote to me that this confirmation of her choice came opportunely. . . . These Arnolds—the young men—are thought to take much on themselves and I hinted to William that Matthew had so acted towards me. However, William, as I said, has high principles, though the religious do not like his book. It is without religion. The interesting trial of Percy the Ensign, just ended, has great resemblance to that of Oakfield, but shows the army in England to be worse than Arnold dared to paint it, even in India. I drank tea with Mrs. Arnold once. . . . I have no complaint to make of inattention, as certainly I did not expect to be invited to the luncheon to which Lord John Russell was invited on the 21st. At the same time I do not think my acquaintance will ever become intimacy.

I found on my arrival at the Mount the family as well as I could expect. Miss Wordsworth more quiet than I have known her for years, and the day of my departure she showed a recognition, and more than that, in tone discriminated between me and Dr. Jackson. Mrs. Wordsworth is unchanged; except a slight lameness or weakness in the knee, in good health. She has great comfort in Mr. Carter, who is chaplain, steward—everything, in fact. An excellent man, but wayward, Mrs. Wordsworth says, and requires attention. John Wordsworth was there several days. . . .

. . . My reading at Rydal was slight. The most interesting part of this was a short account of the family of Mrs. Hutchinson (Miss Monkhouse)—interesting from the simple piety and just sentiments of Mrs. Wordsworth. I looked over several volumes of *The Doctor*. Pleasant gossip, but the book has been very overpraised.

The only book from which I made extracts was Carlyle's *Chartism*, a book read with conflicting feelings. On the whole I dislike it—though full of Mephistophelian truth, at best half-truths. . . . I left Rydal on the Tuesday afternoon with an impression that if I ever see it again it will be with several mutilations. Even that excellent servant, James, is growing old. He is grateful for small favours. . . .

AUG. 25th . . . Began looking over [Peter George] Patmore's *My Friends and Acquaintance*. An interesting chapter about Lamb, Dec. 5th 1826. He writes: 'H.C.R. called at half-past eight. There was an end of general conversation, he took it all to himself!' This, though uncivil, does not offend me, as a report of Hazlitt's abuse of Ayrton does Ayrton. He proceeds, but incorrectly, to report what I said about Spanish names—for the English Reformers—by no means bad if well related. It is good being thick-skinned when one cannot escape the cudgel. . . .

AUG. 26th . . . I called at Rogers's and found from Edmund that he was in his bed and much feebler than ever. He was not expected long to survive. . . . This is another instance. We may live too long. Old age without intelligence is no boon. . . . I began and I finished yesterday Patmore's long paper on Hazlitt. Patmore is a low fellow, booksellers' drudge, and the book will be deservedly despised—perhaps even more than it deserves. His admiration of Hazlitt is even absurd, and betrays a want of refined sense and correct judgment. Yet he has a certain vigour of description. . . .

SEPT. 1st . . . Spent several hours reading *Hard Times*, which, though not one of Dickens's best novels, has an object. I wish him success in his exposure of the matter-of-fact Manufactory System. His ridicule of Mr. Bounderby, the bully of humility who brags of his beggarly poverty, of Gradgrind, the rich man of Coketown, the candidate Harthouse, and Blackpool, the high-minded working hand, are all well drawn. More hereafter. . . .

SEPT. 3rd . . . I devoted the day nearly to the finishing of *Hard Times*. By no means one of Dickens's best novels. The matter-of-fact Gradgrind, his ruined son and nearly ruined daughter, Louisa, are not made out either consistently or probably. Bounderby, the bully of humility, and his really humble mother, who, full of love, conceals that she is his mother, and the obsequious Mrs. Sparsit, the dependant, are original without being good. Coketown is a sort of caricature of Manchester. The strike and popular orators are spirited, and Blackpool is affecting, but not credible. . . .

SEPT. 12th–23rd [*Visit to Masqueriers at Brighton.*] On the day of my arrival Masquerier gave a dinner, for which he fixed me to come. It was to Dr. Croly[1] chiefly. He was the star. Sortain, a sort of antithesis, and Ricardo. Neither of whom could relish him. . . . The Doctor is a character. I met him at Walter's some thirty years ago or more, when I was requested to give him some hints about being *The Times* correspondent at Paris. Walter asking what I thought of his friend, I said: 'Had I met him in the evening in a retired spot I should have fallen on my knees and said: "Take my money and spare my life." ' He has a large person and a fierce physiognomy pitted with the smallpox, and a loud voice. He has made his way in the world at last in the Church, and is a popular preacher at the city church of St. Stephen, Walbrook, where he took an active and laudable part in the legal disputes with Gibbs. He attempted novel-writing and wrote *Salathiel* (the Wandering Jew), and he wrote a tragedy, *Catiline*, and a comedy. Pride will have a fall, at least, I think so. In fact,

[1] The Rev. George Croly (1780–1860).

he has been a literary adventurer. He and I sparred and talked freely. . . . He is growing deaf and is a discontented man—a general fault-finder. He was a Tory, but he spoke now against all parties. He speaks on religious subjects like one whose duty it is to take a part; but he has not the air of a religious man, and I suspect he has no zeal but what proceeds from party spirit. . . . I saw a good deal of Sortain. . . . He spoke of *The Divine Drama* very warmly. . . . Indeed, this book is making way though not yet reviewed.

Sortain told me that he met Carlyle at William Marshall's, where his conversation was so gross that Marshall was obliged to remind him a clergyman was in the room. Before even the ladies left the room, the tone of Carlyle was offensive enough. . . .

. . . Lady Byron . . . I saw almost every day after Sunday. She was more cordial and confidential than ever. Her communications must be carefully noticed, though all were of a kind to do her honour. She is delighted with William Arnold, who is now at Bonn with her grandson Ralph. . . . She is undoubtedly a Unitarian, and yet seems unwilling to acknowledge herself one. . . . She spoke freely of my *Exposure* which I put into her hands. She thinks acuteness in interpretation my *forte*, not continuous writing, and assented to almost all I said in the way of critical remark. Her opinion of the Bishop of Oxford that of everyone [who] honours the name of Clarkson. I must put in cypher what she said of most interest. She confirmed what Goethe says, that Lord Byron was fond of boasting that he had killed a person. On coming out of the church after our marriage, i.e. in the carriage [he said]: 'We must come to a separation sooner or later.' And within the week of the marriage he fell into a violent passion for something she had very innocently [word wanting in MS. ?said or done], drew a dagger, lifted it up as if he would stab her. On which she looked calmly. He paused and said: 'No, I will not imbrue my hands in blood a second time.' 'Yet with all this,' she said, 'we were most fitted to each other of any persons.' He was the victim of imposture. He was weak in will. He professed at times the greatest respect for her, and she can prove that at the time she first proposed a separation he had himself determined on it. She intimated she would write to me, perhaps in a foreign name, when speaking on these family matters. Of her daughter she said nothing; says Lord Lovelace hates her. *Er ist ein Geizhals*,[1] which is the source of his faults. She spoke of her eldest grandson with great affection. My interviews with her were frequent, and have added to my esteem. Of her daughter she said nothing. She seemed to think her husband was unable to resist his impulses, and she said expressly he

[1] A miser.

could not have been happy with any woman. She praised the governess whom Lord Byron so abuses. She spoke highly of Lamb, Wordsworth, etc. Does not seem to know much of Lady Blessington—at least, said nothing. Thought highly of Coleridge. . . .

Nov. 30th . . . The Wordsworth monument is up, without consulting secretaries or committee; but it could be nowhere but where it is. We are to have a final meeting! Boxall is quite satisfied. But the Dean and Chapter have been exorbitant. . . .

1855

Jan. 10th–20th [*Brighton.*] . . . Lady Byron I saw more than any one out of the house. I took tea with her several times quite early, and saw her as often as I could. . . . We talked more about Lord Byron as a poet than ever before. . . .

Jan. 22nd [*London.*] . . . I dined with Kenyon by invitation, and [he] had Boxall whom I was to meet. It was a very agreeable evening. . . . The subjects of talk were Wordsworth's monument, which Boxall had not yet seen. It seems that the artist is most to blame. He fixed the place, and he is the loser thereby—that is justice; had I known of the intention I would have protested against its being placed where it cannot be seen, and would have presented a memorial to the Queen to allow it to be put elsewhere, as the Dean and Chapter have refused to give up their fee of £200. . . .

Jan. 25th . . . A letter forwarded by Miss Fenwick announcing the expected death of Miss Wordsworth. Mrs. Wordsworth can hardly write, still less able to see what she writes. . . .

Jan. 27th . . . From Ambleside I had a letter from William Wordsworth announcing the death of his aunt, an excellent person. But William Wordsworth wrote that I should be shocked to hear of what in itself was rather to be rejoiced at than deplored—she had been many years imbecile —and for which I had been prepared by a letter Miss Fenwick had forwarded from Mrs. Wordsworth received two days before. . . .

Feb. 20th . . . Finished the second volume of Lady Blessington's *Life.* Could I consider it as an honour to be named in such a book I might be vain. It appears there four times—pp. [blank], 346, 367, and 372. Lady Blessington wishes she saw more of me,—says I have a sound head. At least, not so foolish an encomium as the Herzogin von Weimar's *zarte Empfindung.* Landor's good word is worth a good deal more, but not much, from his want of judgment. He calls me the honestest of lawyers, as he used to do. One of his references is to his letters about Wordsworth, which are to be preserved. They may be worth printing hereafter. . . . Landor's letters are the best; but it is a very catch-penny book. . . .

FEB. 25th . . . I have remarked tonight in Jeremy Bentham an excellence I never suspected him of possessing—humour in his family letters.

I have since begun Burton's[1] own summary, and I find *now* no inclination to adopt Bentham's Greatest Happiness principle, though I perceive it to be rather a violation of good taste than logically wrong; and I have not yet found the solution of the riddle as to *selfishness*. Bentham maintains that the greatest happiness is secured by each man attending to his own, which is true only in a state of *perfect wisdom*, in which alone 'true self-love and social is the same.'

FEB. 26th . . . I spent several hours upstairs arranging my books—a disagreeable but necessary work. The quantity is immense. The worthlessness is equally infinite. . . . I went on with Lady Blessington's *Memoirs* —a worthless book, but it makes me lose much time, for it is, after all, attractive. . . .

FEB. 28th . . . I read two chapters of Bentham. It is marvellous how many actual reforms owe their existence to his suggestion. . . . It is just midnight and I am not tired; yet I ought to feel ashamed of so lazy a life, for I spend my days without any real exercise of thought or attention whatever.

MARCH 13th . . . I had also a gratification of my vanity in looking into two volumes of the *Correspondence of Goethe and Knebel*, in which I am spoken of repeatedly by Knebel with great kindness and only a great exaggeration of qualities of which there may be some. . . .

MARCH 16th . . . I also wrote a letter, long on my mind, to Lady Byron about Lord Byron's religious opinions, and the injury done him by his Calvinistic faith, in which I quite agreed with her. . . .

MARCH 23rd . . . Had a short interview with Kenyon. He is still poorly and said he had lived long enough to consider death as a *refuge*. A just thought on many occasions, but it is an evidence of a low state of spirits. Were we to lose him it would be a loss to the community. He makes many happy through his wealth. I should feel it the more on account of his kind expressions about me. *Er meinte es bloss in einem praktischen Sinn —aber nach Mrs. Bayne—sagte er hält mich fur den weisesten der Menschen.* That is, I know how to be happy. . . .

MAY 15th . . . A strange letter received on Tuesday from Lewes,[2] the

[1] John Hill Burton assisted Bowring to edit Bentham's works and to write his life. He published *Benthamiana* in 1843.

[2] G. H. Lewes.

philosopher, though never introduced to me. Yet on the strength of his reputation as a man of letters he asked me to give him some anecdotes about Goethe for a forthcoming Life! I am glad that I have not been induced to send a more favourable answer to his request, which I must now give him. He signs [*sic*] 'Dear Sir,' though we have never seen each other. The only thing I like in the letter is the absence of flattery and compliments. He lives with Miss Evans [George Eliot], and Thornton Hunt [Leigh Hunt's son] with Mrs. Lewes. . . .

MAY 20th . . . [Letter] to George Henry Lewes declining to give him any reminiscences or letters, as the incidents have little value independent of the personal relations, and hinting at my contempt for the modern opinion of Goethe. . . .

JUNE 20th . . . Palmer, my acquaintance in Wales and landscape-painter, sent me a formal introduction to Gilchrist, who is writing a *Life of Blake*. Gilchrist's letter to me I took no notice of before, but now I wrote in a friendly tone to him and asked him to breakfast with me. . . .

JUNE 23rd . . . I had an agreeable [chat] with . . . Monckton Milnes, especially about Blake's biographer. . . . Monckton Milnes has shown him all his engravings and drawings by Blake. . . .

JUNE 28th I had Gilchrist with me four hours talking about Blake. . . . He is a young man, fair in complexion and zealous for his subject. I read him my notes of a conversation with Blake, but I would not trust him with the manuscript. . . . He is desirous to consider Blake as an enthusiast, not as an *insane* man; but such a question, whether he were or not insane, is a mere question of words. . . .

JULY 14th . . . I breakfasted with Kenyon and had a most agreeable two hours with his party. Kenyon was himself apparently in low spirits or not in high health. The Brownings were the attraction. Mrs. Browning when Miss Barrett was an object of compassion. Now, no one would think she had ever been ill. She talks freely and well and does not now affect the invalid. But the conversation was easy and on popular subjects. Browning was talking *tête-à-tête* with Edward Kenyon, and Miss Bayley and Miss Courtenay were the others. I left at half-past twelve.

AUG. 1st . . . William Arnold is engaged on the *Economist*, and is willing to be introduced to the best among my friends here, for he will be much in London. . . . I like William better by far than Matthew. He is quite free in his opinions, and is beloved by his family. . . . I, looking over books and circulars, was able to get to bed at midnight, feeling in good spirits, rejoicing in my safe return [from Rydal], and in very good health, with a consciousness that I am approaching the close. . . .

AUG. 2nd I have now to write memoirs of the last fortnight passed in a visit to dear Mrs. Wordsworth, of which I will give a short account, disregarding as much as will be in my power the diary form, for I find it very hard to break old habits. . . . At the bottom of the Rydal Hill James was in attendance for me, and I was gratified by the pleasing appearance of Mrs. Wordsworth herself—unaltered, except somewhat less active from increased dimness of sight. . . . I laid myself down with a feeling of melancholy comfort. I found at the Mount William from Oxford and Mr. Carter as fresh as ever. . . . I took with me Robertson's *Sermons*, intending to try how they would be relished by so pious, but yet somewhat timid a Christian as Mrs. Wordsworth. I began by reading two a day, but she allowed of interruptions. And though, on the whole, the experiment succeeded, yet I could perceive that she was several times alarmed (as at the Sabbath Sermon) and had some apprehension all might not be right with his orthodoxy. She did not *say* as much, and perhaps it was my fear only. The fame of Robertson has reached this remote district, and I believe his reported discourses will do good here. I read all but five and six, and I think higher of him than ever. The Arnolds and Fletchers, perhaps, will profit by him. . . . I was surprised by a call from Harriet Martineau's niece, a pleasing girl—a general favourite. Harriet Martineau sent her to inquire how I was. . . . I have no doubt she sent that I might *not* call on her. The niece answered my intimation that I should call: 'Miss Martineau will hardly be able to see you. She spends the morning writing—(it is said she is dictating her Life to Atkinson) and in the afternoon she is fatigued.' I replied: 'I will at all events leave my card, and hope I shall see her.' The day before I left Rydal I meant to call, but it rained hard; I sent an apologetic message by Mrs. Gaskell, and on the day of my leaving called on her by her own desire, and found her very comfortable. She manifests great strength of character in her last illness, and will leave not altogether a bad name behind her—but for her infidelity even a good one. She is allowed to be benevolent and sincere, and her faults are presumption and, towards others, overbearing; but I feel respect for her and good will. . . .

SEPT. 13th . . . Reading . . . *David Copperfield*. Certainly this novel has the merit of great truth. It has the general character of Dickens's later novels. Peggotty, the honest servant, the weak mother, the tyrannical stepfather, the old school system in all its worthlessness, the honest seaman, etc., all well exposed. The scene is Blunderstone in Suffolk. Dickens knows, at all events, the Suffolk words: 'mawther' and 'bor' constantly occur. . . .

SEPT. 15th . . . I went on with *David Copperfield*. For its truth it is superior to most of Dickens's tales, and it is less extravagant and wild in its incidents than other tales, which is also a merit. . . .

SEPT. 24th . . . I read several pages in the admirable *David Copperfield.*

SEPT. 29th . . . Finishing *David Copperfield* the forenoon, I wrote a short account of the story, or rather of the characters, and I took from the library the volume of Ruskin's Edinburgh *Lectures.* It begins charmingly and the earnestness is an excuse for the arrogance. . . .

SEPT. 30th . . . I also went [on with] a very exciting book—Ruskin's *Lectures.* . . .

OCT. 2nd . . . I was reading Ruskin's *Lectures*, which I finished. It is an attractive book, though he does not make out his case in honour of the Pre-Raphaelites and Turner as he ought, to use language so dogmatic. But it is a book from which much may be learned.

OCT. 3rd . . . Read in the *National*, an able but an unsatisfactory paper on Tennyson. Over-praised, I think. But *Maud* justly declared to be unworthy of him.

OCT. 19th . . . Concluded the day with Kenyon. Procter, alias Barry Cornwall, a man of sorrows in appearance, most amiable and generous and good—a sort of Christ, without his divinity. Forster, coarse and almost offensive by violence and loudness of voice; but the *Examiner* thrives under his management. . . .

[*Travel Journal: Bath.*] Nov. 8th . . . I called on Landor. . . . He received me most cordially, and was in his usual jovial mood, but with some diminution of strength. He was looking thin. But he became lively. Insisted on my staying to dinner, and I did remain till half-past six with him. We were quite alone. He spoke on the old topics, and was as extravagant as ever in his judgments. He does not forgive Louis Napoleon for restoring the Pope, but cares not for the assumption of power. 'I saw him,' he said, 'on his flight from Ham at Gore House. "I wish you joy, *mon prince*, on a double escape from a prison and a throne. Whether on a throne or in a prison I shall always see you with pleasure." I have written my mind to him since he became emperor. He is the greatest statesman living; much greater than the first Napoleon. He was a low fellow and had no tact.' I avoided unpleasant topics, but not unfriendly names. He spoke with indifference of the world, cares not when he dies. He says: 'I have let Louis Napoleon know that if any man flies to England for refuge, having failed in an attempt to assassinate him, I will allow him an annuity of £15 for his life.' He reads nothing. His house is full of paintings, and he pointed out some half-dozen, each the very finest that ever was painted. He has lost his taste for poetry. A kind expression when I left him.

Hopes always to see me when I come to Bath. His children are all idlers, and will do nothing. They have talent without application.

Nov. 21st . . . I read chiefly in Lewes's *Life of Goethe*. I am better pleased with it than I expected. It is written with more *Germanism* than *spirituality* certainly; but at all events it is a book that fully appreciates the magnitude and superiority of Goethe. I could correct a few points—errors in fact—but of no great moment. . . .

Nov. 25th . . . Went on with Goethe's *Life*; I feel deeply interested in it. Not that I am by any means satisfied with the author as the right man. His moral tone is low. . . .

Nov. 26th . . . I went on with the second volume of Lewes's *Goethe*. I am too much interested by it to proceed rapidly, and I find many things quite new. . . .

Dec. 3rd . . . I finished Lewes's *Life*. A book which has given me much pleasure. On the whole, better than I could have expected. . . .

Dec. 18th . . . The incident of the day is the death of Rogers—long expected. . . . Rogers, without being a poet, was a maker of good verse, and held a place in society which none of the real poets does. His death makes a gap in society. . . . My whole evening was most pleasantly diverted from my intended occupation by looking over the fourth volume of his [Macaulay's] *History*. It is as attractive as a novel. No wonder that the third and fourth volumes have thirty thousand purchasers at thirty-six shillings each copy. Marvellous success! The volumes have indexes. So the book is delightful. . . .

Dec. 19th . . . I borrowed Sydney Smith's *Life* and read it in bed with great pleasure, and I have gone on with it today. I expect great enjoyment from it. The wit is not a mere joker's, but seriously wise. I read early in bed and since till 5 p.m. The day has been spent so that I could not do any work. . . .

Dec. 21st . . . But I could not set to any work, though I had nothing to do beyond reading Sydney Smith's *Life*. The materials make up for the bad workmanship. Yet the close of his life, when he became a defender of the corporation of Dean and Chapter, somewhat lessens him in my esteem. . . . He carried his defence too far. He makes the social relation so great as to render the spiritual influence next to nothing. The Establishment is more than the Church—a word that Sydney Smith uses more as an adjective than a substantive. . . .

Dec. 23rd . . . It is singular Miss Martineau continues to live,[1] and is coming out with a book on the factory question. . . .

Dec. 25th . . . I was engaged reading the *Life of Sydney Smith*, which

[1] She lived until 1876.

I finished. An excellent man certainly. He could as little be acquainted [*sic*] of tuft-hunting as Rogers perhaps, and his love for Lady Holland (the wife of Lord Holland) is a blot on his character. He was neither martyr nor hero nor saint, but, with all his infirmities, an amiable and admirable man. I read in his *Letters* also. . . .

1856

JAN. 8th . . . The *Letters* of Sydney Smith, since finished, impress on me the certainty of my soon being infirm. He said, when seventy-six years old, shortly before his death: 'I can't put off dying much longer, not that I am ill, but old.' This is precisely my case. I must be temperate at meals. Having finished Sydney Smith's *Life*, I must speak of it as a delightful book. . . .

JAN. 16th . . . It makes me melancholy when I think that I am unable to fix my attention on any *lecture*. I cannot listen or recollect. Yet I am as lively as ever, and repeat my old stories, alas! too often. . . .

FEB. 22nd . . . I spent several hours reading Rogers's *Table Talk*. It is certainly amusing. It has not many things which it ought not to have—that is, malignant anecdotes or ill-told *bons mots*. Yet it has a few. . . .

FEB. 28th . . . I finished the *Table Talk*. It is not so bad as the envious pretend, especially *The Times* reviewer, who spites the editor [A. Dyce]. Nor is it excellent. Amusing it must be. The account of Wordsworth's poverty will, I fear, mortify the family, though not with reason, for not to be able to eat meat more than three times a week from poverty is not dishonourable, though, to the feeling, worse. . . .

MARCH 8th . . . Spent the rest of the morning at the Athenaeum. There I read a number of the *Athenaeum*, which . . . led me to read the introduction to Collins's *Dark Hour*.[1] Son of the painter R.A., whom I knew. A promising and powerful writer of fiction. . . .

MARCH 12th . . . I lost several hours afterwards at the Literary Fund. Dilke,[2] Dickens, and Forster appeared as the advocates of a motion against the committee, but suffered a flagrant defeat. They managed their case ill. At the same time, the committee, in justification of an expensive system, so little pleased me that I came away before the vote was taken. Before the committee gained by four only, now by more than one-third,

[1] Wilkie Collins's *After Dark* appeared in 1856.

[2] Charles Wentworth Dilke, proprietor and formerly editor of the *Athenaeum*, and an important influence on his grandson the politician.

about fifteen! Dickens made a bold, clever, but imprudent speech which did harm. Forster was angry and Dilke coarse. On the other side, Bell was tedious and trickish—that is, lawyer-like, evasive; Blackmore[1] dull and offensive; Murray gave offence. Blewitt's[2] personal character was in favour of the committee, and it was alleged that a large capital was given expressly for a house. . . .

MARCH 18th I went on with my Knebel's correspondence, and to my surprise found an extravagant puff of myself which I was not aware of, though I was aware that he had written very flatteringly of me. . . .

MARCH 20th I finished in bed this day the *Correspondence of Goethe and Knebel*, a book that had deeply interested me and which exhibits the condescending love of the superior and the reverential admiration of the inferior most honourably towards both parties. My personal recollections added to my enjoyment, and though the mention of me is not flattering in the way of praise, yet I feel it as an honour to have my name even but written by the great man of his age, accompanied by the expression of or an implied good-will. . . .

MARCH 24th . . . At the Athenaeum. . . . I had a pleasant chat with Matthew Arnold and heard the north country news. . . .

MAY 31st . . . I walked back [from a dinner-party at Mrs. Bayne's] with James Spedding, who talked *tête-à-tête* about his forthcoming *Lord Bacon*. . . .

JUNE 3rd . . . I went to the Athenaeum. There I had a very pleasant chat with Arthur Stanley, biographer of Dr. Arnold. Very liberal in his writings and character. He praised highly Robertson's *Sermons* and he wishes to see my obituary paper on Robertson. Altogether, Stanley is worthy of his father.[3] . . .

JUNE 14th . . . The incident of the day was a dinner at Harness's. . . . A small party of six: one, a stranger who did not to my hearing speak a word. Mitford the writer, rather a morose but intelligent man . . . and Dyce, the repeater of Rogers's *Table Talk*. . . . He is a collector of facts, but has no skill in statement, nor perhaps judgment in selection. . . .

AUG. 14th . . . J. P. Collier . . . by the bye, has a diseased habit of dissenting from others as often as he can and loves finding fault much more than praising. . . . I went to Maidenhead from Reading. . . . At the station was Robert Proctor. He came in a little cart and drove me first to J. P. Collier's, who lives in a small neat house, where, being now in his *own* house, he receives attentions, as a man of letters, from the gentry of the

[1] R. D. Blackmore, the author of *Lorna Doone*.
[2] Octavian Blewitt, Secretary of the Royal Literary Fund.
[3] Edward Stanley, Bishop of Norwich.

neighbourhood, which he had not when he was the inmate of Robert Proctor. This flatters him as it ought, for he feels he is justly appreciated. He perhaps was never so happy as now. . . . The house empty, but I was glad to be with these friends alone.

AUG. 28th . . . Read the *Letters of Southey*, volume three. He . . . speaks of me as the friend of Wordsworth and himself. . . .

AUG. 30th . . . Went on with Southey's *Letters*. Not excellent, but to me interesting. A revival of old fading recollections. The vanity of Southey, of which too much is said, was not an unkind vanity, and his inconsistencies with reference to the Church were all creditable in his moral sense. His humanity would not permit him to believe in Hell. . . .

AUG. 31st . . . Spent all the forenoon finishing the *Letters of Southey*, in which I found nothing particularly excellent except a certain kindliness of disposition. . . .

DEC. 3rd . . . I sent off a letter to Mrs. Wordsworth with an account of the death of the Kenyons [John, Dec. 3rd, and Edward, Nov. 24th, in Vienna]—an event that will very much diminish our social enjoyments here.

DEC. 15th . . . I went to Booth's dinner. Miss Bayley alone there. . . . Towards me very kind. They give me Landor's portrait by Boxall—a handsome present, especially as I have a legacy.[1]

DEC. 17th . . . Have this morning been looking at the portrait of Walter Savage Landor by [William Fisher] sent me yesterday by Booth, the present of him and Miss Bayley. It is not what I supposed it to be, the portrait by Boxall, but more striking as a likeness. The Gallery of National Portraits might not perhaps accept it.[2] . . .

DEC. 25th . . . I dined with the Bootts. Robert Brown [the botanist] was the great, silent man; a man who will live in the memory of the scientific world uttered scarcely a word. He looked infirm, but intelligent. . . .

1857

JAN. 16th . . . I finished the *National Review*, reading last, or rather, glancing my eye over the article on the Crédit Mobilier in France, by Bagehot. Though I do not understand the subject in the least, yet the

[1] John Kenyon's executors were James Booth and Miss Bayley. The legacy was £100. Crabb Robinson had already told them he would have preferred a personal memento to a 'pecuniary legacy.'

[2] Crabb Robinson bequeathed the portrait to the National Portrait Gallery, which did accept it.

tone of it satisfies me that the article is written with intelligence. Bagehot is a man of talent unquestionably, and now a banker in the west of England. One of the best of our University College pupils. . . .

JAN. 23rd [*Manchester.*] . . . The one thing that has eclipsed all others is the Free Library. Availing itself of the Act, the city has obtained a rate for a public library intended for the use of the working class. In a large hall there were some twenty or thirty men, working-men perhaps, reading, not light and idle books. There was no impudence or impertinence or anything objectionable. There is also a news-room, and this is not the most instructive reading, but it is with this and novels, etc., that young men must begin. Above is a library of books not lent out—large, valuable books. We talked with Edwards the librarian. I was pleased with his conversation. He is a Scotchman. It seems that this is a useful establishment in every sense of the word. . . . We saw also Owens College; but neither Professor Greenwood nor Principal Scott in the college, and the naked and empty rooms could give no pleasure to us, knowing that this is an acknowledged failure. It is not in the capital of mechanical industry that the higher branches of learning can be taught. . . .

APRIL 29th . . . The forenoon was sauntered away,—the reading part consisting in a first perusal of the new and enlarged edition of *The Opium Eater*. It is rather a volume of De Quincey's autobiography than anything else, and as a writer he is indisputably one of our best. . . .

APRIL 30th . . . I read a considerable part of the day in De Quincey's enlarged *Opium Eater*. It is delightful, but it is now become more autobiographic. . . .

MAY 4th . . . I was engaged reading *The Opium Eater*, new matter in the new edition making it more like a third volume of the autobiography. Not only eloquent, he is wise, and—sad bathos—useful by drawing my attention to myself and the petty ailments in my body. I have just finished the volume five of the Selections. I long for the rest of De Quincey, and yet I neither love nor respect the man; I admire only the writer.

MAY 10th . . . I breakfasted with a party which agreed very well, and there was no want of talk between the historian Ranke and Mr. Donne for the short time he stayed. . . .

MAY 27th . . . I called on Mrs. Byles. . . . She put into my hands a tale by Anthony Trollope, which I have since read. A singular history. It is a sort of controversial tale[1] with no object clearly made out. It is founded on Whiston's attack on the Deans and Chapters. A reformer occasions a bill to be filed against the Warden of an almshouse, but being in love with his daughter, at her solicitation abandons the suit, and she in

[1] *The Warden.*

gratitude consents to marry him. The Warden, being an extremely conscientious man, resigns the wardenship, though he becomes poor in consequence. The Bishop is also a conscientious man, and will not fill up the Warden's place, to the great annoyance of the Bishop's son, the Archdeacon, who alone answers to the common notion in novels and polemical writings of an archdeacon. There is a sharp satirical description of *The Times* newspaper, called *Jupiter*, and of *The Times* office, called Olympus. It is a singular book—a sort of 'wild-goose' flight. . . .

JULY 8th . . . I began *Tom Brown*—highly praised. It is dedicated to Mrs. Arnold. A school novel. The colloquial style and country dialect are well preserved. . . .

JULY 13th . . . I spent the rest of the day at the Athenaeum reading great part of *Tom Brown*. It turns out a *serious* schoolboy novel, and by not beginning with the religion produces a good effect. One is caught, and the religion is rational. The Doctor and Mrs. Arnold are kept in the background. It will have a good effect and serve to improve public schools. . . .

JULY 15th . . . I finished the *Tom Brown's Schooldays*. It is an excellent book—the author's name, Hughes. The religious tone is not remarkable at the beginning. One acknowledges the fidelity of the description and respects the talents of the writer before one has any inducement to ask: Is this or not *cant*? The author's health was given at the late Rugby dinner. He is a layman. I still think the fagging scandal too lightly treated. . . .

JULY 24th . . . At eight precisely was at St. Martin's Hall. . . . I was at the end of the stalls nearly, so that in a full hall I heard little or nothing. I knew the *Carol* and did not like it. But I had heard Dickens's reading praised highly, and it is mortifying to hear loud laughing or clapping and not be able to join, so that there being a pause at the end of the hour, I made up my mind to leave the hall, but on going down the centre walk I was stopped by Herbert . . . and in the kindest way Herbert insisted on my taking his place. I did enjoy the latter part heartily, and could then perceive the merits of Dickens as a reader. . . . After the reading I had a friendly shake of the hand from the lecturer. . . .

SEPT. 14th . . . I was also engaged reading, what I have this morning been finishing, a remarkable essay on *Oxford Studies*, in the *Oxford Essays*, by Pattison. A remarkable paper in which all the faults of Oxford are freely acknowledged. One wonders that from Oxford such a paper could proceed, especially in connection with other Oxford writers,—really *liberality*. Yet Pattison has no respect for the London party and has the aristocratic attachment for Alma Mater, but so modified I have all respect for it. I am, however, painfully impressed with my own incapacity to sit in judgment upon it. It is almost an impertinence my reading it. Yet something I have learned from it, and I find certain favourite notions of my own confirmed. . . .

SEPT. 15th . . . This day . . . spent in reading a paper on Alfred de Musset by Palgrave, Fellow of Exeter College. Remarkable is the paper from that quarter. How German principles of taste have found their way in our High Church periodical press! The *Oxford Essays* might be called the Oxford magazine. Palgrave praises all the poets, German and French, whom he ought to have abused, true to his party. . . .

OCT. 1st . . . I began to skim a volume of Hugh Miller's *First Impressions of England*. A remarkable man, by far the greatest of the self-educated original characters. This is the least valuable of his books, probably. . . .

OCT. 8th . . . I began . . . *Eöthen*. A very smart book. I think I must have read it before.[1] It is pleasantly written. But Kinglake's levity is such as to make his *serious* passages unpleasant. When he writes in an *orthodox* tone, and even as a *believer*, one cannot help suspecting him of insincerity. . . .

OCT. 9th . . . And I have now just finished it in bed. There is an audacity about the book that amuses the indulgent reader. The traveller says he saw the ruins of Baalbec, but will not disturb the awful impression the name inspires by giving dimensions of pillars, and adds as if chuckling: 'I think I got cleverly out of the Baalbec scrape.' Serjeant Kinglake is an M.P. and an advocate of some repute. . . .

1858

JAN. 3rd . . . Read an interesting paper in the *National Review* making a respectable poet known to me, Coventry Patmore. He is of the Wordsworth school of thought apparently, feebler, of course. . . .

JAN. 15th I began in bed the article in the *National* on Buckle on *Civilization*. The book is by every one said to be very valuable, and from the first half of the article I suspect it is written by Martineau or perhaps by Hutton.[2] It is very interesting—full of thought, but some expressions (a few only) bespeak the writer who *hunts* for the proper *expression*.

I have since found the article is by Hutton. It is highly praised by Tayler and Martineau. He is rising rapidly in public estimation and is fortunate in his private relations. He is about to be married. . . .

[1] He had. See *supra*, Oct. 14th, 1844.
[2] R. H. Hutton, later editor of the *Spectator*.

FEB. 14th . . . This is what I wrote in F. Sharpe's album, which filled the little page, the left side being uniformly to be filled up by the owner: 'Were this my last hour, and that of an octogenarian cannot be far off, I would thank God for permitting me to behold so much of the excellence conferred on individuals. Of woman, I saw the type of her heroic greatness in the person of Mrs. Siddons, of her fascinations in Mrs. Jordan and Mlle. Mars. I listened with rapture to the dreamy monologues of Coleridge, "that old man eloquent." I travelled with Wordsworth, the greatest of our lyrico-philosophical poets. I relished the wit and pathos of Charles Lamb. I conversed freely with Goethe at his own table: beyond all competition the supreme genius of his age and country. He acknowledged his obligations only to Shakespeare, Spinoza, and Linnaeus, as Wordsworth, when he resolved to be a poet, feared competition only with Chaucer, Spenser, Shakespeare, and Milton. Compared with Goethe, the memory of Schiller, Wieland, Herder, Tieck, the Schlegels and Schelling has become faint.'—H.C.R.

MARCH 16th . . . At the request of Scharf,[1] looked at painting by Cary of dear Charles Lamb. In no one respect a likeness; thoroughly bad. Complexion, figure, expression, all unlike. But for 'Elia' on a paper, I should not have [thought] it possible that [it] could be meant for Charles Lamb.

MARCH 30th . . . Read two *Times*. In one a frightful description of the prisons in Canton. This *Times* Special Correspondent is really a power in the state. In every country the marvellous establishment has its representative, and in the Crimean war actually took upon itself to distribute charity which the Government neglected to do. There is much of envy in the hatred of the Press expressed by Paynter, Hunter, etc. During my short connection with *The Times*, fifty years ago, it was in its infancy. . . .

APRIL 27th . . . Lady Byron . . . is reading Hogg's *Life of Shelley*. A bad book, she says, but most interesting to her. She never saw either Shelley or Mrs. Shelley. Has a great [?] sense of Shelley's greatness. . . .

MAY 20th . . . Why do I make such insignificant remarks? It is that, living alone, I gossip in my journal, saying on paper what I have none to *say* to in speech.

MAY 26th . . . We drove to St. Martin's Hall, and being in the front row I heard to perfection what I in a back could not have heard with pleasure. Dickens is an admirable reader—his voice clear and melodious,

[1] Sir George Scharf, as he eventually became, was Secretary and later Director of the National Portrait Gallery. A double-portrait of Lamb and his sister by F. S. Cary was accepted by the Gallery in 1895.

his humour strong. The pathos recording Scrooge's conversion to benevolence by the Spirit's sights was enough to bring a hearer to tears. The large hall was full, and it holds many. This must be a *popular* divertissement not equalled by the evening's entertainment. . . .

JUNE 10th . . . The great traveller Robert Brown died in the forenoon. . . . A great man of science, and morally most excellent, has departed. His simplicity and *naiveté* and benignity were charming. He once breakfasted with me, and was always friendly. . . .

JULY 8th . . . Young men now come to me as an old man who has seen and known great men of a past age. Sixty years ago I sought the company of such persons.

JULY 10th . . . I have gone on with the *National* and read two light articles, one on Kingsley's poetry—a very high appreciation of the author's prose writings, and a subtly discriminating refusal to him of the poetical faculty. A slashing exposure of Martin Tupper, with an ingenious explanation of the cause of his popularity. His bombastic commonplaces suit the taste of uneducated readers, and they are now the greater majority. . . .

JULY 13th . . . I then was again fortunate in finding Miss Coutts at home, also Mrs. Brown, who has been very ill. A very friendly chat about Dickens's unwise advertisement of domestic calamities. Miss Coutts is satisfied there has been nothing criminal—nothing beyond *incompatibilité d'humeur*—to require a separation, which should have been done quietly. Miss Coutts is friendly with both husband and wife. . . . Neither of them [Cookson and Field, his legal advisers] can give me any aid as to the use to be made of my reminiscences hereafter. These and my numerous letters give me a great deal of trouble, and I know no one to whom I can entrust them. . . .

JULY 15th . . . I wrote to Lady Byron returning a letter from one of the Shelley family on the subject of the scandalous *Life of Shelley* by my old acquaintance, Hogg. The family have taken away the papers lent him. My fear now is that there may be a suppression of facts and documents in themselves valuable. Shelley, as I wrote to Lady Byron this morning, was one of the four masters of poetry in that age, viz. Byron, Coleridge, Shelley, and Wordsworth. . . .

JULY 24th [*Rydal.*] . . . In the evening after our early dinner I read parts of *The Prelude* to dear Mrs. Wordsworth. The freedom of this poem, expressed as it is towards the Heads of Houses, robbed the statue of many subscribers. The Dons could not well forgive the personification:

> And blind Authority beating with his staff
> The child that might have led him.

SEPT. 9th . . . I had got interested in *Westward Ho!* A book, however, as little agreeable on the whole as any of Kingsley's writings. . . .

SEPT. 10th . . . Went on with *Westward Ho!* A most unequal work. . . .

SEPT. 14th . . . Now that I have finished *Westward Ho!* I will say that it is one of the least agreeable to my taste of any I have read by him. It may be my fault. The incidents, if invented, are disagreeable; if copied, ill-managed. The Indian maid has no keeping. I fear it has been produced by the wish to produce a vulgar hatred of Popery. His natural history wearies me, and nautical language bores, etc. . . .

1859

JAN. 1st . . . Today I received a letter from Rydal Mount announcing the expected death of Mrs. Wordsworth—a few lines so ill-written as to be hardly legible, and I know not whether written by John Wordsworth or his wife. She is said to be aware of her condition—quite resigned. . . .

JAN. 3rd The early post brought me a most unexpected letter from John Wordsworth, announcing a marvellous change in his mother. Dr. Davy, who had despaired, was full of hope. Her appetite had returned, she had slept well, and there were no bad symptoms! . . . Of course, I sent a few lines of congratulation. One could not wonder were her death announced today, she being in her eighty-ninth year! . . .

JAN. 19th This morning arrived the news of the death of dear Mrs. Wordsworth on Monday night. I wish I could venture down to show my reverence for her! But to attend a funeral would be dangerous in this weather. . . .

JAN. 25th . . . The obituary of Mrs. Wordsworth appeared first in the *Daily News.* A circumstance hardly necessary to satisfy one that Harriet Martineau is the author. It has sly insinuations against the poet, who is throughout referred to only as the 'old husband,' who aggravated Mrs. Wordsworth's grief by his selfish weeping and mourning at the death of Mrs. Quillinan. . . .

FEB. 4th . . . William Wordsworth . . . gave me an interesting account of the last days of his honoured mother. For a fortnight before her death her hearing was partly recovered, also she had some sense of light. She was perfectly happy. She desired five pounds to be given me that I might buy with it a ring. This was given to me as one of the oldest of her friends next to her relations. I accept this with pleasure, but I shall return it to some of the grandchildren. I cannot mix it with other money.

William Wordsworth had to call on Miss Gillies about the portrait of Mr. and Mrs. Wordsworth, etc. I accompanied him to her, but came back alone. William Wordsworth took luncheon with me. I shall see him on Wednesday. This was a very interesting call. The Mount will be quitted in a few months. I shall, I suppose, never see it again! This is a sad rent in the structure of my friendships.

FEB. 15th . . . I could only manage to . . . attend the Photographic Society, where I heard a lecture on Architecture from George Street, Ruskin in the chair. I dare not pretend to say that I brought away any definite ideas on art, and yet I really enjoyed the addresses of both and felt, as I used to feel from the German professors, as if some feelings were sowed in me which would produce fruit hereafter though unconsciously. The meanness of Ruskin's countenance struck me, but it was overpowered by a display of power in style and promptitude of manner. I felt increasing respect for Street. He read his lecture too rapidly. It consisted mainly of an explanation of the photographic representation of the buildings in Venice and Verona. Both were the objects of warm eulogy. Ruskin could not help hinting that the value of these representations is increased by the peril in which the originals were likely to be thrown by their becoming the seats of war—Verona especially. . . .

MARCH 4th . . . Began *Adam Bede*, a much-prized new volume by Eliot. . . .

MARCH 10th . . . I also went on with *Adam Bede*. Its conversational style is admirable, though I know not that its dialect is quite correct historically. . . .

MARCH 15th . . . I went on with *Adam Bede*. It has an established reputation. . . .

MARCH 16th . . . At the Athenaeum I found *Adam Bede* on the table and applied myself steadily to it. . . . I have read one-half. It does not yet become impassioned, but the quiet humour goes on—somewhat less pungent perhaps—till the young Squire's majority is celebrated. . . .

MARCH 19th . . . The day devoted to *Adam Bede*, of which I retain a very high opinion, though the tragic part is not so excellent as the comic. I read a whole volume, tragic description allowing of much skip. . . .

MARCH 22nd . . . I finished *Adam Bede*. Towards the close the interest flags. The dialogue loses its spirit. Adam, falling in love with Dinah, the Methodist, and she returning his affection, become commonplace. Arthur, the repentant seducer, after the interesting interview with Adam, who forgives him, is lost sight of. But with all this the novel will hold its place. . . .

APRIL 1st . . . The thoughtful essay on *Liberty* by John Mill greatly pleased me. The importance Mill attaches to the indulgence of individuality in opposition to following the public taste is to me both new and instructive. In like manner I looked into J. Austin's pamphlet on *Parliamentary Reform*. Pleased that both have greatly modified their opinions and are more conservative than in their youth. . . .

APRIL 16th [*Brighton.*] . . . I called on Lady Byron at three and found a very interesting man, a Mr. MacDonald,[1] author of a poem, *Within and Without*, which I must read. He is an invalid and a German scholar. The talk was altogether interesting. He will call on me. . . . A pleasing letter from the Provost of Eton (Hawtrey) thanking me for recommending him to read *Adam Bede*, which he praises as warmly as every one does, including Lady Byron, etc. . . .

APRIL 17th . . . Will Arnold died at Gibraltar. . . . Matthew Arnold has a mission abroad to see the state of schools, etc. . . .

APRIL 18th . . . I had a call from . . . Mr. MacDonald, who stayed till near two. He is, I know now, a literator by profession, and I have no doubt a meritorious man whom it will be a pleasure to serve. His connections are among the Dissenters—visits Russell Gurney and William Kent—yet is quite liberal. He is a lecturer, and in that way one can serve him. I was named to him by Scott of Manchester. He is married and lives at Hastings. . . . Of his works hereafter. . . .

MAY 13th . . . I read in bed a very pleasing short article in the *Daily News*, on the auction of furniture at Rydal Mount, by Harriet Martineau, done with great propriety and in a better feeling than I should have given her credit for. . . .

MAY 26th . . . I subscribed to Mudie's Library, as I have long intended. My immediate object was to read MacDonald's *Within and Without*, a dramatic poem, dreamy and metaphysical. By no means calculated to be popular. A jumble of sentimentality and speculation. . . .

MAY 27th . . . One of the songs is said to be sung or said *within* the singer. . . .

MAY 30th . . . I went to Mudie's for the poems of MacDonald, which I fear will puzzle more than please me. I have already met with many passages full of thought but hard to retain. I attended his first lecture on Walter Scott. His lecture on Scott was but thinly attended—chiefly ladies. His judgment I concurred in generally. Only Scott's descriptive power was praised. Ruskin's overpraise censured. MacDonald has to manage his voice, which is disagreeable from over-loudness. . . . I was made uncomfortable by the feeling that I was unable to render others the services I wish. . . .

[1] George MacDonald (1824–1905), poet and novelist, author of *Phantastes*.

JUNE 3rd . . . [MacDonald's] lecture on Lord Byron was worse attended than the first on Scott, and MacDonald read so low that he was not audible. . . . His apology for the poet was generous and full of feeling, and this Lady Byron acknowledges, but I fear the general impression was not favourable. . . .

JUNE 7th . . . I heard today the third lecture of MacDonald, on Shelley. . . . Half the time was spent in making a vain attempt to distinguish intelligibly between Imagination and Fancy; Wordsworth, Coleridge, and De Quincey had failed before. He apologised for the atheism of Shelley. . . . I took at Mudie's, volume one of Hogg's *Shelley*, which I have already nearly finished. Meant to skim only, but I have found it better than I expected. Indeed, bad as Hogg's portion may be, Shelley's letters are excellent, at least, much is deeply interesting, and the account of the journey to Scotland by Hogg to meet his friend on his marriage is written with spirit, though evidently spun out. . . .

JUNE 10th . . . MacDonald's lecture on Keats. . . . I . . . wish he could be more popular even though he sacrificed some portion of his philosophical truth. I could not enter into the spirit of much that he said as to Keats's poetical merits. This may well be my fault or misfortune, not *his*. . . .

JUNE 11th . . . I went on with Hogg's *Shelley*. Disliking the book exceedingly, I still went on with it. . . .

JUNE 13th . . . I have just finished it. . . . A worse book was never written. The family have taken away his papers and the present Lady Shelley is to go on with his *Life*. . . .

JUNE 28th Nearly the whole of the morning in bed; in the evening at the Athenaeum; and again this morning have been devoted to Rogers's *Recollections*, which I have finished. W. Sharpe has been fastidious. It wants bulk, and in the fear of being accused of *making* a book, he has not made enough of a book. I wish I had met with it a few years ago, as it has suggested to me how my reminiscences should be treated—*Selections from the Reminiscences of H.C.R.*, and a few letters. But it is too late now for me to do anything, but after my death such a volume double the size might be produced. But by whom? Aye, there's the rub. . . .

JULY 2nd . . . Another unpleasant subject was matter for talk at Hunter's. A very severe attack on J. P. Collier's volume of Shakespeare which he published as an important discovery, containing, as he maintained, *contemporaneous emendations*. The volume being suspected, the Duke of Devonshire, whose property it had become, let it be examined at the British Museum, one of whose officers, Hamilton, puts his name to a charge of fraud, not against Collier, though if all the facts are as he states them—I need not go into the particulars of what will hereafter be easy of reference—they will sadly detract from J. P. Collier's character as a critic. His enemies will, of course, ascribe to him *privity*, though that seems absurd. . . .

JULY 7th . . . I had a kind letter from Collier, and I read in *The Times* his absolute denial of all privity in the fraud, if any. He waives any defence of the genuineness of the document. His letter is short and quiet and so far dignified. . . .

JULY 15th Mr. MacDonald breakfasted with me, and after breakfast he heard from Miss A. Swanwick that he had been actually elected Professor of English Literature at the Ladies' College, a very poorly remunerated office, but he thinks it may lead to something better. . . .

JULY 16th . . . Called on Hunter. We did not allude either to the Collier-Shakespeare question (other writers go on to prove the ungenuineness of the emendations). . . . Lest I forget it, I must now say that MacDonald told me that he had seen a letter in the handwriting of Lewes, who lives with Miss Evans (it was after his wife had run away from him to Thornton Hunt that she took his[1] wife's place), that Miss Evans is the author of *Adam Bede*. I would rather so excellent [?] a book was written by any man than a woman, and worse, that of all women the translatress of Strauss should be the writer. Such a fact destroys all comfortable notions of right and wrong, true and false, as they make the writer quite independent of personal character. Yet I am glad on looking back that I liked her much.

JULY 17th . . . I do not like to state to any one that so admirable a book has been written by a woman whose history is at least so unfortunate as Miss Evans's. It disturbs one's idea that a book should be the reflection of the author's innermost practical feelings. . . .

JULY 23rd . . . I began a new novelist[2] and have found great pleasure in Anthony Trollope's *Barchester Towers*. His picture of the dramatis personae of his cathedral town is quite delightful, as far as the first nine chapters go. It is quite an event falling in with a new favourite author. . . .

JULY 24th I went on with *Barchester Towers* with great pleasure, continuing it in the Hampstead omnibus, and during a short walk on the Heath. . . .

JULY 28th . . . The rest of the day was spent at Stratton Street [Miss Coutts's] and the Athenaeum. There was a crowd of genteel people. . . .

[1] From here to the end of the entry is scratched through after being much corrected. Crabb Robinson got drowsy while writing—a not unusual occurrence, though on this occasion it happened after breakfast. On the following day he rewrites the phrases.

[2] See *supra*, May 27th 1857.

I was sorry to find that in general the public voice is against Collier about his volume of Shakespeare. I can't believe in his being a party to the fraud. . . .

JULY 29th . . . I went on at intervals reading *Barchester Towers*, which I did not finish till past midnight. An excellent novel with a unique character. . . .

AUG. 3rd [*Bury*.] . . . Wrote . . . a letter to Miss Bayley,[1] recommending *Adam Bede*, and writing of Miss Evans, the author. . . .

AUG. 6th . . . I received a very pleasant letter from Miss Bayley, written with her usual strong and sound sense. She means to become acquainted with Mr. Lewes and Miss Evans, who live in her neighbourhood, and, while she acknowledges the necessity of conventionalities, considers theirs as a case of exception. . . .

AUG. 18th [*Bury*.] . . . I also went to the Library, from which I took a volume of *Blackwood* and have begun one of the *Scenes of Clerical Life*. It is cast in the same mould as *Adam Bede*. The same excellent dialogue. The contrast between the ruffianly anti-religious spirit operating on the vulgar commonplace people of the Establishment and the silly Evangelicals betrays in reality a spirit more unfavourable to religion than anything in *Adam Bede* and more like what might be expected from the translatress of Strauss's *Leben Jesu*.

AUG. 21st . . . I finished *Janet's Repentance*. It is so very Evangelical in its tone that it is quite unpleasant thinking of it as the writing of Miss Evans. I have since met in the *Saturday Review* some admirable remarks on this fact, and I suspect with a silent reference to the works of this author—that in this age men write wisely and beautifully but without any actual belief in what themselves write. One excuses this in so great a man as Goethe. He is the perfect artist; as such he represents his class in Emerson's little book of Characteristics.[2] One is not displeased on reading (at least, I am not) Goethe's *Confessions of a Beautiful Soul*, but the *Repentance of Janet* I should have read with some pleasure from a regular Evangelical or pious High Church—Miss Sewell. I was not annoyed by anything in *Adam Bede*, but in *Janet* there is what I cannot think to be other than cant. I should unwillingly impute any actual insincerity to anything that she writes.

AUG. 23rd . . . At night I read *Aurora Leigh*.[3] I cannot take to it.

AUG. 24th I have dozed evening and morning over this poem. It is a weariness and surely loss of time to hunt for passages to copy as evidence

[1] Kenyon's friend.

[2] *Representative Men*.

[3] By Elizabeth Barrett Browning.

of having read the book. The style is very, very strange, and with difficulty could I fix my attention to it. . . .

Nov. 11th . . . I read S. Sharpe's memoirs of his uncle, Samuel Rogers. It has the great merit of being judicious and temperate—no violent praise or puffing—perhaps too brief and dry; but if a fault, on the right side.

Nov. 14th . . . I did nothing but read in Ruskin the lecture on Iron. . . . It is very beautiful. Ruskin gives all the credit to Iron as the oxidising principle, which is found among the kinds of earth. Rust is Iron turned to account. This lecture is full of matter. After treating of its nature, he eloquently expatiates on the Plough as the instrument of labour by which the earth is rendered fertile and on which he gives you an admirable sermon. Though a great anti-Papist, he does not spare the Protestant, in the course of a vehement declamation against the cruelty to the poor practised by our reckless traders, whose failures bring ruin on the masses. . . .

Nov. 19th . . . I began *John Halifax, Gentleman.*[1] . . . It is at the beginning very attractive. . . . I expect a remarkable book. . . .

Nov. 26th I had an hour's reading in bed—in *John Halifax*—with great enjoyment. The election scene, however, is the least correct of any, but it is an efficient one for effect. . . . The latter end, however, is not so interesting as the earlier portion. The interest ceases for the present after the death of Muriel, the blind child. . . .

Nov. 30th I read early and I read late *John Halifax*, and finished it. A capital novel, but it is inartificial, being without unity. It contains the history of several generations and comprehends more than sufficient to explain Miss Mulock's idea of a gentleman. . . .

1860

Feb. 15th . . . I also looked into the attack on Collier by a Museum man. He accuses Collier on grounds purely physical and material of having practised tricks on manuscripts. I have never thought my old friend capable of so unworthy an act. Indeed, if he were guilty I could not call him my friend. . . .

Feb. 19th . . . She [Mrs. Proctor] brought me an *Athenaeum* to read the defence of J. P. Collier against the malignant charges brought against him, in which he has been successful beyond my expectation. His tone is

[1] By Dinah Maria Mulock.

manly and simple, and will propitiate many, and I see no fault in any part of his reasonings, though some faults may have escaped me. The defence is by the editor, Dixon,[1] the defender of Penn against Macaulay, acute and contemptuous—too much so, if it were not for the gentler spirit of Collier himself. . . .

MARCH 26th My attention was this day directed to another subject—the sale by auction of the paintings of the Pattissons at Christie's, King Street. . . . The gems of the sale were several by Turner. One magnificent large picture of Venice fetched 2,400 guineas! The announcement produced a burst of applause. . . .

APRIL 1st . . . I sat up late looking over Smiles's *Self-Help*; a paltry book. . . .

APRIL 5th . . . Here [at the Athenaeum] I was accosted in a friendly tone by Carlyle—Thomas Carlyle. He was called off, and perhaps it was as well, for we might have stumbled on disagreeable topics. . . .

APRIL 12th . . . I read the *Autobiography* [Leigh Hunt's]. I feel somewhat kindly towards Hunt, but very little respect. . . .

APRIL 18th . . . A considerable part of the day was spent in reading the first volume of *The Mill on the Floss* with great pleasure. . . .

APRIL 21st . . . I finished volume two of the novel in bed. . . . The novel absorbed my attention. . . .

APRIL 23rd I finished early *The Mill on the Floss.* A novel of great ability. It is not altogether a pleasant story. The hero and heroine are a brother and sister, Tom and Maggie Tulliver. Their father, a weak man, ruins his family and dies in debt. Tom, proud and insolent, devotes himself to redeem the family honour and succeeds in obtaining possession of the Mill. Maggie forms an attachment to a cripple—Philip, the son of their family enemy Wakem, a lawyer—but has to encounter the curse of her brother if she follow her inclination. And, in fact, this passion is overcome by another for a handsome youth who is betrothed to her cousin, Lucy, a sweet girl, a contrast to her heroic character. Her mother has three sisters, exquisitely drawn characters, true to nature like Miss Austen's—natural figures. This lover, Stephen, seduces her into a boat on the Floss, and then, against her will, she is compelled to take refuge in a vessel; though she acts like a heroine on this occasion, yet, being several days absent, her tale of innocence is not believed, and she is deserted by her brother and every one, living in a hovel with a packman, a capital character. She is alone aware of a rising flood. For the moment saves her brother, but at last both are drowned in each other's arms—from the Mill. As in Bulwer's Greek tale [*The Last Days of Pompeii*?],

[1] William Hepworth Dixon.

a natural event determines the fate of the parties, and no act of theirs. A sad fault. I reproached Bulwer with this, and he had no apology for it. Mrs. Glegg and Mrs. Pullet are admirable comic pictures. Its moral pure. But nothing in it equal to Mrs. Poyser. . . .

. . . Coming home a party at Barrett's was breaking up, one of whom was the poet laureate (Tennyson), who reminded me of having dined together at Rogers's when Mrs. Norton was there.[1] I showed him I had not forgotten the scene, and quoted his words that when she looked at him he felt as if a serpent [?] was crawling down his back. 'A savage speech,' he said. . . .

MAY 2nd . . . A friendly call from J. P. Collier. . . . I confessed my inability to judge of the literary merits of his volume, but that I always asserted my belief in his integrity. . . .

JUNE 8th . . . MacDonald's lecture . . . hardly authorised the sacrifice I made to attend it—on my own account certainly not. It was on Tennyson. Extravagantly praised. It contained elaborately composed sentences. I was for ever whispering: '*May* be so—may be *not*.' I did not feel his eulogy to be true. . . .

AUG. 10th . . . My first call was on Mrs. Dyer, the laundress, wife and widow of George,[2] who attains her ninety-ninth year on the seventh of December. If cleanliness be next to godliness, it must be acknowledged she is far off from being a good woman. Yet what strength of character and animal nature! She was in an arm-chair. The apartment at the top of Clifford's Inn, No. 1, small and seemingly full of inhabitants. A child was playing about—her great-grandchild. It fell out of a window thirty-six feet from the ground and was uninjured by the fall. She has her eyesight, and hearing me, guessed who I was. She spoke in warm praise of Charles and Mary Lamb and her present friends, Mrs. De Morgan and Miss Travers, but nothing servile in her acknowledgments to me. She is a large woman still. I was reminded of Wordsworth's *Woman of Jedburgh* [*The Matron of Jedborough*]. . . .

SEPT. 25th . . . The weather was so bad that we [Crabb Robinson and Miss Bayley] could not well call on the author of *Adam Bede*, whom Miss Bayley very much likes, though perhaps she does not excite so much admiration in her personal intercourse as she does in her writings. . . .

OCT. 19th . . . I paid one social debt, which was also an agreeable act, by taking luncheon with Miss Evans [George Eliot]. She has quite won on me. . . . I began a course of instruction on Wordsworth's poetry,

[1] See *supra*, Jan. 26th, 1845.

[2] Lamb's friend who fell into the New River at Islington, as described in 'Amicus Redivivus'.

repeated to her what I could by heart, and in the evening . . . I devoted several hours to the making out of a list of those of Wordsworth's poems which I thought a beginner ought to read. She will buy his works.

Nov. 3rd . . . Mr. Gilchrist . . . talked an hour with me about Blake, and I have promised to lend him some papers. . . .

Nov. 5th . . . My time not devoted to the very interesting news of the day[1] was spent in reading the beginning of *The Woman in White*. It is highly praised by a very large public, and is praised for the skill with which a mystery is concealed from premature disclosure. But this is not the only merit. The character of a selfish invalid is admirably painted in the first scene in which he is introduced—Mr. Fairlie. He is made grotesque. . . .

Nov. 11th . . . *The Woman in White* . . . established the author at once as a first-rate novelist. Collins has great skill in the arranging his facts. He can keep up the interest, preserving his readers' curiosity and more effectually concealing his secret. . . .

Dec. 17th . . . I read in the *Saturday Review* a successful exposure of the deplorably bad taste of Emerson. But the writer might have, like myself, found himself unable to resist the fascination of Emerson's person and manner. . . .

Dec. 30th . . . Dr. Boott brought with him Lover,[2] the Irish song-writer and novelist, one of the most agreeable of his countrymen. We had none of his songs, of course [at a Sunday breakfast-party], but he was free in his talk. All his sentiments were of a generous and philanthropic cast, and his humour saved his philanthropy from becoming cant, and his warm-heartedness rendered his free sentiments innocuous to the opposite party. I am anxious to read his Irish tales when I have time to go beyond the *Saturday Review*.

1861

Feb. 11th . . . We had an interesting party [at Mrs. Bayne's]. . . . The Bishop of St. David's (Thirlwall), Thackeray the novelist, and Donne were the persons of note; Paget, an eminent surgeon, and Dalrymple, a great solicitor, both good talkers. I felt myself displaced, but was not

[1] *The Times* of the day records the defeat of the Bourbon army and King Victor Emmanuel's entry into Naples. There is also news of the war in China.

[2] Samuel Lover, author of *Legends and Stories of Ireland*, *Handy Andy*, *Rory O'More*, etc.

disturbed by it. . . . Thackeray showed no signs of colloquial ability. . . .

FEB. 21st . . . I began early Leslie's *Memoirs*[1] and read a chapter in the evening. It promises to be what report makes it to be, a great artist's biographical history book. . . .

FEB. 22nd . . . Nearly two-thirds of volume one of Leslie's autobiography has been reached today, and the book is so delightful that I forgive myself too easily.[2]

APRIL 11th . . . I began *Silas Marner*. Manner of Miss Evans. It promises well and induces me to go again [to the Athenaeum] and finish it soon. . . .

APRIL 14th . . . I walked to the Athenaeum solely to read *Silas Marner*, which is a powerful production. The miser seems to be like the plague, a standing theme for first-rate stylists. . . .

APRIL 18th . . . I was engaged at the Athenaeum reading *Silas Marner*. Its object I now see and I find has a great affinity to Coleridge's *Ancient Mariner*. . . .

APRIL 19th . . . My business at the Athenaeum was to finish *Silas Marner*, in which I succeeded. This is certainly an admirable novel, perhaps George Eliot's best. . . .

JULY 22nd . . . I was seduced to read a few chapters in Dickens's *Great Expectations* in consequence of the great praise of the *Saturday Review*, as if it were a revival of his early excellence. I am not sure that I shall go on with it. I do not feel impressed with its truth, though I feel the force of the description of the poverty of the family of the blacksmith and extreme ferocity of the escaped convicts of the prison ship. . . .

AUG. 20th . . . I skimmed volume one of Dickens's last novel. My curiosity was raised by the warm praise of the *Saturday Review*. It is one of the least agreeable by him that I ever read. . . . Why it has been so praised I cannot conceive. Whether I go on with it or not will depend on circumstances. I would rather read a good review of it.

AUG. 25th . . . The second volume, which I skimmed, is less unpleasant than the first. . . .

AUG. 26th . . . I devoted the day to the concluding volume of *Great Expectations*. This third volume is far better than the other two, though at the best a disagreeable story. One feels an interest in volume three, but at the best there is an untruth and improbability in all the incidents and characters that destroys it entirely as a novel. One can't believe that a villain like the convict could feel so romantic a love to the boy, who

[1] *Charles Robert Leslie: Autobiographical Recollections*, ed., with an essay on Leslie and selections from his correspondence, by Tom Taylor, 1860.

[2] i.e. For reading instead of sorting his papers.

partly from terror and for no other reasonable motive keeps his word to him. Miss Havisham has no truth about her character. And why Jaggers the lawyer and Wemmick the clerk should have so much good as well as bad? Were Jaggers a humorist one might reconcile much. The most important incidents are told short. The poetically conceived Estella consents to marry a wretch, and one cares nothing about her when at the very last her brute of a husband, after cruelly treating her, dies, and the hero by chance falls in with her and we are given to understand they never part. I cannot comprehend the praise given to this tale, which at least interested me; but I regret throwing three days away upon it. Herbert, the generous friend, [son] of the scholar by whom the hero is educated, but of which [whom?] we hear nothing, is a fine character, but he is not made out. The scenes are admirably painted in volume three; the endeavour to escape and capture of the convict, whose riches, by the bye, had they been, would have given him ample means of escape. . . .

NOV. 29th . . . Made a beginning of a famous novel by Miss Yonge, a book of great repute with good people, *The Heir of Redclyffe*. Though I have had two short readings, yet I have read enough to be satisfied that the book deserves its reputation. I shall take it up at intervals, and have an indefinite time for the use of it. I presume that the religious tone is genuine, and whatever there may be of cant is kept in the background. The writer wisely resolved to prove her talent before she made use of it for purpose of edification. At present I have only an idea of the character to be exhibited. I hear that the heir is to be a *perfect* character. I am already interested in an amiable family. . . .

DEC. 12th [At the Society of Antiquaries.] . . . I heard of Collier. He was at Ouvry's, but Ouvry could not induce him to come. 'No wonder,' Beesly remarked, 'no wonder. He did not like to show his face.' I said that I believed Collier entirely free of the imputations cast on him. Beesly, who himself had no opinion, said every one was against Collier. . . .

DEC. 13th . . . Recollecting that Collier was at Ouvry's, etc., I cabbed it to Ouvry's, where I found, besides Collier, Mrs. George Street. Collier was pleased with my making the call to see him, and in good spirits. So was I, and glad to have a rubber of whist.

DEC. 19th . . . Read through Dr. Brown's delightful little book *Rab and his Friends* . . . or rather . . . read it again, for I had forgotten it. . . .

DEC. 27th . . . For want of other occupation went on with *The Heir of Redclyffe*; but it is so manifestly didactic that I must pause; it begins to pall on one. . . .

1862

FEB. 15th . . . I was startled on entering the drawing-room [at Sir Francis Goldsmid's] by being accosted by Miss Procter.[1] . . . The poetess is plain. . . . I was also agreeably addressed by the poet Browning. He was very cheerful and friendly in manner. He has been admitted a member by the committee at the Athenaeum. He believes the prospects of Italy are favourable, and that Louis Napoleon is honest in his intentions towards the King. He says we English are unjust in our suspicions. I was in good spirits in spite of giddiness. . . .

APRIL 12th Early I read some of Miss Procter's poems. Very pleasing; but one gets a surfeit of moral and domestic ballads, and one must read sparingly. . . .

JUNE 5th . . . I began Luttrell's *Julia*[2] and finished first *Letter* this morning. A *gentlemanly* poem! That is fashionable verse. I recollect the author at Rogers's. An elegant man.

JUNE 6th Awoke early and finished the first epistle. I do not think I shall go on with it. It is the third edition. The author confesses that the first two editions portrayed loose morality. This is made decent; it is probably dull. . . .

JUNE 25th I have been reading in an old *Saturday Review* on Edward Irving,—I suspect by Thomas Carlyle, who is by no means so simple-minded as he was and whom I knew through Irving. If my memory was not gone so far I should like to write my recollections about him. Irving is the entirely bygone powerful man of irregular and disorderly genius. In Carlyle there is much that is artificial, and it is quite a problem whether he will be more thought of when he has been dead as long. He is neither as sincere nor as benevolent. . . .

JULY 23rd I renewed the perusal of *The Heir of Redclyffe*. . . .

JULY 24th I went on early this morning. . . . I had proceeded so far in the novel, which towards the close was somewhat heavy and more directly commonplace in its piety and very High Church, that I thought [it better] to finish it at once, which I did. . . . I shall scarcely venture on another of Miss Yonge's novels. At least it surfeits. . . .

AUG. 16th . . . I cabbed it to the Athenaeum. . . . My reading there was chiefly confined to a skimming of Clough's poems, which were formerly liked by very few. This posthumous[3] collection, however, afforded me

[1] Adelaide Ann Procter, daughter of B. W. Procter (Barry Cornwall).
[2] *Advice to Julia*, 1820; 3rd ed. entitled *Letters to Julia*, 1822, by Henry Luttrell.
[3] Clough had died at Florence in 1861.

great pleasure, being the poetry of thought and exhibiting a high and pure state of feeling. The editor . . . speaks of him as a disciple of Wordsworth. . . . Clough's editor is Palgrave. . . .

AUG. 22nd . . . At night after looking into the *Golden Treasury*, which is printed so small as to be hard to read, I began to look into Miss Procter's poems—very pleasing for a time, but so monotonous read consecutively as to be wearisome, and I find great difference between them and the masterpieces of the *Golden Treasury*. . . .

SEPT. 29th to OCT. 19th [*At Grasmere.*] . . . I went also to see the Arnolds, from whom I had a kind reception, though Matthew has not much kindness in his nature. . . .

[*Travel Journal: Brown's Hotel, Grasmere.*] OCT. 1st . . . The hotel carriage took Mrs. Cookson, senior, Miss Elizabeth, and myself to the old Rydal Mount, now occupied by Mrs. Hills, the widow of Hills the barrister. . . . Here I saw James, who was glad as ever to see [me]. He is now the butler [of the] house, and has the benefit of showing it. We next drove to the Arnolds. Here were the eldest son, Matthew, and his wife. The only unmarried daughter, once 'little Fan', now a young woman. Mrs. Arnold was very cordial, and Matthew Arnold could not be otherwise than civil. . . .

1863

FEB. 8th . . . I was gratified by a call from Bagehot. Though there is something sarcastic in his general tone, he was kind towards me. . . .

FEB. 22nd . . . I found great pleasure in reading *David Elginbrod*[1] . . . and I stayed up late, nearly finishing the first volume. I found the portion about the education of the unfortunate . . . and mismanaged boy very interesting, and the tale hitherto attractive, though the parts of the narrative ill-joined together.

FEB. 25th . . . As I had already entered on the mystical part of the novel of *Elginbrod* I continued the second volume with interest, though the character which gives the name to the work does not make his appearance after the first volume. . . .

MARCH 13th . . . I finished *David Elginbrod*, and am prepared to call it a bad novel with excellent things in it. The great fault is the want of the constructive faculty. . . . I fear, and so do others . . . that the author speaks from experience of the hard condition of a tutor. . . .

JULY 30th . . . A letter from Field gravely counselling me as a

[1] By George MacDonald, 1863.

preservative not to talk more than two hours consecutively! Was this satire? This does not offend me. It ought to mortify me. . . .

SEPT. 7th . . . I read a chapter of *Romola*, but I found it not at all agreeable. The dialogue heavy. I may go on and like it. . . .

NOV. 6th . . . I hurried through the first volume of Trollope's *Rachel Ray*, a novel of daily life, the characters and manners true to nature. Not a great, but an amusing work. . . .

NOV. 13th . . . My chief occupation was the reading, with considerable skipping, the second volume of *Rachel Ray*—not a first-rate novel. . . . Its truthfulness gives it interest, and I was sufficiently amused. But I had a deeper interest. Here [at the Athenaeum] I found the recently published *Blake's Life*. I was promised a copy by Mr. Gilchrist, which I shall have to write for unless I receive it on Monday. . . . I find free use has been made of what I sent—anecdotes related and long quotations. The only thing I yet see to censure is the mention of my reminiscences and journal. But it treats me politely, without any mention in the preface [of me] as a contributor. It might have been worse. I should hardly say that, as I must read it properly before I can feel any confidence. . . .

NOV. 17th . . . The presentation copy of *Blake's Life* is come. I have no impatience to read what is said even about myself or by myself—a decided proof that I am not a vain man. I can now bear contempt better than I could formerly. . . .

NOV. 20th . . . Read in my bedroom the two chapters, xxvi and xxvii, in which my account of Blake—what I wrote in my journal and reminiscences—is referred to, not always concurring with me. But then, these reminiscences and journal are known both to exist, and it will be in vain that I shall protest—though it is most truly—that no part of these is written *for* the press, and not more than a tenth part fit for *selection*. Nevertheless, what is printed is better than I expected. I am not ashamed of it, though I am by no means proud. . . .

NOV. 21st . . . I have not since read more in *Blake's Life* than what appertains to myself. I am satisfied there is nothing very bad in what bears my name, and as I have now lost all expectation of literary repute my anxiety ceases. . . .

NOV. 24th . . . The *Athenaeum* review of *Blake* is so civil towards me that I cannot but think it is the work of a friend, and who can it be but De Morgan?[1] . . .

DEC. 15th I read a chapter in *Blake*, finding his poetry very beautiful, but I cannot relish his designs. . . .

[1] Augustus De Morgan, the mathematician, father of William De Morgan, the artist and novelist.

1864

APRIL 20th . . . I enjoyed today, especially in reading one piece of refined criticism—Bagehot's article on Shakespeare from the *National.* Parts I did not understand. . . .

APRIL 21st And at five awaking, I went on with the article, which I have heartily enjoyed. . . .

APRIL 29th . . . Went on with what I began a few days since, Bagehot's admirable article on Shelley in his volume of collected reviews. It has already given me great pleasure with his subtle discrimination. I will read it continuously. . . .

MAY 4th . . . I fortunately fell in with a very pleasant man, one of my most agreeable [acquaintances], Erasmus Darwin, the elder brother of Charles Darwin, one of our great thinkers and philosophers, whose doctrine is feared by the theologians. . . .

MAY 22nd . . . Scharf brought the catalogue of the Portrait Gallery and I was engaged great part of the day (the work being slow) in drawing up an improved article on Wordsworth, which I am to insert in the catalogue and let it be submitted to Lord Stanhope.[1] . . .

AUG. 5th . . . I read Charles Knight's passages in the autobiography of a working man. . . . I cannot but feel great respect for the man who has done so much to promote useful knowledge and spread education more widely. Where the surface is so wide it is unreasonable to require great depth. . . .

AUG. 11th . . . I . . . was amused by Charles Knight's passages in the life of a working man. There is an air of integrity about him not spoiled by some bragging. That is hardly to be avoided in a *parvenu*, nor in an upstart ultimately disappointed. I feel interest in his success with envy of his faculties. . . .

AUG. 15th . . . I then went to Street's and took tea with him. A very agreeable incident: Holman Hunt came in. I was much pleased with him. He has a sweet smile and his conversation is unaffected and genial; but I felt my increasing deafness painfully. . . .

SEPT. 17th . . . I went to the Athenaeum. . . . I chatted with but few; there was, however, the librarian, who put into my hands the recently published poems of Praed, extravagantly praised by the editor, Derwent Coleridge, but, from the little I read, well deserving praise. I had time, however, to read little besides Praed's Memoir by Coleridge. He seems to

[1] The President of the Trustees of the National Portrait Gallery.

have been a man of most attractive qualities, with a want of earnestness, and infirm of purpose.[1] . . .

OCT. 6th . . . Finished MacDonald's novel, *Adela Cathcart*; it has various merits in the several tales. The conclusion was anticipated as far as final success was concerned and the means satisfactory.

OCT. 28th . . . I began *Pendennis*, reading two short chapters. There is a free and easy fun in [Dickens?] which gives . . . a gaiety I do not find in Thackeray. There is, however, more of depth, more of design in Thackeray. He is also less amiable. . . .

NOV. 17th . . . I must not forget his [Donne's] epigram in the form of an epitaph [on Landor, who had died at Florence]:

> Beneath this Stone lies Walter Savage Landor,
> Who half an Eagle was and half a Gander.

DEC. 16th . . . I finished one article in the *National*—that by Bagehot on poetry, full of ingenuity, but not so satisfactory as I could have wished, in which he places Wordsworth as the master of a pure style over Tennyson, the head of the ornate, and Browning, the head of the grotesque. . . .

1865

JAN. 13th . . . I was tempted to change the course of my thoughts by the promising headings of *Pendennis*, but the Begum and her daughter have no attractions but that of truthfulness of representation. Thackeray has great skill in the representation of entirely selfish and worthless characters. But Foker, who is not so worthless as the others, is neither so truthful. I should pity Pen had he been caught by Miss Amory, but I shall not care for Foker if he be. . . .

JAN. 21st . . . After dinner a very remarkable call was announced. The name I could not at first recollect—Allsop,[2] whose name has been long forgotten by the public. An extinct volcano. Our acquaintance was never intimate. He was first known only as the generous, though not high-born, friend of Coleridge and Lamb. He knew Hazlitt, Leigh Hunt, Alsager, Southey. He was an admirer of great men. After the death of the most famous of these he went abroad and I had lost all sight of him, when he

[1] The two last assumptions were not justified. Praed had died in 1839, aged 36.

[2] Thomas Allsop (1795–1880), best remembered as the friend and correspondent of Coleridge.

appeared as the accomplice of Orsini and Bernard in the attempt to assassinate Louis Napoleon. Without confessing himself to have been guilty of the most heinous charge, he admitted that he was the friend of Orsini, whom he praised as one of the noblest as well as the handsomest of men. Bernard also he praised highly and boasted of his friendship. He gave like praise to Mazzini as a really high-minded and generous creature. He thought as I do of Gallenga, alias Mariotti, and the rest of the eminent . . . of the day, and has since seen the most eminent of the survivors. He retains more than most do of the old sentiment. He has hopes for Italy, and thinks that [Louis] Napoleon has overreached himself, and that the Italians will at length have independence and perhaps at last the Carbonari their revenge—except on the question of regicide, perhaps, for he said nothing to justify his conviction on that charge. And I was pleased, or rather amused, by his bringing back old times. . . . He talked freely about *The Times* and did not make any difficulties about referring to his former acts. That he does not now feel ashamed of his former connection with the patriots of the last generation is certain. He talked of literature with just opinions, I was glad to perceive. He who is right on questions of taste cannot be quite wrong on questions of morals. . . .

FEB. 23rd . . . I have read again in *Pendennis*. It diminishes in interest as it gets on. . . . But it does not profess to be a sensation tale. It is now more clever than pleasant. . . . The disagreeable part of the story is the mysterious connection between Sir F. Clavering and Altamont. It is very unpleasant. . . .

MARCH 17th . . . I had an interrupted morning of reading at home, but the interruptions were agreeable. One from De Morgan occasioned his leaving with me two [verses] which I characterise as critical doggerel.

THACKERAY

Who sees but ridicule in good like Thackeray
And gloats on human stains in black array
Of heaven's light most surely doth he lack a ray.

DICKENS

A splendid muse of fiction hath Charles Dickens,
But now and then just as the interest thickens
He stilts his pathos, and the reader sickens.

MARCH 30th Whenever I feel dissatisfied with myself and I am uncomfortable I have no more efficacious remedy than a good novel. So I was happy to read in *Pendennis*, a book full of talent, but often I am dissatisfied with his views of man. You seldom can love any one. It becomes a sensation novel towards the close. . . .

April 6th . . . Expected last evening to finish *Pendennis*. . . . I began to read as soon as I could see the small print, and I went on with the volume to the end. . . . I could not hurry over it at the last. Poetic justice is in most respects complete. I understand that some of the family appear in some other tale. The old major is intensely selfish, but one cannot say that he is not truly painted. Lady Rockminster is a happy painting also . . . Helen, Pen's mother, and Laura are, especially the last, really noble characters. If any one is brought to life again it should be Warrington, the 'Bluebeard' of Lady Rockminster. Pen should be shown in Parliament. The author is dead, but Trollope might adopt him. . . .

April 13th . . . I have read one chapter only of *Vanity Fair*. It has fine touches in it, but reading by candle light is so dangerous if I hold the candle in my hand, that I must not go on with it with any hope of finishing it. The first chapter is excellent. . . .

April 21st . . . Awoke very early and being unsettled as to reading at length took to *Vanity Fair*; read chapters ii and iii. Becky Sharp is a gem from the beginning, but more odious morally than I had any idea of.

June 10th I had engaged Rev. Harry Jones to bring Mr. Stopford Brooke to breakfast with me. Mr. Brooke is about to publish a *Life* of Robertson of Brighton, or rather his *Letters* with a Memoir. A pale face and round head, the opposite of Harry Jones's. Liberal he must be or he would not otherwise write such a memoir. He came for anecdotes and facts. I had very little to give him. I foolishly mentioned my memoir and I have offered to let him see what I wrote. He says he will call and read it, but it can be of no use to him, and he will perhaps prefer seeing it elsewhere. He may then conceal his dislike. He means to relate, not emphatically, the history of Wagner's opposition, and I hope he will not be too timid. I had several very agreeable hours' chat with these gentlemen. . . .

Nov. 3rd . . . Went . . . to the Athenaeum. [Read] in the *Fortnightly Review* two chapters of *The Belton Estate* . . . very clever as a novel of character . . . one of Trollope's best. . . . I exchanged a few words with Matthew Arnold. . . .

1866

Jan. 26th . . . I could not resist the temptation to waste nearly a whole day in reading FitzGerald's volume on Charles Lamb—a paltry compilation.[1] He has from Patmore's volume copied a volume of gossip about

[1] *Charles Lamb, his Friends, his Haunts and his Books,* by Percy FitzGerald, 1865.

H.C.R.'s coming in and usurping the whole conversation, and several times copies from other extracts from books of talk; but I doubt whether I ever knew him, FitzGerald. . . .

FEB. 7th I went out in a cab and drove at once to Procter, alias Barry Cornwall. I had an interesting but short chat with him. He spoke with deep interest of Lamb and Wordsworth, and but a mixed feeling of Coleridge. He promises me a copy of his forthcoming little book on Charles Lamb. . . .

FEB. 12th . . . I took a cab straight to the Athenaeum and there remained till near eleven. . . . The most unexpected [acquaintance there] was Thomas Carlyle: he was both kind and respectful, said he and his brother would call. I do not think they will. I was more frank than he: I noticed his having cut me, which he denied. I was not wise in my manner. I confessed to not liking his assertion of Frederick's merits. He said he loved Frederick and he loved Frederick's father. . . .

FEB. 17th . . . I spent several hours in reading Robertson's *Life*—an excellent collection of letters of the genuine religious character. His piety undoubted, his liberality equally unquestionable. An admirable man. . . .

MARCH 12th . . . I cabbed it to the Athenaeum. . . . Chatted with . . . Forster about Landor and the letters I possess by him, which he will read and perhaps make use of according to circumstances. . . . He was very flattering. . . .

JULY 23rd . . . Field brought his old friend Linnell, . . . the friend of Blake . . . a remarkable man of genius as an artist. A mystic in matters of religion, and though interesting at least, I fear would prove troublesome, as all enthusiasts are in danger of becoming. I got tired of him at last. . . .

[*Travel Journal: Brighton.*] AUG. 2nd . . . I read in *Maud*, a most disagreeable, unhealthy poem, a picture of violent passions with no legitimate object. If men be as a class . . . like the family here exhibited, they are not entitled to our love or sympathy. The supposed sufferer from Maud's want of feeling is contemptible for his love of her. . . .

AUG. 3rd . . . I did nothing but . . . finish *Maud*. The only parts that amused me were the force of expressions used to expose the vulgar spirit of the age. . . .

AUG. 21st Looked over some *free* poems by Swinburne. They are queer things: I know not what to make of them, and I doubt whether they are worth the trouble of enquiry. . . .

AUG. 24th . . . My reading was merely of Barry Cornwall's *Life of Charles Lamb*. A charming book with no great merit, perhaps, on the part of the author, though Barry Cornwall is a man of talent and of genius too. My name occurs several times, but merely as a name and person acquainted with Lamb, though once solely called 'one of the most amiable,' but nothing to obviate that this was an amiability compatible with being a dunce. I never was a favourite with him, and his wife hates me. . . .

OCT. 19th . . . Among my stray reading is Clough's *Letters and Remains.* He incidentally names me by no means flatteringly, but not at all offensively. It might mortify men more vain than myself. I am not (now, certainly) anxious for the applause of all men, though the fable of *The Old Man, the Son, and the Ass* [is] sometimes on reflection brought to my mind.

1867

FINAL ROUGH JOURNAL[1]

JAN. 15th . . . Cabbed after early dinner to Athenaeum.[2] There from past two to half-past eight. A pleasant chat with Matthew Arnold; a man of talents and also pretensions. . . .

JAN. 17th . . . Received *Essays in Criticism*, by Matthew Arnold. . . .

JAN. 30th . . . Great part of the day spent in reading Matthew Arnold's first *Essay in Criticism* and was delighted. . . .

JAN. 31st . . . I read a capital paper—the first in Matthew Arnold's volume. If the others are like it in ability and fidelity to principle it will be invaluable. The subject is Criticism. Wordsworth and Goethe he honours both. College matters diverted my mind from its proper object. . . .

FINAL DIARY ENTRY

JAN. 31st During the last two days I have read the first *Critical Essay* on the qualifications of the present age for criticism. He resists the exaggerated scorn for criticism and maintains his point ably. A sense of *creative power*, he declares happiness to be, and [that] Arnold maintains, that genuine criticism is. He thinks of Germany as he ought, and of Goethe with high admiration. On this point I can possibly give him assistance which he will gladly (But I feel incapable to go on)

H.C.R. died 5th February, 1867.—E. W. Field, executor and attached friend.

[1] The rough notes from which the diary entries were afterwards written up.
[2] The last visit.

BIBLIOGRAPHY

Strictures on a Life of William Wilberforce by the Rev. W. Wilberforce and the Rev. S. Wilberforce, with a Correspondence between Lord Brougham and Mr. Clarkson, also a Supplement, containing Remarks on the Edinburgh Review of Mr. Wilberforce's Life. London, 1838. Ostensibly by T. Clarkson, but largely written and edited by Henry Crabb Robinson, the supplement being entirely by him.

Exposure of Misrepresentations, contained in the Preface to the Correspondence of William Wilberforce, by H. C. Robinson, Esq. London, 1840.

Protest against Unitarian advocacy of non-resistance to the Pope's Bull. To the Editor of the *Christian Reformer.* 1851. (Offprint at Dr. Williams's Library.)

The Diary, Reminiscences and Correspondence of Henry Crabb Robinson, ed. T. Sadler. 3 Vols., London, 1869; 2 Vols., 1872.

Literary Studies, by W. Bagehot. Vol. II. London, 1879.

Dictionary of National Biography, 1897. Vol. XLIX. Henry Crabb Robinson, by Fraser Rae.

Blake, Coleridge, Wordsworth, Lamb, etc., being Selections from the Remains of Henry Crabb Robinson, ed. E. J. Morley. Manchester, 1922.

Masquerier and his Circle, by R. R. M. Sée. London, 1922.

Henry Crabb Robinson's 'Essay on Blake', by H. G. Wright. *Modern Language Review.* XXII. 1927.

The Correspondence of Henry Crabb Robinson with the Wordsworth Circle (1808–66), ed. E. J. Morley. 2 Vols. Oxford, 1927.

Crabb Robinson's Opinion of Shelley, by R. W. King. *Review of English Studies*, IV. 1928.

Mme de Staël et Henry Crabb Robinson, by D. G. Larg. *Revue de Littérature comparée*, VIII. 1928.

Henry Crabb Robinson and Madame de Staël, by D. G. Larg. *Review of English Studies*, V. 1929.

Crabb Robinson in Germany 1800–1805. Extracts from his Correspondence edited by E. J. Morley. Oxford, 1929.

Henry Crabb Robinson and Goethe, by P. Norman. 2 Parts. English Goethe Society, 1930–1.

Crabb Robinson and Goethe in England, by B. J. Morse. *Englische Studien*, LXVII. 1932.

The Life and Times of Henry Crabb Robinson, by E. J. Morley. London, 1935.

The History of 'The Times'. London. Vol. I, 1935; Vol. II, 1939.

Henry Crabb Robinson of Bury, Jena, the 'Times' and Russell Square, by J. M. Baker. London, 1937.

Two Little-known References to Henry Crabb Robinson, by M. E. Gilbert. *Modern Language Review*, XXXIII. 1938.

Henry Crabb Robinson on Books and their Writers, ed. E. J. Morley. 3 Vols. London, 1938.

Cambridge Bibliography of English Literature, 1940. Vol. III, p. 678: Henry Crabb Robinson.

English Diaries of the XIX Century, 1800–1850, by James Aitken, London, 1944.

Index to the Henry Crabb Robinson Letters in Dr. Williams's Library, being a supplement to the index in Edith Morley's 'Henry Crabb Robinson on Books and their Writers', compiled by Inez Elliott. London, 1960.

To Hell, with Crabb Robinson, by R. H. Mottram. London, 1962. (Fiction: a fantasy.)

The Correspondent of 'The Times' in Hamburg-Altona in 1807, by S. H. Steinberg (*Festschrift Percy Ernst Schramm*), Wiesbaden, 1964.

Henry Crabb Robinson und seine deutschen Freunde, by H. Marquardt. Vol. I (to 1811). Gottingen, 1964. (Vol. II in preparation.)

Index

KING ALFRED'S COLLEGE
LIBRARY